OXFORD EARLY CHRISTIAN STUDIES

General Editors

Gillian Clark   Andrew Louth

THE OXFORD EARLY CHRISTIAN STUDIES series includes scholarly volumes on the thought and history of the early Christian centuries. Covering a wide range of Greek, Latin, and Oriental sources, the books are of interest to theologians, ancient historians, and specialists in the classical and Jewish worlds.

John of Scythopolis and the Dionysian Corpus

Annotating the Areopagite

PAUL ROREM
and
JOHN C. LAMOREAUX

CLARENDON PRESS · OXFORD
1998

Oxford University Press, Great Clarendon Street, Oxford OX2 6DP

Oxford New York

Athens Auckland Bangkok Bogota Bombay Buenos Aires Calcutta
Cape Town Chennai Dar es Salaam Delhi Florence Hong Kong Istanbul
Karachi Kuala Lumpur Madrid Melbourne Mexico City Mumbai
Nairobi Paris São Paulo Singapore Taipei Tokyo Toronto Warsaw

and associated companies in
Berlin Ibadan

Oxford is a registered trade mark of Oxford University Press

Published in the United States
by Oxford University Press Inc., New York

British Library Cataloguing in Publication Data
Data available

Library of Congress Cataloging in Publication Data
John of Scythopolis and the Dionysian corpus: annotating the
Areopagite / Paul Rorem and John C. Lamoreaux.
(Oxford early Christian studies)
Includes bibliographical references and index.
1. Pseudo-Dionysius, the Areopagite.   2. John, Bishop of
Scythopolis, 6th cent.   I. Lamoreaux, John C.   II. Title.
III. Series.
BR65.D66R65   1998   230'.14'092—dc21   98-20623

ISBN 0-19-826970-6

1 3 5 7 9 10 8 6 4 2

Typeset by Regent Typesetting, London
Printed in Great Britain on acid-free paper by
Bookcraft (Bath) Ltd., Midsomer Norton

ACKNOWLEDGEMENTS

We would here like to acknowledge the aid of a number of colleagues and friends. For reading and commenting upon earlier versions of various chapters we are grateful to Elizabeth Clark, David B. Evans, Alexander Golitzin, Patrick T. R. Gray, Wayne Hankey, Andrew Louth, Joshua Sosin, and Kenneth Paul Wesche, as well as the readers and editors at Oxford University Press. Thanks also to Julian Plante, former director of the Hill Monastic Manuscript Library, for facilitating our access to microfilms of the various manuscripts used in this study. For his invaluable help in collating the Syriac, we wish to acknowledge the grateful appreciation we owe to our dear friend 'Abd al-Masīḥ Sa'dī. Beate Regina Suchla deserves a special measure of recognition: not only has she answered many questions over the years, but also without her seminal researches a study such as this would not even have been conceivable.

P.R. and J.C.L.

CONTENTS

ABBREVIATIONS

AAST	*Atti della accademia delle scienze di Torino: Classe di scienze morali, storiche e filologiche*
ACO	Acta conciliorum oecumenicorum
AHC	*Annuarium historiae conciliorum*
BS	*Byzantine Studies*
BZ	*Byzantinische Zeitschrift*
CAF	T. Kock (ed.), *Comicorum Atticorum Fragmenta*
CCSG	Corpus christianorum, series graeca
CH	*The Celestial Hierarchy*
ChH	*Church History*
CPG	Clavis patrum graecorum
CSCO	Corpus scriptorum christianorum orientalium
DHGE	*Dictionnaire d'histoire et de géographie ecclésiastiques*
DN	*The Divine Names*
DOP	*Dumbarton Oaks Papers*
DS	*Dictionnaire de spiritualité*
DTC	*Dictionnaire de théologie catholique*
EH	*The Ecclesiastical Hierarchy*
EO	*Échos d'orient*
EP	*Epistles*
FGrHist.	C. Müller (ed.), *Fragmenta Historicorum Graecorum*
FHG	F. Jacoby (ed.), *Fragmente der griechischen Historiker*
GCS	Die griechischen christlichen Schriftsteller der ersten drei Jahrhunderte
HJ	*Historisches Jahrbuch*
IEJ	*Israel Exploration Journal*
JECS	*Journal of Early Christian Studies*
JTS	*Journal of Theological Studies*
Lampe	G. W. H. Lampe (ed.), *A Patristic Greek Lexicon*
LCL	Loeb Classical Library
LSJ	H. G. Liddell, R. Scott, and H. S. Jones (eds.), *A Greek–English Lexicon*
Mansi	G. D. Mansi (ed.), *Sacrorum conciliorum nova et amplissima collectio*
MSR	*Mélanges de science religieuse*

MT	*The Mystical Theology*
Mus.	*Le Muséon*
NAWG	*Nachrichten der Akademie der Wissenschaften in Göttingen:* i. *Philologisch-historische Klasse*
OC	*Oriens Christianus*
OCP	*Orientalia christiana periodica*
PG	Patrologia graeca
PL	Patrologia latina
PO	Patrologia orientalis
Prol.	*Prologue to the Dionysian Corpus*
PTS	Patristische Texte und Studien
REB	*Revue des études byzantines*
REG	*Revue des études grecques*
RHE	*Revue d'histoire ecclésiastique*
RSO	*Rivista degli studi orientali*
RSPT	*Revue des sciences philosophiques et théologiques*
RTAM	*Recherces de théologie ancienne et médiévale*
SC	Sources chrétiennes
SchCH	*Scholia on The Celestial Hierarchy*
SchDN	*Scholia on The Divine Names*
SchEH	*Scholia on The Ecclesiastical Hierarchy*
SchEP	*Scholia on the Epistles*
SchMT	*Scholia on The Mystical Theology*
SE	*Sacris Erudiri*
SP	*Studia Patristica*
TDNT	G. Kittel (ed.), *Theological Dictionary of the New Testament* (ET)
TRE	*Theologische Realenzyklopädie*
TU	Texte und Untersuchungen zur Geschichte des altchristlichen Literatur
VC	*Vigiliae Christianae*
ZKT	*Zeitschrift für katholische Theologie*

INTRODUCTION

The book of Acts tells us that Paul's missionary journeys took him to Athens and that there he debated with Jews in the synagogues as well as with passers-by in the city square. Eventually he was brought before the council of the Areopagus. There, prompted by having seen an altar dedicated to an unknown God, he gave a remarkable speech about the God in whom we live and move and have our being. The speech, we are told, was moderately successful, for some became believers on this occasion. Among the converts mentioned by Luke was a certain 'Dionysius, a member of the council of the Areopagus' (Acts 17: 34). Nothing else was heard from this Dionysius for about half a millennium. It was then, in the early sixth century, that there began to circulate in the Christian east a corpus of writings ascribed to him. This corpus was fascinating to its medieval readers not only for the light it shed on apostolic times, but also for the innovative ways it philosophized about the subject matter of Christian theology. Quickly accepted as the authentic works of an apostolic contemporary, their status as such remained almost unchallenged until the beginning of the sixteenth century.

The labours of modern scholars have begun to make clear something of the influence that the writings of Dionysius exercised during the thousand or so years which intervened between the time when they first appeared and the time when their authenticity began first to be suspected. Especially intriguing is what we are now beginning to learn about how the works of Dionysius were a stimulus to further, creative theological reflection. Much of this reflection was enshrined in the various medieval commentaries on the Dionysian corpus. At the head of the long list of commentators stands the obscure figure of John of Scythopolis. This John composed an extensive set of scholia or marginal annotations to the works of Dionysius. These scholia were in turn prefaced by a prologue in which John set out his reasons for commenting on the corpus. A single generation at most separates John's interpretative labours from the earliest appearance of the works of Dionysius. More significant even than their early date, however, is the influence which John's comments exercised on the earliest form of the Dionysian tradition itself.

As documented by the studies of Beate Regina Suchla, the exemplar from which all Greek manuscripts of the Dionysian corpus descend was characterized by a number of distinctive features.[1] This exemplar was provided with interlinear or marginal variant readings. It was, in other words, an *editio variorum*, a primitive critical edition. More notably, however, it was already augmented with John's *Scholia* and *Prologue*. For a number of reasons, Suchla dates this *editio variorum* to the first half of the sixth century. Inasmuch as it and John's labours were contemporary and so closely intertwined, Suchla further argues that this *editio variorum* must be assigned to the circle of John of Scythopolis. It may in fact have been John himself who was responsible for it.

John's scholia were eventually intermixed with comments written by other authors. Hitherto it has been impossible to distinguish John's remarks from those of these later authors. Now, however, thanks again to the labours of Beate Regina Suchla, this situation has begun to be rectified. She has discovered an early recension of the scholia, a recension which contains only those comments authored by John.[2] Her research in this regard has opened up a new world of possibilities for investigating not only John, but also the earliest reception of the Dionysian corpus itself. For subsequent generations did not read the Areopagite; they read the annotated Areopagite—and John had the early monopoly on those annotations. It is hard to overemphasize the significance of this literary phenomenon, this linkage of text and exegesis. It is as if there were no New Testament but that of Erasmus, no Shakespeare but that of Bowdler. This close connection between text and commentary suggests a host of questions which cannot be easily or quickly answered—among these, how did John's work affect subsequent readings of the Areopagite? Or perhaps even, how might the Dionysian corpus have been read and received had it not been intertwined with John's interpretations? Such questions are not answered in this book, but the groundwork for investigating them is here prepared. One must first encounter what John himself had to say and this, at last, is possible.

This book introduces John of Scythopolis and his presentation of the writings of Dionysius. Our primary objective in this study is to survey John's sources, methods, and theological concerns in the hundreds of

---

[1] 'Eine Redaktion des griechischen Corpus Dionysiacum Areopagiticum im Umkreis des Johannes von Skythopolis, des Verfassers von Prolog und Scholien', *NAWG* (1985), 4: 177–93; 'Die Überlieferung des Prologs des Johannes von Skythopolis zum griechischen Corpus Dionysiacum Areopagiticum', *NAWG* (1984), 4: 176–88.

[2] 'Die sogenannten Maximus-Scholien des Corpus Dionysiacum Areopagiticum', *NAWG* (1980), 3: 31–66.

scholia which he appended to the Dionysian corpus. These scholia are sometimes a few words in length; at other times they fill a whole column or more in Migne. They are at times repetitive and not infrequently obscure. At first glance the individual scholia may seem self-contained, atomistic: a comment here, a comment there, each capable of standing on its own, each able to be interpreted by itself. The atomistic nature of the scholia can, however, be misleading. For the individual scholia are embedded within a number of different contexts and the full significance of John's comments can only emerge when read against these diverse backgrounds.

The scholia themselves form one such context. Each of John's comments must be read against the background of all his comments as well as against his own explicit concerns as set forth in his *Prologue*. It is only when they are linked together, compared, or contrasted, that the full weight of John's arguments can emerge. At the same time, one must always keep in mind that John is commenting on another text, the Dionysian corpus. He is weaving his comments around another text, garnishing its margins with his lucubrations, providing his readers with clues to what he considers significant and perhaps at times diverting their attention from potential problems. Any attempt to understand John's strategies as a commentator must read his scholia against the background of the Dionysian text itself. Yet again, John's comments are embedded in a particular theological tradition. The participants in this tradition were most often Christians, but sometimes included Jews and pagans. Whenever John treats of a particular theological problem in his comments one must be careful to attend to the ways that his reflections are caught up in the nexus of this wider historical context. And finally, John was himself an important participant in the theological debates that wracked the eastern churches in the aftermath of Chalcedon. He was the bishop of the metropolis of Palestina Secunda, a large and important see. He could not ignore contemporary controversies, nor could he be ignored by his opponents. This contemporary context presents us with the fourth and final background against which one must read John's comments.

The complexity of the scholia and the many contexts in which they are embedded have presented us with a number of challenges, the primary of these being that of reducing the manifold concerns of the scholia and their fragmentary manner of presentation to some sort of comprehensible order. But order there is. As we hope we have shown, John's *Scholia* are united by a common set of doctrinal concerns and a unified theological methodology. As one begins to see the proverbial forest for the proverbial trees John starts to emerge as a creative theologian in his own right and to take his place among the important theologians of the sixth century. At the same time, it must be emphasized, John's works are themselves a new and important source for the intellectual history of the Greek east in the sixth century and as such offer fresh insights into some of the problems which beset the study of this period.

Accounts of the intellectual history of the Greek east in the sixth century have tended to take one of two forms. To many modern observers this period is one that is consumed by Christological controversies, the particular challenge being to interpret the Formula of Chalcedon in ways compatible with the legacy of Cyril of Alexandria and thus reconcile to the imperial theology those theologians of Egypt, Syria, and elsewhere who revered Cyril and rejected Chalcedon. This is one narrative. But there is another as well. This version tells of the decline and fall of ancient philosophy. The main character in this dramatic narrative is the cruel Justinian; the hapless victims, the last representatives of philosophy. Amidst these tribulations philosophy herself must go into exile or hiding, as the golden chain of the Platonic succession is at last broken. Or such at least is the narrative. In the sixth century, the writings of the mysterious Dionysius suddenly appeared and were quickly accepted as apostolic. The modern, perhaps overly suspicious perspective on this timing is to frame all questions about the Dionysian corpus and its early reception within one or the other of these narratives. *Cui bono?* Someone must after all be profiting from this skilful, deliberate forgery. Were these treatises composed to further a Christological agenda? Or do they perhaps represent a resurfacing of the prohibited philosophical tradition? We would submit that this bifurcated approach to the early history of the Dionysian tradition ignores too much. Not only does it present a selective reading of the Dionysian corpus, but it also passes over in silence a great deal of what we now know about the early reception of the corpus. In short, the formative period of the Dionysian tradition simply cannot be adequately understood on the basis of these two epic narratives.

Our treatment of John of Scythopolis and his reading of the Dionysian corpus will, we hope, add a measure of nuance to the way intellectual history in the sixth-century east has traditionally been conceptualized. It is true that many of John's comments concern Christology, and that some touch on the Areopagite's orthodoxy in other respects, while at the same time other scholia defend the integrity of Dionysius as an apostolic writer in the matrix of a dialogue with Neoplatonism. All of this is fascinating, to be sure, and will be treated below, as fully as space allows. Yet even taken together, Christology and Neoplatonism do not monopolize John's concerns. Just as the insights and complexity of the Dionysian corpus cannot be reduced to a single polemical strategy, so also John's *Prologue* and *Scholia* offer the modern reader more than just another chapter in these two familiar narratives. Rather, they give a rare glimpse of a sixth-century theologian at work, interacting with Scripture and other earlier sources, invoking liturgical traditions, and directing his attention to a myriad of concerns not directly related to Chalcedon or Greek philosophy. Of course, one can argue for a polemical import to any theological comment—an author chooses to say one thing and not another within a particular context of alternatives: indeed, conspiracy theories of the Dionysian forgery will suspect everything of contributing to the fraud. It is equally true that some of the scholia may have polemical subtexts which we have not noticed. But to approach the Dionysian corpus and John's *Scholia* with this hermeneutic of suspicion is, we would submit, reductionistic. We offer this major work of sixth-century theology, previously of uncertain attribution, in hopes that the reader will not simply attend to the dialogue with Neoplatonism, the Christological polemics, or even the debates about the authenticity of the Dionysian corpus, as significant as such issues may be. John is concerned with far more than these issues and we hope that his readers will share something of his broader interests, many of which shaped the reception of the Dionysian corpus for centuries.

Being the first, as far as we know, to write about the overall landscape of John's comments, as clearly distinguished from later additions to the *Prologue* and the *Scholia*, we have sometimes felt like Moses' scouts bringing back an account not only of the terrain ahead but also of the magnitude of the task yet to be accomplished. 'There we saw the Nephalim . . . and to ourselves we seemed like grasshoppers. . . .' Any one of our sections below can and should be superseded by more detailed analyses now that John's interpretative labours can be identified with confidence. For the moment it is enough to share a broad report on the sources and methods, the theological concerns and philosophical perspectives of John of Scythopolis, the first and perhaps the most influential of all Dionysian commentators.

Our study is structured as follows. We begin in Chapter 1 with a re-evaluation of the earliest reception of the Dionysian corpus. In Chapter 2 we analyse the evidence for John's life and reconstruct his now lost theological works, before taking up the question of his *Prologue* and

Scholia to the Dionysian corpus and arguing that his *Prologue* provides an overview of almost all his major concerns in his *Scholia*. Chapters 3 to 5 treat those major concerns. In Chapter 3 we investigate how John uses a diverse body of sources in order to facilitate his interpretative agenda. In Chapter 4 we probe John's treatment of the doctrines of the Trinity and Christology, creation, and eschatology. In Chapter 5 we explore John's defence of the authenticity of the works of Dionysius, paying particular attention to John's handling of philosophical materials in general and Plotinus in particular. Following this, we offer a translation of John's *Prologue* as well as of a large selection of his *Scholia*.

PART I
John of Scythopolis and the Dionysian Corpus

I

The Earliest Reception of the Dionysian Corpus

After fifteen hundred years the identity of the author of the Dionysian corpus remains a mystery.[1] Even an accurate date for the composition of these works is lacking. In order to establish a *terminus a quo* for their appearance, appeals are often made to three factors, none of which, we would submit, can provide anything more than a very rough guide. In *The Ecclesiastical Hierarchy* Dionysius twice seems to allude to the recitation of the Creed in the course of the liturgy.[2] It is usually asserted that Peter the Fuller first mandated the inclusion of the Nicene Creed in the liturgy in 476.[3] But as Bernard Capelle has convincingly argued, this assertion can hardly be maintained. It is far more likely that Timothy the patriarch of Constantinople was responsible for this liturgical innovation toward 515.[4] Secondly, it is often suggested that because Dionysius seems to eschew divisive Christological language, he was probably writing while the *Henoticon* of Zeno was in effect, in other words, sometime after 482.[5]

---

[1] For a survey of the various proposals, Ronald F. Hathaway, *Hierarchy and the Definition of Order in the Letters of Pseudo-Dionysius* (The Hague, 1969), 31–5. For the most recent attempt, Michel van Esbroeck, 'Peter the Iberian and Dionysius the Areopagite', *OCP* 59 (1993), 217–27.

[2] *EH* 3. 2 (80. 21) and 3. 3. 7 (87. 22–88. 9).

[3] Josef Stiglmayr, 'Das Aufkommen der Pseudo-Dionysischen Schriften und ihr Eindringen in die christliche Literatur bis zum Lateranconcil 649', *Jahresbericht des öffentlichen Privatgymnasiums an der Stella matutina zu Feldkirch*, 4 (1894/5), 34–9. Cf. Eugenio Corsini, 'La questione areopagitica', *AAST* 93 (1958/9), 128–227, 135–40, esp. 139 n. 2. For Peter the Fuller, Aimé Solignac, 'Pierre le Foulon', *DS* 12/2 (1986), 1588–90; G. Fritz, 'Pierre le Foulon', *DTC* 12/2 (1935), 1933–5; Heinrich Bacht, 'Die Rolle des orientalischen Mönchtums in den kirchenpolitischen Auseinandersetzungen um Chalkedon (431–519)', in Aloys Grillmeier and Heinrich Bacht (eds.), *Das Konzil von Chalkedon*, vol. ii (Würzburg, 1953), 260–2, 271–2; C. Karalevskij, 'Antioche', *DHGE* 3 (1924), 576; Rudolf Riedinger, 'Akoimeten', *TRE* 2 (1978), 148–53.

[4] See his 'L'Introduction du symbole à la messe', in *Mélanges Joseph de Ghellinck*, vol. ii (Gemboux, 1951), 1003–7, and his 'Alcuin et l'histoire du symbole de la messe', *RTAM* 6 (1934), 258–9. His arguments are based in the main upon the careful weighing of the contradictory testimony of the fragmentary history of Theodore Anagnostes.

[5] Stiglmayr, 'Aufkommen', 39–45. See *Letters* 6 and 7 for a general statement of Dionysius' irenic approach to theology. For the *Henoticon*, L. Salaville, 'Hénotique', *DTC* 6/2 (1947), 2153–78.

To be sure, our mysterious author studiously avoided the traditional Christological formulae, but this may have had little to do with the influence of the *Henoticon*. It may rather have arisen from the Areopagite's attempt to preserve an overall apostolic ambience for his works. At any rate, it must be remembered that the *Henoticon* was not rescinded until the accession of Justin in 519. Finally, thanks in large measure to the labours of Stiglmayr and Koch, it is clear that Dionysius 'borrowed' many of his views, especially on the nature of evil, from the works of Proclus (d. 485), even at times employing passages from Proclus with little or no variation.[6] What of a *terminus ante quem*? Here we encounter some difficulties, for the earliest references to the Dionysian corpus occur in works which are themselves difficult to date. The first firm date, however, is 528, the year in which Severus' treatises against Julian were translated into Syriac, though the treatises themselves may have been composed as many as nine years earlier—exactly when we know not, the chronology of Severus' exile and his controversy with Julian being rather opaque.[7] Be that as it may, the authors of this study are inclined to push the date of composition of the Dionysian corpus well into the sixth century, the closer to the date of their first appearance the

---

[6] H. Koch, 'Proklus als Quelle des Pseudo-Dionysius Areopagita in der Lehre vom Bösen', *Philologus*, 54 (1895), 438–54; idem, *Pseudo-Dionysius Areopagita in seinen Beziehungen zum Neuplatonismus und Mysterienwesen* (Mainz, 1900); Josef Stiglmayr, 'Der Neuplatoniker Proclus als Vorlage des sog. Dionysius Areopagita in der Lehre vom Übel', *HJ* 16 (1895), 253–73, 721–48.

[7] According to Stiglmayr, the earliest theologian to make use of Dionysius was Andrew, the bishop of Caesarea in Cappadocia ('Aufkommen', 45–7). At issue here: his *Commentary on the Apocalypse* (ed. Schmid), a text which Stiglmayr dated to the end of the 5th cent. It is now known that Andrew's commentary was written in the early 7th cent. See Adele Monaci Castagno, 'Il problema della datazione dei Commenti all'*Apocalisse* di Ecumenio e di Andrea di Cesarea', *AAST* 114 (1980), 223–46. Among the earliest works containing references to the corpus, Stiglmayr ('Aufkommen', 47) also signals a treatise against Proclus ascribed to Procopius of Gaza (d. *c.* 528). Later scholars (including Stiglmayr himself) have shown that this refutation of Proclus was in fact written by Nicholas of Methone, a 12th-cent. Byzantine author. Although Johannes Dräseke ('Prokopios' von Gaza "Widerlegung des Proklos"', *BZ* 6 (1897), 55–91) has argued that the similarities between this fragment and the work of Nicholas are to be explained by supposing that Nicholas had plagiarized an original work of Procopius, Nicholas' integrity has been defended so well by Josef Stiglmayr ('Die "Streitschrift des Prokopios von Gaza" gegen den Neuplatoniker Proklos', *BZ* 8 (1899), 263–301) and Giovanni Mercati (*Notizie di Procoro e Demetrio Cidone, Manuele Caleca e Teodoro Meliteniota* (Vatican, 1931), 264–6) that Athanasios D. Angelou can declare, 'the controversy is not alive anymore' (*Nicholas of Methone* (Leiden, 1984), xliii). On this point the CPG (7440) should be corrected. Although it appeals to L. G. Westerink ('Proclus, Procopius, Psellus', *Mnemosyne*, 3rd ser. 10 (1942), 275–80) to support the contention that a tract by Procopius of Gaza against Proclus was in existence up to the 11th cent. and goes on to imply that this tract was identical with the work from which came the fragment in question, such a conclusion is not supported by Westerink's evidence.

better, for it is hard to imagine that the corpus would have left no mark for decades, or that an author as resourceful as the mysterious Dionysius would not have made sure that his work was 'discovered' sooner rather than later.

It is commonly believed that when the works of Dionysius first appeared on the stage of history, they were immediately pressed into service by Monophysite theologians in their attempts to confute the Chalcedonians. Only later were these works able to circulate unproblem- atically in Orthodox circles: it was necessary first that Chalcedonian authors, such as John of Scythopolis and Maximus the Confessor, vaccinate readers against the Areopagite's dubious Christology and cosmology—and this, through lengthy commentaries whose 'dominant *tendenz*', according to Jaroslav Pelikan, 'was to bring Dionysius into con- formity with Orthodox spirituality and dogma'.[8] As we ourselves shall argue in what follows, John's commentary was indeed specifically designed to defend the authenticity and orthodoxy of the Dionysian corpus. But a detailed analysis of the earliest stages of the reception of the corpus does not support the contention that the Monophysites had the early monopoly on it.

In what follows we first examine the scarce evidence for the early use of the corpus by Severus in the 520s, arguing against the common view that he had pre-empted the Dionysian corpus in an offensive strike against the Chalcedonians. Following this we turn briefly to the Collatio of 532 in which Hypatius is said to have objected to Monophysite use of the Dionysian corpus. As we hope to show, Hypatius' rejection of the works of Dionysius as heretical is not nearly as straightforward as is usually suggested. And finally, a brief overview of sixth-century appeals to the Dionysian corpus shows clearly that it was being used by just about all parties in the Christian east and that at no point was it the exclusive pre- serve of the Monophysites.

DIONYSIUS IN THE HANDS OF SEVERUS

Severus of Antioch (d. 538), whose works contain the first datable reference to the works of Dionysius, cited the corpus just three times: twice in his polemics against Julian of Halicarnassus, and once in his third

---

[8] Jaroslav Pelikan, 'The Odyssey of Dionysian Spirituality', in *Pseudo-Dionysius: The Complete Works* (Mahwah, NJ, 1987), 16. We ourselves suggested the same in 'John of Scythopolis on Apollinarian Christology and the Pseudo-Areopagite's True Identity', *ChH* 62 (1993), 482.

letter to John the Hegumen. This is all: nowhere else in his copious extant works do we find him appealing to the authority of Dionysius. Two other passages, however, are occasionally *wrongly* presented as further evidence that Severus made broad and general use of the works of Dionysius. At the Lateran Council of 649, a treatise of Themistius (*fl.* mid-sixth century) against Colluthus was cited in which Themistius referred to the precedent of Severus in defence of his own use of the saying 'theandric energy'.

Of the same [Themistius] from his work *Against Colluthus* the heretic, wherein he bears witness that Severus the heretic also confessed of Christ one theandric energy: 'It is quite easy to see that the blessed Severus similarly desired to confirm the theandric energy (not only the divine energy) in that he says of Christ that "the Same does some things divinely and others humanly." '[9]

From this passage it has been concluded that Themistius was defending his own use of the phrase 'theandric energy' by appealing to Severus' prior use of the same expression.[10] It is rather the case, as our translation of the rather tangled Greek shows, that Themistius was defending his use of 'theandric energy' by reference to Severus' statement that Christ does some of his deeds divinely and others of them humanly.[11] Again, the *Oratio theologica* of Theodosius I patriarch of Alexandria (*sedit* 535–66) has also been signalled in this context.[12] In this oration Theodosius mentions the prior labours of Severus in expounding the works of Dionysius, saying that 'Severus of blessed memory no less than they [scil. the Chalcedonians] and no less diligently read the works of St Dionysius'.[13] From what follows in the oration, however, it is quite clear that Theodosius draws this conclusion not because he has evidence that Severus actually made use of the Dionysian corpus; rather, he has inferred this from the general tenor of Severus' works, naturally fighting as they do against the misinterpretation of the corpus.[14]

Severus twice appealed to Dionysius in his works against Julian, who

[9] ACO ser. 2, 1: 146. 1–7: τοῦ αὐτοῦ ἐκ τῆς κατὰ Κολλούθου τοῦ αἱρετικοῦ γενομένης αὐτῷ συγγραφῆς, εἰς ἣν ἐπιμαρτύρεται λέγων, ὅτι καὶ αὐτὸς Σεβῆρος ὁ αἱρετικὸς "μίαν θεανδρικὴν" ὡμολόγησεν ἐπὶ Χριστοῦ τὴν "ἐνέργειαν"· ὅτι γάρ τοι καὶ ὁ μακάριος Σεβῆρος περὶ Χριστοῦ λέγων, ὡς τὰ μὲν θείως, τὰ δὲ ἀνθρωπίνως ὁ αὐτὸς ἐνήργησε, τὸ τῆς ἐνεργείας θεανδρικὸν οὐ μόνον, μέντοι θεοπρεπὲς ὁμοίως δεῖξαι προήρητο καταθεάσασθαι ῥᾷον.

[10] Stiglmayr, 'Aufkommen', 49.

[11] As will be seen, it is the case that Severus had discussed Dionysius' 'theandric energy', but this was in a private letter to a fellow Monophysite.

[12] Pelikan, 'Odyssey of Dionysian Spirituality', 15.

[13] *Oratio theologica* (tr. Chabot), 52.

[14] *Oratio theologica* (tr. Chabot), 52. 13–53. 20.

was, of course, not a Chalcedonian but Severus' erstwhile anti-Chalcedonian ally and then Monophysite foe. In chapter 41 of his *Contra additiones Juliani*, Severus attempted to defend the proposition that the flesh of God the Word was constituted from the blood of the Virgin Theotokos.[15] In proof of his thesis, in addition to citations from Theophilus of Alexandria, Gregory of Nazianzus, and John Chrysostom, Severus brought to bear the witness of:

Dionysius the Areopagite bishop of Athens whose memory is preserved in the Acts of the apostles, in a treatise concerning *The Divine Names* which he addressed to the bishop Timothy, [who] wrote thus: 'The most evident idea in theology, namely, the sacred Incarnation of Jesus for our sakes, is something which cannot be enclosed in words nor grasped by any mind, not even by the leaders among the front ranks of the angels. That he undertook to be a man is, for us, entirely mysterious. We have no way of understanding how, in a fashion at variance with nature, he was formed from a virgin's blood.'[16]

This treatise is difficult to date. At most one can say that it was written sometime after the beginning of Severus' exile to Alexandria in 518, but before the year 528, when it was translated into Syriac by Paul of Callinicus.[17] A second reference to the works of Dionysius is found in chapter 25 of Severus' *Adversus apologiam Juliani*.[18] For purposes quite similar to those which led him to invoke the authority of the Dionysian corpus in the *Contra additiones Juliani*, Severus cites the same passage from *The Divine Names*. Again this treatise is difficult to date: after 518 and before 528.

The only other place where Severus appeals to the authority of Dionysius is his *Third Epistle to John the Hegumen*, which is only partially preserved in the florilegium *Doctrina patrum de incarnatione Verbi*.[19]

[15] Severus, *Con. additiones Juliani* 41 (ed. and tr. Hespel), 154–9 (t), 130–5 (v). The theological issue at stake has been expounded by Aloys Grillmeier, *Christ in Christian Tradition*, ii/2 (Louisville, Ky., 1995), 108–11.
[16] Severus, *Con. additiones Juliani* 41 (ed. and tr. Hespel), 157 (t), 133 (v), citing *DN* 2. 9 (133. 5–9).
[17] René Draguet, *Julien d'Halicarnasse* (Louvain, 1924), 73.
[18] Severus, *Adversus apologiam Juliani* 25 (ed. and tr. Hespel), 304–5 (t), 267 (v).
[19] *Doctrina Patrum* 41. 24–5 (ed. Diekamp), 309. 15–310. 12. Theological interpretations of this letter have been offered by Grillmeier, *Christ in Christian Tradition*, ii/2, 170–1; Joseph Lebon, *Le Monophysisme Sévérien* (Louvain, 1909), 319–20, 451–3; idem, 'Le pseudo-Denys l'Aréopagite et Sévère d'Antioche', *RHE* 26 (1930), 893–5; idem, 'La Christologie du monophysisme syrien', in Aloys Grillmeier and Heinrich Bacht (eds.), *Das Konzil von Chalkedon*, vol. i (Würzburg, 1951), 488 n. 92; Friedrich Loofs, *Leontius von Byzanz* (Leipzig, 1887), 56–7. Cf. Joseph Lebon, 'Encore le pseudo-Denys et Sévère d'Antioche', *RHE* 28 (1932), 297.

Although a date of 510 was once suggested for this letter and is still occasionally encountered in the secondary literature, there is absolutely *no* evidence which supports it.[20] Lebon maintains rightly that there is at present no way to date the letter.[21] At any rate, Severus writes, again not to a Chalcedonian foe but to a fellow Monophysite:

> We, just as we have already written in greater detail elsewhere,[22] by the saying of the all-wise Dionysius the Areopagite which reads 'rather, by being God-made-man he accomplished for us something new, the theandric energy'—by this we have understood and do now understand *one* composite [energy]. The saying cannot be understood otherwise, in so far as it excludes every dyad. This we confess is the *one* theandric nature and hypostasis, as also the *one* incarnate nature of God the Word. . . . We proclaim as of the one himself one composite nature and hypostasis and energy, anathematizing also all those who teach of him a dyad of natures and energies after the union.

A second fragment of this letter adds:

> It follows therefore from the one composite (as we have understood it) and theandric energy that of such a sort also is the nature and hypostasis which bears it [i.e. this energy], as it can have nothing in its energy which is contrary to its nature.

It should be carefully noted what Severus is here arguing. He is attempting to show that the adjective 'theandric' is not only applicable to the energy (as Dionysius had used the term), but also that it applies to the nature or hypostasis which bears the energy. Furthermore, because 'theandric' is the equivalent of 'composite', according to Severus, Dionysius' phrase expresses the traditional Cyrillian formula, 'one incarnate nature of God the Word'. The language which Severus here uses—

[20] Franz Hipler, *Dionysius, der Areopagite* (Regensburg, 1861), 103, was apparently the first to suggest a date around 510, but he offered no evidence for this contention. Stiglmayr, 'Aufkommen', 48 n. 1, cites the dating of Hipler, but does not seem eager to endorse it; in 1928 ('Der sog. Dionysius Areopagita und Severus von Antiochien', *Scholastik*, 3 (1928), 177) he expressed still more hesitation as to the date. Hipler's suggestion (through Stiglmayr?) lies behind the references to 510 as a *terminus ante quem* for the corpus: Gerard O'Daly, 'Dionysius Areopagita', *TRE* 8 (1981), 772; Hathaway, *Hierarchy*, 4 n. 4, 35; John M. Rist, 'In Search of the Divine Denis', in *The Seed of Wisdom* (Toronto, 1964), 122; R. Roques, 'Denys le Pseudo-Aréopagite', *DHGE* 14 (1960), 267; idem, 'Denys l'Aréopagite', *DS* 3 (1957), 249; Adolf Martin Ritter (tr.), *Über die Mystische Theologie und Briefe* (Stuttgart, 1994), 7 n. 19.

[21] Lebon, 'Pseudo-Denys', 899 n. 4.

[22] It is not known where Severus had already written about this matter. Perhaps in his first and second letters to John the Hegumen (no longer extant). If Severus had discussed this matter in works which were other than private, it is hard to imagine that they would have escaped the notice of Themistius (see above).

'one composite nature and hypostasis'—is extremely rare among the Monophysites. Indeed, according to Lebon, it is only in this passage that Severus uses it, the adjective 'composite' being more commonly applied to Christ or the incarnate Word.[23] Severus is adamant that this is the proper interpretation of the Dionysian text: 'we have understood and do now understand', 'the saying cannot be understood otherwise', and 'as we have understood it'. As Lebon has argued, given the whole tenor of this letter, as well as the extraordinary lengths to which Severus is going to reconcile this Dionysian passage with Monophysite Christological formulae, it must be concluded that Severus has offered this interpretation because his colleague and correspondent had reported to him a dyophysite interpretation of this Dionysian text, an interpretation which he was eager to rebut.[24]

What then of the general nature of Severus' use of the works of Dionysius? It is indeed the case that Severus offers our earliest dated reference to the works of Dionysius. But this fact should not be allowed to overshadow the nature of his appeals to the corpus. Twice he had turned to Dionysius in his polemics against errant, fellow Monophysites. But even then, just a single Dionysian text was at issue. Once again, Severus, in a private letter to a fellow Monophysite, attempted to clarify the proper interpretation of a Dionysian passage, but the nature of his remarks suggests that he was responding indirectly to an earlier dyophysite interpretation of the passage.[25] Nothing in these three appeals to the corpus permits the conclusion that Severus has pre-emptively seized upon the works of Dionysius and has employed them as a key element in his polemic against the Chalcedonians.

THE COLLATIO OF 532

The year 532 found Justinian actively engaged in the attempt to reconcile feuding Monophysites and Chalcedonians. Part of his plans was a meet-

---

[23] Lebon, *Monophysisme Sévérien*, 319.

[24] Lebon, 'Pseudo-Denys', 894–5.

[25] If this is the correct interpretation of Severus' *Third Epistle to John the Hegumen*, it is interesting to examine his *ep.* 22 (PO 12/2: 214–16) in its light. This letter (written probably in 519 or 520) says that the Jebusites (i.e. the people of Jerusalem) have 'in a clumsy fashion and by a new and very crass expression' named the Trinity a *tlitōyūt qnūme* or 'trinity of hypostases'. From the Syriac translation of the letter it is not entirely clear what this 'compounded word' may have been in the Greek original. It is possible, however, that it represents the Greek adjective τρισυπόστατος, a word popularized by Dionysius, if not, however, coined by him. This reading of the letter would again suggest that Severus was on the defensive in his attempts to appropriate the authority of Dionysius.

ing held at Constantinople, attended by leaders of both factions, the so-called 'Collatio cum Severianis'.[26] The Monophysites, having been invited to participate in the Collatio and by now quite on the defensive, sent to the emperor a short letter containing a clarification of their Christological position.[27] In this letter, after opening with praises of the emperor's virtue and prayers for his and the Empire's safety, the Monophysites go on to state that they take their stand on the rulings of the first three ecumenical councils. Then, following a brief statement of faith, they argue that their Christological position falls in the middle between that of Apollinaris and that of Nestorius: it neither compromises the humanity of Christ, nor ignores the reality of the union of natures in him. All this, they claim, is in agreement with what is believed by Justinian, as is clear from the letter he wrote to them summoning them to Constantinople for the purpose of theological discussions. The authors of the letter then proceed to cite in support of their position select passages from the fathers, beginning with a passage from the works of Dionysius, 'who from the darkness and error of heathendom attained to the supreme light of the knowledge of God through our master Paul'.[28]

The Dionysian proof-text cited by the Monophysites occurs in a famous passage (*DN* 1. 4, 113. 6–12) where our mysterious author runs through the various names and attributes by which the thearchy has been celebrated by past theologians (monad and unity, Trinity, cause of beings, wise and beautiful). More appropriate than all these, according to Dionysius, is the title φιλάνθρωπος. This name is especially apropos, according to Dionysius:

because in truth the thearchy shared completely [ὁλικῶς] in our [things] in one of its hypostases, summoning to itself and exalting human lowliness, from which in an unspeakable manner the simple Jesus became composite [συνετέθη] and he who was eternal received a temporal duration and he who supersubstantially

---

[26] For the theological and political background of the Collatio, Jakob Speigl, 'Das Religionsgespräch mit den severianischen Bischöfen in Konstantinopel im Jahre 532', *AHC* 16 (1984), 264–85. We have a number of descriptions of this three-day meeting: a partial Syriac account stemming from Monophysite circles, another Syriac account from Monophysite circles, and a Latin translation of a now lost, Greek account of the conference written by a participant, Innocentius the bishop of Maronia. For the Syriac accounts, Sebastian Brock, 'The Conversations of the Syrian Orthodox under Justinian (532)', *OCP* 47 (1981), 87–121; for the letter of Innocentius, ACO 4/2: 169–84. On the Collatio in general, W. H. C. Frend, *The Rise of the Monophysite Movement* (Cambridge, 1972), 263–8, and Franz Diekamp (ed.), *Analecta Patristica* (Rome, 1938), 109–15.

[27] The most important parts of this letter are preserved in the *Chronicle* of Pseudo-Zachariah of Mitylene, 9. 15 (tr. Hamilton/Brooks), 246–53, repr. by Frend, *Rise of the Monophysite Movement*, 362–6.

[28] *Chronicle* 9. 15 (tr. Hamilton/Brooks), 250.

transcended every natural order entered into our nature while maintaining the unchanged and unconfused foundation of his own [things].

The Monophysites hoped to deduce from this passage two points. First, the union in Christ took place via composition: this is confirmed when Dionysius says that 'the simple Jesus became composite'. Secondly, God the Word joined with a complete human nature, *pace* Apollinaris: this Dionysius implies when he uses the adverb 'completely'.[29] The Monophysites go on to conclude that if God the Word became incarnate by joining to himself ensouled and rational human flesh which he made his own by joining with it in composition, then of necessity one must confess a single nature of God the Word.[30]

So much for the opening fusillade of the Monophysites. When once the battle is joined and the Collatio opens, the arguments take a different turn. As the details of what transpired are recorded by Innocentius, Hypatius the metropolitan of Ephesus acted as the spokesman for the Chalcedonians. It should be emphasized that Hypatius was a strict dyophysite, along the lines of theologians such as Theodoret. Although he adhered to Chalcedon, he would have been rejected by the Chalcedonian *avant-garde* as a Nestorian, in large measure because of his rejection of the theopaschite formula.[31] For our purposes Innocentius' account of the second day of the Collatio is of primary concern. After summarizing the results of the previous day's discussion, Hypatius turns his attention to the proof-texts which the Monophysites had used to support their cause. Hypatius discusses these in some detail, at length suggesting that they had been forged by the heretical Apollinarians of old. When the Monophysites offer to verify them against ancient copies in the archives of Alexandria, Hypatius responds by claiming that because those archives had long been in Monophysite hands, their books could no longer be trusted. Finally Hypatius turns to the Dionysian proof-text.

[29] John himself noted the anti-Apollinarian thrust of this passage, SchDN 196. 4. Moreover, the Chalcedonian patriarch of Antioch, Ephrem of Amid (*sedit c.*527 to *c.*545) cited the passage, 'the simple Jesus became composite' (113. 9), in order to support the Cyrillian expression, 'one incarnate nature of the Word'. See our notes to the translation of *SchDN* 196. 4.

[30] *Chronicle* 9. 15 (tr. Hamilton/Brooks), 251.

[31] Hypatius served as metropolitan of Ephesus from 531 to sometime not long after 537. He was an important player in the Christological controversies which shook Constantinople in the fourth decade of the 6th cent., as well as an accomplished theologian in his own right, at least judging from the remaining fragments of his theological and exegetical works (edited by Diekamp, *Analecta Patristica*, 109–53). For his doctrinal stance, Charles Moeller, 'Le Chalcédonisme et le néo-chalcédonisme en Orient de 451 à la fin du VIe siècle', in Aloys Grillmeier and Heinrich Bacht (eds.), *Das Konzil von Chalkedon*, vol. i (Würzburg, 1951), 661.

Those testimonies which you say are of the blessed Dionysius, how can you prove that they are authentic, as you claim? For if they are in fact by him, they would not have escaped the notice of the blessed Cyril. Why do I speak of the blessed Cyril, when the blessed Athanasius, if in fact he had thought them to be by Dionysius, would have offered these same testimonies concerning the consubstantial Trinity before all others at the council of Nicea against Arius' blasphemies of the diverse substance. But if none of the ancients made mention of them, I simply do not know how you can prove that they were written by Dionysius.[32]

The impression that here emerges is that Hypatius is caught off-guard by the works of Dionysius. He devotes a great deal of attention to the other texts which the Monophysites had cited, whereas his response to the Dionysian passage consists not of theological examination or detailed historical criticism, but of the simple statement that the Monophysites cannot prove these testimonies to be authentic. Moreover, it is only by implication that Hypatius can be said to class the Dionysian corpus among the heretical writings. His statements are directed against its historicity, not its orthodoxy. Hypatius even goes so far as to suggest that both Cyril and Athanasius would have used these works if they had known them. This implies that Hypatius must have been willing to grant the orthodoxy of at least certain parts of the corpus. Whatever Hypatius' final judgement on Dionysius may have been, we should be careful to maintain perspective on the relative weight that was given to Dionysius at the Collatio.[33] Neither party saw the debate to turn upon the witness of this supposed contemporary of the apostles. Of much greater importance were the other well-worn proof-texts, those from Felix and Julius of Rome, Cyprian, Athanasius, and the Gregories.

THE RECEPTION OF DIONYSIUS IN THE SIXTH CENTURY

If now we turn to the larger questions of who was using the works of Dionysius in the sixth century and for what purpose, we shall see that it is impossible to maintain the thesis that the works of Dionysius were

---

[32] ACO 4/2: 173. 12–18.

[33] It has been argued by Ernst Kitzinger ('The Cult of Images in the Age before Iconoclasm', *DOP* 8 (1954), 138) and Jean Gouillard ('Hypatios d'Éphèse ou du Pseudo-Denys à Théodore Studite', *REB* 19 (1961), 63–75) that Hypatius later came to approve of the Dionysian corpus. These claims have been strongly criticized by Stephen Gero ('Hypatius of Ephesus on the Cult of Images', in *Christianity, Judaism and Other Greco-Roman Cults*: part 2, *Early Christianity* (Leiden, 1975), 208–16, esp. 212–13).

primarily being used by the Monophysites against the Chalcedonians. Representatives of just about every major Christological party in the early sixth century at some point appealed to the authority of Dionysius. We have already discussed Severus and the Collatio of 532: other Monophysites to appeal to the authority of Dionysius include Theodosius I (d. 566) and perhaps also Ecumenius (*fl.* 530), as well as Themistius (*fl.* mid-sixth century), founder of the sect of the Agnoetes, and the Tritheist, John Philoponus (wr. between 546 and 549).[34] As for the Chalcedonians, Leontius of Byzantium (d. *c.*543), the patriarch Ephrem (*sedit* 527–45), and Job the Monk (*fl.* mid-sixth century), all made explicit use of Dionysius.[35] Leontius of Jerusalem, probably writing between 538 and 544, betrays a knowledge of the Dionysian corpus in a number of passages, although he nowhere explicitly cites it.[36] Of later sixth-century Chalcedonians, Pamphilus gives Dionysius a place of relative importance in his theological arguments.[37] So also, Leontius the Scholastic, author of the *De sectis*, writing probably in the last quarter of

[34] Theodosius, *Oratio theologica* (tr. Chabot), 50–2. For Theodosius' eventful life, John Meyendorff, *Imperial Unity and Christian Divisions* (Crestwood, NY, 1989), 120, 222–30, 253–8, 260–1, 266–8, 273–4, 279, and Aloys Grillmeier, *Christ in Christian Tradition*, ii/4 (Louisville, Ky., 1996), 53–9. Ecumenius, *Commentary on the Apocalypse* (ed. Hoskier), 46 n. 9. On the doctrinal affiliation of Ecumenius, John C. Lamoreaux, 'The Provenance of Ecumenius' Commentary on the Apocalypse', *VC* 52 (1998), 88–108; but cf. Castagno, 'Problema della datazione', 223–46. Themistius, *Epistula ad Marcellinum et Stephanum* (ACO ser. 2, 1: 144. 35–146. 22). For Themistius' life and theological activity, É. Amann, 'Thémistius', *DTC* 15/1 (1946), 219–22. Philoponus, *De opificio mundi* (ed. Reichardt), 2. 21, 3. 9, 3. 14. For John's life and works, Gustave Bardy, 'Jean Philopon', *DTC* 8/1 (1947), 831–9. A. L. Frothingham, *Stephen Bar Sudaili the Syrian Mystic and the Book of the Holy Hierotheos* (Leiden, 1886), 5 (followed by Stiglmayr, 'Aufkommen', 70), has suggested that Peter of Callinicus, the Monophysite patriarch of Antioch (*sedit* 581–91), made use of the corpus in his *Contra Damianum* (then unpublished). The new edition of this text (CCSG 29), however, shows no references to Dionysius.

[35] Leontius of Byzantium, *Against the Nestorians and the Eutychians* 1. 4 (PG 86/2: 1288), 1. 7 (1304–5), and the florilegium to book two of this work (see the notes to our translation of *SchDN* 288. 13). For Leontius' doctrinal affiliation, Brian Daley, 'The Origenism of Leontius of Byzantium', *JTS* NS, 27 (1976), 333–9. Ephrem, *Apology for Chalcedon, apud* Photius, cod. 229 (ed. Henry), 4: 144. For Ephrem's life, Joseph Lebon, 'Éphrem d'Amid, patriarche d'Antioche (526–544)', in *Mélanges d'histoire offerts à Ch. Moeller*, vol. i (Louvain, 1914), 197–214; Aloys Grillmeier, 'Éphrem d'Amid', *DHGE* 15 (1963), 581–5; and Glanville Downey, 'Ephraemius, Patriarch of Antioch', *ChH* 7 (1938), 364–70. Job the Monk, *Tract on the Incarnation, apud* Photius, cod. 222 (ed. Henry), 3: 175–7. For Job's life, É. Amann, 'Job', *DTC* 8/2 (1925), 1486–7, and Josef Slipyi, 'Die Trinitätslehre des byzantinischen Patriarchen Photios', *ZKT* 45 (1921), 81–7.

[36] Marcel Richard, 'Léonce de Jérusalem et Léonce de Byzance', *MSR* 1 (1944), 87–8. Cf. also Gouillard, 'Hypatios d'Éphèse', 75.

[37] *Dubitationum solutio* (CCSG 19), qu. 2. 108–19 (cf. *DN* 1.5–7), qu. 3. 111–22 (*DN* 1. 4, 113. 6–114. 1), qu. 11. 80–91 (*DN* 1. 2, 110. 2–10); cf. also qu. 10. 121–4 (*DN* 1. 2, 110. 3–4, 6).

the sixth century, mentions Dionysius as one of the ancient fathers.[38] Sergius of Resh'aina (d. 536), the first translator of the works of Dionysius into Syriac, though initially a Severian Monophysite, ended his life a member of the Chalcedonian camp.[39] The only major party not represented here would be the Julianists, though this is surely a result of the relatively few Julianist works surviving to the present. Even thinkers hard to put into a particular theological category, such as Stephen bar Sudaile (d. *c.*550) and Pseudo-Caesarius (wr. *c.*550), were influenced by the Dionysian corpus.[40]

Different parts of the Dionysian corpus were being used for different purposes. In the first half of the sixth century, the majority of open appeals to the authority of the corpus were restricted to the *Divine Names* and the *Epistles*. As would be expected, Christological issues were paramount. Severus twice used the Dionysian corpus against Julian (*DN* 2. 9, 133. 5–9). In their letter to Justinian the Monophysites used it against the Chalcedonians (*DN* 1. 4, 113. 6–12). Leontius of Byzantium appealed to the authority of Dionysius against the Julianists (*DN* 4. 25, 173. 6–7): his other two references carry little polemical value (*DN* 2. 10, 134. 11; 2. 4,

[38] Leontius Scholasticus, *De sectis* 3. 1 (PG 86/1: 1213A). On Leontius, Silas Rees, 'The *De Sectis*', *JTS* 40 (1939), 346–60, and Marcel Richard, 'Le Traité "De Sectis" et Léonce de Byzance', *RHE* 35 (1939), 695–723.

[39] According to Pseudo-Zachariah (tr. Hamilton/Brooks, 266), Sergius had a falling out with the bishop of Resh'aina and as a result took his case to the patriarch Ephrem, who then sent him to Rome in order to persuade Pope Agapetus to intervene in the East. As a result of Sergius' mission and the Pope's intervention, Ephrem was able to proceed against the recalcitrant Monophysites of Syria. In addition to his translation of the works of Dionysius, Sergius was also the author of an introduction to the corpus (ed. and tr. Sherwood), in which he tries to reconcile Dionysian and Evagrian spirituality. For the life and works of Sergius, Anton Baumstark, *Lucubrationes Syro-graecae* (Leipzig, 1894), 358–60; idem, *Geschichte der syrischen Literatur* (Bonn, 1922), 167; P. Sherwood, 'Sergius of Reshaina and the Syriac Versions of the Pseudo-Denis', *SE* 4 (1952), 174–84.

[40] Stephen Bar Sudaile's *Book of the Holy Hierotheus* has been edited and translated by Marsh. Concerning this work, see Frothingham, *Stephen Bar Sudaili*, *passim*; Irénée Hausherr, 'L'Influence du "Livre de Saint Hiérothée"', in *De doctrina spirituali christianorum orientalium* (Rome, 1933), 176–211; Antoine Guillaumont, 'Étienne Bar Soudaili', *DS* 4/2 (1961), 1481–8; G. Widengren, 'Researches in Syrian Mysticism', *Numen*, 8 (1961), 161–98. Pelikan ('Odyssey of Dionysian Spirituality', 15) has pointed to Bar Sudaile as further evidence that the works of Dionysius were popular in Monophysite circles. If the generally accepted account of Bar Sudaile's life is correct, this cannot be maintained, for Bar Sudaile was condemed as a heretic by a number of prominent Monophysites. As for Pseudo-Caesarius, in his *Erotapokriseis* (ed. Riedinger) he often employed distinctively Dionysian vocabulary (e.g. θεανδρικός is found no less than 28 times) and once (at 91. 29–31) mentioned the Areopagite by name. On this text, Rudolf Riedinger, 'Akoimeten', *TRE* 2 (1978), 148–53. It has been argued that the compiler of this work was a Severian (Rudolf Riedinger, 'War der Kompilator der Erotapokriseis des Pseudo-Kaisarios ein Severianer?' *Helikon*, 8 (1968), 440–3), but cf. Grillmeier, *Christ in Christian Tradition*, ii/2: 377–9, who concludes that he was a 'Spät-Henotiker'.

126. 3–128. 7). Ephrem used the corpus against the Monophysites (*DN*
1. 4, 113. 6–12). The Monophysite Theodosius employed it in controversy with the Chalcedonians (*DN* 1. 4, 113. 6–12; 2. 6, 130. 5–11).
Themistius turned it against the Severians (*EP* 4, 161. 9). Other authors,
such as John Philoponus, were attracted to historical references in the
corpus; or like the *Euthymian History* (perhaps stemming from the sixth
century), to its treatment of Mary.[41] What objections were made to the
authenticity of the Dionysian corpus? Hypatius is our only dissenting
voice. But even the assertion that Hypatius rejected the Dionysian corpus
should be nuanced, as we have argued. The more subtle indictment of the
corpus, that it is tainted with the stain of pagan philosophy, is nowhere
explicitly put forward in works to survive from the sixth century.[42]

Given the sheer volume of theological compositions produced in this
time period—massive doctrinal syntheses on the part of both Chalcedonians and opponents of Chalcedon, polemical works of the utmost
rigour, florilegia which tend to reach lengths of tedium—it is perhaps
surprising that the works of a supposed contemporary of the apostles
were not cited a great deal more than in fact they were. Indeed, the few
appeals to Dionysius are almost inconsequential in comparison with the
many thousands of times Athanasius, the Gregories, Cyril of Alexandria,
or Basil the Great were introduced into the controversies of the first half
of the sixth century. For this reason, one ought studiously to avoid con-
veying the impression that the works of Dionysius washed over the theological landscape of eastern Christianity and radically changed the way
theology was being done. Far from it! Apart from John's own work, one
must search far and wide for any evidence that the works of Dionysius
were being read at all.[43]

When John came to compose his *Scholia* between the years 537 and

---

[41] See the fragment of the *Euthymian History* found in sect. 18 of the *Sermo secundus in
gloriosum dormitionem sanctissimae Dei Genitricis ac perpetuae virginis Mariae* (PG 96:
747–52). We follow Honigmann's conclusions as to its date ('Juvenal of Jerusalem', *DOP* 5
(1950), 267–70), cf. M. Jugie, 'Le Récit de l'histoire euthymiaque sur la mort et l'assomption de la Sainte Vierge', *EO* 25 (1926), 385–92. This hagiographical text attempts to
account for why the Virgin left no relics, along the way explaining that both Dionysius
and Hierotheus were present as witnesses of her dormition (*DN* 3. 2, 141. 4–14 is cited
verbatim).

[42] See further the discussion in Ch. 5.

[43] To be sure, the peculiarly Dionysian lexicon, his idiosyncratic use of philosophical
language—this we find seeping into the cracks and crevices of even the most unphilo-
sophical of theological writings throughout the course of the 6th cent.: e.g. the hagiographer
Cyril of Scythopolis could not resist the temptation to use that distinctively Dionysian word
ἱεραρχία (ed. Schwartz, 95. 5, 224. 10). Cf. Josef Stiglmayr, 'Über die Termini Hierarch
und Hierarchie', *ZKT* 22 (1898), 180–7.

543, the Dionysian corpus had already begun to make its way on to the stage of sixth-century theological controversy, albeit in bits and pieces. But let us keep in mind the extent to which the Dionysian corpus was still an open question. Each of the major theological parties was beginning to take its stand on the way the text might be used, but none had yet established an interpretative framework such that questions about the proper interpretation of the Dionysian corpus were fixed and competing readings had to start from within this framework. There was certainly no Monophysite monopoly which needed to be broken. Let us also emphasize how close in time John's comments stand to the earliest appearance of the Dionysian corpus in the Christian east. Ten or twenty years at most separate the earliest references to the corpus from the dates for John's labours. John's exquisitely detailed commentary thus offers modern scholars not only their most vivid evidence for the way the Dionysian corpus entered into the dogmatic controversies of the Christian east, but also insight into the very earliest stages of this process.

2

John of Scythopolis

Sources for an examination of John's life are unfortunately quite meagre, consisting mostly of scattered comments in the theological and hagiographic works of John's near contemporaries, as well as later encomiastic notices relating to his theological activities. From materials such as these it is quite impossible to derive more than an outline of John's life. Furthermore, the vast majority of John's theological works have not survived the corrosive effects of time. The loss of these works has greatly diminished our understanding of the first generation of Neo-Chalcedonian theology in Syro-Palestine. But judging from the praise of his supporters, the condemnation of his opponents, and the information garnered from those parts of his œuvre which do remain, John's theological speculations were profound and his impact upon contemporaries significant. In this chapter we first examine the fragmentary evidence for the course of John's career in general and then present his (largely lost) theological works.[1] Following this we introduce John's *Scholia* and *Prologue* to the works of Dionysius the Areopagite.

JOHN'S CAREER

It is clear that in his activities as a theologian John made a noticeable impression upon his contemporaries and later theologians. Appeal can be made to the materials discussed in the second section of this chapter such as the use of his dogmatic works in later conciliar acts, the existence of at least one of his works in the patriarchal archives of Constantinople, the circulation of his works among contemporary theological opponents such as Basil of Cilicia and Severus of Antioch, as well as among later

[1] Previous treatments of John's biography include: Friedrich Loofs, *Leontius von Byzanz* (Leipzig, 1887), 269–72; Joseph Lebon, *Le Monophysisme Sévèrien* (Louvain, 1909), 71, 147–63 (*passim*); Siegfried Helmer, *Der Neuchalkedonismus* (Bonn, 1962), 176–81; Patrick T. R. Gray, *The Defense of Chalcedon in the East* (Leiden, 1979), 111–15; Lorenzo Perrone, *La chiesa di Palestina e le controversie christologiche* (Brescia, 1980), 240–9; Bernard Flusin, *Miracle et histoire dans l'œuvre de Cyrille de Scythopolis* (Paris, 1983), 17–29; John Binns, *Ascetics and Ambassadors of Christ* (Oxford, 1994), 141–2, 247–8.

supporters such as Photius. But also, a number of near contemporaries, living in the sixth and seventh centuries, offer brief glimpses into the importance of John's theological activities. The patriarch Sophronius made mention of John in the anti-Monothelite florilegium which he attached to his *Synodical Epistle* in the fourth decade of the seventh century.[2] This florilegium is no longer exant: knowledge of it is derived from Photius' brief summary.[3] According to Photius, it contained patristic witnesses to the twofold activity of Christ: some of these fathers living before Chalcedon, others contemporary with it, others living after it. Among the fathers cited by Sophronius: 'John the bishop of Scythopolis, who is among the saints, who wisely and with an inspired mind exerted himself on behalf of the Chalcedonian Synod.'[4] Some forty years later at the Third Council of Constantinople (680) Pope Agatho wrote of John as one of the venerable fathers who defended the doctrine of two natures in Christ and the teaching that there are two natural activities in Christ.[5] The approbation which John received at the hands of these seventh-century authors, who recognized in his work against the Monophysites ammunition for their own struggles with the Mono-thelites, can be set alongside evidence from the work of one of John's Palestinian contemporaries.

Leontius of Jerusalem in the florilegium attached to his treatise *Against the Monophysites* (written between 538 and 544) mentions 'John the bishop of Scythopolis', and associates him with the discovery of certain Apollinarian forgeries.[6] At issue here is a text being used by the Monophysites to defend the doctrine of a single nature in the incarnate Christ. This text was thought by them to be from the pen of Julius of Rome and was of great value because of its statement that from the two elements of Christ a single nature came to subsist.[7] This was obviously a proof-text which Leontius could not concede to the Monophysites. Not only, he argues, is this text not recognized as authentic by the Romans, but also it has been shown to be an Apollinarian forgery by John the

---

[2] For Sophronius' *Synodical Epistle*, Christoph von Schönborn, *Sophrone de Jérusalem* (Paris, 1972), 100.

[3] The text of the epistle is extant, ACO ser. 2, 2/1: 410–96. For Photius' summary of the florilegium, Photius, cod. 231 (ed. Henry), 3: 64–7.

[4] Photius, cod. 231 (ed. Henry), 3: 66.

[5] Mansi 11: 270.

[6] PG 86/2: 1865B–D. For Leontius of Jerusalem, Marcel Richard, 'Léonce de Jérusalem et Léonce de Byzance', *MSR* 1 (1944), 35–88; Gray, *Defense of Chalcedon*, 122–41; Loofs, *Leontius von Byzanz*, 269–72. Gray has convincingly argued (pp. 122–3) that this work should be dated sometime between 538 and 544.

[7] Referring to Julius I bishop of Rome (337–52).

bishop of Scythopolis, 'who laboured long in the most ancient writings of Apollinaris'. In particular, John found the 'Julius' passage in the recognized writings of Apollinaris, while yet another passage from the same text he found to contain manifest Apollinarian views on the replacement of Christ's human soul by the divine word. In the end, Leontius argues, the passage is not a legitimate proof-text for the Monophysites, it being stained with the heresy of Apollinaris.

Perhaps more indicative of John's importance as a theologian is the disdain in which he was held by his opponents. In the second section of this chapter we shall examine some of the opposition which John encountered at the hands of Basil of Cilicia and Severus of Antioch. To this can be added further testimony from the works of Severus. In one of his letters to 'Sergius the Physician and Sophist', dated, according to Brooks, between 515 and 518, Severus writes in defence of the reception given to Eutyches at the Latrocinium (449) by 'the holy Dioscorus'.[8] Severus draws attention to the fact that he had treated the issue at length some time ago, but that because certain men were slandering the council, he thought it good to send Sergius a copy of the former work. With regard to those who were calling into question the Latrocinium, he continues: 'Not only the wretched man from Scythopolis, but many others besides him and after him, employed absurdities, not knowing what they are saying, but made empty-minded fullness of blasphemy against God.' Although John is not here mentioned by name, it seems likely that it is he whom Severus has in his sights, for such an attack on Dioscorus was probably contained in John's work *Against the Aposchists*.[9]

Several sources dating from between 518 and 530 refer to John as a *scholasticus* in Scythopolis.[10] On the other hand, by the time Leontius came to write his *Against the Monophysites* (between 538 and 544), John was already being referred to as the bishop of Scythopolis. We thus gather that before assuming the metropolitan throne of Scythopolis John was a *scholasticus* resident in that city.[11] From Cyril of Scythopolis, we

[8] Severus, *ep.* 31 (PO 12/2: 264–6).

[9] On this work, see below. Brooks ad *ep.* 31 (PO 12/2: 264 n. 1) takes 'the wretched man from Scythopolis' to be a reference to John.

[10] John's *Against the Aposchists* (written post-518) was said by Photius to be written by John the *scholasticus*, with no indication that he was yet a bishop (see below), while Basil of Cilicia (see below), writing between 520 and 530, clearly presents John as a layman, referring to him as a διϰολόγος, a term synonymous with *scholasticus*. Further, John's *Apology for Chalcedon* (see below), written between 515 and 518, contains nothing to suggest that John was yet bishop.

[11] What exactly was a *scholasticus* in the context of the 6th cent.? As argued by Charlotte Roueché, *Aphrodisias in Late Antiquity* (London, 1989), 76–7, 107, the title begins to be encountered with some frequency in the 4th and 5th cents. and indicates that the man so

know of two *scholastici* named John who lived in Scythopolis in the early
sixth century. In his *Life of Sabas*, Cyril mentions a certain layman
named John, a *scholasticus* of Scythopolis, who in the company of
Theodosius (then bishop of that city) had gone out to meet St Sabas
when the latter was visiting the city in 518. Cyril writes: 'There was in
Scythopolis a certain *scholasticus*, John, son of the *compulsor*, a man wise
and enlightened of soul.[12] He came to St Sabas in the bishop's house and
explained for some time the evils and impieties of Silvanus the Samaritan
who had much imperial power and threatened the Christians.'[13] Sabas
then prophesied the eventual downfall of this Silvanus, a leader in the
Samaritan revolt of 529.[14] The other *scholasticus* named John, found in
early sixth-century Scythopolis, is Cyril's own father. Cyril records that
his father made the acquaintance of Sabas during the visit of 518, witnessed one of his miracles, and enjoyed the saint's company at his
house.[15] Elsewhere, when telling of Sabas' second visit to Scythopolis
in 531, Cyril further specifies that his father worked as a judge in the
episcopal court at Scythopolis, a legal assistant and adviser to the bishop
Theodosius.[16] It is unlikely that the second of these *scholastici*, Cyril's
father, is to be identified with our John. It is hard to imagine that Cyril
would not have made specific mention of the fact that his father had taken
up the episcopal throne following the death of Theodosius. But what of
the first John, the son of the *compulsor*? Certainty escapes us, but it is
tempting to identify him with our John.

As for the dates of John's episcopacy, it is possible to be fairly precise.
We know of two other bishops of Scythopolis in the first half of the sixth
century. There is the Theodosius whom we just encountered in the *Life
of Sabas*. He was already bishop in 518 and we last hear of him when he
attended the Synod of Jerusalem in 536.[17] We also know of a bishop

specified had completed the basic course of general studies and was qualified to take up
law as a profession. As such the title 'records a professional qualification, rather than an
officially awarded honour or office' (Roueché, *Aphrodisias*, 77). It was, moreover, not at all
uncommon for *scholastici* to become bishops. Indeed, the Council of Serdica (343) states
quite explicitly that the two most common reservoirs from which bishops could be drawn
consisted of *sive dives, sive scholasticus* (Mansi 3: 14c, cf. 27b).

[12] *Compulsor*s were imperial officials who gathered taxes and arrears from the imperial
domains.

[13] *Life of Sabas* 61 (ed. Schwartz), 162. 20–163. 2.

[14] A second mention of this John, son of the *compulsor*, is made by Cyril when recounting
the fulfilment of Sabas' prophecy. See *Life of Sabas* 70 (ed. Schwartz), 172.

[15] *Life of Sabas* 63 (ed. Schwartz), 164.

[16] *Life of Sabas* 75 (ed. Schwartz), 180. On such judicial advisers, John C. Lamoreaux,
'Episcopal Courts in Late Antiquity', *JECS* 3 (1995), 143–67.

[17] That he was bishop already in 518, *Life of Sabas* 61 (ed. Schwartz), 162. This same

named Theodore, a former abbot of the New Laura and of Origenist leanings, whom Theodore of Cappadocia, supporter of the Isochrists, made bishop of Scythopolis *circa* 548.[18] He must have held the episcopal throne of Scythopolis at least until 558/9, for his name appears in an inscription bearing that date.[19] We know that John did not become bishop after the reign of Theodore, for Leontius, writing between 538 and 544, mentions John as already a bishop. Two indications suggest that John was not the bishop before Theodosius. First, a number of sources dating from between 518 and 530 refer to John as a layman.[20] Secondly, in one of his letters written between 513 and 518 Severus mentions a bishop of Berytus who tended toward a Eutychian Christological position.[21] Severus goes on to state: 'It pleased this man also to deem worthy of honour that man, when he passed away, who was bishop of Scythopolis, that man who was hardly even a Christian, as you also know—an act full of stupidity.'[22] It would appear that the Eutychian bishop of Berytus had admitted to veneration a recently deceased bishop of Scythopolis, also a Eutychian. One can thus surmise that the predecessor of Theodosius on throne of Scythopolis was a strict Monophysite. This could hardly be our John. All told, the evidence converges on a date for John's episcopacy after Theodosius and before Theodore (i.e. after 536 but before *circa* 548).

JOHN'S THEOLOGICAL WORKS

Memory of a first treatise by John is preserved in Severus of Antioch's refutation of John the Grammarian's *Apology for Chalcedon*. Severus composed this work shortly after being exiled to Alexandria in 518, indeed probably in the very first year of his exile.[23] In the process of refuting the Grammarian's treatise, Severus twice mentions a treatise by

year Theodosius signed John of Jerusalem's *Synodical Epistle* against Severus (ACO 3: 79.4). Sometime shortly after 532 he ordained Cyril of Scythopolis as a reader (Flusin, *Miracle et histoire*, 16). For Theodosius at the Synod of Jerusalem, ACO 3: 188.8.

[18] *Life of Sabas* 89 (ed. Schwartz), 197. Toward the end of 552 he addressed to Justinian a tract against Origen, the *Libellus de erroribus Origenianis* (PG 86/1: 231–6). For the date of this text, Franz Diekamp, *Die Origenistischen Streitigkeiten* (Münster, 1899), 128. Cf. also Johannes Irmscher, 'Teodoro Scitopolitano', *Augustinianum*, 26 (1986), 185–90.

[19] M. Avi-Yonah, 'The Bath of the Lepers at Scythopolis', *IEJ* 13 (1963), 325–6.

[20] See above, at n. 10.

[21] On this bishop of Berytus, Ernest Honigmann, *Évêques et évêchés monophysites d'Asie antérieure au VIe siècle* (Louvain, 1951), 32–3.

[22] *Sixth Book of the Select Letters* (ed. Brooks), 1/2: 474.

[23] Lebon, *Monophysisme Sévérien*, 153.

John of Scythopolis, 'a lengthy apology for the Synod of Chalcedon'.[24] What the exact title of John's work was, we know not: let us refer to it as the *Apology for Chalcedon*. While treating the Grammarian's use and 'deliberate corruption' of a passage from St Ambrose, Severus digresses to examine John's use of that same passage, explaining along the way how he had come upon John's apology and giving in passing a number of quotations from John's work. According to Severus, John wrote an apology, but fearing refutation, he did not circulate it openly, but only among friends. Indeed, says Severus, 'he showed great care lest it fall into our hands'.[25] Now and then Severus happened upon portions of this work, and this through the help of zealous friends who surreptitiously copied extracts from it. But because Severus was unable to obtain the full work for the purpose of refutation, he contented himself with the demolition of 'the little work' of the Grammarian. But no matter, for in respect of doctrine 'the two were thought to be as one'.[26] And yet, while in the process of composing his refutation of the Grammarian, Severus was given a full exemplar of John's work, copied out by a friend. Severus was at that very moment engaged in writing his comments on the Grammarian's use of a passage from Ambrose, and by chance when he opened John's work his eyes alighted upon John's use of the very same passage from Ambrose.[27] Severus accuses John of having corrupted Ambrose's original text in three places, each time in favour of the Chalcedonian doctrine of Christ.[28] He also asserts that John was wrongly informed as to the prior appearance of this passage in earlier doctrinal debates.[29]

---

[24] Severus' second reference to John is brief and adds little to the first: 'We have now considered the passages of the famous Ambrose, bishop of Milan; we have also shown that they were corrupted by the Grammarian and by the Scythopolitan, defenders of their own impiety; and we have shown that they do not even agree amongst themselves in this forgery' (*Contra Impium Grammaticum* 3. 2. 13 (tr. Lebon), 139).

[25] *Contra Impium Grammaticum* 3. 1. 17 (tr. Lebon), 201.

[26] *Contra Impium Grammaticum* 3. 1. 17 (tr. Lebon), 202.

[27] The passage in question was from Ambrose's *De fide ad Gratianum* 2. 77 (PL 16: 576B13–C5). It had first come to play a role in 5th- and 6th-cent. Christological controversy when it was cited at the Council of Ephesus (431), and later when Pope Leo included it in the florilegium (fr. 7) attached to his *Tome* before sending it a second time to Constantinople (450), and still later when it was included in the acts of the Council of Chalcedon. On this passage from Ambrose, Marcel Richard, 'Notes sur les florilèges dogmatiques du Ve et du VIe siècle', in *Actes du VIe congrès international d'études byzantines*, vol. i (Paris, 1950), 317–18; Gustave Bardy, 'Sur une citation de saint Ambroise dans les controverses christologiques', *RHE* 40 (1944/5), 171–6; M. Breydy, 'Les Témoignages de Sévère d'Antioche dans l'exposé de la foi de Jean Maron', *Mus.* 103 (1990), 227–8.

[28] *Contra Impium Grammaticum* 3. 1. 17 (tr. Lebon), 203.

[29] *Contra Impium Grammaticum* 3. 1. 17 (tr. Lebon), 202.

Following his examination of this Ambrose citation, Severus moves on to another defect of John's apology, again relating to its use of Ambrose. At question here is John's appeal to an oration entitled 'De fide', ascribed to Ambrose, but in fact, according to Severus, a forgery made by the Nestorians.[30] Among the passages from the 'De fide' cited by John was the following: 'But [Christ], coeternal with his Father, because of the multitude of his goodness deigned to unite to himself the first-fruits of our nature, not by way of mixture, but one and the same being made manifest in each of the two natures.'[31] In response to John's use of this proof-text, Severus lines up in quick succession a number of further citations from the 'De fide' which he in turn compares with material taken from Andrew of Samosata, Nestorius, Theodore of Mopsuestia, Cyril, and others, so as to show not only the affinity of the 'De fide' to works clearly recognized as Nestorian, but also to show its utter discord with the doctrine of Cyril.[32]

As to the general theological position taken by John in his *Apology for Chalcedon*, little that is specific can be gathered from Severus' somewhat random lucubrations. The Ambrose texts which John utilized had long been under consideration on both sides of the Chalcedonian fence: by the Council's defenders (be they strict dyophysites or Neo-Chalcedonians) and by the Council's detractors. In this regard we see John following well-worn paths. When did John compose his text? Clearly he wrote his work within a few years of Severus' exile, let us say sometime between 515 and 518. These dates accord well with John's apparent reticence to circulate his work openly, corresponding as they do with the close of the last period of Monophysite ascendancy under the emperor Anastasius.

Photius offers a summary of a second work by John, his *Against the Aposchists*.[33] The full title of this work, as recorded by Photius, is as follows: *Against Those Who Separate Themselves* [τῶν ἀποσχιστῶν] *from the Church, which is to say, Against Eutyches and Dioscorus and Those Who Think the Same and Refuse to Proclaim Christ in Two Natures.* As to the

---

[30] *Contra Impium Grammaticum* 3. 1. 17 (tr. Lebon), 204. 1–8. Whether this was in fact a forgery is a question not yet resolved. Whereas Gustave Bardy has argued for its inauthenticity, placing its composition during the Nestorian controversy ('L'"Expositio Fidei" attribuée à saint Ambroise', in *Miscellanea Giovanni Mercati*, vol. i (Vatican, 1946), 199–218), Marcel Richard has defended its authenticity ('Notes sur les florilèges dogmatiques', 315–16). This oration had come first to play a role in the Christological controversies following the Council of Ephesus when it was included by Theodoret in the second of his three florilegia appended to his *Eranistes*.

[31] *Contra Impium Grammaticum* 3. 1. 17 (tr. Lebon), 204. 10–13.

[32] *Contra Impium Grammaticum* 3. 1. 17 (tr. Lebon), 206–7.

[33] Photius, cod. 95 (ed. Henry), 2: 48 .

identity of the author of this treatise, Photius specifies simply that John was a scholastic of Scythopolis. Concerning the circumstances which led John to compose this work, Photius gives only two indications: (i) his treatise was written in response to another work, an anonymous treatise with the title *Against Nestorius*, and (ii) 'a certain high priest by the name of Julian' had commissioned it. The treatise, according to Photius, contained twelve books. Photius goes on to report that John fought with not a little energy against the Aposchists and that, although he employed an abundance of scriptural testimonies, he did not disdain the use of logical arguments if they were appropriate to the subject under consideration. As to the theological contents of this treatise, little can be garnered from Photius' summary. From the title of this work, however, it is clear that John must have concerned himself with the circumstances surrounding Dioscorus' reception of Eutyches at the Latrocinium, as well as with a defence of the Chalcedonian expression 'in two natures'.

As for this anonymous treatise *Against Nestorius*, Photius writes that its author had refused to give his name and had intentionally mistitled his work so as to lead astray those who were simple of mind. By this he probably means that Chalcedonian readers, running across a treatise critical of Nestorius would find themselves the unwitting subjects of Monophysite propaganda. Photius moreover suggests that the author of the treatise 'may have been Basil of Cilicia', a tireless opponent of John who also wrote against the latter a dramatic dialogue.[34] What of Photius' suggestion? Some modern scholars have accepted it.[35] All indications as to Basil's theological stand, however, suggest that he was a strict dyophysite adherent to the Council of Chalcedon and not a Monophysite.[36] And yet, from the title of John's work it is clear that the anonymous author against whom he was writing was a Monophysite. For this reason alone, Photius' suggestion cannot stand. Who was this Julian, the high priest who commissioned this work from John? Although one cannot rule out the possibility that he is otherwise unknown, among the Chalcedonians named Julian living in the Christian east during the late fifth and early sixth century, there are two possible identifications: Julian the patriarch of Antioch, or Julian the metropolitan of Bostra in the Province of Arabia.[37] It is quite unlikely that Photius meant the

[34] For this text, see below.

[35] e.g. Honigmann, *Évêques et évêchés*, 81.

[36] See below.

[37] The first Julian, through the help of Gennadius of Constantinople and the emperor Leo, was appointed to the see of Antioch in 471, as a substitute for Peter the Fuller. After a reign of about five years, in 475/6 Julian was replaced on the throne of Antioch by Peter the

patriarch of Antioch.[38] When it is considered that Julian the metropolitan of Bostra moved in the same dogmatic circles as John—Palestinian monastic support of Chalcedon and opposition to its Monophysite critics, especially Severus—there is nothing to hinder the identification of this Julian with the metropolitan of Bostra. When did John compose his treatise? Specific dates cannot be given. Nevertheless, if the identification of Julian with the metropolitan of Bostra is correct, perhaps we can best date John's treatise to sometime shortly after 518.[39]

Consideration of a third treatise by John brings us on to ground less unstable, if not yet terra firma. Again the work is not extant. Nor this time do we have even a direct summary by Photius. Instead, knowledge of this text derives from a detailed summary by Photius of a refutation of John's work, a refutation composed by the same Basil of Cilicia whom we encountered above.[40] What the title of John's treatise was, we know not. Because, however, it was clearly directed against those theologians tending toward a more strictly dyophysite view of Christ, let us refer to it as *Against the Nestorians*. Few details have come down to us concerning this Basil.[41] Although Photius records that he was a priest in Antioch at the time of the patriarch Flavian (498–518) and the emperor Anastasius (491–518), this statement ought not be taken at face value.[42] He is known

Fuller who this time had the support of the imperial usurper, Basiliscus. See C. Karalevskij, 'Antioche', *DHGE* 3 (1924), 576. The second Julian, Metropolitan of Bostra, was an opponent of the Monophysites, most especially of Severus himself. He and Epiphanius of Tyre were the only metropolitans to refuse assent to the consecration of Severus in 512. In 515 we find Julian leaving his see and going to the monastery of Theodosius in Palestine, where he remained until 518, at which point he was rehabilitated to his see. See Honigmann, *Évêques et évêchés*, 76.

[38] He prefaced the term 'high priest' with an indefinite article, implying that he was himself not quite sure of his identity: and yet, Julian the patriarch of Antioch was a fairly well-known person. Moreover, elsewhere in his *Bibliotheca* (cod. 42 (ed. Henry), 1: 26–7) Photius offers dates for Basil much later than the time of the patriarch Julian's reign (see below).

[39] And this for three reasons: (i) John refers to Julian as a high priest, implying that he was not writing during the latter's sojourn at the monastery of Theodosius: perhaps before or perhaps after; (ii) one can conjecture that John came to know Julian during his stay in Palestine, and upon his return to Bostra, the latter requested John's refutation—perhaps in order to undo the effects of the Monophysite Cassien, who had held the see of Bostra during Julian's absence: and (iii) a date around 520 would accord well with what is known of John's other literary activities.

[40] Photius, cod. 107 (ed. Henry), 2: 74–8.

[41] The best account of Basil's life (with bibliography) remains that of Honigmann (*Évêques et évêchés*, 80–1), who maintains rightly that Basil is not to be identified with Basil of Irenopolis. Cf. also P. Godet, 'Basil de Cilicie', *DTC* 2/1 (1932), 463–4.

[42] Photius, cod. 107 (ed. Henry), 2: 77. It is likely that Basil was projecting his work back in time, for he gives undue attention in this work to the theopaschite formula, whereas controversy concerning theopaschism became a major issue of debate in the Christian east

to have written at least two works: his treatise *Against John of Scythopolis* here under consideration, as well as a *History of the Church*.[43] It has been asserted that Basil was a Nestorian.[44] This, however, is unlikely.[45] Rather, Basil is better understood as a strict dyophysite adherent of the Council of Chalcedon, a dogmatic standpoint not likely to ameliorate his opponents, for in their eyes such a position was no better than Nestorianism itself.[46]

Photius offers a fairly comprehensive overview of Basil's refutation of John. He informs us that Basil had composed his refutation in sixteen books against John's treatise which comprised three books. According to Photius, Basil accused John of various moral and theological defects: he was suspect of Manichaeanism; he restricted the forty days of Lent to a mere three weeks and did not restrain himself from eating the meat of birds during this time; he attended Hellenic (scil. Pagan) rites; driven by gluttony, he would never partake of the 'perfected sacred act', but after the Gospel would partake of the mysteries with the children and then hurry off to his table.[47] According to Photius, Basil 'insulted the man by scattering these things throughout just about the whole of his work'.[48] Perhaps the reference to John as an initiate in Hellenic rites can best be

only after 519. Cf. É. Amann, 'Théopaschite (Controverse)', *DTC* 15/1 (1946), 505–12, and 'Scythes (Moines)', *DTC* 14/2 (1941), 1746–53. How would Basil have benefited by falsely claiming to be writing under Flavian? An answer to this question has been suggested by Honigmann and further argued by Perrone (Honigmann, *Évêques et évêchés*, 81, Perrone, *Chiesa di Palestina*, 244). Basil was attempting to arrogate to himself the authority of Flavian, the resolute opponent of Philoxenus, the same Flavian who was eventually exiled (512) to Petra for his defence of Chalcedon.

[43] Basil's *History of the Church* was in three books: the first treating of events in the reigns of Marcian, Leo, and Zeno (from 450 to 483); the second, which alone Photius had read, encompassing what happened between the death of Pope Simplicius in 483 and the death of Anastasius in 518; the third dealing with the events of the reign of Justin I (518–27). Cf. Photius, cod. 42 (ed. Henry), 1: 26–7.

[44] Charles Moeller, 'Le Chalcédonisme et le néo-chalcédonisme en Orient de 451 à la fin du VIe siècle', in Aloys Grillmeier and Heinrich Bacht (eds.), *Das Konzil von Chalkedon*, vol. i (Würzburg, 1951), 656.

[45] Photius writes that Basil '*defends* weakly and wrongly how *we* do not say there are two Christs'. In this is implied that even Photius recognized a certain kinship with the strict Chalcedonians. Photius adds that although Basil was 'sick with the heresy of Nestorius, he did not make Nestorius his friend', instead calling Diodore and Theodore fathers. Photius also says that Basil refrained from 'shamelessly blaspheming the divine Cyril to his face'. See Photius, cod. 107 (ed. Henry), 2: 78

[46] Neo-Chalcedonian objections to the theology of Basil and others like him may perhaps explain two peculiar passages in the *Scholia* (*SchEH* 181. 10, *SchCH* 72. 5) which mention a sect associated with the Nestorians and called 'Basileans'.

[47] For these accusations, Photius, cod. 107 (ed. Henry), 2: 74–5.

[48] Photius, cod. 107 (ed. Henry), 2: 75.

seen as a subtle indictment of John's knowledge of Hellenic learning. The accusation of Manichaean inclinations is not surprising, for such was commonly applied by the strict dyophysites to any and all who in their opinion compromised the humanity of Christ.[49] At the same time, Basil criticized John in the strongest terms for 'urging nothing other than the twelve chapters of Cyril, and especially the twelfth which introduces theopaschism'—as Theodoret says and no doubt Basil as well, 'those Chapters surely grew from the bitter root of Apollinaris'.[50] And finally, Photius notes that Basil had been commissioned to write this work by a certain Leontius, 'whom [Basil] revered as holy and god-beloved and as a father'.[51] Who this Leontius was, we know not, there being a singular lack of strict Chalcedonians by the name 'Leontius'. Photius goes on to give a brief overview of the first thirteen books of Basil's treatise, paying particular attention to the biblical texts being discussed. It is clear both from Photius and from the biblical texts at issue that Basil had placed great weight upon the theopaschite confession of Christ,[52] and further-more, that John seemed to have been intent on showing that the Chalcedonian creed was best interpreted in a Cyrillian sense if Nestorianism was to be avoided.[53]

When did John write his treatise *Against the Nestorians*? The most that can be said is probably sometime after the outbreak of controversy over the theopaschite formula in 519. Because Basil's *Church History* did not go beyond the reign of Justin (518–27), it can be surmised that Basil him-self did not live into the reign of Justinian. If this is the case, it would seem likely that John's work and Basil's refutation of that work probably appeared in the third decade of the sixth century.

We are fortunate to possess a substantial fragment of a fourth treatise by John, his *Against Severus*. The fragment in question is preserved in

[49] e.g. according to Theodoret (*Eran.* 113 (ed. Ettlinger, 117)), whose theological views were probably not all that different than Basil's, not only Simon, Menander, Marcion, Valentinus, Basilides, Bardesanes, and Cerdo, but also Mani himself, 'openly denied the humanity of Christ', and thus became the fathers of the Monophysite heresy.

[50] Photius, cod. 107 (ed. Henry), 2: 78. Theodoret, *Epistle* 151 (PG 83: 1417A).

[51] Photius, cod. 107 (ed. Henry), 2: 78.

[52] In defence of which John appealed especially to John 3: 13, 3: 16, Rom. 8: 32, 1 Cor. 2: 8.

[53] This is implied in John's accusation that strict Chalcedonians were teaching the Nestorian doctrine of the two Christs, and by his claim that 'saying Christ is the same as saying God', an argument meant to emphasize an anti-Nestorian view of the attributes of Christ. It is also clear from some of the biblical texts being debated. These concern John's defence of the contention that the God-Word assumed a human nature, but was not changed into or fused with that nature, such that a *tertium quid* should result which is nei-ther God nor human, which would nullify the central soteriological point of the Incarnation (using especially Isa. 11: 1, John 1: 14, Baruch 3: 35–7).

three places, each time being incorporated in later texts with a view to the seventh-century Monothelite controversy.[54] It was of use to later authors because of its clear confession of 'two activities after the union'. According to the lemma, the fragment being cited comes from the eighth book of John's refutation of Severus. The complete text is as follows:

We see why [Severus] again accuses the most holy Pope Leo, for the [latter] says that 'each form with the union of the other does what is proper to itself'. The Word does what is of the Word; the body does what is of the body.

Since you, [Severus], have presented this sacred saying as absurd, consider Julian of Halicarnassus who refutes you and thus tears to pieces your [arguments]: 'The Word works incorruption, the flesh worked corruption, according to your blasphemy.'

Tell us, my good man, do you believe that the God-Word was united substantially with the flesh and soul to which he was united?

Indeed, [Severus] says.

This God over all, by the distinctive character of his divinity, did he hold sway over heaven and earth and sea, ether and air, angels and archangels, rulers and powers and, to speak in short, the thousands upon thousand and myriads upon myriad of holy servants and invisible beings which are in incorporeal blessedness—did he, I repeat, hold sway over them so as to maintain and providentially protect all things visible and invisible generally and each one particularly?

Indeed, I suppose that you will grant this, since you have not completely separated yourself [from the truth].

Will you not call such providence the activity of God?

And with this you will not dispute, since not even now do you want to fight so openly against the divinity. Therefore you will grant that the activity of the God and Incarnate one is unceasing.

Would you say that the intelligent soul hypostatically united with him thought or was not able to think?

If, on the one hand, it was not able to think, you have fallen in with the blasphemy of Apollinaris, your father, who said that the humanity united with the God-Word was without a mind. If, on the other hand, you say that the mind thought and was not unable to think after the manner of soulless or mindless things, you will grant completely that thought is an activity of the mind, since even now you wish to be consistent in your reasoning.

For example: he knew that he was united with the Divinity, even if he had come into the state of a nature which is the same as men, apart from sin; he knew that in fact he had risen above every creation, seen and unseen, and [that] the soul indivisibly united with God, the creator of the universe, was being worshipped by

[54] It is found in: (i) the *Doctrina Patrum* 13. 13 (ed. Diekamp), 85–6, (ii) the acts of the Lateran Council of 649 (ACO ser. 2, 1: 314. 1–5), and (iii) the acts of the Council of Constantinople of 681 (Mansi 11: 437–40). This last version is the fullest and thus the basis for our translation.

the upper powers; he recalled the virgin Theotokos and birth according to the flesh from her, the passing of time upon the earth, the saving passion, the cross, the grave, the resurrection, the ascension into heaven; he knew that every army of heaven had surrounded it and was worshipping it as the soul of God.

You yourself, I suppose, would say that such thought is the activity of a thinking soul which is indivisibly united with the divinity. You see that we see that our one and the same Lord Jesus Christ, his divinity and his humanity, indivisibly and without change has two activities.

Having cited this passage, the acts of the Council of Constantinople go on to specify that the excerpt was checked against the copy of the book found in the patriarchal residence.

The theological arguments here employed by John in defence of Leo's contention that each nature maintains its prior characteristics even after the union are tangled, but clever. Having adduced the negative evidence of Severus' opponent, Julian, John drew forth from his hypothetical-Severus the admission that after the union Christ's divine nature continued to exercise its providential control of the world, which is to say, after the union the divine nature's activity remained as it was before the union. As to Christ's human nature and its activity after the union, John argued that Christ's human mind was cognizant of the divine nature's attributes and thus that Christ's mind had its own activity, separate from the divine activity. From this it follows that the natures of Christ, although united, maintained intact their natural properties and the activities expressive of those properties, which conclusion John evidently considered to express the same as Leo's assertion that 'each form with the union of the other does what is proper to itself'.

John's knowledge of the Julianist schism implies as a date for this treatise sometime after 518.[55] Because knowledge of the schism between Severus and Julian in its fully developed form would have taken time to reach Palestine (remember that John has even cited a work of Julian), his work was probably written at least a few years after the onset of the controversy—let us say, sometime shortly after 520.

To summarize the results of our investigations thus far: we have knowledge of four works from the pen of John: (1) *Apology for Chalcedon*, perhaps written between 515 and 518; (2) *Against the Aposchists*, perhaps written sometime shortly after 518; (3) *Against the Nestorians*, perhaps written in the 520s; (4) *Against Severus*, probably written shortly after 520. These works show John to have been active on two fronts, fighting against both Nestorians (or those considered by him to be Nestorians,

---

[55] A concern for the Julianists is also seen in John's *Scholia* (e.g. SchDN 221. 8, 229. 5).

such as Basil of Cilicia) and Severian Monophysites. At stake was nothing less than the defence and proper understanding of the Chalcedonian formula. For his efforts, John was attacked by strict Chalcedonians like Basil and by Monophysites like Severus. Less is known of the specific course of John's career, whether secular or ecclesiastical. He was certainly active in controversy with the opponents of Chalcedon before his episcopacy (after 536 but before *circa* 548). His defence of Chalcedon and his refutation of its opponents earned him the praise of contemporaries, as well as the approbation of later theologians. The image of John's theological accomplishments and activities as it has been uncovered in these investigations allows us to place him squarely within the midst of the Christological controversies which troubled Palestine in the early sixth century. Although much has been lost, enough remains to support the conclusion that he was a major player in the debates of his time, even if primarily on a provincial level.

JOHN'S *SCHOLIA* ON THE WORKS OF DIONYSIUS

Our meagre knowledge of John's theological activity can now be augmented. Recent research into the earliest commentaries on Dionysius has in effect resulted in the recovery of a 'new' work by John, his *Scholia* on the works of Dionysius. As has been known for some time, the scholia reprinted by Migne under the title *Scholia sancti Maximi in opera beati Dionysii* are in fact a conflation of the comments of at least two authors, John of Scythopolis and Maximus the Confessor.[56] Until recently it was impossible to distinguish the authorship of individual scholia. This fact more than any other rendered the *Scholia* all but unusable for scholarly purposes. Now, however, on the basis of the work of Beate Regina Suchla this situation is beginning to be rectified.[57] She has discovered an early

[56] In 875 Anastasius Bibliothecarius informed Charles the Bald that in Constantinople he had recently received a copy of the *Scholia* on the works of Dionysius. This text he translated and added to the margins of Eriugena's Latin version of the works of Dionysius. He goes on to state that these scholia were written by two different authors, Maximus and John, and that in his translation he would identify those by Maximus with the sign of the cross (PL 129: 740). The oldest surviving manuscript of the *Corpus Anastasianum*, Berlin Phill. 1668 (10th cent.), no longer preserves Anastasius' crosses accurately, if at all. A collation of this manuscript showed that there are very few such crosses, and furthermore that some of them are affixed to scholia which we otherwise know were written by John, as they are present in the early Syriac and Greek recension of the scholia.

[57] The results of Suchla's labours can be found in the following publications: 'Die sogenannten Maximus-Scholien des Corpus Dionysiacum Areopagiticum', *NAWG* (1980), 3: 31–66; 'Die Überlieferung von Prolog und Scholien des Johannes von Skythopolis zum

Syriac and Greek recension of the *Scholia* which contains only those comments authored by John.

The first translation of the works of Dionysius into Syriac was accomplished by Sergius of Resh'aina sometime before his death in 536. Sergius' translation did not included any scholia. Some two hundred years later in 708, Phocas bar Sergius, being dissatisfied with the quality of Sergius' work, effected yet another translation of the works of Dionysius into Syriac. In the preface to his translation, Phocas informs the reader that he was able to better Sergius' version in large part because of his access to the explications of John, 'an orthodox man, of good and glorious memory, by trade a *scholasticus*, who originated from the city of Scythopolis'.[58] Over against Phocas' translation of the *Scholia* can be set the evidence of a nearly identical early Greek recension.[59] The collective evidence of the early Syriac and Greek recensions points conclusively to the continued existence of an unconflated version of John's *Scholia* into the eighth century and beyond, a version which it is now possible to recover.

To date, Suchla has published the results of her collation only for the scholia on the *The Divine Names*. Using a similar approach, the authors of this study have provisionally identified the comments by John on the rest of the works of Dionysius. We based our collation on a Syriac manuscript written in the year 837, British Library, cod. 626, add. 12,152 (hereafter: Syr.).[60] A number of important scholia adduced in what follows were verified by recourse to the early Greek recension as witnessed in Florence, Biblioteca Laurenziana, Conventi Soppressi, cod. 202 (hereafter: FA), perhaps the earliest of the Greek manuscripts containing the shorter recension. It seemed safe for the purposes of this study to forgo a full collation of the Greek manuscripts, especially given the extreme stability of this early recension, as evidenced in Suchla's collation of the scholia on *The Divine Names*. Of those comments on the *The Divine Names* which are present in the early Syriac recension—of which there

griechischen Corpus Dionysiacum Areopagiticum', *SP* 18/2 (1989), 79–83; *Corpus Dionysiacum I*, 38–54.

[58] See William Wright, *Catalogue of Syriac Manuscripts in the British Museum*, vol. ii (London, 1871), 494.

[59] Suchla signals the following manuscripts in this regard: HA = Jerusalem, Patriarchal Library, Fonds tou Timiou Staurou, cod. 23, 9th cent.; MA = Moscow, Staatliches Historisches Museum, cod. 109, 9th cent., only those scholia written in the first hand being taken into consideration (Suchla, 'Sogenannten Maximus-Scholien', 46); FA = Florence, Biblioteca Laurenziana, Conventi Soppressi, cod. 202, written in 886; PD = Paris, Bibliothèque Nationale, cod. Gr. 440, 11th or 12th cent., only those scholia written in the first hand being taken into consideration (Suchla, 'Sogenannten Maximus-Scholien', 47).

[60] The results of our collation are found in tabulated form in the Appendix.

are 260—only twenty-two are not found, all or in part, in at least one of
the four manuscripts bearing witness to the early Greek recension. Of
these twenty-two comments, seventeen are short marginalia which
simply repeat or summarize the main point of the passage being
commented upon, or alternatively amplify the works of Dionysius
with additional biblical citations.[61] The other five comments exhibit no
particular characteristics which allow us to explain their non-inclusion in
the Greek recension.[62] It should be noted, however, that whatever the
ultimate origin of these twenty-two comments it is quite unlikely that
they originated first with the Syriac translation. In other words, it is far
more likely that they were excluded from the Greek recension.

A definitive examination of the Syriac and Greek manuscript evidence
for the scholia awaits the results of Suchla's labours. None the less, our
provisional identification of those scholia by John will probably not be
reduced in number, if perhaps a few additional scholia will be added by a
detailed collation of the early Greek recension. For this reason, the set of
scholia which we have isolated can form a sure starting-point for an
examination of John's exegetical labours.

The magnitude of John's newly recovered commentary can be gauged
from the following figures. In Migne's edition of the *Scholia* there are
approximately 1,675 individual scholia. These range in length anywhere
from one or two lines to well over a column. Of this total, roughly 600
scholia (all or in part) can be assigned to John with certainty. In other
words, around 36 per cent of the scholia printed in Migne are by John.
Note, however, that this percentage is based solely on the *number* of
scholia. Since the scholia by John tend to be longer than the unidentified
scholia, the total *length* of John's scholia in proportion to the whole of the
commentary is closer to 70 per cent.[63] Thus, of the approximately 225
columns of Greek text in Migne, around 160 columns can be ascribed
with certainty to John.

Various factors converge to determine an approximate date of composition for John's *Scholia*. First, in two scholia John makes mention of
the schism between Severus and Julian.[64] This controversy began shortly
after 518. On the other hand, John evinces no knowledge of the Three

---

[61] *SchDN* 232. 2, 236. 2, 249. 6, 252. 2–4, 261. 1, 296. 3, 308. 4, 340. 4, 356. 5, 360. 6,
364. 2, 385. 2, 413. 4, 416. 2–3.

[62] *SchDN* 220. 1, 224. 4, 292. 11, 400. 7, 401. 3.

[63] We have arrived at this figure by dividing the number of characters in the computer
file containing our translation of John's scholia by the number of characters in that containing a translation of all the scholia.

[64] *SchDN* 221. 8, 229. 5.

Chapters controversy which began to break in 544. Secondly, John refers to the Origenist controversy as a contemporary problem.[65] This implies a date after the death of Sabas in December of 532.[66] On the other hand, the *Scholia* probably appeared before the edict against Origen in 543, in so far as John sometimes refers to Origen and even Evagrius with a measure of approval.[67] This would have been unlikely after 543, especially when we consider that John, as metropolitan of Scythopolis, would certainly have signed the edict.[68] Finally, John notes with approval Antipater of Bostra's work against Origen.[69] This makes it possible to be even more precise, for at the beginning of the hegumenate of Gelasius (537/8) Antipater's anti-Origenist treatises first appear in the sixth-century fight against Origen, being supported by the monks of monastery of St Sabas.[70] We conclude therefore that the *Scholia* were probably written between 537 and 543, in other words, in the first half of John's episcopacy.

JOHN'S *PROLOGUE* AS AN INTRODUCTION TO THE *SCHOLIA*

Closely associated with John's *Scholia* is his *Prologue* to the works of Dionysius.[71] Many themes intimated in the *Prologue* find their full development only in the *Scholia*: indeed, John explicitly defers full discussion of certain issues, saying that they will be treated in the appropriate context in the *Scholia*. Given the integral relation between the *Scholia* and the *Prologue*, it can be concluded that both works were composed at the same time.

John intended his *Prologue* to serve as an introduction not only to the Dionysian corpus but also to his own *Scholia*. A modern parallel would be

---

[65] *SchEH* 173. 8.

[66] Cyril, *Life of Sabas* 83–4 (ed. Schwartz), 188. 3–24. For historical details on the outbreak of the Origenist crisis in 6th-cent. Palestine, Antoine Guillaumont, *Les 'Képhalaia Gnostica' d'Évagre le Pontique et l'histoire de l'origénisme* (Paris, 1962), 128–33.

[67] *SchCH* 76. 7, *SchDN* 337. 5, *SchEP* 549. 6.

[68] For details on this edict, Guillaumont, *Képhalaia Gnostica*, 132; Aloys Grillmeier, *Christ in Christian Tradition*, ii/2 (Louisville, Ky., 1995), 385–402.

[69] *SchEH* 176. 3.

[70] Cyril, *Life of Sabas* 84 (ed. Schwartz), 189. 14–22, cf. Guillaumont, *Képhalaia Gnostica*, 131.

[71] To date the only detailed studies of this text are those by Beate Regina Suchla, 'Die Überlieferung des Prologs des Johannes von Skythopolis zum griechischen Corpus Dionysiacum Areopagiticum', *NAWG* (1984), 4: 176–88; 'Eine Redaktion des griechischen Corpus Dionysiacum Areopagiticum im Umkreis des Johannes von Skythopolis, des Verfassers von Prolog und Scholien', *NAWG* (1985), 4: 177–93; and 'Verteidigung eines platonischen Denkmodells einer christlichen Welt', *NAWG* (1995), 1: 1–28.

an annotated Bible in which the prologue ostensibly introduces the Bible itself rather than the annotations, and yet inevitably previews the concerns which will appear in those annotations. So also, at the same time that it introduces the Dionysian corpus, John's *Prologue* also indirectly reveals his basic interpretative strategies and the issues which will inform his marginal comments.

In his *Prologue* to the Dionysian corpus, John argues first for the integrity of the Areopagite and then for the orthodoxy and authenticity of his writings. He invokes the exalted reputation of the council of the Areopagus as proof of the nobility of Dionysius, even before Paul converted him. Given this background, John's second section argues for the doctrinal orthodoxy of his writings, over against a number of specific charges that they were heretical. The third and final section then builds upon these foundations to argue for the authenticity of the corpus as a whole, in the face of explicit suspicions to the contrary. The *Prologue*'s specific comments on Dionysian integrity, orthodoxy, and authenticity deserve careful attention. As important as they are in themselves, they also constitute a preview of John's concerns in the *Scholia*, for every subject introduced in the *Prologue* is treated in the course of the *Scholia*, even as every major concern evident in the *Scholia* is explicitly mentioned in the *Prologue*. Thus, our observations here on the character of John's *Prologue* serve as an introduction to our subsequent chapters on the range of sources and doctrinal concerns which characterize the *Scholia* overall. Because they are presented in scholia, John's doctrinal concerns are scattered throughout the margins of the Dionysian corpus: there is thus no inner necessity for presenting his main topics to the modern reader in any particular order. Accordingly, the rationale for our arrangement below emerges not from any order internal to the *Scholia*, but from the order of topics in the *Prologue*.

John's *Prologue* begins with an invocation of Dionysius as an 'Areopagite' and greatly expands the biblical account of his conversion, making it into a foundation for the defence of his personal character and doctrinal orthodoxy. John cites the book of Acts and paraphrases the account of Paul's experiences in Athens, before quoting the reference to 'Dionysius the Areopagite and a woman named Damaris'. John has chosen to emphasize Acts and especially its reference to the council of the Areopagus because it helps establish the prestige and personal integrity of Dionysius. To this end, John alludes to Paul's discussion of wisdom and foolishness and embellishes the biblical narrative so that the unbribed

[72] *Prol.* 17C.

judge 'cast his vote for the truth delivered by the spirit-bearing Paul'.[72]
This use of Scripture is entirely indicative of John's exegetical strategy
throughout the *Scholia*. When he pauses to add or even amass biblical
citations, or to elaborate upon a biblical phrase, such labours usually serve
larger purposes that are not always readily apparent. This holds true
especially in the many extended biblical excursions in the *Scholia* which
serve John's particular concern to support the orthodoxy of Dionysius'
Christology and the legitimacy of his use of Neoplatonic terminology.

Still pressing his point about the prestige of the council of the
Areopagus, John's *Prologue* shifts from the biblical sources to the
historians of ancient Athens. At issue here is the history of the Areopagite
council, its composition and exalted reputation. Androtion and Philochorus are mentioned, with reference to their cumulative *Athenian
History*, as external proof of the aristocratic virtue of any Areopagite.
John here anticipates his use of non-Christian authors in the *Scholia* on
selected issues of history, grammar, philology, and philosophy. As will be
seen below, he displays a wide range of reading in non-Christian poetry
and prose. Some of this display is quite gratuitous, such as the *Prologue*'s
etymology of 'Areopagus' or various scholia on obscure words, but
perhaps these excursions served to establish an aristocratic air of erudition for the corpus as a whole, its author, and its commentator.

Besides Scripture and the writings of classical antiquity, the *Prologue*
invokes a third type of literary authority, namely, the church fathers. The
use of the fathers in the *Prologue* involves an argument over authenticity
which is never revisited in the *Scholia*. John must explain why Eusebius
and Origen never mentioned the Areopagite's writings. His explanation is
most intriguing, not least because Origen is mentioned without any overtones of controversy. That Eusebius did not mention the Dionysian
corpus is no barrier to its authenticity, argues John, since the historian
himself freely admitted that he did not cover everything, even authors
from his own land such Hymenaeus and Narcissus. John extends his
argument by pointing out that Eusebius and even Origen missed some of
the letters of the Roman Clement. In his *Scholia* John evinces a broad
knowledge of the major patristic sources and seems to have had a special
penchant for those from the earliest period. Although the nature of
John's comments do not allow us to fathom just how fully he understands
these authors or the extent to which he had acquainted himself directly
with their works, none the less there are few pre-Nicene eastern theologians who have escaped his purview.

To return to the order of topics in the opening section of the *Prologue*, beyond the scriptural sources and the historical documentation of the prestige of the council of the Areopagus, John has yet another argument for the integrity of Dionysius. The Areopagite had apostolic authority inasmuch as he was appointed by the apostle Paul. Not only was Dionysius converted by Paul, he was also 'pedagogically educated under Hierotheus the great'.[73] Most importantly, however, he was 'seated by the Christ-bearing Paul as bishop of the faithful in Athens'.[74] Dionysius received his authority through proper hierarchical channels, in particular, from the apostle Paul. This fact is used by John to support Dionysius' integrity. It also coheres with one of John's broader concerns in the *Scholia*, that of a strict hierarchical order which safeguards the prerogatives of bishops. The *Scholia*'s wide-ranging liturgical interests are not directly previewed in the *Prologue*, but John's insistence here that Dionysius received proper hierarchical authorization anticipates in part this major liturgical concern in the *Scholia*.

Upon the carefully constructed foundation of Dionysius' personal integrity, the *Prologue* begins to build a case for the Areopagite's doctrinal orthodoxy and the legitimacy of his use of philosophy. John is explicit about this double agenda, as he moves immediately from the orthodox 'traditions of the Church' to the issue of the 'Greek philosophers'.[75] When John rails against those ignorant and presumptuous accusers of non-Christian learning and of the Dionysian corpus itself, he is clearly asserting the integrity of Dionysius in the face of some who suspect the writer of being a heretic. He goes on to itemize several areas of concern. As already acknowledged, there may be other ways to order John's doctrinal concerns in the *Scholia*. But the presentation in the *Prologue* conveniently organizes them into four general areas: Trinity, Christology, creation, and eschatology.

'For what could they say of his theology of the only-worshipped Trinity?'[76] John begins his list with the doctrine of the Trinity. This may seem surprising at first glance, since the sixth-century eastern Mediterranean context had no serious Trinitarian controversies, at least nothing comparable to its warfare over Christology.[77] In his attention to the issue of the Trinity John seems more intent on establishing solid doctrinal foundations for other concerns, especially Christology. In any case, a substantial number of scholia do present Trinitarian concerns.

---

[73] *Prol.* 17C.   [74] *Prol.* 17C.   [75] *Prol.* 17CD.   [76] *Prol.* 20B.

[77] Questions of the Trinity most often came to the fore in the Origenist controversy (Grillmeier, *Christ in Christian Tradition*, ii/2: 392, for the condemnation of Origen's subordinationist tendencies) and in the later problem of the so-called 'tritheists' (Aloys Grillmeier, *Christ in Christian Tradition*, ii/4 (Louisville, Ky., 1996), 131–8).

John is careful to point out the explicit Trinitarian language in the Areopagite's own vocabulary, as well as those Dionysian passages which presciently opposed Arius and Eunomius. John can also add a specifically triune note to the Areopagite's generic language for God, and enlarge upon distinctively Dionysian and Neoplatonic ways of talking about God's unity and triunity.

John's next item, Christology, receives a fuller statement in the *Prologue*, thereby indicating more specifically which Christological concerns he had in mind. Christology is perhaps the most important issue explicitly addressed in the *Scholia* overall, as would be expected given John's involvement in the doctrinal controversies of sixth-century Palestine. In the course of his remarks, John mentions many Christological heresies, usually in tandem as opposite enemies of the orthodox *via media*. Here in the *Prologue* he indicates a particular concern for Christ's full humanity, including a rational soul and earthly body—echoes of the fourth-century Apollinarian controversy. So also, in his *Scholia* John offers many observations on Dionysian Christology and on specific Christological heresies, with a particular focus on Apollinaris.

The third doctrinal concern itemized in the *Prologue* is somewhat less apparent. 'For what error could anyone rightly blame him, with respect to intelligible and intelligent and perceptible things?'[78] These terms are a familiar part of the Neoplatonic vocabulary: the *noetic* (that which is conceived or thought), the *noeric* (that which conceives or thinks), and the *aesthetic* (that which is perceived by the physical senses). Dionysius used this language throughout his corpus, and one might well expect John to comment on such terminology.[79] When John's *Prologue* mentions 'the intelligible and intelligent and perceptible' as an issue of orthodoxy and heresy, the reader may well think of the entire cosmological realm of the invisible and the visible, the eternal realm of the mind and the temporal world of the senses. Within this vertical hierarchy, however, John's *Scholia* provide more detailed discussions at the lower end, that is, the doctrine of creation. One scholion in particular identifies the creation as 'the intelligibles, intelligents, sensibles'.[80] The *Prologue*'s cryptic

[78] *Prol.* 20B.

[79] On the face of it, the language of *noetic* and *noeric* links some of Proclus' terminology about lofty 'minds' to the Dionysian description of the angels. While John notices and approves of this nomenclature in the Areopagite (*SchCH* 109. 2, *SchEH* 120. 0, *SchDN* 240. 3, 269. 2, 309. 3, 344. 3, 345. 3), it does not really seem to be of much doctrinal significance to him. Certainly the *Scholia* do not accord angelic minds the measure of attention they give to the doctrines of the Trinity and of Christ.

[80] *SchDN* 316. 4, cf. 329. 1 and 332. 1.

reference thus previews John's concern for the doctrine of creation, for the world brought forth by God *ex nihilo*.

John's list of doctrinal issues concludes with a reference to the 'general resurrection' of body and soul and the judgement of the just and the unjust.[81] The resurrection is of major interest to John in the *Scholia*, especially as it concerns the errors of certain Greek philosophers and the heresy of Origen. As suggested above, Origen is an ambiguous figure in John's *Scholia*. While sometimes cited in the *Scholia* as an authoritative father, as in the *Prologue*, Origen is also and more often explicitly treated as a heretic, especially with regard to the resurrection of the body. Below we treat the theological, historical, and textual dimensions of this situation, as well as a similar ambiguity in John's treatment of Evagrius.

John's *Prologue* continues by taking up the objection already mentioned: if these works are genuinely apostolic, why did Eusebius not mention them?[82] That Eusebius was unfamiliar with many works is a historical argument which is never revisited in the *Scholia*. But there are other charges against the authenticity of the Dionysian corpus which John does counter in the *Scholia*. When the *Prologue* moves from a rebuttal of this particular charge to a positive argument for the authenticity of Dionysius' writings, John does anticipate the *Scholia*'s concerns. That Dionysius writes to Timothy and refers to Paul verifies the authenticity of his works. The *Scholia* themselves also note Dionysius' references to Timothy and Paul, but John does not make much of them. The *Prologue*'s stronger form of this argument, however, receives more pointed attention in the *Scholia*: 'That these writings truly belong to Dionysius is confirmed by the fact that he offhandedly mentions the sayings of men who were his contemporaries, and who were also mentioned in the divine Acts of the apostles.'[83] In the *Scholia*, John makes a point of noting most of the Areopagite's 'offhand' references to ostensible contemporaries (Peter and James, Bartholomew, Justus, and even Paul's opponent Elymas) and takes these as occasions to assert the antiquity and thus the authenticity of these writings.

Mention of Timothy, the ostensible recipient of these writings, allows John to broach the question of Greek philosophy. The entire corpus, he argues, is Dionysius' response to Timothy's plea for help in refuting the Greek philosophers who surrounded him in Ephesus. 'There is nothing unreasonable in this', he adds, for Paul did the same.[84] Here John has explained away both the extensive use of Greek philosophy in the Dionysian corpus and also its apparent goal of opposing these non-

[81] *Prol.* 20B.   [82] *Prol.* 20C.   [83] *Prol.* 21A.   [84] *Prol.* 21A.

Christian philosophers. Of course, Dionysius' use of Platonic philosophy and John's commentary on the same are both much more complicated than John here allows. The *Scholia* make positive and negative remarks about the philosophers, and the sharpest critique comes not at the higher end of the hierarchical spectrum, when it is a question of God and the angels, but at the lower end, when John treats of matter and evil, a case in point being John's unacknowledged use of Plotinus on these subjects.

In summary, John's *Prologue* is informed by three major themes: the integrity of Dionysius, the orthodoxy of his theology, and the authenticity of his writings. As John treats these subjects in the *Prologue* he also raises many of the issues which will in turn be broached in his *Scholia*, in most cases explicitly and in considerable detail, and in some cases more implicitly and sporadically. Inasmuch as the sequence of John's concerns in his *Prologue* offers an appropriate overview of his concerns in his *Scholia*, we have taken it as the organizing principle for the chapters which follow. In Chapter 3 we examine how John uses a diverse body of sources (scriptural, pagan, patristic, and liturgical) in order to facilitate his interpretative agenda. In Chapter 4 we turn to John's treatment of the Trinity, Christology, creation, and eschatology. And finally, in Chapter 5 we explore John's defence of the authenticity of the works of Dionysius, paying especial attention to John's handling of philosophical materials in general and Plotinus in particular.

3
Sources of the *Scholia*

In order to explicate the meaning of the Dionysian text, John makes use of a wide variety of sources. He most often cites the Christian Scriptures, but he also invokes non-Christian authors, an assortment of church fathers, and the liturgical traditions of the eastern and western churches. In this chapter we examine John's formal patterns for using such materials. In the course of this examination we also introduce some of John's more substantive concerns in interpreting the Dionysian corpus.

BIBLICAL SOURCES

John's use of scriptural sources is extensive and sometimes quite sophisticated, both in identifying some of the biblical allusions in Dionysius and also in supporting his own overall interpretative programme. We need to note briefly what John used, that is, the issues of text and canon, but especially how he used it, that is, his subtle agenda of using Scripture to present a particular reading of the Dionysian corpus.

That God can be described as 'small', to start with a Dionysian example from the Old Testament, is only possible on the basis of the Septuagint's version of 'the still, small breeze' in which God was present to Elijah in 1 Kings 19: 12, as John notes.[1] Only in the Septuagint version of Isaiah, furthermore, can we locate John's own biblical sources for three separate scholia.[2] But John, unlike the Areopagite, is not limited to this Greek version of the Old Testament. In contrast to Dionysius himself, who admits and displays his ignorance of Hebrew, John shows an interest in the several Greek versions and in the Hebrew text of Exodus regarding

[1] *SchDN* 369. 2. Other examples of the *Scholia*'s awareness of Dionysius' use of the Septuagint: *SchCH* 60. 1 re Isa. 9: 6; 64. 7 and 73. 3 re Isa. 6: 2; 88. 3 re Deut. 32: 8; *SchDN* 385. 4 re Ps. 24: 7, 9; and *SchEP* 549. 6 re Deut. 16: 20.

[2] Namely, *SchEH* 32. 4, 88. 3, and *SchDN* 189. 3 which employ the Septuagint texts of (respectively) Isa. 10: 12, 14: 13–14, and 40: 13. There are many other examples of John's own use of the Septuagint text: *SchEH* 132. 11 re Ps. 88: 5; *SchDN* 224. 7 re Zech. 4: 12 (discussed below); 252. 7 re Zech. 9: 17; 277. 1 re Gen. 32: 30; 301. 4 re Amos 3: 6–7; 332. 3 re Ps. 103: 31 and Prov. 8: 30; 364. 1 re Ps. 73: 8; 380. 3 re Hab. 3: 8; and *SchEP* 560. 4 re Ps. 45: 10.

their words for 'darkness'. 'It is necessary to know that in Exodus where it is written that Moses entered into the darkness where God was, the Hebrew text has *araphel* [Exod. 20: 21]. The Septuagint renders *araphel* as "darkness" [γνόφος], as do Aquila and Theodotion. Symmachus, however, translates *araphel* as "fog" [ὁμίχλη].'[3] John is apparently using Origen's *Hexapla*.

As for the New Testament, John's biblical citations reflect a stable Greek text, with a few signs that he also knew a relative of the Western manuscript, Codex Bezae or D, at least for Luke and Acts. For Acts 1: 26, John explicitly discussed the variant readings 'they cast lots for them' and 'they cast their lots', preferring the former rather than the latter (Western) reading as more consistent with the witness of Dionysius.[4] Dionysius himself seemed to use a Western (or the Alexandrian) text for Luke 23: 44–5, regarding the eclipse, which interested John greatly.[5] Where Dionysius only alluded to Luke 9: 51–5, John supplies a quotation from the fuller text of Luke 9: 55 ('You do not know what manner of Spirit you are of') which is attested only in the Western reading.[6]

Regarding the canon of scriptural books, we must keep the ostensible chronology in mind, for John is remarking in the sixth century on what he understands (and wants his readers to understand) as a first-century text. The intervening centuries had seen many discussions about the canonical standing of several books, as John himself surely knew. Eusebius, for example, reported in the early fourth century that certain texts were disputed, that is, James, 2 Peter, 2 and 3 John, Jude, and probably Hebrews and Revelation.[7] Evidence that any of these texts were used as Scripture in the first century would be of interest to a later commentator, and John makes several remarks in this vein. When Dionysius appealed to James, the scholiast adds: 'Note that the blessed Dionysius made use of the catholic epistle of St James, for the passage in question is taken from that source. Note also that [the epistle of James] had already been put into circulation [in the time of Dionysius].'[8] The Areopagite's heavy use of Revelation prompts a similar comment from

---

[3] *SchMT* 421. 1. Dionysius' ignorance of Hebrew is evident in his use of 'seraphim' as a singular noun (*CH* 13. 1, 43. 21) and is explicitly acknowledged in *CH* 7. 1 (27. 6–7), *EH* 4. 3. 10 (101. 10–11), 4. 3. 12 (103. 19–20). John mentions the Septuagint by name here and in *SchDN* 224. 7.

[4] *SchEH* 168. 4.

[5] *SchEP* 541. 5.

[6] *SchEP* 552. 11.

[7] Eus. *h.e.* 3. 25 (SC 31: 133–4), cf. 3. 38. 2 (SC 31: 152–3).

[8] *SchCH* 29. 3. That it was already put into circulation also contributes to John's argument about the antiquity of the Dionysian corpus.

John: 'One must note that he accepts [as canonical or authentic] the Apocalypse of St John the Evangelist.'[9] *Letter One* to 'Gaius' prompted from John a comment which indicates his own acceptance of 3 John: 'I conjecture that this Gaius is the one to whom the divine evangelist John wrote his third letter.'[10] John also acknowledges, without reservation, Dionysius' use of Jude as Scripture.[11] The single occasion when Dionysius quoted 2 Peter also prompts John to give his approval to the use of this controversial epistle: 'The divine Peter said in his catholic epistle: "Until the morning star rises in your hearts . . ." [2 Pet. 1: 19].'[12] John goes beyond Dionysius in his own explicit use of 2 Peter, especially in quoting twice what became the *locus classicus* for the developing doctrine of theosis ('being partakers of the divine nature').[13] He made no editorial comments upon the frequent use by Dionysius of the epistle to the Hebrews, which he also used freely as Scripture and accepted as by 'the apostle' Paul.[14] John made explicit comment on only one of the disputed Old Testament books: 'Concerning the Song of Songs, note that it was considered holy by these holy men, for Theodore of Mopsuestia disparaged it, with great foolishness.'[15]

Whereas the Song of Songs, James, and Revelation receive just one comment each, the case of the Wisdom of Solomon is more complex, partly because it is somewhat ambiguous within the Dionysian corpus itself. The Areopagite used Wisdom as Scripture, but also qualified this usage. When Dionysius quoted what he called the 'introductory Scriptures', John adds: 'One must understand that he calls the writings of Solomon the "introductory divine Scriptures", from which also this saying comes.'[16] Here the word 'introductory' probably refers, for Dionysius and for John, to the Old Testament as introductory to the New, rather than to any sort of deutero-canonical status. On a couple of other occasions, when Dionysius quoted or alluded to the Wisdom of Solomon, John notes this usage and adds some further citations of his own from the same source, treating it naturally as a scriptural text.[17]

---

[9] *SchDN* 212. 6.   [10] *SchEP* 528. 1.   [11] *SchDN* 289. 4.   [12] *SchCH* 45. 4.

[13] 2 Pet. 1: 4, in *SchEH* 152. 2, and *SchDN* 193. 1.

[14] *SchCH* 33. 4 and *SchEH* 132. 11.

[15] *SchEP* 561. 2. Following Dionysius, John also mentions the Song of Songs in *SchEH* 140. 9.

[16] *SchDN* 265. 1.

[17] On the phrase 'introductory Scriptures', see Paul Rorem, *Biblical and Liturgical Symbols within the Pseudo-Dionysian Synthesis* (Toronto, 1984), 13. In *SchEH* 145. 4, John says that Dionysius is citing the Wisdom of Solomon; he may mean Wisd. 3: 1–10 or 5: 15, but the allusion is obscure at best. At *SchDN* 353. 2 John quotes Wisd. 7: 22, regarding the discussion at *DN* 7. 4 (198. 23–199. 1) of wisdom (with quotation from Wisd. 7: 24).

John follows and expands upon Dionysius' use of other texts of disputed canonical standing. Dionysius explicitly quoted Susanna 42, for example, and on two different occasions John used the same passage ('He who knew all things before their generation').[18] John quotes Baruch 3: 3 ('seated/enthroned forever') among several biblical verses while commenting upon a passage which may or may not have intended such an allusion.[19] Similarly, John refers directly to 'Jesus ben Sirach . . . in his hymn of the fathers' while commenting on the treatment of Joshua 10 in *Letter 7*, where Dionysius may have also reflected a reading of Sirach but gave no such direct acknowledgement.[20] When the Areopagite referred to the 'elder angels', John provides an explicit reference to Tobit 12: 15, and he elsewhere creatively invokes Tobit far beyond the Dionysian text.[21] In another category entirely is John's use of the *Shepherd of Hermas*, since Dionysius appears not to have used it at all, and John himself seems to cite it not as Scripture but as one of the fathers.[22]

John's specific interpretations of Scripture are often quite subtle. The Areopagite's biblical allusions are numerous and yet often oblique, and only twice did Dionysius himself identify a biblical book by name.[23] John selectively ignored many of the Areopagite's unidentified scriptural allusions, but he did pick out certain passages for thorough biblical annotation. His apparent reasons for such choices are varied. He may choose a passage simply because the allusions were particularly compressed and therefore difficult for the reader to appreciate. When the Areopagite mentioned in passing the biblical symbols for God as sun, morning star, unconsuming fire, water, and ointment, John identified and amplified the texts in question.[24] Similarly, when *The Divine Names* said that God is great and small, same and different, like and unlike, standing, sitting, and moving, John supplies the pertinent biblical quotations with thorough precision.[25] Sometimes the challenge is not in unpacking a compressed set of clear allusions but rather in a single but oblique reference, the kind that

---

[18] Dionysius quoted Sus. 42 at *DN* 7. 2 (196. 17), where there is no comment from John, and may have alluded to it at *DN* 1. 6 (119. 1) and 7. 2 (196. 6). John used it as Scripture, without qualification, at *SchDN* 200. 3 and *SchMT* 429. 3, in comments upon Dionysian texts which did not themselves use this passage.

[19] *SchDN* 369. 2.

[20] *SchEP* 537. 6.

[21] *SchDN* 225. 3. John uses Tobit 2: 10 and/or 6: 8 at *SchDN* 349. 4, in order to illustrate the Areopagite's general comment about angelic knowledge.

[22] *SchDN* 241. 6 and 244. 1.

[23] Genesis and Song of Songs, see *EP* 9. 1 (196. 2) and *EH* 3. 3. 4 (83. 19).

[24] *SchCH* 45. 4.

[25] *SchDN* 369. 2, cf. *SchCH* 40. 9.

has puzzled many modern annotators of the Areopagite. For example, Dionysius said that according to the Scriptures God is clothed in the 'armour of barbarians', a phrase seemingly without a direct biblical connection. John ponders this phrase with considerable insight, draws also upon the help of a Greek historian, and finally offers his suggestions as to the biblical verse at issue.[26]

Many of John's biblical references occur in the course of his own argument, when he brings in a biblical passage or phrase which was not explicitly invoked in the Dionysian text under consideration.[27] When Dionysius alluded to the biblical language about God's standing or sitting, for example, John quickly quotes six specific verses in explicit support and explanation of the text in question.[28] When the Areopagite went on to remark that the scriptural writers say that 'God goes out into everything' and yet does not quote or allude to any specific passage, John supplies another six texts.[29] When the Areopagite sampled the scriptural variations on the theme of 'eternity', John supplies yet another ten pertinent quotations.[30] When Dionysius mentioned the baptismal ointment's 'sweet odour', John connects 2 Corinthians 2: 14–16 to the bowls of incense (Rev. 5: 8), the foul odours of the devil (Ps. 38: 5), and the pleasing fragrance of Noah's offering (Gen. 8: 21).[31] The same pattern is seen in his biblical embroidery on the Dionysian language of 'otherness', the joys of heaven, the word 'ungenerated' in its various meanings, and God as the 'limit'.[32] As a final sample of this sort of biblical expansion, when Dionysius referred to Jesus' death, John embellishes the comment with quotations from the Gospel of John, Hebrews, Isaiah, Acts, and the Psalms.[33]

This last example of John's biblical expansions upon selected Dionysian topics raises the deeper question of John's interpretative agenda, especially regarding Christology. John has here made the most out of a passing reference to Jesus' death. A single word in the Dionysian text, such as 'whole', can become John's starting-point to refute both a soteriology which saved only the soul and a Christology which involved only the body of Christ and not a rational soul, namely, the Apollinarian heresy directly combated on various occasions and the subject of a

---

[26] *SchEP* 560. 4.   [27] e.g. *SchCH* 56. 1.   [28] *SchDN* 380. 3.

[29] *SchDN* 381. 1.

[30] *SchDN* 385. 4, see also *SchDN* 208. 2.

[31] *SchEH* 133. 2.

[32] 'Otherness' in *SchEH* 141. 18, 'the joys of heaven' in *SchEH* 177. 13, 'ungenerated' in *SchDN* 372. 3, and 'limit' in *SchDN* 253. 1.

[33] *SchEH* 132. 11.

major discussion below.[34] When the Areopagite's *Letter 4* touched briefly and famously on the 'new' activity of the God-man, beyond the simply human or the simply divine activities, John gave this tripartite format some biblical evidence.[35] An especially impressive *tour de force* of biblical annotation occurs when Dionysius, with characteristic brevity, mentioned the 'divine frailty', presumably in the Incarnation. This prompted John to supply numerous biblical allusions and quotations to document the frail humanity of Christ.[36] The pattern sampled so far pertains to Christology: John often made the most of a slim Dionysian reference to Christ's humanity by filling the page with biblical citations and references to a concrete historical Incarnation with all of its suffering and death.

There is a second pattern. John occasionally decided to give biblical annotation to some of Dionysius' vocabulary and concepts which a reader might associate with Neoplatonism. John's *Scholia* do not openly refute any such associations, but they do make a point of emphasizing the Christian and especially the biblical connections. John, for example, supplies biblical warrant for the figure of Hierotheus, whom the suspicious reader might mistake for Proclus. Going beyond Dionysius, John calls Dionysius' mentor 'Saint Hierotheus' and links him directly to Paul and to Acts, even though Hierotheus made no appearance in the Scriptures.[37] When Dionysius referred to his 'sacred initiator', which consistently means Hierotheus, John once preferred to understand this as a reference to Paul and his experience of the 'third heaven' in 2 Corinthians 12: 2.[38] We note seven other examples of John's scriptural strategy regarding Dionysian uses of Neoplatonic terminology: 'home' [ἑστία],[39] offshoots, flowers, and lights,[40] not learning but suffering,[41] the presence of God,[42] theurgy,[43] remaining, procession and return,[44] and paradigms.[45] In some of these cases, John is merely explicating the biblical warrant which Dionysius had himself invoked for using these unacknowledged loans from Neoplatonic terminology. In other cases, it is John himself who finds the scriptural support. Since John was quite selective in his choice of occasions to provide a comment and especially an explicit biblical support, this pattern of scriptural warrant for expres-

---

[34] *SchEP* 545. 8. See Ch. 4. [35] *SchDN* 536. 1.

[36] *SchDN* 236. 10, cf. *SchDN* 340. 5.

[37] *SchDN* 232. 2. Hierotheus is also called 'saint' and linked to Paul in *SchDN* 340. 4; also 'saint' in *SchEH* 136. 1; 'blessed Hierotheus' in *SchEH* 124. 1. Cf. *SchDN* 236. 5, 385. 1.

[38] *SchCH* 64. 4. John recognizes the 'sacred initiator' as Hierotheus in *SchDN* 385. 1.

[39] *SchDN* 209. 1. [40] *SchDN* 224. 7. [41] *SchDN* 228. 2. [42] *SchDN* 233. 3.

[43] *SchCH* 57. 2, cf. *SchDN* 197. 1. [44] *SchDN* 220. 1. [45] *SchDN* 329. 1.

sions associated with Neoplatonism would suggest that John was trying to prevent such associations. That he himself could have recognized this Neoplatonic vocabulary and that he might have engaged in intentional literary manipulation is not at all hard to imagine, given his own surreptitious use of Plotinus in the course of commenting upon *The Divine Names*.[46] And yet, these scholia do not by themselves justify the conclusion that John knew that the Areopagite used earlier Neoplatonic authors. He may have recognized some similarities, but we should not therefore conclude that he considered the Dionysian texts to be dependent upon the Neoplatonic ones.

NON-CHRISTIAN SOURCES

As already observed in our comments on the *Prologue*, among his sources John occasionally cites the venerable voices of ancient Greece. These references are not especially numerous, about ten texts, and some may in fact depend upon earlier citations by other Christian authors. Normally, these citations provide minor pieces of information in order to illuminate Dionysian concepts or vocabulary items. At a Dionysian reference to poetic imagery, for example, John casually adds: 'By "poets" understand . . . those admired by the Greeks, such as Homer, Hesiod, and so forth.'[47] John's one reference to Aristotle includes his apparent approval.[48] While discussing funerals, Dionysius itemized various mistaken notions about death. In his comments on this passage, John dismisses a certain Bias as among the more irrational of the Greeks for believing that the soul is mortal like the body. Although Plato is listed among the more rational, his denial of the resurrection of the material body earns him John's disapproval.[49] Beyond these few references to poets or philosophers, John's favoured genre of literature from antiquity is history. As seen in the *Prologue*, he used the *Athenian Histories* of Androtion and Philochorus, albeit probably at second hand.[50] At the end of a long scholion on *Letter 7*'s reference to the eclipse during the crucifixion, John cites the Greek chronographer Phlegon, although he here is surely copying what he had read in an earlier patristic authority.[51] John also uses

[46] See Ch. 5.   [47] *SchCH* 36. 3.   [48] *SchDN* 377. 1.   [49] *SchDN* 173. 8.

[50] *Prol.* 17AB. Jacoby has argued that John was dependent here on a legal handbook (no longer extant) in which the homicide courts of Athens were treated (ad *FGrHist* 324F3–4).

[51] *SchEP* 541. 5. This passage from Phlegon was often cited by earlier authorities: e.g. Or. *Cels.* 2. 33 (GCS 2: 159–60); Afric. *chron.* fr. cited at PG 10: 87–9; Eus. *chron.* a. 19 Tiberii imp. (Latin version, GCS 24: 174–5; Armenian version, GCS 20: 213).

the historian Phylarchus to help him comment on 'the armour of barbarians'.[52]

On four occasions John linked Dionysian ritual vocabulary to its usage among the pagans of Athens and Rome. *The Ecclesiastical Hierarchy* mentioned the clergy as 'secret beholders [θεωροί] of the intelligible'.[53] 'Beholder' is not a technical term for the hierarch in Dionysius.[54] Nevertheless, John applies the word 'beholder' to the bishops, based upon his awareness of its usage among the Greeks. 'He calls the bishops "beholders" because the Greeks use the name "beholders" with reference to those who are nominated by all to inquire of God about the future, to offer sacrifices for them, and to propitiate God for them.'[55] How did John know this? He elsewhere refers to a work by a certain Demophilus entitled *Sacrifices and Feasts among the Ancients*.[56] This may stand behind his comments here as well. John makes a similar remark when Dionysius used the unusual title 'harmost' with reference to the hierarch. John points out that the Spartans used to use this term with regard to the governors of their cities and that the Athenians themselves used to call the inspectors of public morals by this name.[57] The latter he knows from Plato the Comic's play entitled the *Ambassadors*.

The remaining two examples concern the vocabulary used in the story of Carpus at the end of *Letter 8*. Although Dionysius normally used the word προτέλειος to mean 'beyond perfection', in this passage he applied it to the prayers which precede communion: such prayers are literally 'pre-perfecting'.[58] This peculiar usage may derive from an earlier version of the story, but John gives the credit to Dionysius, suggesting that he had adapted Greek ritual vocabulary to a Christian context.[59] John correctly points out that among the Athenians the prayers and sacrifices which preceded the rite of marriage were said to be 'pre-perfecting'. He then offers a variety of etymologies for this adjective: he knows that marriage was itself called a τέλος among the Greeks, for he had read this in many comedies; moreover, the comic Cratinus in his play the *Pulaia* had used related verbs to mean 'being ready for a mystery'. In the very next sentence of *Letter 8*, John encounters another Dionysian word

---

[52] *SchEP* 560. 4.   [53] *EH* 4. 3. 2 (97. 16).
[54] It can apply to the angels (*CH* 7. 2, 29. 6), to laity (*EH* 5. 3, 106. 15), and to providence (*DN* 12. 3, 225. 12).
[55] *SchEH* 153. 6.   [56] *SchEP* 556. 1.   [57] *SchEH* 152. 9.
[58] On the sources of the Carpus story, see Rorem, *Biblical and Liturgical Symbols*, 138–40, and Ronald F. Hathaway, *Hierarchy and the Definition of Order in the Letters of Pseudo-Dionysius* (The Hague, 1969), 93–9.
[59] *SchEP* 553. 9. See also *SchCH* 32. 10.

which precipitates a similar comment.[60] The Areopagite's story about Carpus refers, with apparent innocence, to 'the joyful days' [τῶν ἱλαρίων ἡμερῶν] after baptism. But John knows and shares with his readers the more complicated history of these festival days. After discussing their nature among the Greeks, he then goes on to point out that 'there was also a particular feast of the Romans which was called a *hilaria*. It was to honour the mother of their gods—or more properly, their demons. Demophilus speaks of it in his work *Sacrifices and Feasts among the Ancients*.' Here again John explicates Dionysius' ritual vocabulary with reference to usage among the pagans.

It must be admitted that John's acknowledged use of classical sources is not terribly extensive. Most often such materials are called upon for rather minor purposes: to illuminate Dionysian vocabulary and to provide occasional bits of historical information. Moreover, some of these sources were almost certainly being cited at second or third hand (e.g. Plegon, Androtion, and Philochorus). This presentation should be contrasted with earlier assessments of John's relationship to classical sources, treatments which were based upon all of the scholia found in Migne. Both von Balthasar and Flusin concluded on this basis that John was quite learned in classical sources, that he had a taste for such erudition, even (in the words of von Balthasar) that he was a 'Polyhistor'.[61] Such conclusions should be tempered in light of what we now know to be John's scholia.[62]

THE FATHERS AS SOURCES

As John comments on the Dionysian corpus, he occasionally calls upon the witnesses of the patristic past. This should in no way be surpris-

---

[60] *SchEP* 556. 1.

[61] Bernard Flusin, *Miracle et histoire dans l'œuvre de Cyrille de Scythopolis* (Paris, 1983), 24; Hans Urs von Balthasar, 'Das Problem der Dionysius-Scholien', in *Kosmische Liturgie* (Einsiedeln, 1961), 666. Cf. John Binns, *Ascetics and Ambassadors of Christ* (Oxford, 1994), 142, who takes John's extensive knowledge of classical sources as evidence of the 'influence of classical learning on the Church'.

[62] There are four other scholia of uncertain authorship which cite Homer and other poets regarding accents, spelling, and unusual words (these are attested in FA but not Syr.): *SchMT* 420. 3, a quotation from the *Iliad* illustrating an accent; *SchMT* 421. 4, from the *Odyssey* regarding 'statue' (with Euripides and Dionysius the Poet); *SchEP* 553. 1 on the *Iliad* regarding the word and accent for 'temple' or 'head'; *SchEP* 572. 11, on the spelling and meaning of 'child-rearing'. It is conceivable that these also are by John, for the Syriac translator may have had a hard time rendering such materials and thus thought it better to leave them out.

ing, for in the sixth century doctrinal disputes often pivoted upon the authoritative sources invoked, the fathers having become in a very real sense the guarantors of orthodoxy.[63] But in many respects John's use of patristic sources differs greatly from what was normal in his context. As we shall argue, John is primarily interested in the fathers as they touch on certain historical issues and on the question of Origen. Otherwise it can hardly be said that he actively engages the fathers on theological issues. They function for the most part as minor annotations for his own comments. On the other hand, the manner of John's patristic citations suggests that he was seeking to imbue the corpus and his own comments with a pre-Nicene ambience, and this by actively avoiding later patristic authorities.

We begin with John's invocations of the fathers as historical sources. A total of seven scholia use the fathers in this manner.[64] Troubled by the fact that Dionysius referred to himself by the pre-Christian title 'Areopagite', John notes that Justin also had signed his work *Against the Greeks* with his pre-Christian title 'philosopher'.[65] Twice John invokes patristic sources to oppose Simon Magus' doctrines. In this regard he appeals to Irenaeus (twice), Hippolytus (twice), Origen, and Epiphanius.[66] John also uses the witness of Africanus, Eusebius, Irenaeus, and Clement in order to clarify the chronology implied in the letters as it touches upon the date of the eclipse which accompanied the crucifixion and the exile of the evangelist John to Patmos.[67] When Dionysius addressed a letter to Polycarp, John invokes Irenaeus to establish that this same Polycarp later became bishop of Smyrna.[68] In a similar vein, to show that Dionysius himself became bishop of Athens, John refers to the authority of the *Apostolic Constitutions*.[69] In each of these passages, John appeals to the fathers to clarify the historical personages or events mentioned within the Dionysian corpus. Most of these references to the fathers are brief asides with little or no polemical force. Indeed, many of these same historical references had already been cited by Eusebius in his *History of the Church*.[70]

---

[63] See the important studies of Patrick T. R. Gray, ' "The Select Fathers" ', *SP* 23 (1989), 21–36; idem, 'Forgery as an Instrument of Progress', *BZ* 81 (1988), 284–9.

[64] To these we might add John's reference to Philo as a witness to the therapeutae (*SchEP* 528. 1).

[65] *SchCH* 113. 10.   [66] *SchDN* 337. 5, *SchEP* 545. 8.   [67] *SchEP* 541. 5, 573. 7.

[68] *SchEP* 536. 5.

[69] *SchEP* 552. 11, the same passage is also cited in *Prol.* 17C.

[70] On the exile of John, Eusebius cites the same two passages from Irenaeus and the same passage from Clement (*h.e.* 3. 23, SC 31: 126–9). On Polycarp, Eusebius also cited the same passage from Irenaeus (*h.e.* 4. 14, SC 31: 179–80). John could have learned from Eusebius

If now we turn to John's treatment of the question of Origen, a some-what different pattern emerges. Here at least John is eager to provide a detailed description of the errors of Origen and Evagrius. In fact, the only extended patristic citations which John gives in his scholia are from Origen and Evagrius.[71] At issue here is their treatment of the fall. When John comes to cite those authors who had opposed Origen on certain key questions, he contents himself with simply noting the fact that such authors had written such works. 'Read what has been written about his views on the resurrection by Methodius the martyr and bishop of Olympus in Lycia, by Ammon the bishop of Adrianople, and by Antipater the bishop of Bostra.'[72] 'Ammon of Adrianople presents this more fully in his treatises *On the Resurrection* which he wrote against Origen.'[73]

John's treatment of these anti-Origen works is very similar to his over-all pattern of invoking patristic authorities on points of doctrine. After having expounded his own interpretation of the Dionysian text at issue, he is usually content simply to throw out for further consideration the fact that one of the fathers had also treated this issue or had used this language or had expressed a similar idea. Let us consider here a few indicative examples. Commenting upon Dionysius, John pauses to note that the first gift which humans receive from teaching is the ability to know ourselves. He then adds: 'The divine Basil also said this.'[74] In another scholion John notes that Christ conquered Satan by an act of judgement and righteousness. He then adds: 'Gregory of Nyssa also says this in his *Catechism*.'[75] When Dionysius used the expression 'elder angel', John cites some parallels from the Apocalypse and Tobit and then adds that Clement also spoke this way in the fifth book of his *Hypotyposes*.[76] To explicate the Dionysian idea that just things ought to be pursued in a worthy manner, John cites a parallel from Deuteronomy and says that Dionysius will himself clarify his meaning in what follows. John then adds as an aside: 'Origen explicates this quite well in the tenth of his homilies on the Lamentations of Jeremiah.'[77] As these examples suggest, John really makes little or no attempt to engage his patristic sources. More often than not, he cites them as parallels to the Dionysian

---

(*h.e.* 4. 16, SC 31: 190–2) that Justin called himself a 'philosopher'. Even Philo on the therapeutae had already been cited by Eusebius (*h.e.* 2.17, SC 31: 72–7). That Dionysius had been bishop of Athens was not controversial: Eusebius had also mentioned it (*h.e.* 3. 4. 10, SC 31: 101).

[71] *SchEH* 172. 11.   [72] *SchEH* 176. 3 (corrected from Syr.).   [73] *SchCH* 65. 6.
[74] *SchEH* 129. 6.   [75] *SchEH* 149. 4.   [76] *SchDN* 225. 3.
[77] *SchEP* 549. 6.

text or to his own comments. They are, if you will, patristic footnotes to his own footnotes on the Dionysian text.

To which of the fathers does John appeal? Most often cited are Basil (seven times) and Irenaeus (six times).[78] Clement of Alexandria is appealed to on four occasions.[79] Origen is cited positively twice and negatively four times.[80] The Gregories are each cited twice, as are Africanus, Ammon of Adrianople, the *Shepherd of Hermas*, Hippolytus, and Papias.[81] Evagrius also is cited twice, once positively, once negatively.[82] The following are each cited once: Antipater of Bostra, Polycarp, Eusebius, Methodius, Symmachus (from the *Hexapla*), Athanasius, the *Apostolic Constitutions*, Sextus, Aristo of Pella, Justin, Chrysostom.[83] We might add that John cites three Jewish authors, once each: Aquila and Theodotion (both from the *Hexapla*), and Philo.[84]

This rapid survey of John's patristic sources leads to several general observations. John seems to have a special penchant for pre-Nicene authors: Africanus, Aristo of Pella, Clement of Alexandria, Hermas, Hippolytus, Irenaeus, Justin, Methodius of Olympus, Origen, Papias, Polycarp, Symmachus, and the *Apostolic Constitutions*.[85] Apart from the Cappadocians (in particular Basil), John expresses almost no interest in post-Nicene patristic authorities. John uses a fifth-century authority only once: Antipater of Bostra over against Origen. Although he names heretics from the fifth and sixth centuries often enough, John's use of the fathers more or less ends with the Cappadocians. Cyril of Alexandria in particular is strikingly absent from John's *Scholia* even though he figured prominently in contemporary Christological debates. Similarly, John never refers explicitly to any of the authoritative church councils. He does note that certain more recent fathers have proposed *homoousion* as a

---

[78] Basil: *SchCH* 44. 6, 68. 1, 108. 5, *SchEH* 129. 6, *SchDN* 248. 4, 413. 1, 309. 3. Irenaeus: *SchEH* 176. 4, *SchDN* 337. 5, 377. 1, *SchEP* 536. 5, 545. 8, 573. 7.

[79] *SchCH* 48. 7, *SchDN* 225. 3, *SchMT* 421. 1, *SchEP* 573. 7.

[80] Positively: *SchDN* 337. 5, *SchEP* 549. 6. Negatively: *SchEH* 172. 11, 173. 8, 176. 3, *SchEP* 548. 8. *SchCH* 65. 6 is not so much a reference to Origen, as to Ammon.

[81] Greg. of Nyssa: *SchEH* 149. 4, *SchDN* 413. 1. Greg. of Nazianzus: *SchDN* 221. 1, 413. 1. Africanus: *SchEP* 532. 4, 541. 5. Ammon: *SchCH* 65. 6, *SchEH* 176. 3. Shepherd: *SchDN* 241. 6, 244. 1. Hippolytus: *SchDN* 337. 5, *SchEP* 545. 8. Papias: *SchCH* 48. 7, *SchEH* 176. 4.

[82] *SchCH* 76. 7, *SchEH* 172. 11.

[83] Antipater: *SchEH* 176. 3. Polycarp: *SchEP* 536. 5. Eusebius: *SchEP* 541. 5. Methodius: *SchEH* 173. 3. Symmachus: *SchMT* 421. 1. Athanasius: *SchEP* 565. 5. *Apostolic Constitutions*: *SchEP* 565. 5. Sextus: *SchMT* 429. 1. Aristo: *SchMT* 421. 1. Justin: *SchCH* 113. 10. Chrysostom: *SchDN* 340. 4.

[84] Aquila: *SchMT* 421. 1. Theodotion: *SchMT* 421. 1. Philo: *SchEP* 528. 1.

[85] Although the *Apostolic Constitutions* probably stem from the late 4th cent., John surely considered them to be of much greater antiquity.

term for the divine nature, meaning the fourth-century fathers who are 'more recent' than Dionysius.[86] But that is as 'recent' as John goes with his invocation of the fathers. The slight allusions to Chalcedonian Christological formulae are never framed as an appeal to authority.[87] Perhaps John is intentionally avoiding references to more recent authorities in an attempt to ground his arguments in the voices of a more distant past. If he emphasizes the pre-Nicene canon of authors with more appeal to all parties in the contemporary debates, in this he seems to have shared some of the Dionysian strategy itself.

This leads to a general question about John's sources: did he know each of these authors directly, or did he know some of them as cited and preserved in the works of others? It is fairly clear that John is picking up many of his citations at second hand. His reference to Papias' views on the gustatory pleasures which will accompany the resurrection is surely derived from Irenaeus.[88] When John linked Clement's *Can a Rich Man be Saved* and Irenaeus on the question of the date of the exile of the evangelist John, he was only following the prior example of Eusebius.[89] Irenaeus' account of Polycarp had also already been cited at length by Eusebius.[90] The Christian translator Symmachus and the Jewish translators Aquila and Theodotion were surely known to John through Origen's *Hexapla* or even through other authors who had used the *Hexapla*.[91] Philo's reference to the therapeutae was probably derived from Eusebius.[92] On the other hand, it is possible that John had independent access to the work of Africanus, for neither of John's references can be paralleled in other extant fragments of his *Chronographies*.[93] Similarly, his two references to Clement's *Hypotyposes* cannot be paralleled in any other extant fragments of that work.[94]

---

[86] *SchMT* 424. 3. The phrase 'light from light' (*SchDN* 224. 7) seems to be a Nicene allusion.

[87] *SchEH* 149. 15, *SchDN* 197. 2, 229. 5. See below on Christology.

[88] *SchEH* 176. 4, cf. Iren. *haer.* 5. 33. 3–4 (SC 153: 411–21).

[89] *SchEP* 573. 7, cf. Eus. *h.e.* 3. 23 (SC 31: 126–9).

[90] *SchEP* 536. 5, cf. Eus. *h.e.* 4. 14 (SC 31: 179–80).

[91] *SchMT* 421. 1. We have been unable, however, to locate parallel discussions of the word *araphel*. The following authors were searched: Origen, Gregory of Nyssa, Gregory of Nazianzus, Basil, Chrysostom, Clement, Theodoret, Athanasius.

[92] *SchEP* 528. 1, cf. Eus. *h.e.* 2. 17 (SC 31: 72–7).

[93] *SchEP* 532. 4, 537. 6.

[94] *SchMT* 421, *SchDN* 225. 3.

LITURGICAL SOURCES AND CONCERNS

In his comments on the Dionysian corpus, John demonstrates a selective interest in Christian worship and other rituals, especially in the strict hierarchical order which regulates the duties of the clergy. Because John cannot comment on every liturgical item, his chosen occasions for any remark at all, even a simple repetition or reinforcement of the Dionysian point, can be significant. Many such remarks function as an outline in the margins rather than as a commentary.[95] Certain scholia, however, bring into the discussion items or terms not in the text being commented upon, at least not explicitly. Most importantly, John is clearly eager to reinforce the author's strict hierarchical principles about ritual duties and authority, especially those of the bishop.

John often specifies what he considers to be assumed or intentionally concealed in Dionysius' discussion of a liturgical item. He acknowledges but did not imitate the Areopagite's strict discipline of silence when it came to the actual words used in a rite.[96] Whereas Dionysius would only paraphrase certain liturgical texts, even the single word 'Alleluia' or the biblical words of institution in the anaphora, John shows no such reservation. He freely identifies the 'Alleluia', some of the biblical phrases in the anaphora, the name of the 'Trisagion hymn', the liturgical announcements of ordination, and the words used at the elevation.[97] When the Areopagite obliquely surveyed the various biblical books used in the liturgical readings, John pauses to point out which words indicated the Old Testament books and which particular phrase was an allusion to the Song of Songs.[98] When John identifies the references to the New Testament books, he also ventures a guess at the cryptic allusion to a writing by the beloved disciple: 'I think he means the Apocalypse of the divine John, or his Gospel, which is even more likely.'[99]

Although these identifications of rites and biblical books seem accurate enough, some of John's assumptions about Dionysian liturgical practices reveal more about his own liturgical context than about the Areopagite's text. That the Dionysian deacons placed the bread and cup on the altar was considered indicative of his antiquity and of 'the custom which prevails in Rome'.[100] Similarly, 'note that the deacons at that time kept

[95] See e.g. *SchEH* 125. 3.

[96] *SchEH* 184. 1, cf. *SchEH* 133. 2.

[97] Alleluia: *SchEH* 125. 10. Anaphora: *SchEH* 137. 4. Trisagion: *SchCH* 76. 7. Ordination: *SchEH* 165. 13. Elevation: *SchEH* 136. 20.

[98] Old Testament books in *SchEH* 140. 7. Song of Songs in *SchEH* 140. 9.

[99] *SchEH* 140. 11. New Testament books in *SchEH* 140. 10.

[100] *SchEH* 136. 16.

the doors', and 'note that at that time the deacons alone divested them for baptism, whereas the presbyters did the remaining rites, which now the deacons do'.[101] The apparent use of the Creed in the communion liturgy occasions a comment about such continuity, even though the Creed was not used in that context until just before John's time.[102] Even if John was aware of the relative novelty of the practice, he comments only on its antiquity 'even then' in Dionysius.[103] To John, any such discontinuities are minor, especially in comparison with the continuity which he affirms between the liturgy of his own day and this apostolic witness from the first century.

Also noteworthy are the occasions when John's interpretations differ from the Areopagite. John, for example, considers the highest of the celestial beings to be the Thrones, whereas in *The Celestial Hierarchy* the highest order is that of the Seraphim.[104] John also thought that the lower clerical orders included exorcists, even though there is no such office mentioned in Dionysius.[105] Furthermore, John spoke of 'hierarchies' within the churchly hierarchy, including 'a hierarchy of deacons' headed by the 'archdeacon'.[106] Although Dionysius once mentioned the 'first of the liturgists', he never used the word 'hierarchy' in this plural sense and never spoke of a hierarchy of deacons. More significantly, John was once constrained to equate 'presbyter' and 'bishop', despite his overall concern to keep the orders distinct: 'Note that the name "presbyter" can be applied to a bishop, for the bishop is also a presbyter.'[107] This relationship of different clerical orders is partially correct, even on Dionysian terms, since the higher order contains the lower within itself, but it could introduce confusion, for a presbyter does not have the authority of a bishop. John is prompted to make this comment, however, because of the subtitles to *The Celestial Hierarchy* and other treatises: 'From Dionysius the presbyter to Timothy the co-presbyter'. John has concluded from other passages that Dionysius was a hierarch, and he must reconcile that overall judgement with this wording.

In certain areas, John does not so much supply what seems assumed in Dionysius as he builds extensively upon what is explicitly in the text. Only on specific issues does he take the trouble to expand significantly

---

[101] *SchEH* 165. 1, 125. 7.

[102] For the date of this innovation, see our discussion in Ch. 1.

[103] *SchEH* 136. 17.

[104] *SchCH* 64. 7, 65. 1, and 65. 9.

[105] *SchCH* 52. 3, cf. *SchEP* 549. 5.

[106] *SchEH* 117. 14. Dionysius mentioned the 'first of the liturgists' in EH 7. 2 (123. 6).

[107] *SchCH* 29. 2.

upon the Areopagite, and these occasions always reward further examination. Upon the Dionysian mention of a triple immersion in baptism as imitating Christ's three days in the tomb, John supplies three consecutive brief comments on death in general and then adds a fuller exposition of the biblical references to Christ's death.[108] His interest in death and the afterlife is yet more apparent and explicit in his expansions upon the Dionysian chapter on funerals.[109] The *Scholia* demonstrate a particular concern to underscore what Dionysius says about symbolism and the superior knowledge available to the hierarch. On the one hand, this emphasis is simply faithful to Dionysius, who discusses at length the interpretation of biblical and liturgical symbolism and entrusts this spiritual process to the hierarch. John can paraphrase the text or ask us to note that Dionysius 'by "original symbol" of the current mysteries means . . . the mysterious supper of the Lord'.[110] On the other hand, John shows his own interests here too. To the Dionysian language of the interpretative move from effects to causes regarding liturgical interpretation in general, John adds an eschatological note which is not part of the Areopagite's hermeneutic:

by the expression 'from the effects to the causes' he means from the perceptible symbols to those which are intelligible and intelligent, that is, from those which are less perfect to those which are more perfect: for example, from the types to the image, and from that to the truth, even as the things of the Old Testament are shadows, those of the New, an image, and the state of the things to come, the truth.[111]

To be sure, the Dionysian method of interpretation is a movement from the perceptible to the intelligible; but this distinction of types, images, and truth is John's own, especially when the Testaments and the eschaton are attached. John also goes beyond the Areopagite when it comes to the role of the hierarch regarding symbolism. For Dionysius, all humans, including the hierarch, need symbols and divine inspiration for interpreting them. Although the hierarch is indeed the one through whom the interpretation flows to others, he is not somehow exempted by the Areopagite from the need for the symbolic. Compare John on this point:

the covering of the divine myron does not include the bishop himself, but, as the apostle has said [2 Cor. 3: 18], with 'unveiled face' he contemplates the mysteries, whereas for those who are not perfect there is need of symbols. It is for this reason

---

[108] *SchEH* 132. 8–11. See our discussion in Ch. 4.
[109] Especially *SchEH* 173. 8. See also *SchEH* 173. 7, 176. 2–4, 176. 6, as well as Ch. 4.
[110] *SchEH* 137. 4. For another example of paraphrasing, see *SchEH* 121. 5.
[111] *SchEH* 137. 7. John seems here to echo Hebrews 10.

that the holy myron of God is covered with folds by the hierarch, who thus intervenes between the things of God and those of the laity and reveals the symbols
through his interpretation.[112]

In *The Ecclesiastical Hierarchy*, the consecration of the myron ointment
by the hierarch is seen only by himself and by those clergy immediately
around him. It is not seen by the laity, and the folds of the cloth do veil
the ointment during most of the service. But there is no suggestion in
Dionysius that the hierarch does not need symbolism because he is
among the 'perfected'. This exaltation of the hierarch, even beyond the
Areopagite's already high view, is John's own emphasis. It seems to be
part of his special attention to the hierarchical authority of the bishop.

A great number of John's scholia express his concern for clerical duties,
hierarchical order, and ecclesiastical authority, especially that of the
bishop. Such may seem self-evident, in so far as the issue of hierarchical
authority permeates the Dionysian corpus itself, but the sheer quantity of
John's comments here is significant. Almost thirty separate scholia consider the proper ranking and duties of the clerical or lay orders. Of the
many topics covered in the *Scholia* as a whole, only Christology receives a
significantly higher number of remarks.

John's concern for ecclesiastical authority operates within certain pre-
suppositions about Dionysius and about the idea of hierarchy in the first
place. The very word 'hierarchy' is naturally of interest to John, and he
pauses to note the Dionysian definition in his scholion on the title of *The
Celestial Hierarchy*.[113] Not only are the members of a hierarchy all carefully situated under a higher human source or authority, but the human
hierarchy as a whole is strategically located, both for Dionysius and for
John, as a 'mean term' half-way between the heavenly hierarchy and the
legal.[114] Beyond these definitions and the larger context of the human
hierarchy, there is yet another parameter for discussing hierarchical
authority. John specifies why Dionysius himself can speak an authoritative word: 'By "master" he means St Paul the apostle, since it was he who
ordained him high-priest of the church of the Athenians, as it is written
in the sacred *Apostolic Constitutions*.'[115] Thus, the Areopagite's own
authority came through proper hierarchical channels.

The first step in delineating good clerical order is to clarify the terms
used for the various ranks of clergy: 'by "hierarch" he means the one who
is the source, not of priests, but of sacred things, the one who cares and
provides for them'.[116] John freely equates this term with 'bishop' even

[112] *SchEH* 153. 6.   [113] *SchCH* 29. 1.   [114] *SchEH* 161. 3.
[115] *SchEP* 552. 11, cf. *Prol.* 17C.   [116] *SchCH* 29. 1.

though the Areopagite never mentioned the common designation of 'bishop' among his occasional synonyms for the title 'hierarch'. John also clarifies the Areopagite's nomenclature for the other ranks of clergy: 'In what follows you will also discover that by "liturgists" he means the deacons, and by "priests", the presbyters'.[117] Thus the Dionysian triad of hierarch, priests, and liturgists is naturally accepted by John as bishop, presbyters, and deacons. The nomenclature for the laity also needs clarification, especially the Dionysian term for monks. John attached his most thorough comment on that word to the title of *Letter 1*,[118] but goes out of his way to repeat this equivalence of 'monks' and 'therapeutae' on two more occasions when he comes to *Letter 8*.[119] That letter to an insubordinate monk involves John's (and the Areopagite's) most direct and impassioned arguments for hierarchical authority, over against the evils of disorder. In asserting that the rank of monks should be distinguished from the rest of the laity regarding marriage, the military, and the market-place, John adds specific details to the Dionysian distinction.[120] The Areopagite's other lay classifications, that is, the faithful, the catechumens, penitents, and possessed, also receive individual reinforcement in John's scholia.[121]

John's general interest in hierarchical order stems from his concern for clerical duties and for episcopal authority in particular. Sometimes he carefully adds his marginal signposts to the pertinent sections of *The Ecclesiastical Hierarchy*.

Note what is the order of hierarchs.

Note what is the order of priests, i.e. of presbyters.

Note what is the order of liturgists or of deacons.[122]

On some of these occasions he takes the time and the space to paraphrase Dionysius rather fully, more so than on other subjects.[123] The Dionysian view of hierarchical authority, that the higher ranks contain all the authority and insight of the lower ones but not vice versa, is especially important when it comes to the role of the bishop. For example, the priests operate only within the limited authorization given to them by the hierarch.[124] John frequently finds it worth while to repeat and to reinforce the strong Dionysian view of authority and clerical duties within the churchly hierarchy, especially the dominant role of a hierarch or

---

[117] *SchEH* 125. 7.   [118] *SchEP* 528. 1.   [119] *SchEP* 544. 1, 548. 6.
[120] *SchEH* 172. 1 (marriage not mentioned in Syr.).
[121] e.g. *SchEH* 141. 8–9, 169. 1–5.   [122] *SchEH* 164. 12, 164. 14
[123] e.g. *SchCH* 92. 4.   [124] *SchEH* 164. 8.

bishop.[125] He can sometimes put it quite strongly, more forcefully than the Dionysian text in question. When *The Ecclesiastical Hierarchy* merely mentioned clerical orders and allotments, John adds some detail: 'because each clerical order has its own distinctive sacred ministries in some sense allotted to it, which it is not able to transgress'.[126] Similarly, a general comment on *The Celestial Hierarchy* prompts John to restate these principles ('someone enrolled in the clerical order ought not do anything greater than his own proper rank') and to add a double biblical warrant.[127]

This concern comes to a head in *Letter 8*, both for the Areopagite and also for John. The intensity of John's commitment to these principles is apparent in the first scholion, which he attaches to the opening words of the epistle about disorder. John hears the Dionysian irony in addressing the rebel monk as 'noble Demophilus', and wants the reader to note that such 'evil things' took place even and also in apostolic times.[128] Such a violation of good order is, indeed, a sin.[129] Like Dionysius himself, John is concerned to protect the prerogatives not so much of the priests as of the hierarch. If a monk like Demophilus should not have transgressed the prerogatives of a priest, 'how much more is it not to be permitted that bishops be accused by anyone'.[130] Whether there is any human authority above the rank of hierarch is an ambiguous question in Dionysius. On the one hand, the Areopagite said that the hierarchs should 'bow to the apostles and to the successors of the apostles'. On the other hand, and in the very next sentence, he also said that an erring hierarch 'should be set right by his peers'. John chooses to reinforce the former scenario rather than the latter, which could imply a college of equal bishops.[131]

In summary, John spends an extraordinary amount of time and space reinforcing the Dionysian principles of hierarchy, sometimes with fervour, and even goes beyond the Areopagite at some points. Perhaps John asked the reader to 'note that these evils *also* took place in those [apostolic] times' because he was himself pitted against insubordinate monks. His interest in this subject would confirm the dating of the corpus

---

[125] Besides those discussed, there are several other reinforcements of hierarchical authority: *SchCH* 49. 12, 69. 7, 96. 4, *SchEH* 160. 7, 165. 1, 165. 3, 165. 5, 165. 6.

[126] *SchEH* 160. 7. See also *SchEH* 153. 6 on the hierarch not needing symbols.

[127] *SchCH* 49. 7.

[128] *SchEP* 544. 1.

[129] *SchEP* 552. 4.

[130] *SchEP* 548. 2.

[131] *SchEP* 552. 1. See also the other scholia regarding episcopal power in *Letter 8*: *SchEP* 548. 1, 548. 6–7, 549. 6–7.

to John's own episcopate. Not only was he himself as a bishop responsible for good order in the Church, but also as the bishop of Scythopolis around 540 he may have had his own conflicts with disobedient monks, especially given the Origenist controversy swirling about Palestine at that time. Of course, overreaching monks were common enough earlier as well, but John's concern to refute them may have been particularly acute given his own context.

4
Doctrines of Salvation and Charges of Heresy

John's *Prologue* announced his concern for the 'doctrines of salvation' and for a number of specific charges of heresy which were being levelled against the Dionysian corpus. He made it clear that he was out to defend his author, since 'some dare to abuse the divine Dionysius with charges of heresy, being themselves absolutely ignorant of matters of heresy'.[1] The *Prologue* specified four such areas of concern: the Trinity, Christology, cosmology (creation), and eschatology (resurrection and future judgement). When John discusses any of these subjects in his *Scholia*, we must remember his overarching concern to defend Dionysius, even when he does not stress this agenda. John approaches these issues of heresy from a second perspective as well. He frequently names the various heretics whose errors he considers to be exposed by the Areopagite's writings. On a variety of issues, not just those listed above, Dionysius had presciently refuted erroneous doctrines which came centuries later. When John attacks heresy in this way, Dionysius is not the defendant but the principal apostolic witness for the prosecution.

The names and viewpoints of various heretics are scattered throughout the *Scholia*, since widely dispersed texts may occasion John's remarks, sometimes in unexpected places. Such a format rules out John's systematic treatment of one heretic or issue at a time. Nevertheless, one topic with its set of heresies dominates John's polemics. Twice as many scholia name Christological heresies as treat all other heretics combined. Approximately forty items overtly identify his Christological opponents, with roughly twenty on all other heretics taken together. Furthermore, even some of these other heresies turn out to have connections to John's Christological opponents.[2] As John's quartet of doctrinal topics is

---

[1] *Prol.* 20A, cf. 'doctrines of salvation' in 17C.

[2] To give just two examples, when John discussed Papias' views on the pleasures of food in the resurrection, John links him with Apollinaris (*SchEH* 176. 4). Similarly, John's discussion of the Marcianists would have carried Christological overtones in the 6th cent. (cf. *SchEH* 169. 19 with the comments of Tim. of Constantinople, *haer.* PG 86/1: 45–52, who classifies the Marcianists as Monophysites).

dominated by Christology, his treatment of the overall subject of orthodoxy and heresy is characterized by a concern for salvation itself. As the
Prologue draws to a close with the subject of salvation, we also conclude
this chapter with the soteriological dimensions of these four interrelated
doctrines: the Trinity, Christology, cosmology, and eschatology.

THE TRINITY

Approximately thirty-five scholia employ language that is explicitly
Trinitarian. Many of these scholia do not address the actual doctrine of
the Trinity: they simply name God in a Trinitarian way where Dionysius
was not so explicit. But there are some important scholia which do
discuss Trinitarian doctrine. John's context had no serious theological
dispute over the nature of the Trinity, certainly nothing like its raging
Christological controversies. Yet the latter often presupposed a careful
foundation in an orthodox doctrine of the Trinity. Concepts of hypostasis, essence, etc., needed to be handled well from the beginning in
order to assure an overall orthodoxy in Christological issues.[3] Furthermore, the indirect dialogue with Neoplatonism involved specific points
of Trinitarian thought and nomenclature. Thus, even John's passing
references to God as the Trinity can be part of his overall strategy for
interpreting and implicitly defending the Areopagite's text.

As here broadly defined, the 'Trinitarian' scholia can be separated into
four groups, with some overlap: first, those which briefly note the Trinitarian language in the Dionysian text; secondly, those which condemn
Arius and Eunomius; thirdly, those which add a specifically triune note to
the Areopagite's generic language for God; and fourthly, those which
enlarge upon distinctively Dionysian and Neoplatonic ways of understanding God's unity and triunity.

1. Some of John's scholia on the Trinity simply point out or repeat the
Trinitarian nomenclature in the Dionysian passage at hand. For example,
John calls attention to the only explicit Trinitarian reference ('tri-
hypostatic') in all *The Celestial Hierarchy*.[4] When Dionysius named the
Trinity early on in the next work, *The Ecclesiastical Hierarchy*, John
commented: 'Note what is the source of hierarchy, and concerning the
Trinity.'[5] John sometimes presented an updating of the Areopagite's

---

[3] Cf. Leon. Schol. *sect.* 1 (PG 86/1: 1193–6).
[4] *SchCH* 76. 7 on *CH* 32. 9 (212C).
[5] *SchEH* 120. 1.

'apostolic' language for the Trinity, as in the very next scholion: 'Note that the holy Trinity knows its own subsistence, as something "obvious", even as we now say that it alone understands its own essence.'[6] Similarly, when *The Mystical Theology* apparently summarized the contents of an earlier book on God as one and as triune, John identified the orthodox contents of the lost (or fictitious) *Theological Representations*, and provided the ostensibly more recent nomenclature: 'It knows how "the divine nature is one"—certain more recent fathers have proposed *homoousion*—how it is "triune"—which we call "thrice-hypostatic". It knows the properties of the persons and what they signify—that is, "Fatherhood and Sonship".'[7] John also commented on some of the Areopagite's more creative terminology. Regarding the divine persons, he says: 'Note that he calls the Father the "god-begetting divinity"; and the only-begotten, "the filial divinity".'[8] When Dionysius linked the language of Trinity to 'fruitfulness', John invoked 'Basil and the Gregories' and remarks that 'the name "Trinity" signifies a "divine-begetting".'[9] These scholia, wherein John underscored Dionysius' use of Trinitarian language, might suggest a fundamental strategy of maximizing the Areopagite's Trinitarian orthodoxy at every opportunity. This possibility is not confirmed, however, by a survey of the fuller range of references to the Trinity in Dionysius. Although John did note most of the locations where the Dionysian text itself used Trinitarian language, he did not comment upon all of them. Twice he passed by the language of 'three persons' without comment, and once he ignored the Areopagite's reference to a 'triadic henad'.[10] Furthermore, the most striking invocation of the Trinity in the entire corpus received no remark at all from John, namely, the prayerful opening of *The Mystical Theology*: 'Trinity! Higher than any being, any divinity, any goodness!'[11]

2. John occasionally refers to the Nicene struggle over the doctrine of the Trinity. As noted above, he remarks in passing that 'certain more recent fathers have proposed *homoousion*'.[12] He cites Athanasius by name only once, while treating the general subject of images.[13] Even this, however, is not a direct discussion of the doctrine of the Trinity. Yet John does make three direct references to Arius and Eunomius, with their theological errors and heretical heirs, all in scholia on *The Divine Names*.

---

[6] *SchEH* 120. 2.   [7] *SchMT* 424. 3, cf. *SchDN* 196. 1.
[8] *SchDN* 212. 10.   [9] *SchDN* 413. 1.
[10] 'Three persons': *EH* 2. 2. 7 (73. 1) and 6. 2 (117. 12–13). 'Triadic henad': *DN* 1. 5 (116. 8–9). The same idea, in different terms, is also passed by in *DN* 3. 1 (138. 3) and 5. 8 (186. 5).
[11] *MT* 1. 1 (141. 2).   [12] *SchMT* 424. 3.   [13] *SchEP* 565. 5.

When Dionysius called God 'unbegotten', John adds to the Areopagite's own caution about the various uses of this term and he named the Arians and Eunomians as the blasphemers who were anticipated by Dionysius.[14] John also turns a Dionysian reference to the Thearchy 'beyond thought and beyond being' into an occasion to oppose Arius: 'From these things it is quite possible to overcome the madness of Arius and Eunomius, who made bold to quibble about the essence of the only-begotten, an essence which is in fact ineffable and beyond being itself.'[15] John has here given the Areopagite's generic God-language a prescient anti-Arian specificity.

For John, the Areopagite's general principle, that all the divine names refer to the whole triune God, subtly contains within itself an argument against Arius and Eunomius. To treat a biblical name for the Father as equally applicable to the Son is to treat the two persons equally and to oppose all subordination.[16] Thus when the second chapter of *The Divine Names* began with a reference to the 'entire divine subsistence', John quickly puts the phrase to an anti-Arian use, and more: 'In this chapter he fights especially against the Arians and Eunomians, both of whom maintain the inequality [of the Father and the Son], but also against the Nestorians and Acephalians.'[17] The three explicit refutations of Arius and Eunomius do not constitute a large subgroup of Trinitarian scholia, nor do they distort the Areopagite's meaning. Nevertheless, an orthodox doctrine of the Trinity, complete with condemnations of the appropriate heretics, was foundational for all other theological formulations.

3. When Dionysius named God with the general term 'divinity', John drew on considerable patristic precedent in noting that this was a reference to the Trinity: 'He customarily calls the revered Trinity the "entire divinity".'[18] The pattern of interpreting the Dionysian phrase the 'entire divinity' to mean 'the Trinity' continues in other scholia as well.[19] Furthermore, that the Areopagite's most characteristic term for God, 'thearchy', is also an orthodox synonym for the Trinity, is not merely assumed by John but is explicitly explained to the reader, perhaps because it was a relatively unusual word.[20] Beyond reading 'divinity' and 'thearchy' to mean the Trinity, John adds Trinitarian nomenclature to several other passages where Dionysius was speaking generally about God. When Dionysius invoked Paul to the effect that God cannot deny himself, John interprets the phrase to mean, among other things, that the

---

[14] *SchDN* 372. 3.
[15] *SchDN* 192. 5. See also 209. 11 on Arius and the Nestorians.
[16] See *SchDN* 212. 3 and 216. 2.   [17] *SchDN* 209. 11.
[18] *SchDN* 209. 11.   [19] *SchDN* 212. 5, see also 216. 1, 189. 4, 312. 1.
[20] *SchDN* 192. 7, cf. 192. 5, 409. 6.

Father and the Son will always want or will the same thing.[21] Where Dionysius simply referred to God with the minimal pronoun, translated by unfortunate necessity as 'it' and often referring back several sentences to the noun 'thearchy' or another such term, John has no hesitation in identifying the subject as the Trinity.[22] Even when the overall import of Dionysius' argument is to deny any assertions about God, including the designations 'one' and 'three', John disregards the Areopagite's programmatic preference for non-descriptive language such as 'it'. He can even identify the subject of *The Mystical Theology*'s final and forceful negations as the Trinity.[23] In this case, John does not follow or perhaps even recognize the more radical Dionysian application of negative theology to all terms and concepts, even to the name 'Trinity'. John affirms the general apophatic principle, and adds 'Sextus the philosopher' in support, but he effectively exempts the name 'Trinity' from the negations.[24]

In summary, when it came to 'divinity' and 'thearchy', John openly stated his conviction that Dionysius himself meant these terms to designate the triune God. This is not an unwarranted assumption, since the Areopagite said as much himself and used the language of the Trinity often enough. Nevertheless, in his articulation and application of this assumption and in his refusal to apply negative theology to the Trinitarian language, as Dionysius ultimately did, John persistently interpreted the Areopagite's corpus as orthodox Christian theology, and presented it to his readers accordingly.

4. The scholia also reveal glimpses of John's own doctrinal understanding of God as triune. One of John's comments on the doctrine of the Trinity has little to do with the interpretation of Dionysius.[25] More significant is the cluster of passages in which John joins Dionysius in interpreting the Christian doctrine of the Trinity with the help of Neoplatonic nomenclature and concepts. This pattern can help account for some otherwise puzzling scholia. For example, when *Letter 8* mentioned 'transcendent lights', John makes a rather abrupt association with the Trinity: 'By the expressions "lights transcendent, intelligible, and divine" he means the pure and holy Trinity.'[26] John can make this linkage because Dionysius elsewhere talks about the Trinity in terms of lights. Biblically, this could be linked to 'the Father of lights' in James 1: 17. Modern Dionysian scholarship, however, has noted the Proclean origins

---

[21] *SchDN* 361. 1, cf. 213. 6, 373. 1.   [22] *SchDN* 193. 1.
[23] *SchMT* 432. 1.   [24] *SchMT* 429. 1.
[25] *SchDN* 344. 2.   [26] *SchEP* 569. 2.

of the phrase 'divine offshoots, the flowering and transcendent lights', as used by Dionysius for the Son and Spirit in their relationship to the 'Father [as] the originating source of the Godhead'.[27] When John commented upon this text, he pointed out the nomenclature but gave it extensive biblical warrant.[28]

Beyond the name 'lights' to speak of the persons of the Trinity, Dionysius used the analogy of lamps quite creatively, and with another Neoplatonic imprint. The Areopagite's example of one light through three lamps draws approval from John: 'The whole mind of the father is thus disposed. He is giving an example regarding the holy Trinity.'[29] The issue here is not so much the actual symbolism of lights and lamps. The real issue is the Neoplatonic way Dionysius and John describe the unity and the differentiations involved in the Trinity, namely the language of 'abiding' or 'remaining' [μονή] as opposed to 'procession and return'.[30] Dionysius called the unity of God the 'abiding' and called the differentiations the 'processions'.[31] The idea that God 'abides' first as one and then 'proceeds' to the three divine persons results from the Areopagite's application of Neoplatonic logic. On some occasions, John provided thorough biblical warrant for these terms and ideas, as if aware of their ambiguity and eager to give them proper Christian credentials.[32] Nevertheless, on other occasions he points out and seems to endorse without any disclaimers this way of speaking about the Trinity.[33] For Dionysius, the counterpart to the unity or remaining of God as one is the differentiations or processions associated with the persons of the Trinity. The Neoplatonic nomenclature of 'procession', used by the Areopagite in one of his key presentations of the Trinity, was taken up by John: 'Note the "thrice-hypostatic Trinity". By "fecundity" he means the paternal procession beyond thought unto the revelation of the Son and the Holy Spirit.'[34] The phrase 'paternal procession' is John's own felicitous summary and seeming commendation of the idea that the Father 'proceeds' into the Son and Spirit. On another occasion when Dionysius spoke of God's unity and differentiations, John expanded upon this complex theme.[35] John's apparent endorsement of this conceptual framework and its Neoplatonic nomenclature offers further testimony that he could integrate Neoplatonist thought into his own as smoothly as Dionysius himself.

---

[27] *DN* 2. 7 (132. 1–3), see Proc. *de mal. sub.* 11. 23–4.
[28] *SchDN* 224. 7. [29] *SchDN* 220. 1. [30] *SchDN* 216. 10.
[31] *DN* 2. 4 (126. 10). [32] e.g. *SchDN* 220. 1. [33] *SchMT* 424. 3, *SchDN* 216. 7.
[34] *SchDN* 196. 1. [35] *SchDN* 221. 1.

John's dominating Christological interest regarding the Dionysian corpus also relates to his other stated interests in the Trinity, creation, and eschatology, to his overall concern for salvation, and even, albeit indirectly, to his concern to defend the authenticity of the Dionysian corpus. We begin with the opposition to Apollinarian Christology already seen in the *Prologue*, then move to John's presentation of various Christological heresies, and finally to his own doctrinal position and agenda in interpreting the Areopagite's Christology.

The anti-Apollinarian agenda

In the *Prologue*, John's explicit reference to a 'fully human' Christ, with 'rational soul and earthly body like ours' introduces the general direction of his comments on Christology.[36] We find echoes of this terminology in several scholia which identify John's opponents quite explicitly and lead us into John's Christology, its historical context, and its relationship to eschatology and soteriology. That the funeral rites as presented by the Areopagite are concerned for the 'entire person' prompted this comment from John:

Note that by an 'entire person' he means one composed of a *rational* soul and a body, as is suggested by the expression 'in pure contemplation and under-standing'. Note also that he refers to the 'whole salvation' of soul and body. One should pay careful attention to these two points so that you might under-stand the Incarnation of a rational soul *and* body when he elsewhere says that 'the transcendent Jesus *wholly* took on our human substance'.[37]

Observe first of all the direct linkage of Christology and soteriology: just as the whole Christ is affirmed as fully human with rational soul and body, so the whole person is saved, soul and (resurrected) body. John elsewhere puts it very briefly: 'By "as a whole" he means the Lord who by taking both soul and body has saved us "as wholes" [composed] of both soul and body.'[38]

Since resurrection and soteriology will concern us below, we stay for now with John's anti-Apollinarian scholia. *The Ecclesiastical Hierarchy* had explained the meaning of the sacramental unveiling, fraction, and

[36] *Prol.* 20B.
[37] *SchEH* 181. 17. 'Elsewhere' is *DN* 2. 6 (130. 5–6), which also receives comment by John (*SchDN* 221. 8).
[38] *SchEP* 545. 8.

distribution in highly significant terms: 'Out of love for humanity Christ emerged from the hiddenness of his divinity to take on human shape, to be utterly incarnate among us while yet remaining "without confusion".'[39] This Dionysian passage provided John with an excellent opportunity for a comment upon the Areopagite's orthodox Christology: 'He says "utterly" [incarnate] since he took on both a rational soul and an earthly body. {Rightly does he speak of an unconfused Incarnation, for when he appeared as a human, he remained God and preserved the properties of each of the two natures.} Note also that this is against the Apollinarians.'[40] Certainly the reference to 'rational soul' is against the Apollinarians, even though John must extrapolate this polemic from the more general Dionysian comment about Christ being 'fully' or 'utterly' incarnate. But the full text of this scholion goes beyond Apollinarianism to invoke Chalcedonian Christology quite directly. In fact, in opposing the Monophysite descendants of Apollinaris, the scholion here sounds strikingly dyophysite. The phrase 'preserving the properties of each nature' clearly echoes an expression from the Formula of Chalcedon and from Leo's *Tome*. In general, John does not mention Chalcedon, and the Dionysian text itself usually avoids that Formula's specialized vocabulary. Nevertheless, assuming that this text is by John and was omitted by the Monophysite translator for its Chalcedonian ring, John rightly saw an opening here to interpret the Areopagite's own Christology in a Chalcedonian, anti-Monophysite direction, since the original Dionysian text quoted above did use one of the Formula's famous negative modifiers ('without confusion'). This precise term is used four times in the Dionysian corpus regarding the Incarnation so as to safeguard the distinction between Christ's humanity and divinity. In addition to the text just quoted, the Areopagite said elsewhere that Christ came into our human nature 'unconfusedly'. There, too, John alerted the reader to the orthodox pedigree of this terminology, claiming that Dionysius had marvellously anticipated the language of Chalcedon: 'Note also that the expressions "without confusion" and "without change", which he used, are from the apostles, as also is the expression "the whole man".'[41] While this last phrase continues the anti-Apollinarian agenda of the *Prologue*, the overall strategy in John's scholia is far broader and deeper than this one polemic.

---

[39] *EH* 3. 3. 13 (93. 16–17).

[40] *SchEH* 149. 15. Bracketed materials not in Syr., but present in FA. Cf. *SchDN* 397. 2.

[41] *SchDN* 197. 2. This issue is further complicated by the Neoplatonic background to some of the Chalcedonian expressions such as 'without confusion'. In this regard, see Ruth M. Siddals, 'Logic and Christology in Cyril of Alexandria', *JTS* NS, 38 (1987), 341–67.

A Chalcedonian via media?

The passages cited so far could give the mistaken impression that John was a strict Chalcedonian or a dyophysite whose only concern was to oppose a Monophysite confusion of natures. This is perhaps the unavoidable result of using the *Prologue*'s anti-Apollinarian slant as our starting-point, but John's overall Christological agenda is far more nuanced. When Dionysius again said that the Incarnation was 'without change or confusion', John pointed out the significance of the passage and said that it opposed the 'Nestorians, Acephalians, and Phantasiasts'.[42] We see an even broader panorama of opponents when John comments upon another Dionysian usage of the term 'unconfused' and thereby provides us with an occasion to assess his overall strategy.

Note the precision of his teachings, a precision that is expressed in a multitude of passages and fights against all heretics. On the one hand, that God's providential care for us was 'self-working' implies that God the Word was one and the same, and not one in another, as some rave with Nestorius. On the other hand, the phrase 'in a true sharing of *all* our properties, yet sinlessly' refutes the Manichaeans, the Eutychians, the Apollinarians, the Acephalians, and all other heretics at once.[43]

There truly are a 'multitude of passages', at least in John's *Scholia* if not in the original Dionysian text, and they may seem to oppose 'all other heretics at once' without differentiation. Over forty separate scholia explicitly name these errant Christologies. Most of them identify more than one heretic, and several oppose quite an array of enemies. Amid these numerous names and doctrinal complications, however, there is a clear pattern to John's naming of Christological heretics. The scholion just quoted is a clear example of this format: the truth stands over against the Nestorians *and* the Acephalians (i.e. the Monophysites).[44] These two groups are frequently named together as the opposing errors on either side of Chalcedonian orthodoxy, which thus occupies a *via media*. As part of this overall pattern, John has several variations on the nomenclature for the Nestorians and the Acephalians. For Nestorians, John may once have substituted 'Basileans'.[45] For the Monophysites John usually

---

[42] *SchDN* 229. 5.   [43] *SchEH* 149. 2.

[44] The name 'Acephalians' refers to those who were initially 'headless' (without a patriarch), namely, the Monophysites or Cyrillian anti-Chalcedonians who refused to follow Peter Mongus when he compromised on the question of the *Henoticon*. Their leader, Severus, later did become patriarch of Antioch, and gave the name 'Severians' to this Monophysite group.

[45] *SchCH* 72. 5, cf. *SchEH* 181. 10 (not Syr./FA) which also mentions the 'Basileans'.

employs the label 'Acephalians', but within this basic category, he included three references to Eutychians, and two to the Phantasiasts.[46] These occasional references to the Basileans, to the Eutychians or the Phantasiasts may have their own historical interest, but when it comes to John's theological discussion these are simply variations in wording. They appear only as explicit synonyms for and always adjacent to the dominant names, 'Nestorians' and 'Acephalians'.[47] Before moving on to the substance of John's Christological polemics, we must first appreciate the overwhelming domination of this format when he mentions such heresies. Of the seventeen times he names the Nestorians, he places them in tandem with the Acephalians ten times. Even more strikingly, of the eleven occasions when he mentions the Acephalians, ten of them are these same passages which pair them with the Nestorians. In other words, in only one out of eleven passages does John mention the Acephalians without also naming the opposite error of the Nestorians.[48]

To move from format to content, to John's actual critique of the Nestorian and Eutychian positions, we return to the scholion quoted above (*SchEH* 149. 2). Over against the Nestorians, Christ is to be identified with God: 'God the Word was one and the same, and not one in another, as some rave with Nestorius'. Over against the Acephalians, Christ fully shared our complete humanity. The 'Nestorian' distinction of Christ's human and divine natures which is implied in the phrase 'the one in another' is never fully analysed by John. Once, while discussing the God–carrying celestial thrones, he invoked Basil regarding the God-carrying flesh of Christ: 'The flesh of the Lord was united in both essence and person to God the Word.'[49] This union he there calls 'unseparated', which is in the spirit (but not the letter) of the Chalcedonian language against Nestorius, even while adding (against the other opponents of Chalcedon) that this flesh has its own proper and true existence. But usually John is content to oppose Nestorius with the bald assertion that Christ is God. For example, to quote a brief but illustrative scholion in its

From Photius, we know that Basil of Cilicia, a 'Nestorian', had often attacked John (see Ch. 2).

[46] The Phantasiasts, also called 'Aphthartodocetists', were Monophysite followers of Julian of Halicarnassus, who split from Severus over the incorruptibility of Christ's body. Eutychians are named in *SchCH* 72. 5, *SchEH* 149. 2, and *SchDN* 216. 3. The Phantasiasts are mentioned in *SchDN* 221. 8 and 229. 5. They may be implied in *SchDN* 197. 6 and *SchEP* 533. 1.

[47] Even the one exception to this rule, *SchDN* 216. 3 which names Eutyches apart from any mention of the Acephalians, places him in the familiar pairing over against Nestorius.

[48] *SchDN* 397. 2.

[49] *SchCH* 68. 1.

entirety: 'Note that Christ is God, against the Nestorians.'[50] Once John even added the phrase 'as God' to a Dionysian mention of Christ in order to oppose Nestorius.[51] John similarly linked the Nestorians explicitly with the Arian heresy of inequality, and at least once aimed his theopaschite sentiments against the Nestorians, since this too assumes that Christ is God and a unified subject.[52] Although John surely knew a more nuanced critique of Nestorianism, his references to Nestorius are usually objections on the grounds that Christ is God.[53]

John's polemic against the Acephalians is more nuanced. Part of it is already seen in his remarks against the Apollinarians.[54] It was usually a Dionysian reference to Christ's sharing of our humanity which provided John the opportunity to oppose the Acephalians, along with the Apollinarians. But John has other strategies for maximizing the reality of Christ's incarnate human nature. Dionysius' reference to Jesus in terms of Melchizedek drew this from John: 'As human, Christ also became the high priest. Note this against the Acephalians and Nestorians.'[55] Upon the Dionysian use of Psalm 24, John first points out that calling Jesus 'the Lord' is against the Nestorians and then adds: 'Against the Acephalians and Eutychians, note that although he is the "Lord of Dominions", he is nevertheless flesh and manifestly human.'[56] Even the brief Dionysian phrase 'visible theophany' regarding the transfiguration is for John a summary of orthodox opposition both to the Nestorians (since it is a sight of God) and also or especially to the Acephalians (since it is visible humanity).[57]

John's own Christology

Despite John's formal Chalcedonian *via media*, his own position on the spectrum is not at the original 'centre' of Chalcedon itself but with the Neo-Chalcedonians. Although he can (apparently) say 'in two natures' and even oppose (Monophysite) talk of 'one nature', he shows a loyalty to Cyril of Alexandria's insistence upon the unity of the active subject in

---

[50] *SchEH* 132. 3.

[51] *SchDN* 216. 3, see also *SchCH* 57. 2, *SchEH* 116. 5, 181. 10, 165. 18, and *SchDN* 225. 3.

[52] *SchDN* 209. 11, 221. 8. We should here recall that the 'Nestorian' Basil of Cilicia found John's theopaschism most objectionable (see Ch. 2).

[53] Still further examples: *SchDN* 209. 11 and *SchMT* 425. 2.

[54] *SchEH* 149. 2. 'Without change' in *SchCH* 57. 3. 'Without confusion' in *SchDN* 229. 5.

[55] *SchEH* 165. 18.   [56] *SchCH* 72. 5; cf. 57. 3.   [57] *SchDN* 197. 6.

Christ's Incarnation.[58] This suggests the deeper question: how far would John go in stating this unity of Christ's person when it came to the contemporary litmus test of theopaschism? The phrase 'one of the Trinity suffered' preserved Cyril of Alexandria's insistence upon the unity of the (divine) subject in Christ, even in his passion and death. Some defenders of Chalcedon, those now called 'Neo-Chalcedonians', could also accept this wording, as long as the suffering and death did not apply to his divinity. On this front, two of John's remarks reveal this particular Christological position and suggest his strategy for interpreting the Areopagite's Christology. In *The Divine Names* Dionysius affirms that the transcendent Word wholly and truly took on human nature, including suffering. Although the Areopagite's use of 'suffering' here could mean merely 'experiencing' in general, instead of suffering pain and death in particular, John adds his approval, with an important reservation. God the Word is in truth the one who suffered 'in the flesh' (i.e. not in his divinity).[59] John's reservation that this suffering only occurs in Christ's flesh, is discussed more fully in another theopaschite scholion. Under the divine name 'power', the Areopagite asked whether there is anything beyond God's power, such as to 'deny himself'. John inserts into this discussion the Christological question from 'Arabia', whether God has the power to suffer in his divinity. Here is John's theopaschism with the key qualification explicitly spelled out: 'Jesus Christ, God the Word, suffered for our sakes in the flesh, but not in his divinity.'[60] This distinction may have excluded a very few Patripassionists, in 'Arabia' or elsewhere, but the Neo-Chalcedonians' overall strategy of affirming the theopaschite formula was designed to appeal to the more moderate and more numerous Cyrillians, yet without sacrificing the individuality of Christ's humanity and the reality of his suffering and death. The Fifth Ecumenical Council (553) ratified this moderate Chalcedonianism, but its proponents never did win over the 'Acephalians'. Nevertheless, with this strategy in mind, we turn to a final set of scholia in which John directly interprets Dionysius' Christology without explicit reference to contemporary heretics.

John's interpretative strategy

To uncover John's deeper agenda in influencing the reader's impression of the Areopagite's Christology, we need to inquire yet further into his argument. John has established Dionysius as a Chalcedonian, or rather, as

[58] *SchCH* 57. 3.   [59] *SchDN* 221. 8.   [60] *SchDN* 360. 7.

a prescient forerunner of Chalcedon's middle way between heresies. Nevertheless, the apparently even-handed treatment of Chalcedon's enemies on both fronts, Nestorians and Acephalians, must yield to John's own *via media* between Chalcedon and the so-called Monophysites. As a Neo-Chalcedonian, John is prepared to go part-way toward the Cyrillian Christology, as evident in the theopaschite scholia. For John's interpretative agenda, however, the conventional reservation that God the Word suffered not in his divinity but in the flesh has a deeper significance than the protection of an impassable divinity. Not the negation, that Christ did not suffer in his divinity, but rather the affirmation, that God the Word truly suffered in the flesh, has a clear emphasis in John's overall presentation of the Areopagite's Christ. Even as John may work for a Neo-Chalcedonian compromise with the Cyrillians, he must also show how Dionysius is orthodox on the specific issue of Christ's distinctive humanity in his passion and death. This agenda builds upon his anti-Apollinarian comments and goes beyond them.

Amid the familiar condemnations of Apollinaris, Eutyches, and Nestorius, John's own agenda in presenting the Areopagite's Christology can also be seen in this comment on a brief Dionysian reference to Jesus:

Note that God the Word alone became incarnate. He says that [the Incarnation] is 'perfect'—against Apollinaris, since it is from an intelligent soul and our body. This he makes clear by saying 'according to us', which is also against Eutyches. It is also against Nestorius, because he speaks of 'the . . . unchangeable subsistence of Jesus' as God 'according to us'. Note also that he says that his mysteries in humanity are 'real'—hunger, thirst, walking on water, passing through closed doors to his disciples, raising the dead, the passion itself, and so on.[61]

John has expanded the Dionysian text at two crucial points. First, he added the reference to Jesus 'as God', in order to oppose Nestorius. Secondly, and to the point at hand, the Areopagite's brief mention of Jesus called his mysteries 'real'. John freely added the concrete human dimensions of hunger and thirst, along with the miracles which combined human conditions with divine power. John's strategy of supplementing the Dionysian text is summed up in the addition of the word 'passion' in the positive sense of Christ's suffering and death. For Dionysius the word 'passion' is most often used in the plural with a negative meaning, as in the 'destructive passions' of this world. His comments about Christ are frequent enough, with sufficient stress on a complete Incarnation to

[61] *SchDN* 216. 3.

satisfy John, but the Areopagite's concrete references to the humanity or suffering or death of Jesus are few and fleeting. What John has to say on such occasions is of prime importance. For example, in his interpretation of the baptismal rite, Dionysius naturally related the triple immersion to the three-day 'divine death' of Jesus. John takes the opportunity of this rare mention of Jesus' death in the Dionysian corpus to expand upon it biblically. Adding material about death first from the Gospel of John, Hebrews, and Isaiah, he then closes with two more quotations from Acts and the Psalms.[62] A reader who encounters this passage by the Areopagite with John's comments over part of the page would be impressed with the emphasis on Jesus' death and its scriptural expressions. But this impression would be due to John, not to the brief mention in the Dionysian text of baptismal immersion and the divine death.

Since the Areopagite's comments on Christ are scattered throughout his corpus, so too are John's pertinent scholia, with the single exception of *Letter 4*, which has received considerable attention ever since the Dionysian corpus first surfaced. John, naturally, wants to claim it for his version of orthodoxy: 'Note the whole of this letter, since it is against every heresy, old and new.'[63] Despite the initial reference to heresies, John's scholia on this epistle never mention any particular heretics, but concentrate on presenting Dionysius to the reader as biblical and orthodox. First of all, he underlines the Areopagite's assertion that the transcendent Jesus is called human not merely as the cause of humans but as an individual human being. Citing Julius Africanus as support, he paraphrases the passage and adds a biblical text.[64] That Jesus was a particular, individual human being is an essential part of John's argument against the Acephalians, although he does not here name them or pursue the argument. But a scholion on the Acephalians elsewhere may also shed some light on John's interest in Jesus' individual humanity. Discussing 'peace' near the end of *The Divine Names*, the Areopagite made reference to 'the individuality of each being'. For John it is the occasion to denounce a heretical Christology: 'Note what he means by "individuality", namely, each thing's being as it is by nature and remaining as it was when it came into being. These things are against the Acephalians who do not even understand the nature of individuality.'[65] This comment does not explain the connection of 'individuality' to Christology and to the human nature of Christ, but the Formula of Chalcedon had done so in a key phrase paraphrased elsewhere by John: the Incarnational union 'preserved the

---

[62] *SchEH* 132. 11.   [63] *SchEP* 532. 4.

[64] *SchEP* 532. 3–4.   [65] *SchDN* 397. 2.   [66] *SchEH* 149. 15.

properties of each of the two natures'.[66] As seen throughout his work, including these scholia on *Letter 4*, John was concerned to safeguard the concrete, historical individuality of Christ, especially in his passion. Thus, in the ostensibly non-Christological scholion on the divine name 'peace', John's critique of the Acephalians regarding individuality may well have involved the individuality of Christ's humanity, which is affirmed in *Letter 4*.

To continue with the scholia on *Letter 4*, the particular part of Christ's anatomy here under discussion was his feet, for the two Dionysian examples of divine and human activity were the virgin birth and the walking on water. Both show the interplay of affirmation (it is human to be born or to walk) and transcendent negation (it is superhuman or divine to be born of a virgin or to walk on water).[67] *Letter 4* concludes: 'but rather, by the fact of being God-made-man he accomplished something new in our midst—the activity of the God-man.' John adds new biblical examples of Jesus' humanity, distances himself from contemporary Neoplatonic language of 'theandrite', and distinguishes in Christ the human, the divine, and the combined.[68] In this tripartite distinction, John is making explicit what he considers to be implicit in Dionysius, namely, a belief in the individual integrity of Jesus' complete humanity, including suffering and death. The scholion brings this out with concrete examples of 'eating and grieving', whereas the Areopagite, here and generally, gave examples only of the divine nature or the mixture of divine and human, never of the human nature on its own.

There is an extraordinary example of this same pattern in *The Divine Names*. In the apparent context of the dormition of the Virgin Mary, Dionysius said that each one present praised 'the omnipotent goodness of that thearchic weakness', and his mentor Hierotheus did so best of all. This oblique expression may well refer to the Incarnation, but it receives no emphasis from Dionysius. All the more striking then is John's scholion, which immediately claims the phrase for his Christology and then discusses it at extraordinary length, with more biblical examples rhetorically piled up on one another than in any of his other scholia.[69] There is no mention of Apollinaris, Nestorius, Eutyches, the Acephalians, or any other historical context; it is simply that Dionysius mentioned the 'thearchic weakness' and John amasses biblical testimonies to the historical details of Christ's poverty and passion. A small sample: 'the piercings of nails, the lance wound in his

---

[67] *SchEP* 533. 2, 533. 3.   [68] *SchEP* 536. 1.   [69] *SchDN* 236. 10.

side, the slaps on the face, the spittings, the vinegar, the bitter drink, the crown of thorns, the mockery and laughter, the genuflections, the cheap funeral and grave'.[70]

The listing of historical details of Christ's Incarnation and passion is especially striking because such lowly and degrading experiences in the flesh are missing in the Areopagite's text, not only in this passage but throughout his corpus. There are sufficient references by Dionysius to Christ's Incarnation in general, but John needs to emphasize each one, for on the whole they lack the very concreteness and individuality which he has here supplied so abundantly from the Scriptures. The concluding portion of the scholion leads us even further into John's Christological interpretation of Dionysius, for he connects the Dionysian language of divine weakness to the Pauline assertion that Christ was 'crucified in weakness', going beyond the Areopagite in explicit identification of the passion.[71] As a whole, the passage is a dramatic example of John's strategy in maximizing the Areopagite's references to Christ in terms of his concrete Incarnation, his earthly suffering, and death on the cross.

The reference to St Paul takes us yet one more step into John's interpretation of Dionysian Christology. Not only did certain scholia emphasize the Areopagite's references to Jesus and especially his rare allusions to Christ's suffering and death, others also supplied this theme even where Dionysius was not discussing Christ. The long passage just discussed mentioned the foolishness of God, which in the Pauline context is the foolishness of the cross. But when the Areopagite cited this same verse (1 Cor. 1: 25) later in *The Divine Names*, there is no discussion of Christ or the cross, but rather of the principles of negative theology. 'It is customary for the theologians to apply negative terms to God, but contrary to the usual sense of a deprivation.'[72] In the Areopagite's apophatic method, the 'foolishness' of God is like a transcending negation, in that God is not wise on the human scale, but more-than-wise. This general principle of interpretation is entirely Dionysian, but it is an epistemological abstraction when compared to the original Pauline emphasis on the foolishness of God in Christ crucified. Nevertheless, where Dionysius ignored Paul's Christological context, John restores it, for his scholion on this passage discusses both the general principle of negative theology *and* its concrete application to the Incarnation.[73] Where the Areopagite

---

[70] *SchDN* 236. 10.

[71] *SchDN* 236. 10, citing 2 Cor. 13: 4, 1 Cor. 1: 25, Phil. 2: 7, Isa. 53: 5, 1 Pet. 4: 1, and 1 Cor. 2: 8.

[72] *DN* 7. 1 (193. 11).   [73] *SchDN* 340. 5.

turned Paul's Christology of the cross into an abstract principle about apophatic theology, John turned the reader's attention back to Incarnation, *kenosis*, the cross, and the resurrection of the dead. Along with the huge gloss on 'thearchic weakness', this insertion of incarnational Christology is John's strongest presentation of the Dionysian position on Christ as orthodox. And yet, John also openly admits that 'other fathers' did not take Paul's 'foolishness of God' to apply to negative theology in such general terms: 'Note how the father understood the saying of the Apostle, for Chrysostom and the other fathers understood it to apply to the cross.'[74] With stunning brevity, John has opened up an enormous (and probably unintentional) critique of the Areopagite's Christology, not over Christ's person and natures but over the centrality of Christ's work in salvation.

For the Areopagite, negative theology became an interpretative technique or a spiritual epistemology, providing the means for ascending toward union with the transcendent God. For Paul and many orthodox interpreters, such as John Chrysostom and John of Scythopolis, negative language about God is not itself a means of ascent, but is meant rather to turn one's sights from the divine transcendence 'down' to the revelation of God as incarnate in Christ, indeed, in Christ crucified. In this light, the problem with Dionysian Christology is not finally over the person of Christ and the relationship of his natures. On that point, John of Scythopolis is probably right to argue throughout that the Dionysian corpus is compatible with orthodox Christology of the Neo-Chalcedonian variety, that is, the theopaschite *via media*. Even if the Areopagite neglected the concrete individuality of Christ's human nature, especially regarding his passion and death, John's scholia consistently attempted to make this part of Dionysius' Christology more explicit. That John never mentioned Chalcedon directly or Cyril or Leo and his *Tome* is curious, but it may reflect an irenic intention: as testimony to his success, note that the Syriac translator of his work only needed to make a few minor deletions before offering it to a non-Chalcedonian audience. But John's deeper objection to the view of Christ in this corpus is rather over the centrality of Christ's death and resurrection in the economy of salvation, relative to the general Dionysian programme of negations and silence.

[74] *SchDN* 340. 4.

CREATION

When John's *Prologue* itemized the areas of his doctrinal concerns, it named the Trinity, then Christ, and then 'intelligible and intelligent and perceptible things'.[75] One scholion, moreover, confirms the linkage of this terminology to the doctrine of creation, for John distinguishes between the 'cause of all' and that which depends 'demiurgically' upon it, namely, 'the intelligibles, intelligents, sensibles'.[76] Overall, his comments on creation are often very complex and usually pertain to equally difficult passages in *The Divine Names*. A scholion on this subject in *The Celestial Hierarchy* is unusual both for its location and also for its direct and simple language. The Areopagite himself brought up the subject of creation: 'the transcendent Deity has out of goodness established the existence of everything and brought it into being'.[77] Prompted by this comment, John says: 'For God made all things out of non-beings, so that they might enjoy his goodness.'[78] John's statement here provides us with an introductory outline for this section.

1. 'God made.' It may seem self-evident for a theology of creation to assert that it is God who is the creator, but John needs to assert that God alone is the creator of all things, and not any other creative divinities: 'The cause of all things is one, and not many; and rightly does one divinity, the holy and blessed Trinity, produce all things, and not many creative divinities.'[79] This scholion goes on to indicate the complex and multifaceted polemic John is conducting: against 'the Greeks', including those we would call Neoplatonists, against Simon, the father of all heresies, and especially against the cosmological dualism which John associated with the Manichaeans. The scholion just cited calls the 'one Divinity' the creator or the 'cause' of all things, which means that none of these caused or created things has any independent power of causation or creation in and of itself. Dionysius himself had said this often, and John is here commenting upon such a text.[80] *The Divine Names* demonstrates a major philosophical difference between its author and contemporary Neoplatonism: all causation and all creation is attributed to the one God, and there are no lesser divinities or hypostases (e.g. Nous or Soul) or entities of any kind which have their own powers of causation or creation. John was happy to point out the Areopagite's orthodox doctrine of

---

[75] *Prol.* 20B. [76] *SchDN* 316. 4. Cf. 324. 1.
[77] *CH* 4. 1 (20. 9–11), cf. *DN* 1. 4 (113. 3–4) and *EP* 8. 1 (174. 1).
[78] *SchCH* 52. 7. [79] *SchDN* 312. 1.
[80] *DN* 5. 2 (181. 7–21).

creation in this respect, here and elsewhere. He claims that Dionysius has exposed a defect of 'the Greek philosophers' who believed that there are three 'powers who came into being from another three powers before them, but were not created particularly by God'. John summarized their position, and added that 'the great Dionysius' wisely opposed such error, by asserting that these powers, and all else, 'were established demi-urgically by God'.[81] On this general foundation, that God alone is the creator of all, John builds his whole doctrine of creation.

2. When John says that 'God made all things', this includes matter. This position pits him against opponents on two distinct fronts: those who attribute the existence of matter to another source or power which is opposed to God, such as the Manichaeans, and those who believe that matter as a primal substance was not created at all but is coeternal with God, namely, some of the Greek philosophers. John attacks the Manichaeans a half-dozen times, usually in conjunction with other enemies. Opposition to an ultimate cosmic dualism was inherent in the Areopagite's own Christianity and in his sympathies with a Platonic (and Stoic) monism. John seems to enjoy identifying the occasions when the Areopagite had marvellously exposed such heretics in advance, such as the Greeks, the Valentinians, and the Manichaeans.[82] That God is the 'one source of all' is also asserted elsewhere against the Greeks and against 'the Manichaeans who are pre-eminent in bad doctrine'.[83] When Dionysius flatly ruled out 'two mutually opposing sources of beings', John again named the enemy as the Manichaeans.[84] Many of John's scholia on *The Divine Names* build upon the Areopagite's own monist explanation of evil as the privation of good, and as therefore not inherent in matter. Occasionally, John names the followers of Mani, as when he reinforced his author's specific comments about the demons not being evil by nature and about the example of light and darkness.[85] A corollary to this anti-Manichaean position is that what we call evil, the absence of good, results from the wrong choices of the free will. This conclusion Dionysius himself appended to the end of his discussion of evil in *The Divine Names*, and illustrated with the story of Carpus in *Letter 9*. In the latter case, John adds the expression: 'One should not suppose that he is positing a certain coercive power (i.e. the devil), such as that affirmed by

---

[81] *SchCH* 77. 5, with *SchDN* 316. 4, 332. 1, 408. 2.
[82] e.g. *SchDN* 397. 8.
[83] *SchDN* 272. 1.
[84] *SchDN* 285. 3 on *DN* 4. 21 (169. 3–4).
[85] Evil by nature: *SchDN* 288. 13. Light and Darkness: *SchDN* 348. 6.

the Manichaeans and Messalians.'[86] An even more important corollary to this anti-Manichaean polemic is the pervasive Dionysian assertion that everything, including matter, has some share of the Good. For John, more explicitly than for Dionysius, this entails the value and integrity of the human body in particular, both Christ's and the believer's. Thus John can lump the Manichaeans together with the Eutychians, Apollinarians, and the Acephalians because they all deny the full Incarnation of the divine Word as a complete sharing of our human properties.[87] Just as John's Christology pertains to his soteriology, so his condemnation of the Manichaeans concerns our salvation as well, for among the heretics who deny the resurrection of the body can be numbered Mani himself.[88]

To say that everything, including this material world, is created by God is also to oppose those who would assert the eternity of the world alongside the eternal God. This venerable debate among the various followers of Aristotle finds significant expression in the Dionysian corpus and in John's *Scholia*. The Areopagite argued effectively that the biblical expression 'eternal doors', for example, means merely 'old' or 'everlasting' in the sense of temporal duration, and certainly did not mean 'coeternal with God'. To this, John adds 'as the Greeks say in their silliness, when they assert, "At the same time God, at the same time all".'[89] Who these Greek philosophers may be, John does not say; but that he is quoting a technical phrase is confirmed by the identical wording in another scholion on *Letter 9*'s image of a bowl's round and thus endless rim. There, too, he opposes the 'the fools who say "At the same time God, at the same time all".'[90] Whatever John's source and opponents, to deny the eternity of the world is to assert its beginning or creation, not out of some primal matter but out of nothing. Thus, that God made *all* things, even prime matter, means that God created *ex nihilo*.

3. 'God made all things out of non-beings.' The notion of creation 'out of non-beings' was for John a mark of difference between the Christian doctrine of creation and the various cosmogonies of other belief systems and philosophies, including the Platonic tradition. Dionysius did not make much of it, but when he says that 'God brought everything into being', John takes this to mean 'out of non-beings'.[91] Furthermore, John explicitly understands the 'everything' which is made 'from nothing' to include matter: 'For even matter was produced by God from non-

---

[86] *SchEP* 557. 4, cf. 557. 2. [87] e.g. *SchEH* 149. 2.
[88] *SchEH* 173. 8. [89] *SchDN* 388. 4 on *DN* 10. 3 (216. 16), cf. 332. 4.
[90] *SchEP* 569. 9.
[91] *SchCH* 52. 7 on *CH* 4. 1 (20. 10–11). See also *DN* 1. 4 (113. 3–4) and *EP* 8. 1 (174. 1–2).

beings—but not as some suppose, as something formless and shapeless.'[92] John knows this distinction well, but he does not really emphasize it or show much interest in it.

4. 'God made all things out of non-beings, so that they might enjoy his goodness.' Why did God create everything? The short answer is 'so that they might enjoy his goodness',[93] but such a formulation only introduces further complexities. When the Areopagite said that 'the good is the cause even for the sources and the frontiers of the heavens', John adds a comment pertinent to our current inquiry: 'He says that the goodness of God is the cause of the "sources and frontiers of the heavens", for God produced these through the abundance of his goodness.'[94] John has here expanded significantly upon the original text. Dionysius was simply saying that God as the good was the cause of these things, whereas John adds the overtone of a motive when he identifies the cause of creation as the goodness of God. Furthermore, the expression 'abundance of his goodness' can carry the connotation of an 'overflow' of goodness. If the world is an 'overflow' of God's own being, the oft-debated issue of Dionysian pantheism arises. At certain points the Areopagite could be read this way, as seen in the *Book of the Holy Hierotheus*, and John can use similar language: 'the procession of God into the multiplicity of the visible and invisible creation through the abundance of his goodness'.[95] But John is concerned to avoid suspicions of pantheism and does so in part through his complex discussions of the ideas or paradigms of God.

5. John's most extensive and complicated comments on creation concern the 'how' of God's creating, the precise way the world was made. Deep in the background is the Areopagite's own custom of talking about the creation as a result of God's 'being-making procession' or 'overflowing'.[96] Pantheism is a controverted issue in the interpretation of Dionysius, although he can, arguably, be cleared of such charges, since he also says that 'as effects they [created things] fall so very far short of their Cause and are infinitely and incomparably subordinate to him'.[97] John's overall concern for pantheism is clear from a scholion early in *The Divine Names*:

For when he said that God is all things and that in him are all things, someone might lower his mind to composition and fall away from the truth by supposing

[92] *SchDN* 272. 1.   [93] *SchCH* 52. 7.   [94] *SchDN* 244. 9.
[95] *SchDN* 221. 1.
[96] 'Being-making procession' in *DN* 5. 1 (180. 12–13), 'creative procession' in 5. 9 (188. 18), 'overflow' in 11. 2 (219. 23).
[97] *DN* 9. 7 (212. 14–15).

that all things are piled up inside God, or that God is all things by way of some sort of composition.[98]

John has two ways of avoiding the error of pantheism. The first way, that of emphasizing God's choice or will, receives a few brief but clear comments; the second, that of clarifying the ideas or paradigms pre-existing in the mind of God, receives numerous lengthy and sometimes obscure discussions. At issue is the free will of the creator over against the necessity of creation. When the Areopagite spoke of creation as the effects caused by God's beneficent providence, John names the error thereby exposed, the ignorant opinion 'that the creative faculty is in God by nature, as also weaving is in spiders'.[99] Thus, the act of creating is not some natural necessity in God, like an animal instinct, but is freely chosen out of goodness. The key word 'will' does not appear in this interesting reference to a spider, but John elsewhere explicitly says that creation is by an act of God's will.[100] John never emphasizes the distinction between will and necessity in God's creation, and never appeals to the fathers for support regarding this or, interestingly, any other facet of the doctrine of creation. He can say simply in passing that God 'brings forth beings by his will'.[101] One such statement brings us the final step into John's complex theology of creation.

Now then, one must know that the production of all things depends upon him as cause and principle, since all beings are from him. Reasonably, just as all future things will happen through his unknowable act of will, they also pre-existed in him who knew both what he would produce and when he would produce it.[102]

Although John knew and used the language of God's free will over against any necessity in creation, he concentrated his remarks on something more specific: what God willed to do in creation was to bring into existence that which already pre-existed in God's own mind. More than a dozen lengthy scholia treat the subject of pre-existent paradigms. The starting-point is characteristically Dionysian: even though we cannot know God in his nature, creation's 'order possesses certain images and semblances of his divine paradigms'.[103] John often pursues the theme of the revelation of God in the order of creation, in terms of paradigms as the 'eternal thoughts of God' and as 'rational principles' [λόγοι].[104] Of the

---

[98] SchDN 209. 1.   [99] SchDN 205. 2.   [100] SchDN 316. 4.
[101] SchDN 224. 6, cf. 193. 4, SchEP 569. 9.
[102] SchDN 200. 3.
[103] DN 7. 3 (197. 21–2), cf. 4. 4 (149. 7–8).
[104] Eternal thoughts of God: SchDN 349. 5. 'Rational principles': SchDN 353. 3, cf. 296. 5, 325. 3.

many observations which could be made on this theme, we here confine
ourselves to two: John's obsessive linkage of the two words 'idea' and
'paradigm', and his firm qualification on this strikingly Neoplatonic
language.

John found the words 'idea' and 'paradigm' often enough in the
Dionysian corpus, but not so tightly linked together or applied to the
process of creation. John, however, rarely mentions the one term without
the other; fourteen times in ten scholia he pairs them, often in the
formula 'ideas, that is, paradigms'.[105] His interest in the latter term
probably stems from the single occasion when Dionysius discussed the
word 'paradigm' more fully instead of just using it casually to mean 'an
example'.[106] With a famous and anachronistic reference to Clement the
philosopher, the Areopagite said: 'We give the name of "paradigm" to
those "rational principles" which pre-exist as a unity in God and which
produce the essences of things.'[107] In one particularly packed scholion,
John explains the word 'paradigm', couples it no less than four times with
'idea', provides a slight scriptural foundation, underscores the orthodox
doctrine of creation, and still has space to comment on this Clement.[108]
It is hard to believe that John mistook the teaching of Clement of
Alexandria for that of the apostolic Clement mentioned by Paul,
especially since he openly cited Clement elsewhere.[109] In any case, he here
indicates his major reservation or qualification regarding the overall
concept. An idea or paradigm, he says, is a product of God, not to be
worshipped; they are the thoughts of God, 'who alone ought to be
worshipped', as he concludes in the next, equally pertinent, scholion.[110]

John consistently explains 'ideas and paradigms' as thoughts in the
mind of God.[111] The effect of this emphasis on God and God's thoughts
is to keep the 'ideas' in their subordinate place, in other words, in the
mind of God.[112] On one occasion John is yet more explicit about his
qualification on talk of ideas and paradigms, and about the position he
opposes.

---

[105] *SchDN* 316. 4, 324. 1, 325. 3, 329. 1 (four times), 332. 1, 332. 4, 349. 5 (twice), 353. 3,
384. 6, and *SchEP* 569. 9.

[106] Dionysius uses the word 'idea' with no particular significance in *CH* 15. 6 (56. 7),
15. 7 (56. 20), *EH* 2. 3. 7 (78. 4), and *DN* 9. 3 (209. 2). 'Paradigm' means simply 'example' in
a casual sense in *CH* 13. 3 (44. 24), 13. 4 (48. 22), *DN* 2. 4 (127. 5), 2. 8 (132. 17).

[107] *DN* 5. 8 (188. 6–9).

[108] *SchDN* 329. 1.

[109] *SchMT* 421. 1, *SchEP* 573. 7, *SchDN* 225. 3, *SchCH* 48. 7.

[110] *SchDN* 332. 1.

[111] See also *SchDN* 324. 1, 384. 6.

[112] *SchDN* 320. 3.

Since some said that the ideas and paradigms are self-subsistent beings, he now smites those Greeks, saying: if the ideas should not exist simply and unitedly, in so far as they are the super-simple thoughts of a super-simple and super-united God, then God would be a compound of a paradigm and himself, which he called 'duplication'.[113]

Perhaps the extraordinary attention John gives to 'ideas and paradigms' should be understood in this polemical context. John may use the Neoplatonic language of ideas and paradigms, but he will not grant any self-subsistence to these ideas or paradigms, as 'the Greeks' do. They are merely ideas in the mind of God, who is not a composite being, and who alone is to be worshipped as the creator. There are other nuances to John's discussions in these scholia, but this particular emphasis brings us back full circle to the initial point that it is God alone who is the creator. This means, for John, that God shares no creative powers with any other, whether a rival Manichaean god or subordinate divinities or self-subsistent 'ideas and paradigms'. No matter what the Dionysian ambiguities and no matter how John may use Neoplatonic categories, he wants finally to assert the orthodox Christian dogma of the one God who created everything, including matter. His soteriological interest in a particular form of matter, namely, our bodies and their resurrection, was identified in the *Prologue* as a separate concern, and thus receives its own treatment next. But a belief in the resurrection of the body presupposes this foundational doctrine of creation.

ESCHATOLOGY, EVAGRIUS, AND ORIGEN

Last in the *Prologue*'s list of doctrinal concerns were two aspects of eschatology: 'our general resurrection which will happen with both our body and our soul . . . and the judgement then of the just and the unjust'.[114] John's theology of creation, wherein our bodies and matter generally are not alien or opposed to God but rather created by God, is the necessary foundation for affirming the resurrection of the body. His soteriology, specifically his concern for the resurrection, appears in the *Prologue* with an eschatological emphasis: the general resurrection which *will* happen, and the judgement *then* of the just and the unjust. The scholia themselves show only minimal concern for the judgement of the just and the unjust, but provide about ten major comments on the resurrection, many of them at the natural Dionysian location regarding funerals and the afterlife.

[113] *SchDN* 332. 4.   [114] *Prol.* 20B.

This is a modest number of scholia, compared with the larger totals devoted to other doctrinal issues. Nevertheless, John's scholia on the resurrection of the body are usually longer than average and are packed with highly significant references: to the Greeks, to fathers both major and minor, and to heretics such as Simon Magus, and especially to Origen.

Ambiguity over Evagrius and Origen

John's scholia made two explicit references to Evagrius, and seven to Origen. In one very unusual scholion, John actually quotes both Origen and Evagrius with reference to a Dionysian comment on the angels' purity. The issue is whether the celestial beings have some kind of bodies and why they need purification. 'For me', insisted Dionysius, 'to say that the angels are not totally pure and that they do not possess the plenitude of transcendent purity would be to have lost all sense of the sacred.'[115] The Areopagite argued throughout his writings that the angelic beings do not have ethereal bodies, weighted down according to the measure of their impurity and resultant fall. For him, they are completely bodiless and need purification only from relative ignorance. In this the Areopagite may have been intentionally opposing an Origenist viewpoint. To the text just quoted, John adds a lengthy scholion, pointing out the contrast between the heretical Origenist angelology of partially fallen 'subtle bodies' and the orthodox Dionysian assertion that they are 'pure and incorporeal'.[116] In this scholion, unusual for its length and unique for the full quotations of opposing views, John declares himself not only against Origen and Evagrius but also against 'those initiated by Origen' or 'those who think his way', those indeed who seem to consider the Dionysian passage to support his and their position. Origen and Evagrius are clearly presented as opposed to the true teachings of Dionysius regarding the angels and their purity, and so are their unnamed followers who were apparently contemporaneous with John.

To start with Evagrius, this particular scholion immediately leads us into a much larger historical question. Its combination of two quotations from different parts of the *Kephalaia Gnostica* is the precise combination used in the fifth anathema which condemned Evagrian Origenism at the Fifth Ecumenical Council in 553.[117] The two passages are there cited in

---

[115] *EH* 6. 3. 6 (119. 18–20), see also *CH* 7. 2 (28. 23–6), 7. 3 (30. 22–31. 5).

[116] *SchEH* 172. 11.

[117] *ACO* 4/1: 248. For the questions concerning whether the condemnation of Evagrian

the opposite order, but the quotations are otherwise identical. Other scholars have noticed this, but because of their mistaken attribution of the scholion to Maximus the Confessor, they simply assumed that Maximus used the text from the Fifth Council.[118] The relationship between John's use of these two texts around 540 and the anathema in 553 can hardly be coincidence. Was it John's own pairing of these two texts which was taken over by the council? In that case, John must be credited with a specific and hitherto unrecognized influence on an Ecumenical Council. But perhaps an earlier or contemporary opponent of Evagrian Origenism had already seized upon these passages and had circulated them in tandem as illustrative of this particular Evagrian heresy. In that scenario, the double quotation of Evagrius was adopted both by John in the scholia and also, but independently from John's work, by the council of 553.

There is another side to the story, however, for both Evagrius and Origen can be cited more positively in other scholia. Another comment, apparently by John, invokes Evagrius by name, not as a heretic but as a witness to the truth. When Dionysius said that 'the Godhead is a monad, that it is one [a henad] in three persons', the scholion explains the word 'henad' by way of Jesus' prayer for unity in John 17 and Evagrius' use of this term 'in the third chapter of his second century'.[119] There are three difficulties in establishing the original text of this scholion. First, the entire section which starts with the mention of Evagrius is not in Syr., although it is attested in FA. It may not be by John at all, but it is more likely that John's positive use of Evagrius was deleted by the Syriac translator. Secondly, FA does not call Evagrius 'impious'. Such a characterization was common enough for Evagrius after the 553 condemnation, which could explain its addition to John's text in other manuscripts. Thirdly, the Migne edition erroneously put quotation marks around a passage which is not by Evagrius. As Guillaumont has pointed out, when the scholion reads 'Evagrius said this', it is not introducing a quotation, but referring back to the language of 'henad and monad'.[120] The sentence which follows is a comment by the scholiast himself, not a quotation from Evagrius.

Origenism took place during or immediately before the Council of 553 and what its exact status was as an authoritative document, see the summary discussion by Aloys Grillmeier, *Christ in Christian Tradition*, ii/2 (Louisville, Ky., 1995), 402–4, as well as the classic treatment of the question by Franz Diekamp, *Die Origenistischen Streitigkeiten* (Münster, 1899), 129–38.

[118] Antoine Guillaumont, *Les 'Képhalaia Gnostica' d'Évagre le Pontique et l'histoire de l'origénisme* (Paris, 1962), 158, cf. 23, 27, 30, 40 n. 70.

[119] *SchCH* 76. 7.

[120] Guillaumont, *Képhalaia Gnostica*, 165 n. 140.

But any positive reference to Evagrius, with or without the qualification 'impious', is striking when the subject and the language is 'henad'.
The word 'henad' was doubly delicate in the sixth century. First, calling
the angels 'henads' could remind readers of the Neoplatonists Syrianus
and Proclus in their description of the 'henads' or 'gods' who come just
below the one.[121] Secondly, and pertinent to this scholion, calling God a
'henad' could imply a specifically Evagrian heresy, for he used this word
to characterize the original unity and identity of all pre-existent souls
before they fell into bodies, except the one (Christ) who remained pure.
This notion of 'henad' was explicitly condemned in the anathemas of the
Fifth Council.[122] John had to work with this term elsewhere as well, for
Dionysius used the word a half-dozen times. The scholion citing
Evagrius used the word as Dionysius usually did, only for the unity of the
triune God and for those who will unite with him. John elsewhere
specifies the Areopagite's orthodox use of such terminology for God:
'Here he makes clear what he especially wishes to signify by predicating
"henad and monad" of God. He says that the theologians said this in
order to establish the undividedness of God.'[123] When Dionysius elsewhere used the plural expression 'angelic henads', modern readers
such as Saffrey may forcefully argue an echo of Syrianus and Proclus
regarding the henads below the one, but John passes the text by without
comment.[124] But when Dionysius used the word in both senses in the
same line, 'the henad unifying every henad', John did have a comment
which pertains to the issue at hand: 'He calls God a "henad", but adds
"unifying every henad", that is, the creator of all simple beings, such as
angels and souls.'[125] To go back to our text, if the heretical Evagrian use
of 'henad' to encompass all pre-existing souls in God was known to John,
why would he make a positive reference to Evagrius regarding this very
word? Perhaps he meant to distinguish an innocent Evagrian use of the
word 'henad' from the usage being condemned, but it is also possible that
John simply did not yet know how inflammatory this language was.
Whatever our unanswered questions, the two scholia that name Evagrius
present a mixed picture. Once John quotes him as a heretic who agrees
with Origen; once he cites him, albeit perhaps grudgingly, as a theologian
who agrees with Dionysius himself, although here John installs significant safeguards on the terminology involved.

[121] Henri-Dominique Saffrey, 'Nouveaux liens objectifs entre le Pseudo-Denys et
Proclus', *RSPT* 63 (1979), 15.   [122] ACO 4/1: 248. 5–13.
    [123] *SchDN* 193. 4.
    [124] *DN* 8. 5 (202. 11), cf. Saffrey, 'Nouveaux liens objectifs', 15.
    [125] *SchDN* 189. 3.

The other references to Origen, beyond the condemnation introduced above, reveal a similar situation. We have already noticed the *Prologue*'s casual mention of Origen, without any overtones of heresy or controversy.[126] In one scholion, John was apparently using Origen's *Hexapla*, without attribution.[127] At another point, John explicitly invoked Origen's interpretation of the Lamentations of Jeremiah as a helpful confirmation of the point which he and the Areopagite were making, again without any qualifications about Origen as heretic.[128] As in many evaluations of Origen, ancient and modern, his biblical exegesis could still be appreciated even where his more speculative theories were not followed. A mixed use of Origen and Evagrius was moreover quite natural during the 530s, when they were both associated with controversy but not yet formally condemned. This was dramatically the case with Evagrius, according to other witnesses. Barsanuphius (d. 540) reported that a certain monk was puzzled and troubled by Evagrius' views of pre-existence and final restoration. When his abbot condemned these ideas and the audacious pride of such speculation, the monk then asked if he should therefore read none of the works of Evagrius. The abbot replied that some Evagrian works were good for the soul, and to apply the parable of the fishing net: keep the good fish and throw away the bad.[129] In this story and in John's scholia, we encounter not a general ambivalence over Evagrius, but rather a specific separation of his truth from his errors. While John's use of Evagrius coheres in general with the account of the discrimating abbot, the particulars do not match, for John's scholion cites Evagrius positively from the text most closely associated with his heresy, the *Kephalaia Gnostica*, and on a point or at least on a word most pregnant with heretical associations.

On the resurrection, against Origen

Even with a positive use of Origen's exegesis, John's main approach toward Origenist theology is adversarial, especially regarding the resurrection of the body. The Areopagite's references to the resurrection are strong enough for John, but are largely confined to the discussion of funerals and the afterlife in *The Ecclesiastical Hierarchy*. In John's soteriological concern to affirm the resurrection, he sometimes discusses it elsewhere as well, going beyond the Dionysian text at hand. For example,

---

[126] *Prol.* 20D.   [127] *SchDN* 421. 2.   [128] *SchEP* 549. 6.

[129] Guillaumont, *Képhalaia Gnostica*, 125–6. Cf. Elizabeth A. Clark, *The Origenist Controversy* (Princeton, 1992), 248–50.

when Dionysius discussed the divine name 'life', he made no mention of the new life in the resurrection, although there is one allusion to our composite human nature of souls and bodies. Nevertheless, this indirect reference prompts John to praise Dionysius for his orthodox confession of the resurrection, over against 'the foolish opinion of the Greeks'.[130] This scholion shows John's general concern to make explicit the Christian confession of the resurrection over and above the Areopagite's text.

John's awareness of the controversy over Origen's views on the resurrection is apparent even while he is discussing other topics. While considering the angels, he refers to Ammon of Adrianople and his arguments against Origen in *On the Resurrection*.[131] This is not John's own explicit opposition, nor even a discussion of the resurrection, but it shows his familiarity with the wider controversy. John provides several other explicit, polemical discussions of Origen and the resurrection. When Dionysius discussed mistaken views of the afterlife, John named names: a certain Bias, Plato, Simon Magus, Menander, Valentinus, Marcion, Mani, and Origen. Here, too, the issue is of current concern in John's own historical context: 'Even *now* there are some who take their stand on the myths—not teachings!—of Origen.'[132] We see here the heart of John's objections to Origen, and his strategy for refuting the heretic. At issue was the general resurrection of the body, such that salvation itself was at stake. John's strategy was to associate Origen and his followers with the arch-heretic, Simon Magus: 'See with whom they wish to be numbered.' In the next scholion, John again associates Origen with Simon Magus regarding erroneous views of the resurrection, and this time he lines up some orthodox correctives to such heresies. Whether Origen taught no bodily resurrection at all, or that it would take place with an ethereal body, John firmly rejects his 'monstrous and foolish fables'.[133] In John's polemical strategy, even more important than his authorities are his chosen heretics. The scholia which condemn Origen's viewpoint on the resurrection *all* attach to him and to his error the name of Simon. Since Simon goes back to the apostolic age, John points out several of his own apostolic (i.e. Dionysian) refutations of such a denial of the resurrection, and he regularly uses these occasions to condemn Origen in particular. There is yet another comment on the resurrection in which John invokes Irenaeus and Hippolytus against Simon and 'those who follow Origen'.[134]

---

[130] *SchDN* 337. 2, cf. *SchEH* 173. 8, 176. 3–4, *SchDN* 337. 5, as well as *SchEH* 173. 7, 176. 2.   [131] *SchCH* 65. 6, cf. *SchEH* 176. 3.

[132] *SchEH* 173. 8.   [133] *SchEH* 176. 3.   [134] *SchEP* 545. 8.

John's strategy here coheres closely with what has been presented above. John is both consistent and emphatic: Simon's denial of the resurrection of the body was shared by Origen and by his followers, but is directly opposed by Scripture and Dionysius, as well as by later patristic authorities.

One further text on the same subject may seem at first glance not to fit with this picture of John's treatment of Origen. When Dionysius referred to 'the faulty arguments of the mad Simon', John lists Origen with Irenaeus, Epiphanius, and Hippolytus, among those who opposed Simon on the question of the resurrection, refuting the supposition that the resurrection of bodies is contrary to nature.[135] If we take John's comment at face value, his invocation of Origen as an authoritative father on the question of the resurrection would seem quite inconsistent. Although all four patristic authorities at numerous points in their writings opposed Simon and his followers, an examination of their criticisms shows that at no point did they actually bring up the issue of the resurrection as it pertains to Simon.[136] We thus gather that John's reference to Origen here is not to be taken too seriously. It is more a general invocation of those who had refuted Simon than a specific reference to the question of the resurrection. Moreover, even if we do take John at face value, we must remember the nuance which he introduced in other of his comments. Even John was willing to admit that not everything which Origen said on the issue was unorthodox. Concerning Simon and his followers, that they claimed souls would have an ethereal body in the resurrection, John comments as follows: 'One must know that Origen too says the same thing in one of his works, whereas in other of his works he completely denies this, teaching that every bodily nature passes into non-existence.'[137]

The last judgement and the afterlife

Affirming the resurrection of the body was the main item in John's eschatology, but not the whole of it. After naming the resurrection, the *Prologue* promised coverage of the future judgement of the just and the unjust. In its literary and historical context, this remark seemed to preview some significant commentary on two fronts. First of all, the *Prologue* claimed to be naming areas where the Dionysian writings had been

[135] *SchDN* 337. 5
[136] For the relevant passages, see the notes to the translation.
[137] *SchEH* 176. 3.

attacked for heresy. Indeed, the Areopagite is quite non-committal about the final judgement, at least damnation. We can thus expect John to find places to defend or at least accentuate Dionysius on this point. Secondly, in the context of the Origenist controversy, any affirmations of the judgement of the just and the unjust might well carry an attack on a final *apokatastasis* or universal restoration of all. Both dimensions of the issue of final judgement, that is, defence of Dionysius or attacks on Origenists, would have made for fascinating reading, if John had indeed pursued them. But the fact is that very few scholia pertain to the final judgement of all. Only once does John mention and reject a final restoration, but with no mention of Origen.[138]

The Ecclesiastical Hierarchy's presentation of funerals consigns sinners not to a definite judgement, but to a pitiable state of uncertainty. Nevertheless, John brings out what he considers to be the orthodox meaning implicit in this passage: he explicitly named what Dionysius never mentioned here or anywhere else, Hades and Gehenna.[139] In a similar context, a vague Dionysian reference to an 'invisible' realm after death prompts John to name it as 'Hades'.[140] In much the same fashion, when Dionysius mentioned the angels in passing, John adds explicit references to the devil, his angels, and eternal fire.[141] This pattern holds true for the celebrated vision of heaven above and hell below by Carpus in *Letter 8*. For the Areopagite this story does not really make an eschatological point; it rather serves to reinforce his exhortation to a general generosity of spirit, although he does make a reference near by to future blessedness and to those who will be 'victims of cruel demons here and after they die'.[142] But the story of Carpus could be taken to support a final restoration of all, since it concludes with Jesus generously saving even those already in the demons' clutches. But John finds only traditional eschatology here, explicitly naming 'the devil' where Dionysius mentioned only demons. In fact, in all of his works the Areopagite never named the devil, Hades, or Gehenna, but John seems to take little notice, smoothly assuming all of this in his author.[143] John's final comment here ('May the Lord free us from such men!'), shows his fervent soteriology, whereas Dionysius presents the whole story almost playfully, and only to illustrate a hierarchical generosity of attitude in general. But again, John's affirmations of a final judgement of the unjust are too few and fleeting to

---

[138] *SchEH* 173. 1.   [139] *SchEH* 176. 6.   [140] *SchEH* 132. 9.
[141] *SchDN* 349. 4.   [142] *EP* 8. 5 (187. 11–188. 2).
[143] *SchEP* 557. 3. John also added an eschatological note in *SchEH* 137. 7 and *SchDN* 345. 3.

constitute an intentional defence of Dionysius' orthodoxy. This part of the Origenist controversy is almost absent from the *Scholia*, despite the promise implied in the *Prologue*.

There is, finally, an anti-chiliast aspect to John's eschatology. The Areopagite had asserted that human words and ideas fall short of the blessed rewards of the saints, and John confirms that even the biblical language about the afterlife is symbolic and not literally true: 'And yet, the good things there are not this, but are truly unknown and incomprehensible to us.'[144] The polemical edge of this argument is quite apparent elsewhere, implicitly in Dionysius and explicitly in John. John's scholion on the Areopagite's rejection of foods in heaven immediately identifies the chiliastic heresy which had already been attributed to Papias of Hieropolis by Irenaeus, but it also condemns Apollinaris for the same teaching.[145] It was a natural part of Dionysian exegesis, and therefore John's interpretation, to consider the heavenly banquets, etc., as symbolic of purely spiritual pleasures, and not as material food. The truly new item in this scholion, however, is the aside about Dionysian authorship, which is the proper subject of our next chapter.

SALVATION

John's interest in soteriology applies not only to the eschatological items just covered, but also to the other doctrinal issues discussed in this chapter. According to the *Prologue*, Dionysius learned the 'doctrines of salvation' from Paul himself.[146] John's concerns for the doctrine of the Trinity, for Christology, for the intelligible and perceptible in creation, and for eschatology, were all summarized in the *Prologue* in terms of soteriology. Referring back to this entire roster of doctrinal issues, its conclusion reads: 'To speak in short, our salvation is focused on these points, which it would not be right to go through in detail, since the *Scholia* explicate all of these things at the proper time.'[147] We should not press this claim too hard, for not everything to do with the doctrine of the Trinity or John's theology of creation was explicitly linked to salvation. But John is consistently concerned for an explicit, traditional soteriology, and his interest in salvation does link together the several doctrinal subjects named in the *Prologue* and sketched in this chapter. Soteriological dimensions are obvious in the eschatological topics of the resur-

---

[144] *SchEH* 177. 13. [145] *SchEH* 176. 4.
[146] *Prol.* 17C. [147] *Prol.* 20B.

rection and final judgement, but less self-evident when it comes to the
Trinity, Christ, and creation. The pivotal affirmation is John's soteriological Christology: that as one of the Trinity, Christ became wholly
incarnate, of rational soul and material body, and thus saves us whole, of
soul and created, material body. In this light, the doctrine of the Trinity
provides the appropriate context for orthodox Christology, as the
doctrine of creation does for the teaching on resurrection. What connects
Christology and the general resurrection is John's wholistic anthro-
pology: Christ's Incarnation applies to the whole person, soul and body;
humanity's afterlife applies to the whole person, soul and body. His
doctrinal concerns for Christology and resurrection are explicitly
connected to each other and are both essential to his soteriology:
'the Lord who by taking both soul and body has saved us "as wholes"
[composed] of both soul and body'.[148]

[148] *SchEP* 545. 8.

5

Authenticity, Platonism, and Plotinus

John's *Scholia* add yet another layer of complexity to the long-standing debate over the identity of the author of the Dionysian corpus and his relationship to Neoplatonism. John has some comments in defence of the Areopagite's apostolic authorship, still more which demonstrate his own assessment of Platonic philosophy (both positively and negatively), and yet others which link these issues together. Furthermore, just as Dionysius had used the ideas and a few phrases of Proclus, John himself quoted numerous passages from the *Enneads* of Plotinus, without attribution. These three subjects—authenticity, Neoplatonism, and Plotinus— each have their own significance for John's overall strategy in commenting upon the works of Dionysius and are sometimes intertwined in complex ways.

AUTHENTICITY

John's *Prologue* explicitly acknowledges that there were already critics who accused the author of the Dionysian corpus of lying, and who asked the enduring question: if these writings are by the apostolic Dionysius, why did Eusebius, for example, never mention them? John has a ready answer for this question: 'Against them, one must say that Eusebius omitted mention of many things which had not come into his hands, nor indeed did he say that he had collected everything once for all.'[1] John's point here is to neutralize this historical argument against the authenticity of these works by asserting and illustrating that Eusebius did not know every previous book. Therefore, Eusebius' silence about the writings of Dionysius is no proof that this corpus is by someone else, presumably a more recent writer. This argument never appears in the *Scholia* themselves. As an external, historical argument about Eusebius, it would have no natural location within the interpretative flow of John's marginal comments on the Dionysian text. The *Prologue* continues with additional attempts to defend the authenticity of these works—with argu-

[1] *Prol.* 20C.

ments which do preview some of John's concerns in the *Scholia*. John first explains that Timothy had requested these treatises from Dionysius in order to further his own refutation of the Ephesian philosophers. Here John explicitly links the questions of authenticity and philosophy by mention of Timothy's apparent need for philosophical counter-arguments.[2] This reference to Timothy leads to a fuller argument for authenticity, for John goes on to conclude that these works must have been written by the apostolic Dionysius because they offhandedly mention the sayings of contemporaries of the apostles who also appear in the book of Acts and the writings of Paul.[3]

On certain occasions, John pauses in his commentary to emphasize Dionysius' connections with the apostolic figures of the New Testament, often with the explicit conclusion that such references establish the antiquity and therefore the authenticity of the corpus. The main connection in the *Prologue* is to Paul, a linkage repeated in the *Scholia*. Dionysius had called Paul 'our most divine master', and John explained the connection: 'By "master" he means St Paul the apostle, since it was he who ordained him high priest of the church of the Athenians.'[4] In *The Celestial Hierarchy*, chapter 6, Dionysius credited 'my sacred initiator' and 'famous teacher' for the organization of the angelic beings into three triads.[5] The terminology and overall context both point to Hierotheus. John recognizes this possibility but prefers to see a reference to the apostle Paul. Even though Dionysius never referred to Paul in these terms, and indeed never quoted or mentioned Paul's comment about being taken up into 'the third heaven', John has diverted the reader's attention from the obscure figure of Hierotheus to Paul and his heavenly vision.[6] It is remarkable that the Areopagite himself never attributed his insights into the celestial ranks to some privileged communication from Paul, based upon the apostle's direct experience of the third heaven. But John makes this association, and brings in the same scriptural text elsewhere.[7] In yet another scholion, even though *The Celestial Hierarchy* is speaking about Hierotheus, John takes the occasion to assert that the apostle Paul passed on secret traditions to Dionysius and others.[8]

There are other apostolic contemporaries, and the *Prologue* previewed John's keen interest in these 'offhanded' references. Although such passages are now considered to be an intentional part of the Dionysian

---

[2] On this point, see *SchDN* 373. 1. [3] *Prol.* 21A.
[4] *SchEP* 552. 11, *Prol.* 17C and 21A. [5] *CH* 6. 2 (26. 12, 20).
[6] *SchCH* 64. 4, quoting 2 Cor. 12: 2. [7] *SchCH* 56. 1.
[8] *SchCH* 64. 10, as well as 60. 1.

pseudonym, they were usually presented by John as evidence for the historical authenticity of these writings. At the complex narrative about Hierotheus and the other apostles gathering around 'that mortal body, that source of life, which bore God', John makes several quick comments, one of them about Dionysius as part of the apostolic age: 'Note also that this divine man was present with the apostles Peter and James.'9 At the reference to Bartholomew in *The Mystical Theology*, John builds an argument upon the tense of the verb. If the comment by Bartholomew had been part of an unwritten tradition passed down later to Dionysius, the Areopagite would have used the past tense, 'said'. But since Dionysius used the present tense, 'says', the reader should take this as proof that he was a contemporary of Bartholomew.10 Further, that Dionysius used a written or unwritten saying of Justus establishes, according to John, the antiquity of Dionysius.11 Similarly, when the Areopagite cited a criticism by 'Elymas the magician', John considers this too as evidence of antiquity.12 In all these cases, John has taken at face value Dionysius' references to first-century people, treating them as proofs of the author's own provenance in the apostolic age. There are two related cases. First, when it came to *The Divine Names*' reference to 'Clement the philosopher', John is not so eager to bring up the question of authenticity. He merely says: 'Moreover, he introduces the blessed Clement bishop of Rome, whom the apostle mentioned [Phil. 4: 3] . . . . He does not indicate where St Clement said these things.'13 Paul did mention someone named Clement, but John may also have recognized here a view of paradigms taught by Clement of Alexandria, which would have undermined rather than reinforced his own arguments for the authenticity of this work. Secondly, when Dionysius mentioned and quoted the second-century Ignatius, another chronological anachronism, John passed the text by without comment.14 Later scholia grapple with this apparent inconsistency, but John does not remark on it.15

Not that John was adverse to explaining apparent discrepancies in Dionysius' chronology. Ostensibly biographical details revealed in the corpus called forth careful explanations at least twice. The Areopagite called Timothy his 'child', and yet the biblical record documents that Timothy had become a Christian first. John offers several possible explanations: that Dionysius was the elder chronologically, or the mentor, or the more experienced in pagan learning, or because we are all God's

---

9 *SchDN* 236. 8. The Dionysian passage is *DN* 3. 2 (141. 6).
10 *SchMT* 420. 2.   11 *SchDN* 393. 1.   12 *SchDN* 360. 7.
13 *SchDN* 329. 1, 332. 1.   14 *DN* 4. 12 (157. 10).   15 *SchDN* 264. 6–7.

children.[16] More seriously, the potential conflict between *Letter 7* and *Letter 10* sparked a long explanation. According to *Letter 7*, Dionysius was with one Apollophanes when they observed the eclipse which shadowed the crucifixion of Jesus, whereas he wrote *Letter 10* to the evangelist John in exile on Patmos under the emperor Domitian and thus a good sixty years after the crucifixion. To span this chronological gap, John laboriously concludes that Dionysius was a young man of perhaps 25 when he saw the eclipse and that he was a very old man of around 90 when he wrote to John the evangelist.[17] In yet another type of comment, when John noticed a difference between the Christian rites as he knew them and those recorded by Dionysius, he attributed this to the historical distance between the apostolic age and his own.[18] Occasionally, this explanation is also an explicit argument for the authenticity of the works of Dionysius, as when John comments concerning certain specific duties of the deacons: 'Note also from this passage the antiquity of the father.'[19]

It may seem at first glance that these references to apostolic contemporaries, their words and deeds, or to minor differences in liturgical practices are hardly convincing proofs of the authenticity of the works of Dionysius. After all, a clever forger could easily have introduced such materials to lend credibility to his labours. And indeed, given our own historical perspective, John's defence is frequently banal. But there may be a more complex level to this discussion. John probably intended his comments to be an adequate answer to certain specific questions which had been raised as to the authenticity of the Dionysian corpus. Indeed, it is only when we attempt to reconstruct those questions that the full significance of John's comments becomes clear. Two passages are essential in this regard.

In *The Celestial Hierarchy* Dionysius referred in passing to the Gentiles or the other nations 'from whom we ourselves are come'. This autobiographical allusion sparks John's interests. He comments:

Note in this passage more than any other how the inopportune and indiscriminate ignorance of some is curbed, those bold to say that these divine books were written by Apollinaris. From the people whom he mentions [in the body of these works] they do not infer the antiquity of the author, instead they say that Dionysius' greetings [at the beginning of these works] are spurious. [They do] not [recognize these works as authentic] even when he here says that he was converted from among the idolaters—and yet, Apollinaris was never one of them.[20]

---

[16] *SchCH* 48. 7.
[17] *SchEP* 573. 7 .
[18] See the more detailed discussion in Ch. 3.
[19] *SchEH* 136. 16, cf. 125. 6, 165. 1.
[20] *SchCH* 85. 6, cf. 32. 2.

Our translation of this key passage deserves a word of defence, in particular when John says (according to our translation) that 'instead they say
that Dionysius' greetings [at the beginning of these works] are spurious'.
The Greek here reads: ἀλλὰ ψευδεπίγραφον λέγοντες τὴν Διονυσίου
προσηγορίαν. The key word προσηγορία can at times bear a more generic
sense such that its meaning approaches the English words 'name' or
'appellation'. But it can also mean 'salutation' or 'greeting'. In this regard,
Christian authors at times used it with reference to the salutations
attached to certain of the Pauline epistles.[21] If we were to translate the
passage as 'instead they say that Dionysius' name is not genuine', it is
rather difficult to make sense of the logic of John's argument, for he is
clearly trying to contrast the content of the works and their προσηγορία.
But if we take προσηγορία in its more specific sense, the logic of John's
argument is clear, as well as the overall nature of his defence of the
Dionysian corpus. John is here making an extraordinary distinction.
Those who rejected the corpus as in fact a work of Apollinaris appear to
have suggested that the texts of the treatises were by Apollinaris, whereas
only the titles or salutations involving Dionysius had been added at a later
date. John's favourite defensive move now begins to make more sense. He
is in fact arguing that the treatises cannot have been written by
Apollinaris. In other words, his point is not that the Dionysian corpus
could not have been a conscious forgery by some later author of
Apollinarian leanings, but that Apollinaris himself could not have been
the author of the bodies of the treatises, writing *sub proprie persona*. John's
arguments would not have satisfied the truly sceptical since such arguments assume the veracity of the author's personal references. They
would, however, have been more than sufficient for anyone who claimed
that the titles alone were forgeries, whereas the treatises themselves were
works by Apollinaris. Those who were raising this objection to the
authenticity of the Dionysian corpus must have carried out a very selective reading of the treatises at hand, if indeed they had read them at all. It
is the case that the name 'Dionysius' appears only once in the body of the
Dionysian corpus, though it does appear in the salutations of the *DN*,
CH, *EH* (according to the new edition).[22] But this objection could have
been brought forward as reasonable only by ignoring most of the biographical allusions, especially in the *Epistles*. It is in fact these very allusions that John takes such pains to point out.

   In yet another scholion John explicitly attempts to counter the charge
that the Dionysian corpus was written by Apollinaris. In *The Ecclesiastical*

[21] Lampe, s.v., paragraph A.   [22] *EP* 7. 3 (170. 4).

Hierarchy Dionysius rejected certain errors about the afterlife, including the belief that it would be accompanied by the pleasures of food. John notes this passage in opposition to the errors of Papias and then quickly moves on to a related subject. He writes: 'Later, Apollinaris believed in this teaching (as is clear in his writing) which some call "chiliasm". How, therefore, could these writings of St Dionysius, writings which oppose Apollinaris, be by Apollinaris, according to the idiocies of some?'[23] The original text of this scholion is not easy to establish, for Syr. says only that 'Apollinaris believed in this teaching', and lacks the rest. Nevertheless, FA contains the key passage: 'How, therefore, could these writings of St Dionysius, writings which oppose Apollinaris, be by Apollinaris, according to the idiocies of some?' We therefore take it to be John's own comment.

Taken together, these two scholia constitute the first defence of the Dionysian corpus over against a charge that it was written by a particular, named author, Apollinaris of Laodicea. But who were these 'bold and ignorant' accusers who harboured such 'idiocies'? It may be that John had his sights on certain Chalcedonians like Hypatius of Ephesus who just a few years earlier, at the Collatio of 532, had objected to the historical authenticity of the Dionysian corpus.[24] Hypatius never explicitly claimed that the corpus was an Apollinarian forgery; he had, however, made this very claim about other of the proof-texts which the Monophysites had brought forward at the Collatio, suggesting not that his opponents at the meeting had themselves falsified them, but that this was done by 'the heretical Apollinarists of old'.

Whatever the origins of this criticism of the works of Dionysius, we know that it was not wholly silenced by John's exegetical labours. Phocas' translation of the works of Dionysius included as prefatory material not only the *Scholia* and *Prologue* by John of Scythopolis, but also a second *Prologue* by a certain George of Scythopolis.[25] This George composed his *Prologue* specifically in order to defend the authenticity of the Dionysian

---

[23] *SchEH* 176. 4. See also our separate discussion of these items in 'John of Scythopolis on Apollinarian Christology and the Pseudo-Areopagite's True Identity', *ChH* 62 (1993), 469–82.

[24] See our overview of the early reception of the Dionysian corpus in Ch. 1, as well as Irénée Hausherr, 'Doutes au sujet du "Divin Denys"', *OCP* 2 (1936), 484–90.

[25] This second *Prologue* is still largely unpublished, though excerpts were printed by William Wright, *Catalogue of Syriac Manuscripts in the British Museum*, vol. ii (London, 1871), 494–5. Our description of George's *Prologue* makes use of British Library, cod. 626, add. 12,152 (copied in 837). The *Prologue* by George begins fo. 5ʳ, col. 1, and ends fo. 8ʳ, col. 2. The first fragment of the letter by Dionysius of Alexandria begins fo. 5ᵛ, col. 1, and ends fo. 6ʳ, col. 2; the second begins fo. 6ʳ, col. 2, ends fo. 6ᵛ, col. 3.

corpus.[26] Such an apology was needed, Phocas writes, for there are many who impugn the authenticity of these writings, supposing them to be by Apollinaris or some unknown heretic of more recent times. George at any rate thinks such slanders groundless, as he knows of a letter written by Dionysius of Alexandria (d. 264/5) which shows that the latter knew of the Areopagite's works and even in his own age had had to defend them against those who were condemning them.[27] After citing two fragments of this letter, George goes on to offer other arguments in favour of the Dionysian corpus, arguments which very much resemble those of John. The authenticity of these writings is confirmed, writes George, by all the knowledge Dionysius displays of the people and events of the apostolic age. Furthermore, those who ask why Dionysius' works were not mentioned by any of the early church fathers should be aware that the patristic heritage has not come down in full or in its original form, for many books have been corrupted and destroyed by persecuting pagans, Jews, and heretics. With these arguments George draws his *Prologue* to a close.

Insight into some of the criticisms being levelled against the Dionysian corpus can also be glimpsed in a work written by a certain Theodore and entitled *That the Book of St Dionysius is Authentic*. Unfortunately we know nothing as to the identity of the author of this work, not even when he was writing. Moreover, this text is no longer extant, though Photius provides a short summary.[28] According to Photius, Theodore's work set itself to counter four possible objections to the authenticity of the corpus. Why did the fathers not mention it? In particular, why was Eusebius silent about it? Why does Dionysius as a contemporary of the apostles seem to show a knowledge of doctrinal developments which took place at

---

[26] Other than what Phocas himself tells us, we know nothing about the identity of this George. We can be sure, however, that he was writing before Phocas made use of his *Prologue* in the 8th cent. The *terminus ante quem* can perhaps be brought forward to the end of the 7th cent., in that Anastasius of Sinai in a rather confusing passage (*hod.* 22. 3. 40–8, CCSG 8: 298–9), mentions Dionysius of Alexandria in the context of interpreting the Dionysian corpus, perhaps, though not certainly, implying that he knew of George's work. As for George's doctrinal affiliations, although Phocas calls him 'orthodox' (i.e. Monophysite), this should not be given too much weight: after all he says the same of John of Scythopolis. On the other hand, because George's *Prologue* first appears in Monophysite circles, it seems reasonable to suppose this as its point of origin.

[27] George goes on to cite two rather lengthy fragments from this letter addressed to Pope Sixtus II. The two fragments can be found in Jean Baptiste Pitra, *Analecta Sacra*, vol. iv (Paris, 1883), p. xxiv (translation), p. xxiv n. 2 (text), 172–3 (text), 414–15 (translation). The letter is clearly a forgery. It is not, however, known whether George himself was its author. With regard to this letter, see the comments of Wolfgang A. Bienert, *Dionysius von Alexandrien* (Berlin, 1978), 50–1.

[28] Photius, cod. 1 (ed. Henry), 1: 3.

later dates in the Church? And finally, how is it that Dionysius can make reference to the letter of Ignatius? Photius concludes his brief summary with a bland remark which could be interpreted to suggest that Photius himself was not totally convinced by the arguments which Theodore had mustered in defence of the corpus: 'These are the four problems which Theodore has attempted to resolve, thereby confirming to his own satisfaction that the works of the great Dionysius are authentic.'

NEOPLATONISM

Long before the onset of modern debates about its origins, the Dionysian corpus had been censured for its use of pagan philosophical terminology and concepts. Naturally, such censures also entailed additional conclusions as to the origins of the corpus. Echoes of these debates have left a few traces in the literary record. Before turning to the way John himself attempted to deflect such criticisms, let us briefly consider two other attempts at reconciling Dionysius' use of philosophical materials with his apostolic persona. Although both of these attempts post-date the work of John, they do none the less offer considerable insight into some of the debates occasioned by the philosophical aspects of the Dionysian corpus.

We turn first to comments which may well stem from John Philoponus (d. *circa* 580). As Suchla has shown, the *Prologue* to the Dionysian corpus as printed in Migne contains near the end a rather lengthy passage that is a later interpolation into the authentic *Prologue* by John of Scythopolis.[29] In form, the passage probably originated as a marginal note or scholion on John's own *Prologue*.

One must know that some of the non-Christian philosophers, especially Proclus, have often employed certain concepts of the blessed Dionysius. . . . It is possible to conjecture from this that the ancient philosophers in Athens usurped his works (as he recounts in the present book)[30] and then hid them, so that they themselves might seem to be the progenitors of his divine oracles. According to the dispensation of God the present work is now made known for the refutation of their vanity and recklessness. . . . Some say that these writings do not belong the saint, but to someone who came later. Such as say this must likewise agree that the forger of these works was an abandoned wretch—and this, because he falsely

[29] Beate Regina Suchla, 'Die Überlieferung des Prologs des Johannes von Skythopolis zum griechischen Corpus Dionysiacum Areopagiticum', *NAWG* (1984), 4: 185–7, *vis-à-vis* PG 4: 21. 12–37, 21. 38–24. 16: the proper order of these two fragments has 21. 38–24. 16 coming first, followed by 21. 12–21. 37.

[30] Cf. *EP* 7. 2 (166. 7–11).

presented himself as a companion of the apostles and as corresponding with men he was never with and never corresponded with. That he invented a prophecy for the apostle John in exile, to the effect that he will return again to Asia and will teach as was his wont—this is the act of a marvel-monger and a prophet hunting madly after glory. There are yet other instances. He said that at the time of the Saviour's passion he was with Apollophanes in Heliopolis, theorizing and philosophizing concerning the eclipse of the sun, in so far as it had happened at that time neither according to nature nor custom. He said that he was present with the apostles at the conveyance of the divine relics of the holy Theotokos, Mary, and that he proffers the usages of his own teacher, Hierotheus, from his funeral orations on her. He also asserts that his own letters and treatises contain the proclamations of the disciples of the apostles.

The manuscript tradition of the *Prologue* gives this short commentary a number of titles (either 'from the scholia of Philoponus' or simply 'scholia'), or sometimes transmits it without title. A number of considerations have led Suchla to suppose this passage to be by John Philoponus. Philoponus was an expert in the works of Proclus and would have been well able to note the verbatim similarities between the Dionysian corpus and the works of Proclus.[31] Furthermore, this short commentary must have entered the manuscript tradition rather early on, given its broad manuscript basis.[32] To these two points of Suchla, we can also add the following. First, Philoponus knew of the Dionysian corpus, believed in its authenticity, and had read at least parts of it. Secondly, of the three times that Philoponus cites the Dionysian corpus, twice it is to draw attention to Dionysius' account of how the eclipse at the time of the crucifixion happened contrary to nature.[33] This can be paralleled with the material cited above, where the author writes that the eclipse happened 'neither according to nature nor custom'. All in all, the evidence leads us to concur that John Philoponus may well have been the author of this short commentary.

On this same topic, another set of interesting comments can be found in the *Questions and Responses* of Joseph Hazzaya, an eighth-century Nestorian author.[34] In the fifth book of this text Joseph takes to task those

---

[31] Recall that Philoponus was the author of a lengthy text treating of the subject of the eternity of the world against Proclus (CPG 7266). We might add that John also knew other aspects of the Neoplatonic philosophical tradition, as is evidenced by his having written a refutation of Iamblicus on the subject of the use of statues, whether they can be bearers of the divine presence (Photius, cod. 215 (ed. Henry), 3: 130–1).

[32] Suchla, 'Überlieferung des Prologs', 186.

[33] See Jo. Phil. *opif.* 2. 21 (ed. Reichardt), 99. Cf. the parallel passage at *opif.* 3. 9 (ed. Reichardt), 129. As for John's third citation, this is found in *opif.* 3. 14 (ed. Reichardt), 149, an exegesis of Gen. 1: 6–8 containing an appeal for theological humility.

[34] For an overview of Joseph's life and literary activity, Robert Beulay, 'Joseph Ḥazzāyā',

who claim that it is the Seraphim who first receive the knowledge of future events. Such as claim this are relying upon the authority of the blessed Dionysius, 'who says in his book that the Seraphim have the knowledge of things before the Cherubim'. What they do not know, Joseph writes, is that this passage was not written by Dionysius but by the person who first translated the Dionysian corpus from Greek into Syriac (i.e. Sergius of Resh'aina).

For scribes, especially those who translate from one language to another, often interpolate the divine books, and the most celebrated interpolator is that writer who translated the book of Mar Dionysius. As wicked as he was wise, he changed the passages in the divine books to his own profit. If I had the time, I myself would translate it and eliminate from it all the errors which this translator has there inserted.

Furthermore, Joseph is quite convinced that it was not Dionysius but the translator who endowed the work with its elevated style. After all, the style of this saint would surely have been as simple as that of the apostles whose disciple he was. Joseph's proof was that one need only examine the commentaries of this translator on the works of the philosophers, for there 'one finds the same beauty of style as in the work of St Dionysius'. It is not hard to admire the logic and candour of Joseph. Still, questions remain. Among these: if in fact Joseph had access to the Greek original, did he not see that not only the Syriac version, but also the Greek contains the elevated style?

Like the Dionysian corpus itself, John's commentary and its relationship to the Neoplatonic tradition has engendered 'suspicions' among its interpreters. Henri-Dominique Saffrey, most notably, has pointed out several occasions when John's explanations of unusual Dionysian vocabulary items suggest his own familiarity with the late Neoplatonism of Proclus. Saffrey's first example concerned the scholion on the adjective 'theandric' in the Areopagite's *Fourth Letter*.[35] Saffrey provided extensive documentation regarding Proclus and the god 'Theandrites', concluding that John's comments on this term inadvertently revealed his own independent familiarity with Proclean Neoplatonism. Saffrey then turned

DS 8 (1974), 1341–9, and E. J. Sherry, 'The Life and Works of Joseph Ḥazzāyâ, in *The Seed of Wisdom* (Toronto, 1964), 78–91. Our knowledge of this text is drawn from two summaries by Addai Scher: 'Joseph Ḥazzâyâ: Écrivain syriaque du VIIIe siècle', *RSO* 3 (1910), 45–63, esp. 59–61; 'Joseph Ḥazzâyâ: Écrivain syriaque du VIIIe siècle', *Académie des inscriptions et belles-lettres, Paris: Comptes rendus des séances* (1909), 300–7. What follows relies on the selections translated into French by Scher in the first of these articles.

[35] *SchEP* 536. 1. Henri-Dominique Saffrey, 'Un lien objectif entre le Pseudo-Denys et Proclus', *SP* 9/3 = TU 94 (1966), 98–105.

his attention to several other items, some of them discussed below, and gave special care to John's comment on the Dionysian phrase 'divinely-named statues'. This wording itself links the Areopagite to Proclus, but the scholion adds an explicit discussion of Hermes, a discussion which in Saffrey's opinion reveals an echo of Plato's *Symposium* and a familiarity with the late Neoplatonic understanding of these statues and the Hermes.[36] Saffrey draws some conclusions from these texts, conclusions to which we shall return below, but we must first survey the whole panorama of John's implicit and explicit dialogue with Neoplatonism. We begin with a brief analysis of John's approximately thirty explicit references to the Greeks, the philosophers, and several individual authors. Secondly, we summarize more generally John's overall relationship to Neoplatonic philosophy. This entire discussion is merely introductory to future, more detailed studies of John's connections to Neoplatonism, especially since many of his debts to that tradition were unacknowledged and quite subtle. Although such detail is not possible in this space or at this early stage of analysing John's overall contribution to the interpretation of the Dionysian tradition, we do offer, finally, some more detailed observations on the way John attempted to interpret Dionysius on the problem of evil with resources drawn from the works of Plotinus.

Explicit references to the Greeks

In John's *Scholia*, of the approximately thirty open references to 'the Greeks', the 'ancients', or 'the philosophers', half are clearly negative or critical, while the other half function positively as helpful background for the clarification of difficult Dionysian terminology.[37] Having once cited Aristotle with approval on another subject, John also notes twice the Dionysian usage of the Aristotelian technical term 'mind' [$\nu o\hat{v}\varsigma$] for the angels.[38] Strategically, at the very beginning of his comments on *The*

---

[36] *SchDN* 368. 8. Henri-Dominique Saffrey, 'Nouveaux liens objectifs entre le Pseudo-Denys et Proclus', *RSPT* 63 (1979), 3–16.

[37] Fifteen scholia will be presented under the category of 'positive': *SchCH* 32. 4, 32. 10, 96. 6, 113. 10, *SchEH* 152. 9, 153. 6, *SchDN* 188. 4, 216. 10, 308. 7, 372. 3, 377. 1, 393. 1, *SchMT* 417. 2, *SchEP* 553. 9, 556. 1. Fifteen scholia are considered 'negative' or critical: *SchCH* 77. 5, *SchEH* 173. 8, *SchDN* 281. 4, 288. 13, 297. 4, 312. 1, 332. 4, 337. 2, 340. 5, 368. 8, 373. 1, 388. 4, 392. 3, 397. 8, with *SchEP* 569. 9 (where the 'fools' make the same comment as the Greeks in *SchDN* 388. 4). See also *SchEP* 537. 2. Related materials have already been discussed in Ch. 3.

[38] *SchCH* 32. 4, *SchDN* 188. 4. Aristotle is named in *SchDN* 377. 1, regarding our bodies as composite (similar and dissimilar) but God as 'similar'.

Celestial Hierarchy and *The Divine Names*, John endorses and extends the
Dionysian use of the νοῦς nomenclature taken from 'the philosophers'.
He does not here add any biblical and patristic warrant for this term, but
rather seems content simply to cite the Greeks. He elsewhere clarifies the
Areopagite's use of the term 'ungenerated' by way of reference to the
Greeks.[39] These passages may be peripheral to the substantive conceptual
issues at stake in the Dionysian corpus. Indeed, some of them are more
philological than theological, such as the observation that the phrase
'not completely inappropriate' is used by Dionysius 'according to philosophical custom'.[40] But John's positive use of the Greek philosophers
extends to certain central doctrinal issues as well.

John cites the Greek philosophical tradition regarding such key
concepts as God as one and the distinction between being and non-being.
Although he never mentions Plotinus by name, he does refer more
generically to the 'ancients' and to their reasons for calling God 'one':
'The ancients called God the "one", not because he is the source of
numbers, but because he transcends all things and because none of the
things after him is connumerated with him, but also because he is uncompounded and simple.'[41] Our point here is not the actual discussion of God
as the 'one', conducted more fully elsewhere by John (and by Dionysius),
with Plotinus clearly supplying the conceptual framework and even some
of John's language, but rather the fact that in this passage John does not
hesitate to credit this nomenclature to 'the ancients'. Similarly, the
Dionysian partnership of the intelligible and the perceptible is interpreted by John as an antithesis of being and non-being, with an invocation of 'the ancients'. Here John uses some substantial philosophical
material from 'the ancients', who seem to be equivalent to 'the philosophers'.[42] That Dionysius himself used such philosophical phrasing to
talk of God was once openly asserted by John: 'Note that even these
divine men [Dionysius and Justus] used the phrases of philosophers, as
when they referred to the peace of God as "ineffability" and "motionlessness"'.[43]

John's critical references to the Greeks are sometimes put rather
mildly, as in the reference to Plato as a Greek who was less irrational than
others but still short of the truth.[44] More often, however, the scholia
which oppose some aspect of Greek philosophy do so with strong

[39] *SchDN* 372. 3.   [40] *SchCH* 96. 6.   [41] *SchDN* 308. 7.
[42] The 'ancients' only in *SchDN* 308. 7 (God as 'One') and in *SchDN* 272. 1 (discussed
shortly) and *SchMT* 417. 2 (on non-being).
[43] *SchDN* 393. 1.   [44] *SchEH* 173. 8.

language: Dionysius refutes, fights, attacks, and smites the foolish opinions, defects, errors, and silliness of the Greeks and related heretics. There is no shortage of polemical rhetoric. But John is quite selective in his critique, since only certain aspects of the Platonic tradition are condemned, and he even seems to use certain Neoplatonic concepts against 'the Greeks'. Although the Dionysian discussion of evil as a privation is notably Neoplatonic, John argues that the Areopagite is here opposing the Greeks.[45] Another pair of scholia presents a similar ambiguity regarding evil and matter: 'In order to refute the Greeks and Manichaeans, he says that not even demons are evil by nature', and 'In a wonderful manner he brings to naught the opinions of the Greeks and such heretics as the Valentinians and Manichaeans, who suppose matter to be a source which bears in itself contraries to the things of God.'[46] In these cases, it is misleading to identify 'the Greeks' with the Neoplatonists, since a Neoplatonic position is here advanced against them. And yet, John here condemns the Greeks, the Gnostics, and the Manichaeans all as one group. This may be polemical hyperbole, at least on the specific point about evil as privation over against Manichaean dualism. But one of John's most cherished theological convictions does pit him against the Valentinians, the Manichaeans, *and* the philosophers among the Greeks, including Plotinus, namely, his convictions as to the nature of the creation as it pertains to the resurrection of the body.

According to John's theology of creation, even formless matter is wholly produced by God; it is neither coeternal with God, as in the Platonic–Aristotelian tradition including Plotinus, nor is it the product of another divinity, as in Gnosticism and Manichaeanism. Some of John's harshest language against the Greeks and their philosophical errors concerns the doctrine of creation and the closely related belief in the Incarnation and the resurrection of the body. After all, said John in the *Prologue*, 'our salvation is focused on these points'.[47] Many such comments about creation and resurrection have been discussed already; the point here is the nature of John's critique of the Greeks or the philosophers. John's criticism occurs at both ends of the ontological spectrum, namely, that God and no one else is the creator, and that all

---

[45] *SchDN* 281. 4.

[46] *SchDN* 288. 13, 397. 8. See also *SchDN* 297. 4 on demons, as well as 300. 1 and 304. 2 on evil and privation, although without reference to the Greeks or philosophers. John's half-dozen attacks upon the Manichaeans are surveyed in the discussion of creation in Ch. 4.

[47] *Prol.* 20B. Scholia on creation, usually against Greek philosophical opponents: *SchCH* 77. 5, *SchDN* 205. 2, 272. 1, 312. 1, 388. 4, and *SchEP* 569. 9. Scholia on the resurrection against the Greeks include *SchEH* 173. 8 and *SchDN* 337. 2, as well as *SchDN* 340. 5.

things, including matter, are made by God. Regarding the specific question of whether the 'ideas and paradigms' involved in creation have any self-subsistent reality, John advances a Dionysian argument which 'smites' the Greeks.[48] Here John's orthodox monotheism requires him, and Dionysius before him, to reject any independent subsistence and/or creative powers below God himself. Of particular interest in a similar scholion is the Neoplatonic provenance of two expressions: 'world-makers' and the 'sediment of all'.[49] Similarly, in two other scholia, John quotes and derisively dismisses an Aristotelian-sounding phrase regarding the language of eternity.[50] It is in reference to the word 'ungenerated' and on this same issue of the eternity of the world that John brought up again, as in the *Prologue*, the supposed reason for the Areopagite's interest in philosophy, namely, that Timothy needed philosophical counter-arguments.[51] Of related interest is John's dismissal of the errors of certain unnamed opponents who present the act of creation as a necessary or natural activity of God, like a spider's web-making, rather than a freely chosen act of goodness.[52]

Amid these critical references to the Greeks on the doctrine of creation comes John's declaration that both he and Dionysius can also use certain Greek concepts in opposition to the Greeks.

Since he said that even non-being somehow desires the good and wishes to be in it (which also you will find that he said a few pages earlier)—granted that it is being declared on the basis of Greek doctrines, for he is fighting against the Greeks especially, as well as the Manichaeans who are pre-eminent in bad doctrine—it is necessary to explain in greater detail why it is called non-being and why it is pious and necessary that there be one principle of beings.[53]

Here John uses Greek doctrines about non-being (presumably the Neo-platonic notion of evil as lacking existence) against the Manichaeans regarding the one principle or source of all things, namely, God; but he here as elsewhere lumps 'the Greeks' in with the Manichaeans regarding this form of dualism. He seems to blame the Greeks for a Manichaean dualism elsewhere as well. In explaining that despite the discord in the world, God is both the maker and uniter of the universe, John claims that

[48] *SchDN* 332. 4. See *SchCH* 77. 5 for a condemnation of the philosophers on the same issue.

[49] *SchDN* 312. 1. See the notes to the translation for parallels in Neoplatonism.

[50] *SchDN* 388. 4, *SchEP* 569. 9.

[51] *SchDN* 373. 1.

[52] *SchDN* 205. 2.

[53] *SchDN* 272. 1. Other associations of 'Greeks and Manichaeans' in *SchDN* 288. 13 and 397. 8.

Dionysius 'refutes the great errors of the Greek philosophers, transferring these errors to piety . . . transferring their coinages to correctness'.[54] Yet even if we discount the rhetorical tarring of the Greeks with a
Manichaean brush, John's posture toward genuine Neoplatonism is consistently negative regarding the doctrine of creation. This opposition has
consequences for other theological issues as well.

There are corollaries to the Christian position on creation which also
pit John against the Greeks in explicit comments. When Dionysius discussed the 'foolishness of God' only in terms of the epistemology of
negations, John escorts the reader back to the Pauline context of the
Incarnation and the cross. Since the Incarnation implies a certain view of
the created human body, this passage is also an occasion to oppose the
Greeks.[55] Yet more explicit and more polemical are the two direct condemnations of the Greeks regarding the resurrection of the dead.
Although the Dionysian text at hand did not refer explicitly to the
resurrection of the body, staying with the general subject of immortality,
John's attack on the 'foolish opinion of the Greeks' echoes the original
narrative of Acts 17 where it was Paul's proclamation of the resurrection
of the dead, not immortality in general, which prompted most of the
Athenians to scoff.[56] John's most direct discussion of the resurrection,
however, occurs in his scholia on the Areopagite's own references to
various mistaken views about the afterlife. Most of them concern
Christian heretics, such as Origen, Papias, and Apollinaris, as already discussed. But he starts off with the Greeks, namely, the irrational Bias and
the more rational Plato.[57] Here John directly sets up the resurrection of
the body against the immortality of the soul alone, and explicitly names
Plato as an opponent on this point.

In summary, John's thirty explicit references to the Greeks are divided
evenly between what we have called the positive and the negative uses. In
the positive uses, John invokes the Greek intellectual tradition to clarify
and support difficult Dionysian terms. While many of these terms seem
incidental to the larger philosophical questions at stake, some are conceptually crucial. In the negative uses, John explicitly attacks the mistakes of
the Greeks, especially touching the doctrine of creation and the resurrection of the body. Many of John's positive comments refer to the upper
end of the ontological spectrum, such as God as the one, whereas his
negative remarks treat of the lower end, namely, matter. This pattern is
instructive: yet only a glimpse of John's complex relationship to Neo-

---

[54] *SchDN* 392. 3.   [55] *SchDN* 340. 5.
[56] *SchDN* 337. 2.   [57] *SchEH* 173. 8.

platonism is in view so far, indeed, only the glimpse he chose to reveal in explicit references to the philosophical tradition.

Implicit or unacknowledged references to the Greeks

Far beyond the overt references, positive or negative, John's implicit and artfully concealed dialogue with Neoplatonism will occupy the scholarly community at length, now that his own comments can be identified with confidence. We here sketch out some of the occasions when John made use of Neoplatonic philosophy, beginning at the top of the hierarchy, with God as the one, reserving for the next section his specific use of Plotinus on the question of evil. In addition to his explicit comment on the pedigree of the name 'one' for God, John freely used this Plotinian nomenclature elsewhere as well.[58] The related language of 'henad' occurs in Dionysius and in John for both God and the angels. Where the Areopagite once referred to 'the henad unifying every henad', John explained the phrase as 'the creator of all simple beings, such as angels and souls'.[59] When Dionysius said that the Scriptures called God 'monad or henad', John explained that this simply indicates the 'undividedness of God'.[60] In general, John presented this terminology not as laden with any technical significance, but as merely another way of saying, with the Scriptures, that God is simple, undivided, and united. Of the various activities of God, or dynamics within the divine Trinity, we have already noted the categories of 'procession and return' to describe the unity and trinity of God, even beyond the Dionysian use of this basic framework.[61] Although John does not make much of the Areopagite's use of procession and return to interpret the hierarch's censing procession in the synaxis or divine liturgy, he does apply it more fully where Dionysius only hinted at it, namely, regarding the overall process of Christian initiation including baptism.[62]

Alongside these examples of John's use of Neoplatonic categories in his doctrine of God, there are also signs of dissent. The 'ideas and paradigms' are not self-subsistent beings, against the Greeks, but (merely) the thoughts of God, the sole creator. The same doctrinal concern is apparent in another set of scholia, but with perhaps a more specific

---

[58] *SchCH* 49. 5, *SchDN* 308. 7, *SchMT* 425. 8, 429. 1.
[59] *SchDN* 189. 3. Saffrey noted the parallel in Proclus: 'Nouveaux liens objectifs', 15. Cf. *SchDN* 189. 2.
[60] *SchDN* 193. 4.
[61] See the discussion in Ch. 4.
[62] *SchEH* 128. 1.

opponent among the Greek Neoplatonists. In *The Divine Names*, chapter 4, Dionysius made thorough use of the example of the sun, with the careful qualification that the sun has no powers of reason or choice. At the first such reference, John amplifies the qualification: 'Let no one suppose that the great Dionysius judges the things of God wholly on the example of the sun. . . . [it] being neither equipped with a soul, nor having choice . . .'.[63] Shortly thereafter, John makes a point of commenting that even if Dionysius used the Platonic pun in speaking of the sun, he did not mean to admit the Neoplatonic association of the sun with a god.[64] Apparently John has a particular concern for possible distortions of such Dionysian passages, judging from these and other scholia as well.[65] That the sun is not God is quite easily dismissed; but that it does not have a soul or any creative powers is a more substantive argument, apparently against a particular strand of late Neoplatonism. The emperor Julian, as an example, was partial to the theurgic side of Neoplatonism stemming from Iamblichus, and wrote a 'Hymn to King Helios' which honours the solar deity Helios. John seems eager to prevent such associations, and in these scholia he reinforces his urgent exhortation to 'think well and do not distort'. When Dionysius mentioned the sun elsewhere, purely in passing, John nevertheless sounds the same warning: 'Be careful! Do not suppose that he claims that the sun gives its own lights. How can something without a soul give anything? An act of giving arises from an act of choice.'[66] Whether John had Julian's work in mind or not, he shows a specific interest in denying that the sun has a soul or any creative powers.[67]

Regarding angels and humans, minds and souls, John follows the Dionysian and Neoplatonic hierarchy which places them in a careful continuum.[68] Beyond these general Dionysian categories, John's own dialogue with Neoplatonism regarding the angels can be clearly seen with respect to two specific terms: the angels as 'henads' and as 'minds'. We have already discussed John's use of 'henad' to name God, but the

---

[63] *SchDN* 240. 2.

[64] *SchDN* 249. 4 on *DN* 4. 4 (149. 1–8) where Dionysius cites the 'sun/sum' pun from Plato's *Cratylus* 409A and denies the 'old myth' that 'used to describe the sun as the provident god and creator of this universe'.

[65] *SchDN* 248. 1, 248. 2. See also 248. 4, 249. 4.

[66] *SchEH* 180. 2.

[67] There might also be an echo here of the Origenist controversy, for Origen was condemned in both 543 and 553 for teaching that the sun, moon, and stars, were part of the henad of rational beings. See Aloys Grillmeier, *Christ in Christian Tradition*, ii/2 (Louisville, Ky., 1995), 393, 404.

[68] *SchDN* 336. 4.

same term can mean the angelic beings: 'Since the intelligibles are the henads of God beyond mind and God himself is one or rather beyond the one.'[69] Calling God the 'one' and the angels the 'henads' in the same sentence is a highly condensed appropriation of Neoplatonic categories, in which John is actually following the Areopagite's use of Proclus.[70] Elsewhere, Dionysius referred to the 'angelic henads', a passage which has already attracted Saffrey's attention regarding the link with Proclus.[71] At this phrase John comments: 'Or, he is calling the simplicities and incorporealities and immaterialities of beings themselves "henads".'[72] The scholia which name the angels 'henads' are not numerous, but this usage is so clearly derived from late Neoplatonism, from Simplicianus through Proclus, that any such text raises the basic question of John's independent use of Proclus.

When it comes to the angels as 'minds', there is also a significant group of comments. As mentioned above, John credits the 'outside philosophers' or 'Greek philosophers' for this terminology.[73] The point is not that the Neoplatonists meant to incorporate Judaeo-Christian angelology into their discussions of the divine mind or minds, but that Dionysius at least had already used their language of 'mind' for the angels. Once John tried to support this naming with biblical material: 'The Scripture also calls them by this name, as in Isaiah: "the great mind, the ruler of Assyrians", that is, the devil'.[74] John never makes very much of this weak biblical allusion, but in various places he simply uses the Dionysian and Neoplatonic terminology of 'minds' for the angels without reference to the philosophers or the Scriptures. When the Areopagite discussed the divine peace and unity given to minds and souls, John explains the activities of the angelic minds in terms of a Neoplatonic epistemology: that which thinks (the intelligent) is united with that which is thought (the intelligible). The dynamics of this activity are also reminiscent of procession and return, as implicit in Dionysius and more evident in John's scholion.[75]

The set of cognates of *nous* relative to the angels, namely *noetic* (intelligible) and *noeric* (intelligent), are familiar to all readers of Proclus. He

---

[69] *SchMT* 425. 8.

[70] Cf. *DN* 1. 1 (109. 13), 1. 4 (112. 11), with Proc. *Plat. theo.* 3. 7.

[71] Saffrey, 'Nouveaux liens objectifs', 15. Cf. I. P. Sheldon-Williams, 'Henads and Angels', *SP* 11/2 = TU 108 (1972), 65–71.

[72] *SchDN* 360. 1.

[73] *SchDN* 188. 4, *SchCH* 32. 4.

[74] *SchCH* 32. 4.

[75] *SchDN* 393. 9. John also explains how Isaiah's angels both stand and fly around God, all in terms of the 'motions' of thinking minds (*SchCH* 73. 3).

posited certain superior beings related to the Nous as *noeta*, certain inferior beings as *noera*, and some in between as mean terms who are both *noeta* and *noera*, both passively intelligible to the inferiors and actively intelligent regarding their superiors.[76] John provides several discussions explaining this Dionysian and Proclean idea. For example, at the beginning of chapter 4 of *The Divine Names*, the Areopagite, amid a strikingly Neoplatonic passage, mentions the *noetic* and *noeric* beings; John shows no reluctance to use and to affirm this vocabulary.[77] The same terminology can be used to discuss the angels and human souls. Several times John repeats the point about the angels being both 'intelligible' and 'intelligent', whereas only the latter category applies to humans.[78] That angels and humans share intelligence in some way is vital for the Dionysian epistemology as also championed in one particular passage by John: the knowledge by the angels, which occurs from within and simultaneously in the realm of eternity, is a goal for human knowledge as well.[79] This part of John's comment simply paraphrases Dionysius, and not very well at that. Where John adds something new is in the concluding eschatological point that in the resurrection we shall fully share this unified and perfect knowledge.

There are several other scholia which reveal John's implicit use of late Neoplatonism regarding the human mind. Some of this could have come purely through the Dionysian texts themselves, but certain specialized terms suggest John's own familiarity with Neoplatonic materials. John uses some specific nomenclature for different parts or aspects of the human mind.[80] He takes the Dionysian term 'peak' from another context to say that 'the soul's mind (i.e. that which is most pure) is its "peak"'.[81] Even more to the Neoplatonic point at hand is the nomenclature of 'bloom' [$\H{\alpha}\nu\theta\text{os}$] regarding both the 'mind' [$\nu o\hat{\text{u}}\text{s}$] and the soul. At the very outset of his scholia on *The Divine Names*, John indicates that the mind has a supreme faculty, the 'bloom' of the 'mind'.[82] Not only does the 'mind' have the 'bloom' as its supreme component, but from the lower perspective of the soul the 'mind' also *is* the 'bloom' of the soul. Where

---

[76] e.g. Proc. *Plat. theo.* 4. 38–9, cf. Werner Beierwaltes, *Proklos*, 2nd edn. (Frankfurt am Main, 1979), 89–92.

[77] *SchDN* 240. 3 on *DN* 4. 1 (144. 6). Cf. also *SchCH* 109. 2, *SchEH* 120. 9, *SchDN* 205. 2 and 269. 1.   [78] *SchDN* 309. 3, 344. 3.

[79] *SchDN* 345. 3. See also 257. 4.

[80] *SchCH* 92. 2. Other discussions of the soul emphasize its faculties, i.e. intelligence, sense perception, imagination (*SchDN* 201. 2). Cf. Carlos G. Steel, *The Changing Self* (Brussels, 1978), *passim*.

[81] *SchCH* 33. 10.

[82] *SchDN* 185. 4.

the Areopagite began a discussion of the division of the soul into its passive and impassive aspects, John understood the latter to mean 'the most pure part of the soul . . . its bloom, that is, its mind'.[83] Apart from the Neoplatonic psychology or doctrine of the soul, the most striking feature of these comments concerns the term 'bloom'. It was this very word, in tandem with another, which helped to prove that the author of *The Divine Names* had used Proclus, the argument which inaugurated modern 'Pseudo'-Dionysian studies in 1895.[84] When John commented upon that text, he mustered biblical support for other parts of the phrase, but said nothing about the 'bloom'.[85] Not that he avoided the word everywhere, for we have just noted the two places where he went beyond the Dionysian texts to add the vocabulary of 'bloom' to designate the highest part of the mind.

In summary, John seems to know late Neoplatonism in some detail, beyond the Dionysian corpus itself; he embraces some of its themes and terms regarding the upper end of the ontological spectrum, in particular regarding God and the angels, and yet opposes them vociferously at the lower end, especially regarding matter, creation, and resurrection. Most of his usage of Neoplatonic vocabulary, however, is not accompanied by clear acknowledgements, and much of it is yet to be documented. But does John's familiarity with Proclus and his use of certain Neoplatonic materials require us to conclude with Saffrey that he was an 'accomplice' to the 'Dionysian fiction'? To Saffrey, John had attempted to disarm the reader's suspicions regarding *every* strange Dionysian expression, and so 'shows his true colours'.[86] This is surely an overstatement, since there are many 'suspect' Dionysian passages which John ignores and there is no conclusive evidence that John was aware of the recent, Neoplatonic provenance of the corpus, much less its true author. On the other hand, John certainly did know and use the late Neoplatonism of the Athenian school, concealed most of his borrowings from that tradition, and occasionally seemed intentionally to mute the Neoplatonic overtones of the Dionysian corpus or at least to divert the reader's attention away from them.

---

[83] *SchEP* 565. 2.

[84] H. Koch, 'Proklus als Quelle des Pseudo-Dionysius Areopagita in der Lehre vom Bösen', *Philologus*, 54 (1895), 438–54, and Josef Stiglmayr, 'Der Neuplatoniker Proklus als Vorlage des sog. Dionysius Areopagita in der Lehre vom Übel', *HJ* 16 (1895), 253–73, 721–48.

[85] *SchDN* 224. 7 on *DN* 4. 7 (132. 2–3). Dionysius also used ἄνθος in *EP* 9. 1 (194. 13), but John does not make any comment there.

[86] Saffrey, 'Nouveaux liens objectifs', 5: 'montre le bout de l'oreille'.

JOHN'S USE OF PLOTINUS ON THE PROBLEM OF EVIL

That John quietly incorporated quotations from Plotinus into his comments on Dionysius has long been recognized, though the nature and extent of this process is only beginning to be appreciated.[87] In this section we examine only a small part of this phenomenon: namely, John's use of Plotinus' *Ennead* 1. 8 (*On the Nature and Source of Evil*). It is not enough simply to cite parallel passages showing John's dependence on Plotinus; rather, we are concerned to offer a number of discrete glimpses into John's use of this tractate of Plotinus, glimpses designed to indicate both the complexity of the philosophical issues at stake and the many layers of intertextuality involved in John's analysis of those issues. One must, in other words, show *how* John was using Plotinian materials in his attempts to explicate the works of Dionysius. Using this method we shall see that there is more at issue in John's comments than simple literary dependence on Plotinus. Rather, John is engaging both Dionysius and Plotinus in a philosophically sophisticated manner, often using Plotinus' work to argue for points antithetical to Plotinus' position but in accordance with the position of Dionysius.

Beginning in section eighteen of the fourth chapter of *The Divine Names*, Dionysius takes up the problem of evil. The discussion is for him of cardinal importance, maintaining his attention through to the end of chapter 4 and thus forming the longest extended treatment of any single topic in the corpus. The importance of this issue is also highlighted by the fact that Dionysius returns to it in chapters 8 and 9 of *The Divine Names*, as well as in his eighth *Epistle*. The reason given for his consideration of this issue in book 4 is that he is attempting to defend the proposition that God is an object of longing on the part of all creatures: 'For if the beautiful and the good is an object of eros and of desire and of charity . . . how is it that the demons do not desire the beautiful and the good?'[88] Such demons instead, through their attention to matter and as a result of their fall, have become the cause of all evils, both for themselves and for as many other things as have become evil.[89] This is the main problem. But other corollary questions are entailed as well, though to be sure on a more general level of consideration.[90] Among these: if the

[87] Werner Beierwaltes and Richard Kannicht, 'Plotin-Testimonia bei Johannes von Skythopolis', *Hermes*, 96 (1968), 247–51; Werner Beierwaltes, 'Johannes von Skythopolis und Plotin', *SP* 11/2 = TU 108 (1972), 3–7; Richard M. Frank, 'The Use of the *Enneads* by John of Scythopolis', *Mus.* 100 (1987), 101–8.   [88] *DN* 4. 18 (162. 6–7).

[89] *DN* 4. 18 (162. 9–12).

[90] *DN* 4. 18 (162. 12).

demons were produced by the good, why did they not remain good, what is evil, in what beings is it present, and so on? [91] Dionysius treats these problems as a list of difficulties to be resolved, as an ἀπορῶν λόγος.[92] But in the course of answering them he spends most of his time showing what evil is not. It is only in the course of these negative arguments that he formulates a more positive doctrine. Dionysius wishes to show first that evil does not originate from the good, and secondly, that absolute evil cannot exist. Evil is instead a lack in that it hinders creatures from the performance of what for them is their natural potential. To be sure, some creatures in the hierarchy of beings are granted more natural potential than others. And yet, this gradation is not of itself evil: God's providence granted to each as much as each could handle. Instead, evil consists in the failure to attain the potential granted. Even so, this lack is not complete. Such would lead to total corruption or non-being. What sort of reality then does evil have? Evil is 'imperfect good'.[93] It is 'parhypostatic'.[94] It is accidental.[95] This in brief is Dionysius' account of the origin and nature of evil.

In its contours as well as in some of its specific formulations Dionysius here follows the work of Proclus, especially his *De malorum subsistentia*.[96] The latter was concerned to defend the unity of the one against the theories of Plotinus on the nature of evil. Proclus was intent upon refuting the belief that there were two principles, one of good and the other of evil, as well as that one could identify matter as a principle of evil. At most he would grant it the status of being 'parhypostatic'.[97] According to critics such as Proclus, Plotinus had taught that evil has some sort of independent existence and that it was to be identified with matter, absolute formlessness. One can therefore say that Dionysius' views on the nature of evil (in so far as they depend upon Proclus) are directed against the formulations of Plotinus. This presents the readers of John's *Scholia* with something of a paradox, for John uses Plotinus' writings on evil precisely in order to exposit a text that is in effect directed against Plotinus' writings on evil.

---

[91] *DN* 4. 18 (162. 12–163. 4).   [92] *DN* 4. 19 (163. 7).   [93] *DN* 4. 20 (168. 7).

[94] *DN* 4. 31 (177. 1).   [95] *DN* 4. 32 (177. 3).

[96] For the use of Proclus in Dionysius, see the classic works of Stiglmayr, 'Neuplatoniker Proclus', 253–73, 721–48; idem, 'Das Aufkommen der Pseudo-Dionysischen Schriften und ihr Eindringen in die christliche Literatur bis zum Lateranconcil 649', *Jahresbericht des öffentlichen Privatgymnasiums an der Stella matutina zu Feldkirch*, 4 (1894/5), 25–34; Koch, 'Proklus als Quelle', 438–54; idem, *Pseudo-Dionysius Areopagita in seinen Beziehungen zum Neuplatonismus und Mysterienwesen* (Mainz, 1900). Cf. Eugenio Corsini, 'La questione areopagitica', *AAST* 93 (1958/9), 154–88.

[97] *De mal.* 49. 11, 50. 2, 50. 29, 50. 51, 54. 22.

SchDN 276. 1

In *DN* 4. 19 Dionysius gives a summary and negative statement as to the nature of evil. Evil, he says, is not a being: if it were, it would not be completely evil.[98] Whatever exists does so because of the good; thus, if something is a being, it has some share of the good. Neither is evil a non-being: for there is no such thing as absolute non-being. Such would perforce corrupt itself. One may, however, speak of absolute non-being in the sense that it is predicated of God in a manner that is beyond being.[99] Neither is evil in beings or in non-beings, rather it is something still more removed from the good and still more insubstantial.[100] To this, however, someone might object, as Dionysius himself explicitly states, that if evil is so lacking in reality, if it does not exist, then virtue and vice will be the same thing.[101] And yet, there is in the soul this opposition between virtues and vices, even before the outward manifestation of the differences. Thus 'it is necessary to posit something evil that is opposed to the good'.[102] From this one must conclude, says the hypothetical objector, that evil is in beings and is a being.[103] Dionysius' answer is to be found in *DN* 4. 20. It is not his answer that is here of interest, but rather John's exposition of and response to this possible objection.[104]

In his comments on this passage, John's first goal is to make sure that his readers understand that this is only a possible objection, it is not a position which Dionysius himself advances, no matter how positive the exposition may sound. 'After putting forward an objection, he expounds it at great length, as if it were probable.' Following this crucial distinction, John restates the objection: 'If we do not grant that there is something contrary to the beautiful (i.e. evil), then virtue is not recognized as good, but rather all things are indistinguishably mixed together.' It is here that John pulls a remarkable but characteristic sleight of hand, connecting these abstract issues of ontology with an analogous but very different situation from the Scripture. He adds: 'just as apart from the Law there will be no sin'. The allusion to Paul's Epistle to the Romans is unmistakable.[105] But it should be emphasized that the addition of this scriptural reference is a supplement to the text of *The Divine Names*. John is in effect pegging the philosophical aspects of the works of Dionysius to questions relating to the exposition of Scripture.

John returns to the objection and summarizes it in greater detail: 'Unless we grant that evil is the opposite of the good, the good itself will

[98] *DN* 4. 19 (163. 21–2).   [99] *DN* 4. 19 (163. 22–3).   [100] *DN* 4. 19 (164. 1–3).
[101] *DN* 4. 19 (164. 4–5).   [102] *DN* 4. 19 (164. 12).   [103] *DN* 4. 19 (164. 16–17).
[104] *SchDN* 276. 1.   [105] Cf. Rom. 4: 15.

be contrary to itself in those who sin by a lack of the good. But even before the activity of virtue of a virtuous person we see in his soul that evils are distinguished from virtues.' This carries us no further than the text of the objection as exposited in *The Divine Names*.[106] But John does not leave it at this. He goes on to explain, apparently still developing the objection, the physiological and psychological foundations for virtue and vice in the soul before their outward manifestation. But it must be noted that the foundations which he describes are not Dionysian: neither the language nor the exact concepts are to be found in the works of Dionysius.[107] Its origins are instead to be found in the Platonic tradition, more specifically in the writings of Plotinus.

John distinguishes two aspects of soul, a rational part [τὸ λογικὸν μέρος] and an irrational part [τὸ ἄλογον μέρος]. When the rational part acts as it should, it is not hindered in the performance of any good thing. On the other hand, when the irrational part of the soul (the part which is mixed with matter and body) overcomes the rational part, at this point the rational part is hindered from the performance of its proper activities. It follows that it is the irrational part which becomes corrupted from its intermixture with matter. The rational part, however, is corrupted not by mixture with matter, but rather by its inclining towards matter [τῷ νεύειν εἰς ὕλην], submitting to the irrational part and not overcoming it. The yielding of the rational part to the irrational part, John continues, is similar to what happen 'when it is dark and the eye is thus hindered from seeing [κωλύεται ὁρᾶν]'.

This doctrine of the two parts of the soul is unmistakably Plotinian. In *Ennead* 1. 8. 4 we find a discussion of primary and secondary evil, the latter being characteristic of bodies alone in that they participate in matter (i.e. primary evil). As for the soul, it is not evil in and of itself, nor can it be all evil. Rather, only the irrational part of the soul [τοῦ ἀλόγου τῆς ψυχῆς εἴδους] can be receptive of evil, in so far as it is receptive of matter or fused with a body that has matter. The reasonable part of the soul [τὸ λογιζόμενον], on the other hand, is hindered from seeing [ὁρᾶν κωλύεται] when by its passions it looks upon matter and inclines itself toward it [πρὸς ὕλην νενευκέναι]. Not that it is mixed with matter like the irrational part of the soul, but rather 'the nature of matter . . . is so evil that it infects with its own gaze that which is not in it but only directs its

---

[106] *DN* 4. 19 (164. 9–12): 'for long preceding the visible evidence for the virtuous man or his opposite is the distinction made within the soul between virtue and evils, and the inner conflict between passion and reason.'

[107] Although *EP* 9. 1 (198. 8–10) is conceptually similar, the language differs substantially from that employed by John.

gaze to it'.[108] The verbal reminiscences are strong enough to suggest direct literary dependence.

The physiological and psychological origins of evil are thus explained, thereby also the process by means of which virtues are distinguished from vices in the soul, even before their outward manifestation. John's positive exposition has augmented and apparently strengthened the opinions of the hypothetical objector. This is not, however, to say that John would deny the doctrine of the two parts of the soul, for elsewhere in the *Scholia* he shows his clear approval of it.[109]

But are the arguments of this hypothetical opponent valid? The objection stated is that there must be something contrary to the good if virtue and vice are to be distinguished in the soul. Not just any type of evil, but evil existing on the same level as the good: absolute evil and absolute good, two contrary principles of existence. But according to John, 'this [argument] does not demonstrate whether absolute evil exists'. In fact it has almost nothing to do with absolute evil. The objector, if he wants to show a contrary to the good, must demonstrate the existence of evil itself, not this or that form of evil resident within part of the soul. Or as John puts it: the evil which has been demonstrated is not 'evil for something', which is to say, evil as a source of evil for something else, which is equivalent to 'absolute evil', but rather, such 'vice exists by being a species and accident of the evil'. Again John is introducing distinctions which are not present in the Dionysian text, the latter being more concerned to explain the non-existence of evil as a principle by way of reference to its corrupting of the good.

But things get even more confusing when John proceeds to explain what he means in greater detail. The passage is worth citing at length:

By the additions it turns into this or that particular [evil]: for example, injustice of the soul is wickedness. And again, the species of injustice [stand in relation] to the matter of desire: for some happen with respect to money and others with respect to honours. Also, by additions the species of evil come about also from the parts of the soul: cowardice or audaciousness from the appetitive part, boldness or silliness from the desirous part. Species of evil also come from the activities: for example, cowardice is a lack with respect to impulse, audaciousness is an excess with respect to impulse, and licentiousness [is an excess] with respect to experiencing.[110]

---

[108] *Enn.* 1. 8. 4. 20–2 (tr. Armstrong). Here and in what follows, translations of Plotinus will be taken from Armstrong's version found in the Loeb Classical Library.

[109] *SchDN* 277. 4, 277. 5, 280. 4. Even in a number of other instances (*SchDN* 297. 4, 300. 1) where he seems to be setting himself against the doctrine, a close reading shows that he is opposed rather to the view that this inclination toward matter happens of necessity.

[110] *SchDN* 276. 1.

Some light is thrown upon this difficult text when we recognize that John is here not so much commenting upon Dionysius as upon a passage from Plotinus. It is a question here of yet another passage from *Ennead* I. 8. In the fifth section of this tractate Plotinus attempted to clarify the difference between primary evil or matter and secondary evil, between that which wholly lacks the good and that which only partially lacks it. These distinctions were initially raised by Plotinus in answer to an objection to his own theory of evil, that matter is evil. His hypothetical objector argues that if the soul's looking toward matter is the origin of its evil, there must already exist in the soul some lack such that the matter itself is only a secondary cause, the lack in the soul being primary. To this Plotinus responds that evil is not just partial lack, but total lack: such utter dearth can only be identified with matter. For matter has no being such that it might have a share in the good.

On this principle one must not think of evil as this or that particular kind of evil, injustice for instance or any other vice, but that which is not yet any of these particular evils; these are a sort of species of evil, specified by their own particular additions; as wickedness in the soul and its species are specified by the matter which they concern or the parts of the soul, or by the fact that one is like a sort of seeing, another like an impulse or experience.[111]

The direct literary dependence of John on this passage is unmistakable. This holds not only with regard to the logical distinctions being made (even the very order of those distinctions), but also with regard to the very language in use, as is best seen by a comparison of the Greek texts. See Table 1.

It is clear what John intends by his use of the Plotinian passage and the distinctions which it draws. Vice is a species of evil. There are, according to John, three senses in which this is so. First, it can be specified in regard to the matter at which its desire is directed. Secondly, it can be specified by the faculties of the soul from which it arises. Thirdly, it can be specified as to the activities which it engenders. But again it must be emphasized that John is arguing thus solely with a view toward refuting the hypothetical objection raised within the works of Dionysius such that evil might be granted the status of an independent principle. Neither Dionysius nor John would be willing to admit that such is the case. But the strategies of each in the attempt to disqualify this objection are radically different. As also Dionysius' anonymous objector would agree, John argues that, if virtues and vices are not to be the same, it must be the

---

[111] *Enn.* I. 8. 5. 14–19 (tr. Armstrong).

Table 1

SchDN 276. 1 (25–36)	Plot. *Enn.* 1. 8. 5. 14–19
ταῖς γὰρ προσθήκαις καθίσταται εἰς τὸ τόδε τι εἶναι, οἷον ἀδικία μὲν ψυχῆς ἐστι πονηρία·	τῷ χρὴ δὴ τὸ κακὸν νοεῖσθαι μὴ τόδε τὸ κακόν, οἷον ἀδικίαν ἢ ἄλλην τινὰ κακίαν, ἀλλ' ἐκεῖνο ὃ οὐδὲν μέν πω τούτων, ταῦτα δὲ οἷον εἴδη ἐκείνου προσθήκαις εἰδοποιούμενα· οἷον ἐν μὲν ψυχῇ πονηρίαν καὶ ταύτης αὖ εἴδη ἢ ὕλῃ περὶ ἥν,
καὶ πάλιν, τῆς ἀδικίας εἴδη πρὸς τὴν τῆς ὀρέξεως ὕλην· ἡ μὲν γὰρ, περὶ χρήματα, ἡ δὲ περὶ τιμὰς συμβαίνει. γίνεται δὲ καὶ κατὰ προσθήκας εἴδη κακῶν καὶ ἀπὸ τῶν μερῶν τῆς ψυχῆς· δειλία μὲν γὰρ, ἢ θρασύτης ἀπὸ τοῦ θυμικοῦ, ἀκολασία δὲ ἢ ἠλιθιότης ἀπὸ τοῦ ἐπιθυμητικοῦ.	ἢ τοῖς μέρεσι τῆς ψυχῆς,
γίνεται δὲ καὶ ἀπὸ τῶν ἐνεργειῶν εἴδη κακῶν· ἡ μὲν γὰρ δειλία οἷον περὶ τὸ ὁρμᾶν ἐστιν ἔλλειψις· ἡ δὲ θρασύτης περὶ τὸ ὁρμᾶν ὑπερβολή· ἡ δὲ ἀκολασία, περὶ τὸ πάσχειν.	ἢ τῷ τὸ μὲν οἷον ὁρᾶν εἶναι, τὸ δὲ ὁρμᾶν ἢ πάσχειν.

case that evils are distinguished from virtues in the soul even before their outward manifestations. For John this is so, however, not because evil is a principle which exists in opposition to the good, as the hypothetical objector would say, but rather because such opposition is inherent in the make-up of the human person and in the perpetual struggle between the rational and irrational parts of the soul.

Furthermore, John writes of the specification of evil in order to establish that evil does not have an independent existence. As for Plotinus, the situation is quite the opposite. He draws these same distinctions in order to establish the existence of matter as the principle of evil. It is as if John were drawing upon philosophical building blocks of the Plotinian system, but putting them together in such a way as to arrive at a system of a different nature. Lastly John brings his philosophical speculations back to the Scripture, to Paul's Epistle to the Romans (7: 23): 'He shows that these things of the irrational part are another law which attacks us in our minds, as the apostle said.' Again John is taking us beyond the Dionysian text.

We can see in this one scholion the many layers of intertextuality involved in John's reading of the works of Dionysius. He always has one eye on the scriptural text and one eye on Dionysius. He weaves these two together through a polemical, if unacknowledged, use of Plotinian materials—in the end, to arrive at conclusions antithetical to those of Plotinus, if faithful to the general thrust of Dionysius' arguments. At issue here is something much more complex than mere borrowings of Plotinian materials by John. Nor are such complexities distinct to this scholion.

SchDN 281. 4

As discussed earlier in this chapter, John suggests on a number of occasions that Dionysius' teachings on evil are directed against the Greeks—and this, even though 'it is being declared on the basis of Greek doctrines, for he is fighting against the Greeks especially, as well as the Manichaeans who are pre-eminent in bad doctrine'.[112] This is so in the main because Dionysius was directing himself against the doctrine that there might be two principles, one of good and one of evil. It makes no difference whether this principle be a lesser God as in Manichaeanism, or matter as an independent principle of evil as in Plotinus (as interpreted by John). In DN 4. 20 Dionysius offers in summary fashion some of his lucubrations on the nature of evil. Anything which exists must thereby have some share in the good. Granted this principle, he can establish a sliding ontological scale such that some beings share more in the good and less in evil, while others share less in the good, but more in evil. God of course stands at the top of the scale; but nothing whatsoever stands at the bottom. 'For that which totally lacks a share in the Good has neither being nor a place in existence.'[113]

These passages, according to John in SchDN 281. 4, are directed against the 'opinions of certain Greeks concerning evil'. Why? If every-

---

[112] SchDN 272. 1. Cf. also 285. 3, 288. 13.   [113] DN 4. 20 (167. 16–17).

Table 2

SchDN 281. 4 (15–19)	Plot. Enn. 1. 8. 5. 14–19
οὐ γὰρ ἐν τῇ ὁπωσοῦν ἐλλείψει, ἀλλ' ἐν τῇ παντελεῖ ἐλλείψει τοῦ ἀγαθοῦ τὸ κακόν. τὸ γοῦν ἐλλεῖπον ὀλίγῳ τοῦ ἀγαθοῦ οὐ κακόν· δύναται γὰρ καὶ τέλειον εἶναι ὡς πρὸς τὴν ἑαυτοῦ φύσιν·	ἢ οὐκ ἐν τῇ ὁπωσοῦν ἐλλείψει, ἀλλ' ἐν τῇ παντελεῖ τὸν κακόν· τὸ γοῦν ἐλλεῖπον ὀλίγῳ τοῦ ἀγαθοῦ οὐ κακόν, δύναται γὰρ καὶ τέλεον εἶναι ὡς πρὸς φύσιν τὴν αὐτοῦ.

thing must have some share in the good, everything must have some share in being. There can be no absolute evil, in that such evil would corrupt itself. Thus, absolute evil could only be essential by having no share whatsoever in the good. This means that absolute evil can nowhere be found, 'not even in formless matter itself'. We thus see right at the outset of this scholion that John is out to argue against the teachings of Plotinus and the like on evil. John continues, whatever was produced by God has some share in the good: this would of course include matter. Such beings are by nature mixed, being partly being (because of their participation in the good) and partly non-being (because they lack in some ways the good). But they are not for that reason evil. 'For evil is not in just any lack, but in a complete lack of the good. Therefore that which lacks the good only slightly is not evil. For it can also be perfect as to its nature.' In case the meaning of this last phrase is unclear, John goes on to explain that it is imperfect as regards the good, but perfect as regards its own nature: 'which is to say, it is good and in no way evil, though participating in a lack as to the first good.' In this passage we again find John drawing upon the works of Plotinus. A comparison of the Greek texts will made this manifestly clear. See Table 2. John continues by expositing in greater detail the nature of this sliding ontological scale. Things closer to evil share less in the good; things less near the good share less in the good. And yet, for all that, it is not possible to find anything which is completely without some share in the good. Such a thing simply could not exist. 'For where the good is not, neither is there anything in the nature.' To make an analogy: 'Take away bodies and light, and there will be no shadows'. He means thereby: evil does not exist independently, but in a derivative fashion from the good, even as the shadow is a derivative product of the sun.

John is clearly dependent upon the works of Plotinus in this scholion, but the nature of that dependence is rather problematic. The passage in question occurs in the same context as was exposited above: Plotinus responding to a hypothetical objector who argues that the soul's looking toward matter is an evil prior to that of matter itself. 'Yes, but evil is not in any sort of deficiency but in absolute deficiency; a thing which is only slightly deficient in good is not evil, for it can even be perfect on the level of its own nature. But when something is absolutely deficient—and this is matter—this is essential evil without any share in good.'[114] We are thus left with another situation in which John is using Plotinus to argue for a position on the nature of evil antithetical to that of the latter. For whereas Plotinus had argued that matter had no share in the good, John explicitly affirmed that 'not even formless matter itself, even if it seemed good to some of the Greeks', is lacking a measure of the good.

SchDN 293. 3

In *DN* 4. 24 we find Dionysius turning his attention to the nature of evil in the soul, answering objections which would make the soul itself evil and not evil by a falling away from the good. Should someone claim that the soul is evil, this might be taken in two senses. Either it is evil because it consorts with evil things when exercising providential and salvific care for them[115]—'this is not evil, but good and from the good which turns to a good purpose even evil'.[116] If, on the other hand, one says that souls themselves can become evil, it must be admitted that the only way this could happen is through privation—a situation that is analogous to the darkening of air when it is deprived of the light. In the final analysis, evil is not some sort of being, but merely a lack.

When John comes to comment upon this passage we find him engaged in a series of very complex intertextual relations with Dionysius and with Plotinus. First he must establish that there cannot be a complete privation of the good in beings. He argues this point as follows:

there is not a complete privation of the good in beings, since there would also be complete corruption, even of corruption itself, but rather privation takes place through a partial lack of the good. For this reason, neither does the soul have

---

[114] *Enn.* 1. 8. 5. 5–9 (tr. Armstrong).

[115] That this is the correct interpretation of Dionysius' rather terse Greek (προνοητικῶς καὶ σωστικῶς) is confirmed by a scholiast, probably not John (the beginning of *SchDN* 293. 3, not present in Syr.).

[116] *DN* 4. 24 (172. 13–14).

complete evil, rather it will have and not have. Also, the good is essential, whereas evil is from without.[117]

The distinctions being drawn are simple enough, until it is realized that this passage is directly dependent upon the works of Plotinus.

In *Ennead* 1. 8, beginning at section 11, Plotinus defends his doctrine of evil, that it is to be identified with matter, against the teachings of Aristotle on the nature of privation.[118] For the latter argues that privation of necessity belongs to something other than itself. Thus, says the hypothetical objector, 'if evil consists in privation, it will exist in the thing deprived of form and have no independent existence'.[119] That such a view has untoward consequences can be shown, according to Plotinus, by a consideration of the nature of evil in the soul. Assume that evil in the soul is simply a privation and not something with an independent existence. Such an assumption would of necessity imply that evil is to be found in the soul through a privation of the good, and would thus deny matter as the locus of evil. But this view cannot be maintained, he continues. For if privation is merely the privation of some form which ought to be present, then in the case of the soul this would mean that the soul has nothing good within itself, in that it produces its vice by the operation of its own nature. And if soul has no good, it has no life. Without life, it is soulless. 'Thus, although it is soul, it will not be soul.' And this, he argues, is absurd, for the soul has life by its very nature, and cannot thus contain within itself the very negation of the good. In the end we must conclude that the soul is something good and not evil of itself. 'It is not then primary evil, nor is primary evil an accident of it, because the good is not altogether absent from it.'[120] Plotinus must next respond to a variation on the above objection which would argue that vice and evil in the soul are not a complete privation but only a partial privation. Could that proposition be maintained, the *reductio ad absurdum* explained above would not be valid. Assume then that there is only a partial privation:

the vice and evil in the soul is not absolute privation of good, but only a [particular, limited] privation of good? In this case, if it has some good and is deprived of some, it will be in a mixed state and the evil will not be undiluted, and we have not yet found primary, undiluted evil: and the soul will have good in its very substance, but evil as some kind of accident.

This passage forms the backdrop to the material cited above from John's scholion. It is abundantly clear that John is here again dependent upon

---

[117] *SchDN* 293. 3.
[119] *Enn.* 1. 8. 11. 3–4 (tr. Armstrong).
[118] Cf. e.g. *Physics* 1. 9.
[120] *Enn.* 1. 8. 11. 17–19 (tr. Armstrong).

Table 3

SchDN 293. 3 (6–11)	Plot. Enn. 1. 8. 12. 1–7
(1) . . . μὴ παντελῆ στέρησιν γενέσθαι τοῦ ἀγαθοῦ ἐν τοῖς οὖσιν,	. . . εἰ μὴ παντελῆ στέρησιν λέγοι ἀγαθοῦ τὴν κακίαν καὶ τὸ κακὸν τὸ ἐν ψυχῇ,
(2) ἐπεὶ καὶ παντελὴς ἐγένετο ἂν φθορὰ καὶ αὐτῆς τῆς φθορᾶς,	
(3) ἀλλὰ κατ᾽ ἔλλειψιν τοῦ ἀγαθοῦ μερικήν.	ἀλλά τινα στέρησιν ἀγαθοῦ;
(4) οὐκοῦν κατὰ τοῦτο οὔτε ἡ ψυχὴ παντελὲς ἔχει τὸ κακόν, ἀλλὰ τὸ μὲν ἕξει, τὸ δὲ οὐχ ἕξει.	ἀλλ᾽ εἰ τοῦτο, τὸ μὲν ἔχουσα, τοῦ δὲ ἐστερημένη, μικτὴν ἕξει τὴν διάθεσιν καὶ οὐκ ἄκρατον τὸ κακόν,
(5)	καὶ οὔπω εὕρηται τὸ πρῶτον καὶ ἄκρατον κακόν·
(6) καὶ τὸ μὲν ἀγαθὸν οὐσιῶδες, τὸ δὲ κακὸν ἔξωθεν.	καὶ τὸ μὲν ἀγαθὸν τῇ ψυχῇ ἔσται ἐν οὐσίᾳ, συμβεβηκὸς δέ τι τὸ κακόν.

Plotinus. See Table 3. John's use of the Plotinian text, however, is extremely complex. For this reason let us take the numbered propositions in Table 3 one at a time. (1) John asserts that there cannot be a complete privation of the good among beings. Plotinus asserts the same, but not as an opinion to which he would consent; it is rather the view of a hypothetical objector. (2) John offers a further explication as to why there cannot be complete privation. Because evil is a form of corruption, complete privation would thus corrupt even itself. That John should add this material points up how greatly his use of the Plotinian materials is being applied to a different context, with different conclusions. (3) Evil is not complete privation, but it is better seen as a partial privation of the good. This ultimately is the essence of John's views on the nature of evil. But again it must be noted that this corresponds not to Plotinus' own views, but those of the hypothetical objector. (4) For John this proposition represents a further logical conclusion to be drawn from the first three propositions. The soul is not wholly evil: it falls somewhere in the middle of the sliding ontological continuum. For Plotinus this proposition is the beginning of a *reductio ad absurdum*. Assume the validity of the distinctions made in propositions 1 and 3, then it follows that the soul has a mixed disposition, and this cannot be identified with the undiluted evil for which he is searching. (5) John leaves this proposition out, because he is concerned precisely to refute the proposition that there can be some undiluted evil, especially if it should be identified with matter. (6) For John the good in the soul must be seen as essential, whereas evil is derivative, a mere shadow. Plotinus is concerned to defend the identification of evil with matter by arguing that evil must be more, much more, than a mere accident. This is after all the natural implication of Aristotle's theory of privation as being always in something else and having no existence of its own, a view with which John would no doubt agree.

John brings this scholion to a close by introducing yet another topic, a hypothetical objection which seems to arise from nowhere, bearing as it does no relation to the arguments of Dionysius in this section, but which comes, by now not surprisingly, from Plotinus.

Someone might also argue as follows: evil is merely an impediment for the soul, [which impedes] its natural activity. Now then, though this impediment is external, this impediment will none the less be responsible for the production of evil deeds, even as the soul is hindered from seeing when it is dark.

To this one must respond as follows: on the basis of the principles already laid down it is clear that such an impediment produces evil, but is not evil itself. For vice is not absolute evil, but merely a species of evil,[121] even as virtue is something which helps to produce good, but is not for all that the absolute good.

To summarize what seems to be the main import of these arguments. One might posit that evil is something outside the soul which hinders it from the performance of its proper actions—in some sense analogous to darkness when it hinders the eye from seeing. Such a concept of evil, according to John, is inadequate. Although this outer impediment can be said to be responsible for the production of evil, it cannot be identified with absolute evil. This distinction, he continues, is comparable to the situation encountered above, where vice is contrasted with evil, the former being a mere species of the latter, and for that reason not capable of being identified as the principle of evil.

Again John is dependent upon Plotinus for the arguments of this passage. In Armstrong's translation we read:

---

[121] Cf. *SchDN* 284. 3: 'For to be a particular evil . . . is not absolute evil, but a species of evil.' *SchDN* 273. 3: 'Absolute evil—I do not mean vice, which is as it were a species and quality, sometimes present in the rational creature and sometimes not, but rather I mean that which is evil *simpliciter* . . .'. *SchDN* 276. 1: 'For [this] is not 'the evil for something' (i.e. absolute evil), but rather, even vice exists by being a species and accident of the evil.' *SchDN* 277. 4: evil *per aliud* 'is a species and accident of vice'.

Table 4

SchDN 293. 3 (12–20)	Plot. Enn. 1. 8. 13. 1–7
ἀλλὰ καὶ οὕτως ἐρεῖ τις κακὸν εἶναι τῇ ψυχῇ τὸν ἐμποδισμὸν τῆς οἰκείας κατὰ φύσιν ἐνεργείας. εἰ καὶ ἔξωθεν τοίνυν ἦν ὁ ἐμποδισμός, ἀλλ᾽ οὖν ὡς ἐν σκότῳ βλέπειν κωλυομένη ψυχὴ, ποιήσει κακά.	εἰ μὴ ἄρα τούτῳ τὸ κακὸν ᾖ ἐμπόδιον, ὥσπερ ὀφθαλμῷ πρὸς τὸ βλέπειν.
	ἀλλ᾽ οὕτω ποιητικὸν κακοῦ ἔσται τὸ κακὸν αὐτοῖς, καὶ οὕτω ποιητικόν, ὡς ἑτέρου τοῦ κακοῦ αὐτοῦ ὄντος.
πρὸς ὃ λεκτέον, ὅτι ἐκ τῶν εἰρημένων εὑρίσκεται ὁ ἐμποδισμὸς ποιητικὸν κακοῦ, οὐ μὴν αὐτόκακον·	εἰ οὖν ἡ κακία ἐμπόδιον τῇ ψυχῇ, ποιητικὸν κακοῦ,
οὐ γὰρ ἡ κακία πρῶτον κακὸν, ἀλλ᾽ εἶδος κακοῦ, ὥσπερ ἡ ἀρετὴ συνεργόν τί ἐστι πρὸς ἀγαθὸν, οὗτοι πρῶτον ἀγαθόν.	ἀλλ᾽ οὐ τὸ κακὸν ἡ κακία ἔσται· καὶ ἡ ἀρετὴ δὲ οὐ τὸ ἀγαθόν, ἀλλ᾽ ἢ ὡς συνεργόν· ὥστε, εἰ μὴ ἡ ἀρετὴ τὸ ἀγαθόν, οὐδ᾽ ἡ κακία τὸ κακόν.

But perhaps evil is an impediment to good, as the eye has impediments which prevent its seeing. Yes, but in this way evil will be what produces evil for the things where it occurs, and produces it in such a way that the actual evil produced is different from the evil which produces it. If then vice is an impediment to the soul, it is not evil but something which produces evil; and virtue is not the good, except in so far as it helps to produce it, so if virtue is not good, vice is not evil.[122]

The direct literary dependence is best seen through a comparison of the respective passages in Greek. See Table 4. In this context, however, we are not so much concerned with the mere fact of literary dependence, as with the use to which the Plotinian materials are being put by John in his attempts to comment upon the works of Dionysius. Recall the original Dionysian context: souls can become evil only through a privation of the

---

[122] Enn. 1. 8. 13. 1–5 (tr. Armstrong).

good. It is only the removal of the good that is to be considered evil, not some sort of evil principle with an existence of its own. John first comments upon this passage on the basis of the arguments of Plotinus, *Ennead* 1. 8. 12, his purpose being to show that souls cannot be completely evil, that the good is present in them 'essentially', whereas evil is only present 'from without' (i.e. accidentally). His reading of the immediately following Plotinian text (*Enn.* 1. 8. 13) raised in his mind yet another possible objection to the Dionysian thesis, one which would have evil be 'from without' and yet still the source of evil: that is, an objection which would identify evil as some sort of impediment to the soul. To this he responds, weaving together the arguments of Plotinus, that such an impediment is capable of occasioning evil, but cannot be identified with evil itself. The two are quite different sorts of things, even as vice is different from evil.

But what relations do these lucubrations of John bear to the original Plotinian context. Little at best! For Plotinus cites this objection (i.e. that evil is merely an impediment to the soul) only in order to refute it. To be sure, it is an occasion of evil; but it must not for that reason be identified with absolute evil (i.e. matter). Vice impedes the soul and is thus an occasion of evil, but is not evil. So also virtue co-operates with the good but is not to be identified with the good itself. An attempt to identify vice with evil is simply insufficient for explaining the nature of evil and the fall of the soul, the latter being a question which will occupy Plotinus' attention for the duration of this tractate.[123] For Plotinus such a view of evil as an impediment does not account for the reality of evil as a principle identified with matter; for John, on the other hand, such a view of evil grants to it too much reality, not recognizing that it is merely a species of evil (i.e. of privation).

CONCLUSIONS

Let us conclude this preliminary examination of John's use of Plotinus by stepping back from the details and turning our attention instead to a more general presentation of John's treatment of the question of evil, one that will draw together the diverse strands of his thought found scattered throughout the *Scholia*. John is motivated in his presentation of the problem of evil first and foremost by the desire to avoid the errors of the Greeks and the Manichaeans.[124] The ultimate dualism of the latter is an

---

[123] *Enn.* 1. 8. 13–15.   [124] *SchDN* 272. 1, 281. 4, 397. 8.

obvious difficulty. As for the former, John is directing himself primarily against a certain Greek or group of Greeks who would identify matter as evil. Not just any evil but evil as an independent principle of evil: one that is essential, auto-hypostatic, en-hypostatic, or hypostatic.[125] Whether fairly or not, he has Plotinus in mind. Of course, Plotinus' teachings on evil were rather more nuanced than John would have it.[126] It would seem that John, by concentrating on certain parts of the *Enneads* to the exclusion of others, has missed the subtlety of Plotinus' arguments. This is especially true in that he nowhere seems to recognize that even for Plotinus matter ultimately depends on the one for its generation and is in the last resort 'an essential component of the infinite variety of the universe'.[127] John's perspective on Plotinus is partly explained by his tendency to concentrate on Plotinus' views on matter as formulated in *Ennead* 1. 8, to the exclusion of other treatments: a tractate which admittedly *implies* that matter is ungenerated.[128] Straw man or not, it was this view of evil against which John sets himself.

This one-sided and excessively narrow treatment of Plotinus may also in part be ascribed to John's tendency to read Plotinus a little too seriously, if you will. As Plotinus worked through his problems, he often proposed preliminary solutions only to cast them away as fruitless. He frequently digressed with lengthy hypothetical objections. All told, these tendencies sometimes make it difficult to determine what we are to think of as Plotinus' own views. John Dillon has aptly characterized Plotinus' approach to philosophy as 'open-ended, "aporetic"'.[129] The *Enneads* are not systematic: and yet, we sense that John reads them as if they were Proclean *Elements*.

Be that as it may, in the opinion of John, good must be essential and evil something less. But how to be more specific? The primary focus of his attention, the point to which he returns again and again—there can be no principle of evil, not even matter.[130] Matter is not pre-existent, something formless and shapeless, a mere 'reflection' of true being.[131] Matter

---

[125] Essential, *SchDN* 281. 4, 301. 8, 277. 4; auto-hypostatic, *SchDN* 305. 3; en-hypostatic, *SchDN* 304. 2; hypostatic, *SchDN* 301. 1.

[126] Cf. John M. Rist, 'Plotinus on Matter and Evil', *Phronesis*, 6 (1961), 154–66; John Dillon, 'Plotinus at Work on Platonism', *Greece & Rome*, 39 (1992), 189–204, esp. 202–3.

[127] Dillon, 'Plotinus at Work', 203. According to Rist, *Plotinus* (Cambridge, 1967), 119, 'Matter therefore is to be accounted for as the last production in the stream of products deriving ultimately from the One'.

[128] Dillon, 'Plotinus at Work', 202.

[129] Dillon, 'Plotinus at Work', 189.

[130] *SchCH* 44. 9, *SchDN* 272. 1, 273. 3. Cf. the discussion above.

[131] *SchDN* 272. 1.

was created by God and is a product of his creative act.[132] Even if John is willing to call it 'lowliest matter' or the 'ἔσχατον of all things', he insists that it shares in God's goodness and always bears the forms granted it by God.[133] He is even willing to grant that matter is infinite in so far as it is always subject to change, as long as it is remembered that it is bounded by God who endows it with forms.[134] It simply is not possible, according to John, for matter to exist as something formless and shapeless.[135] Nevertheless, John is still willing to grant that matter is 'non-being' [μὴ ὄν], if this is interpreted correctly. For matter is 'non-being' only in relation to God who is being in the strictest sense of the term.[136] Matter as 'non-being' is such through a lack of full participation in goodness.[137] But, even so, it does have *some* share in the good, for without the good it could not exist.[138] In the end John takes refuge in the Dionysian formulations, but does little to develop them. Absolute evil cannot exist. Not only would its existence entail two principles and thus a dualism (however ill-defined), but also its existence is quite simply impossible, for evil is corruption and absolute corruption would corrupt even itself.[139] An apt analogy: take away heat from heated iron and the iron will still exist; take away its share in the good and there will be nothing.[140] Instead, argues John, we must think of evil as a privation and a 'slipping in' [παρείσδυσις] that takes place through that privation.[141] It is the absence of a form that ought to be present.[142]

But John does not leave the Dionysian text as he found it; there is at least one major change in emphasis that he introduces. This is his concern for the moral aspects of evil. When John turns his attention to human beings and the reasons for their sin he is adamant that this results not of necessity but through their own inclination. Freedom of the will and its defence are essential to his conception of evil. This is not to say that Dionysius himself ignored such matters in his treatment of evil, but in his desire to defend the proposition that all beings desire the good, he is forced to treat privation as a necessary result of a creature's position in the ontological hierarchy—but 'evil' in this sense is strictly amoral: it involves no occasion of choice on the part of creatures. To be sure, he grants at times that some sort of 'moral sin' occurs through a desire for

---

[132] *SchCH* 44. 9, *SchDN* 273. 3.

[133] *SchCH* 44. 9, *SchDN* 277. 5.

[134] *SchDN* 332. 1.

[136] *SchDN* 272. 1, 277. 1. In much the same way it is without being and form only in relation to God who has these qualities absolutely (see again *SchDN* 277. 1).

[137] *SchDN* 273. 3.   [138] *SchDN* 280. 4.   [139] *SchDN* 277. 1.

[140] *SchDN* 280. 4.   [141] *SchDN* 277. 4.   [142] *SchDN* 301. 1.

lesser goods 'in direct proportion to irrational urges'[143] and that this is a turning aside for which we are responsible.[144] But such considerations do not bulk large. Indeed, our mysterious author expressly deflects such criticism by reference to another work entitled *Concerning Justice and the Judgement*, a work wherein such matters are ostensibly treated at some length. But in *The Divine Names* at any rate he is rather concerned with 'lifting up a hymn of praise to the Good . . . the Source and the end of all things'.[145]

John is not willing to leave the matter without elaboration. He wants to know the mechanism by which human choice is responsible for moral evil—hence his doctrine of the two parts of the soul. There is a rational part that is unmixed with matter or the body. Sometimes he identifies this as the undivided *summa mentis* [ἄνθος] or 'mind' [νοῦς], which alone is able to perceive the truth without the use of symbols, in contrast to the divided part of the soul which is connected with the body through spirit, is carried down by sense perceptions to sensible objects, and for that reason can receive the truth only through symbols.[146] Elsewhere in his *Scholia* John identifies the 'mind' with the Pauline 'inner man'.[147] Between these two parts of the soul, the rational and irrational, there stands a great gulf which can only be crossed by an act of will on the part of the rational part of the soul such that it inclines toward the irrational part and thus toward matter. The process does not, however, work in reverse, for the irrational part of the soul cannot in and of itself cause this inclination to occur. Two arguments are critical for John in this connection. Consider first the angels: although they were not endowed with a body, some of them nevertheless fell into sin.[148] Alternatively, one has the saints: for such as these have overcome the irrational part of their soul.[149] The initiative for the inclination thus comes from the higher or rational part of the soul, and never vice versa. The frequency with which John takes up this topic should alert us to its importance for him.[150]

We have in John's *Scholia* not a complete treatment of the problem of evil, but rather select topics. For all that, there is present a certain unity of exposition, method, and thought. This unity points up the integrity of the newly isolated stratum of the scholia and confirms that John was the author of a creative piece of religious and philosophical

---

[143] *DN* 4. 20 (167. 3).   [144] *DN* 4. 35 (179. 17).
[145] *DN* 4. 35 (180. 1–2).   [146] *SchEP* 565. 2, *SchDN* 185. 4.
[147] Rom. 7: 22–3, Eph. 3: 16.
[148] *SchDN* 297. 4, in this John is simply repeating Dionysius, *DN* 4. 27 (173. 20).
[149] *SchDN* 301. 1.   [150] *SchDN* 276. 1, 277. 4, 277. 5, 297. 4, 300. 1.

reflection with its own thematic agenda. Some years ago W. Beierwaltes devoted his attention to the use of Plotinian materials in John's *Scholia* on the works of Dionysius. Discussing quite briefly John's use of Plotinus' *Ennead* I. 8 he proposed the following: that John, through his knowledge of the Plotinian texts, was able to attain a better understanding of the 'problematic against which Proclus and Dionysius were polemicizing', and that as a result John for the most part 'differentiated the Proclean-Dionysian question' on the basis of Plotinus, in the process going to some extent beyond the Dionysian texts themselves.[151] With these observations it is necessary to agree. But there was more at stake in John's use of Plotinus. As we have seen, he uses Plotinian hypothetical objections and other materials to argue for theses antithetical to those acceptable to Plotinus, but which supported those offered by Dionysius. John's tacit polemics with Plotinus must not go unnoticed in any attempt to assess his use of Plotinian materials.

But the question remains: why does John, a man not adverse to parading his knowledge of arcana, nevertheless refuse to admit openly his dialogue with Plotinus? It remains a subtext, quite unlike his explicit intertextual relations with the Scripture and the fathers, or for that matter the historians and poets of antiquity. Could it be that such open dialogue in the case of a Greek philosopher would contaminate the aura of primitive simplicity and authenticity with which he is trying to endow the works of the great Dionysius? It was proper to engage certain unnamed Greeks. As for Scripture and the fathers, there is after all a deposit of the faith. But Plotinus! Here was a problem. How to bring him into the world of a first-century author and yet preserve the aura of antiquity surrounding the works of Dionysius.

[151] 'Johannes von Skythopolis', 6–7.

PART II
Selected Translation of John's *Scholia*

On the Translation

Our partial translation of John's *Scholia* on the Dionysian corpus includes those comments which we considered representative of the major themes and methods of the work as a whole. In practical terms, this means that we have included about two-thirds of John's commentary.[1] As for those materials which we decided not to include, we were guided by three general principles. First, we have largely avoided scholia of a strictly philological nature, especially those which explain the meaning of innocuous terms in the Dionysian corpus and those which explicate points of grammar. Secondly, we have decided not to include the fairly numerous scholia which do not offer much by way of substantive content. Many of John's comments (especially on *The Ecclesiastical Hierarchy*) are in fact marginal *nota bene*s: 'Here the father says such and such' or 'Note, on the subject of such and such'. Thirdly, we have been rather selective in our inclusion of repetitive materials. John often returns to the same subject on numerous occasions. When he develops in significant ways his earlier arguments we have been careful to include these materials. If, however, his additional comments add little of note, we have usually chosen only the more systematic of his comments on any particular subject for inclusion.

Without being slavish, we have tried to maintain the translation of technical terms as much as possible in accordance with the Paulist Press translation of the works of Dionysius. Although this did at times present certain problems, for in the interests of fluid style the Paulist Press translation is occasionally rather periphrastic, this procedure seemed to offer the most benefit to readers with little or no knowledge of Greek, while at the same time not being an undue hindrance to more advanced readers. It was necessary, however, to introduce one major change. The Paulist Press translation consistently renders νοητός and its various derivatives as 'conceptual'. John, however, often treats of what is νοητός in terms of its correlative, what is νοερός, making specific reference to the passive nature of the former and the active nature of the latter. For this reason we have

---

[1] We have, however, supplied a complete translation of John's scholia on *The Mystical Theology*.

decided to employ the English cognates 'intelligible' and 'intelligent', respectively. Though they may jar on the ear, especially in their substantival plural, they do at least preserve the active and passive distinction upon which John places so much weight.

Several items of information are included at the beginning of our translation of the individual scholia. First, we note the column and paragraph number from Migne's edition of the *Scholia* (e.g. '29. 1' indicates that this scholion is found on column 29, at paragraph 1).[2] Secondly, we indicate with page and line number (e.g. 7. 2) (according to the PTS edition) the Dionysian passage upon which John is commenting. This is followed by the column and section heading of Migne's edition in parentheses, e.g. 120A. Finally, we offer in italic in the Paulist Press translation the word or words being commented upon. Occasionally we expand the lemma printed in Migne. These expansions are included within parentheses: e.g. at *SchEH* 145. 10, *The sacred (bath)*. Occasionally we add an alternative, more literal, rendering in square brackets: e.g. at *SchCH* 72. 6, *Divine work* [lit. theurgy].

Within the translation of the scholia themselves the reader will encounter the symbols shown below.

( )   normal parentheses mark parenthetical remarks present in the original Greek text.

[ ]   square brackets mark editorial comment: biblical references, cross-references to other passages in the Dionysian corpus (cited according to the PTS edition), expansions added by the translators, section headings and Migne divisions (in the translation of the *Prologue*), and Greek words.

{ }   curly brackets indicate material not present in the Syriac recension of the *Scholia*. Normally, such materials were not included in our translation. We note their excision with the symbol '{ . . . }'. Sometimes we have argued that such materials are in fact by John. Such passages we include in the text of the translation between curly brackets, offering in the notes our reasons for thinking them authentic.

{{ }}   doubled curly brackets are used in the translation of the *Prologue* to note a number of passages whose authenticity is problematic.

---

[2] As there are no paragraph or scholia numbers in Migne, the reader needs to count. Migne's 'edition' (a reprint of that of Corderius) can be found in PG 4 under the title *S. Maximi scholia in opera B. Dionysii* (cols. 13–576).

$\langle \ldots \rangle$ angled brackets with ellipses mark materials by John (i.e. in Syriac) but not included in this translation.

Finally, a single scholion often functions as a running commentary on a long passage of the Dionysian corpus. As John introduces new materials from the corpus in the course of his comments, we have put those materials in quotation marks, followed by the page and line number from the PTS edition in parentheses.

The reader will also find in what follows a complete translation of John's *Prologue* to the Dionysian corpus. We have translated in accordance with the corrected version of the text published by Suchla.[3] Within our translation, however, we offer page numbers and section divisions only according to the older edition found in Migne.[4]

---

[3] 'Verteidigung eines platonischen Denkmodells einer christlichen Welt', *NAWG* (1995), 1: 20–2.

[4] For those using Suchla's corrected version of the *Prologue*, this should not be a problem, for she provided cross-references to the page and section divisions of Migne.

Prologue

[PART I: THE INTEGRITY OF THE AREOPAGITE]

[16A] In and of itself, the Athenian council over which the great Dionysius was appointed to judge establishes his noble birth and illustrious wealth. For this man was one of the Areopagites, as the divine Luke made clear while narrating the sacred acts of the sacred apostles [Acts 17: 16–34]. He says that when the most holy apostle Paul was in Athens, he argued with some Epicurean and Stoic philosophers. After proclaiming faith in the Lord Jesus Christ, the resurrection of the dead, and the universal judgement, Paul was seized by these non-philosophers and brought to the Areopagus. After he had made a public speech, he won over some of them on the spot and converted them to the light of truth. 'So Paul went out from their midst. [16B] But some men joined him and believed, among them Dionysius the Areopagite and a woman named Damaris and others with them' [Acts 17: 33–4].

Of all those who believed at that time through the divine Paul, it is not without reason that I hear named by the god-bearing author [Luke] only the excellent Dionysius, as befits his worthiness. For they call him an 'Areopagite', and I would add moreover that he was mentioned with his house because of his extraordinary wisdom and select and blameless way of life among the Athenians.[1] One must know, as I have already said, that it was not the part of every man to belong to the council of the Areopagus. [16C] Only the leading Athenians who were distinguished in family, wealth, and good life judged at the council of the Areopagus. It was necessary earlier to appoint Areopagite judges from among the nine archons seated in Athens, [17A] as Androtion says in the second book of his *Athenian History*. Later on, the council of the Areopagus was composed of more men, that is, fifty-one of the most illustrious men, who had to be of the aristocracy, as we have said, and distinguished by wealth and a prudent life, as Philochorus reports in the third book of the same

---

[1] The reference to Dionysius 'with his house' suggests that John read the biblical phrase 'a woman named Damaris' to mean 'his wife named Damaris'. That Damaris was the wife of Dionysius was the explicit conclusion of Amb. *ep.* 63. 22 (PL 16: 1247) and Chrys. *sacer.* 4. 7 (PG 48: 669).

Athenian History.[2] The court of the Areopagus was outside the city. {{According to Athenian mythology, it was called the 'Areopagus' after the council held between Poseidon and Ares on the very peak of the city's mountain. Poseidon presented his case against Ares in this place, according to ancient myths among the Athenians, claiming that his own son, Halirrothios, had been carried off by Ares. Thus, that hill [πάγος] was called 'Areios' after Ares.}}[3] The Areopagites judged nearly all errors and crimes, [17B] all as Androtion says in the first book, and Philochorus in the second and third books of the *Athenian History*.[4]

Accordingly, as the truth-loving Luke records, the lovers of that wisdom which God has made foolish [cf. 1 Cor. 1: 20] dragged the most divine Paul to the council of the Areopagus, as if he were the preacher of new divinities [cf. Acts 17: 18]. But among the Areopagites at that time there was one ruling as an uncorrupted judge, the great Dionysius. Unbribed, he cast his vote for the truth as delivered by the spirit-bearing Paul. After bidding farewell in all matters to the mindless dignity of the Areopagites, and coming to know the true and all-seeing judge, Jesus Christ, the only begotten Son and Word of God the Father, whom Paul was preaching, immediately he took hold of the light.

[17C] Even though the Romans then ruled, they granted the Athenians and Spartans self-rule; whence even now the council of the Areopagites governs among the Athenians.[5]

Dionysius was perfected in all the doctrines of salvation by the most excellent Paul; he was pedagogically educated under Hierotheus the great, as he himself says; and then Dionysius was seated by the Christ-bearing Paul as bishop of the faithful in Athens, as is recorded in the seventh book of the *Apostolic Constitutions*.[6]

[2] Androtion (d. 340 BC) wrote a history of Athens down to 343. His work was the main source for Philochorus (d. *c*.260 BC), who brought the history of Athens down to more recent times. The Philochorus fragment is found in Jacoby, *FGrHist*. 328F20B; the Androtion fragment, *FGrHist*. 324F4. Müller combines them, fr. 58 (*FHG* 1: 394). Basing himself on a number of parallel passages and taking into consideration a number of other factors, Jacoby has argued that John knew neither Philochorus nor Androtion at first hand, but rather was dependent here on a legal handbook (no longer extant) in which the homicide courts of Athens were treated (Jacoby ad *FGrHist*. 324F3–4).

[3] Some manuscripts omit the words in brackets, but Beate Regina Suchla considers them original. See 'Die Überlieferung des Prologs des Johannes von Skythopolis zum griechischen Corpus Dionysiacum Areopagiticum', *NAWG* (1984), 4: 182.

[4] Jacoby, *FGrHist*. 324F3, 328F4, 328F20A. Müller combines the testimonies (fr. 17, *FHG* 1: 387).

[5] This sentence on Athenian governance seems out of place; it would fit more naturally within the previous paragraph on that subject, perhaps at its conclusion.

[6] *Const. App*. 7. 46. 11 (SC 336: 110). Cf. *SchEP* 552. 11. Here Migne's edition of the *Prologue* adds: 'Dionysius, the ancient bishop of the Corinthians, also mentions the

[PART II: THE ORTHODOXY OF THE AREOPAGITE]

Whoever has been trained with a true knowledge of the invincible traditions of the Church can marvel at the orthodoxy and erudition of Dionysius and [17D] can contemplate how the bastard teachings of the Greek philosophers have been restored to the truth. One can feel only pity and sorrow for the carelessness of a few examiners of learning, that they measure by their own ignorance the disposition to love knowledge as it is found in other people. [20A] Such men, when they happen upon certain writings and perhaps do not follow the argument in what is said, straight away accuse the author of lying. And yet, since they are wholly unable to correct and refute the follies of those with whom they disagree—'follies' is their word, not mine—they ought rather to be angry with themselves. Even more, they ought to be grieved that they also do not know anything about knowledge, and this through having put some efforts into studying, or to speak freely, that they were not freed from their doubts through concourse with such as know about these things. Rather, some dare to abuse the divine Dionysius with charges of heresy, being themselves absolutely ignorant of matters of heresy. For certainly, if they were to compare his teaching in these works with each of the items condemned among the heretics, they would discover that there is as much distinction between his teachings and those idiocies as there is between true light and darkness.

[20B] For what could they say of his theology of the only-worshipped Trinity? Or what about Jesus Christ, one of this all-blessed Trinity, the only begotten Word of God who willed to become fully human? Did [Dionysius] not expound upon the rational soul and the earthly body like ours, and all the other items mentioned by the orthodox teachers? For what error could anyone rightly blame him, with respect to intelligible and intelligent and perceptible things? Or, concerning our general resurrection which will happen with both our body and our soul? And concerning the future judgement of the just and the unjust? To speak in short, our salvation is focused on these points, which it would not be right to go through in detail, since the *Scholia* explicate all of these things at the proper time.

Areopagite, as does Polycarp, in his letter to the Athenians.' Suchla ('Überlieferung des Prologs', 182–3) considers this a marginal gloss on the reference to the *Apostolic Constitutions*. Polycarp's letter to the Athenians is otherwise unknown.

[PART III: THE AUTHENTICITY OF THE AREOPAGITE'S WRITINGS]

[20C] {{To be sure, they say, but Eusebius Pamphili does not write of his books, nor in fact does Origen.}}[7] Against them, one must say that Eusebius omitted mention of many things which had not come into his hands, nor indeed did he say that he had collected everything once for all. On the contrary, he confessed rather that there were far more books which he had not seen. I can recall many which he did not possess, and these even of his own land, such as the works of Hymenaeus and Narcissus who were priests in Jerusalem.[8] I, none the less, have happened upon some works of Hymenaeus. Nor, in fact, did [Eusebius] record the labours of Pantaenus, or of the Roman Clement, apart from just two of his *Epistles*, but not most of the others.[9] I do not know whether Origen made mention of all of them, or four at most. [20D] But a certain Roman deacon, by name of Peter,[10] has told me that all the works ascribed to the divine Dionysius are preserved in the library of the sacred [books] in Rome.[11]

He writes most of his works to the thrice-blessed Timothy, companion of the apostle St Paul, and bishop of the Ephesians, who apparently suffered many things {{at the hands of the foremost men of Ionian philosophy at Ephesus}}[12] and inquired [of Dionysius] so that he might

[7] Some manuscripts omit this sentence, but Suchla considers it to be original ('Überlieferung des Prologs', 183–4).

[8] Hymenaeus of Jerusalem presided over the Council of Antioch in 264–8 and was one of six bishops to sign an admonitory letter to Paul of Samosata. No works by Hymenaeus are known. As for Narcissus of Jerusalem, he succeeded Dolichmanus as bishop of Jerusalem between 180 and 192, and then with Theophilus of Caesarea presided over the Synod of Palestine in 195 which dealt with the problem of the correct date of Easter. He died sometime after 212. Fragments of one of his synodal letters seem to have been preserved in Eus. *h.e.* 5. 25 (SC 41: 72). No other works are known. For more information on the fragments of the synodal letter found in Eusebius, cf. Pierre Nautin, *Lettres et écrivains chrétiens des IIe et IIIe siècles* (Paris, 1961), 85–91.

[9] For Clement's two letters, see Eus. *h.e.* 3. 3 (SC 31: 152–3). Pantaenus was the teacher of Clement of Alexandria. No works of his are known.

[10] The reference to a deacon Peter is intriguing and is perhaps related to John's familiarity with the liturgical responsibilities of Roman deacons (see *SchEH* 136. 16).

[11] At this point, it is tempting to emend the received text. If the reference to Dionysius is original, this passage is part of John's overall defence of Areopagitic authenticity; but in that case the shift to Rome is rather abrupt. If, however, the original text read 'all the works of Clement', then the sentence is part of the *sub-point* about Clement and his works, and the reference to Rome is perfectly natural.

[12] Some manuscripts omit the words in brackets, but Suchla considers them original ('Überlieferung des Prologs', 184). That Timothy was bishop of the Ephesians is not

become learned in non-Christian philosophy, and thus contend still more. [21A] There is nothing unreasonable in this! Even the god-beloved apostle Paul employed the sayings of the Greeks, {{having by chance heard these from his companions}} who were well-versed in {{Greek}} philosophy.[13]

That these writings truly belong to Dionysius is confirmed by the fact that he offhandedly mentions the sayings of men who were his contemporaries, and who were also mentioned in the divine Acts of the apostles. Moreover, the beneficial epistles of the god-beloved Paul show the authenticity of these writings, and most especially the faultlessness of all these teachings. {{ . . . }}[14]

[21C] There was need for exegetical comments, as detailed as possible, for the interpretation of his erudition. Failing this, with God's help, I have set down more briefly, as [the margins of] the book could hold, by means of scholia, the thoughts which occurred to me, according to the order of the treatises which have chanced to come my way thus far.

scriptural, but was extrapolated by the tradition, e.g. Eus. *h.e.* 3. 4. 10 (SC 31: 101). Ephesus, in Ionia, was known for its Greek philosophers ever since Thales and Anaximander. That Timothy and the Christians in Ephesus had disputes with philosophical rivals could be concluded from 1 Tim. 4: 1 and Rev. 2: 2. Cf. *SchDN* 373. 1.

[13] Some manuscripts omit the words in brackets, but Suchla considers them original ('Überlieferung des Prologs', 184).

[14] Suchla ('Überlieferung des Prologs', 185–7) omits the text from 21A12 to 21C37 as not by John. See Ch. 5 for further discussion.

The Celestial Hierarchy

29. 1 on 7. 2 (120A): *Hierarchy*: Since the title has 'hierarchy', we can conclude that he was wont to call the bishops 'hierarchs'.

You should know that by 'hierarchy' he means the source [ἀρχή] of the order of sacred things [ἱερῶν], and in some sense the care [which is shown for them], and that by 'hierarch' he means the one who is the source [ἄρχων], not of priests [ἱερέων], but of sacred things [ἱερῶν], the one who cares and provides for them. A hierarch is not the high priest, but the one who properly disposes sacred things, not only the order [of such sacred things], but also that of the Church and the mysteries. In what follows, in his book *The Ecclesiastical Hierarchy*, the great Dionysius himself sets out this interpretation.[1]

29. 2 on 7. 1 (120A): *The Elder* [lit. **presbyter**]: Note that the name 'presbyter' can be applied to a bishop, for the bishop is also a presbyter. This is also suggested by the Acts of the apostles, in the passages where St Paul the apostle organized his churches in Asia [e.g. Acts 20: 17, 28].

1

29. 3 on 7. 3 (120B): *'Every good endowment'*: Note that the blessed Dionysius made use of the catholic epistle of St James, for the passage in question is taken from that source [Jas. 1: 17].

Note also that [the epistle of James] had already been put into circulation [in the time of Dionysius].

32. 2 on 7. 12 (121A): *Paternally transmitted*: By 'fathers' he here means, not physical fathers, but those who taught him, for he was a convert from among the Greeks, as the Acts of the apostles indicates [Acts 17: 34], and as he himself indicates in his letter to St Polycarp.[2]
{ . . . }

---

[1] *EH* 1. 3 (65. 22–66. 19).   [2] *EP* 7 (165–70), cf. *SchCH* 85. 6.

32. 4 on 8. 1 (121A): *Intelligent* [lit. **minds**]: The Greek philosophers also call the intelligents (i.e. the angelic powers) 'minds'. { . . . } The Scripture also calls them by this name, as in Isaiah: 'the great mind, the ruler of Assyrians', that is, the devil [Isa. 10: 12 LXX]. { . . . }

32. 5 on 8. 2 (121A): *Primal, indeed much more so* [ὑπεράρχιος]: God is ὑπεράρχιος, in so far as he is beyond every source [ἀρχή].

He is also a 'thearchical light' [8. 2], in so far as he is the source [ἀρχή] of those called gods [θεῶν], i.e. angels and righteous persons.

32. 8 on 8. 12 (121B): *Veils*: { . . . } Note that in so far as we are endowed with flesh we cannot look upon immaterial and bodiless things without types and symbols. The veils in the tabernacle also suggest this, as he hints here.

32. 10 on 8. 14 (121C): *The source of perfection*: According to the Greek philosophers, the act of participating in the mysteries is called a 'perfection' [τελετή], in so far as it perfects the initiate and renders perfect those who approach such mysteries.[3]

By 'sacred institution and source of perfection' [8. 14] he means the divine order of our sacred mysteries—the source of this perfection coming from God through the apostles who render good things perfect, for the divine apostle Paul calls those who are initiated 'perfect', saying 'let those of us who are perfect be thus minded' [Phil. 3: 15].

33. 10 on 9. 14 (124A): *Peaks*: This blessed man does not use words at random, but learnedly and (to speak more correctly) piously. Thus when he says that through detailed material symbols and images our sacred arrangement was brought to perfection in a manner appropriate to us and that our sacred arrangement is an imitation of the sacred order among the angels, he rightly calls the divine presence among them [i.e. among the angels] a 'peak'. Experts in these matters use the word 'peak' to refer to the purest part of each essence, that to which the essence is connected immediately (i.e. right next to it).[4] One can say, for example, that the soul's mind (i.e. that which is most pure) is its 'peak', and that a burning love for transcendent and divine things is the 'peak' of love. Thus also, the purest part of our hierarchy and mysterious order and that part of it which stands closest to immateriality is its 'peak'. In the same way, the purest symbol among us is the 'peak' of those mysteries which are without type, simple, and

---

[3] Cf. *SchEP* 553. 9.

[4] This important Neoplatonic term 'peak' [ἀκρότης] is used with reference to that from which the orders proceed and that upon which they revert (cf. Proc. *Elem.* 146). See also *SchCH* 97. 3 for another use of the term.

bodiless, being connected with which the hierarchy transcends in some sense the divine presence among humans. { . . . }

2

36. 3 on 10. 9 (137AB): *Poetic (imagery)*: Note that Scripture also uses poetic imagery to guide human reasoning—but only in so far as human reasoning is unable to receive the teaching of the greater things—for the heavenly symbols [of Scripture] resemble what the poets imagine, as this sacred man himself says.

By 'poets' understand either those admired by the Greeks, such as Homer, Hesiod, and so forth, or [that Dionysius is using the word as a metaphor]: poetic models in the sense of imaginary [models]. { . . . }

37. 5 on 10. 20 (137C): *Godlike*: He says that intelligible beings are 'god-like simplicities', for they are entirely immaterial and uncomposite, in that they are not a mixture or a compound of elements. For bodies are from such [elements], whereas they are without bodies.

37. 7 on 11. 3 (137C): *Lions*: These shapes of the divine and holy cherubim were described by the divine Ezekiel [Ezek. 10] and the divinely voiced John in the Apocalypse [Rev. 4: 8].

37. 10 on 11. 4 (137D): *Other animals*: By 'other animals' he means, for example, horses, mules, and the like.

'The more dishonourable material things' [11. 4–5] are, for example, thrones seemingly made of wood, wheels, iron swords like the drawn sword [which confronted] Balaam [Num. 22: 23], that which David saw, as recorded in 2 Kings [2 Sam. 22: 9–15], and chariots seemingly made of wood.

37. 11 on 11. 5 (137D): *Emotional*: He says 'emotional', since the lion's form signifies something angry, and the shape of a calf, something concupiscent. These are both great emotions.

By 'similarities' [11. 7] he means figurative meanings. Ezekiel thus says that he saw the similitude of a throne [Ezek. 10: 1] and the similitude of a lion [Ezek. 1: 10, 10: 14]. These signify the imaginal and illusional quality of the things which appeared to him, wherefore mention is also here made of 'dissimilar similarities' [11. 6–7], for the prophet does not see all things as similar, but some in this way and others in that way. But also, they are entirely dissimilar for those to whom they appear to be [only] similar, for they actually have nothing of the lion or the calf or the rest.

What 'the dissimilar' signifies, you will find in what follows.[5]

40. 9 on 12. 6 (140C): *Form of 'Word'* [lit. 'reason']: In what way God is said to be 'reason' [λόγος] and 'mind' [νοῦς]. In this verse: 'Who has known the mind of the Lord?' [Isa. 40: 13] And in this one: 'And the word of the Lord came to me, saying . . .' [Jer. 1: 4].

He ascribes 'rationality' to God, not because he wishes to call God 'rational', in the sense of one who participates in reason, for this is already well known, but rather because [God] is rationality itself, being wholly reason. ⟨ . . . ⟩

40. 12 on 12. 20 (141A): *Incomprehensible*: By 'incomprehensible' he means, not that which is foolish, but that which is not understood by someone.

God is 'unlimited' [12.20] in so far as he is subject to no limit, but is himself the limit of all things and limits them all in himself. But [again] he is not subject to a limit. { . . . }

41. 1 on 12. 20–13. 1 (141A): *The way of negation*: This is applicable not only to God himself, but also to all divine things (i.e. all the intelligibles around God). Of these he says that there are both 'true negations' [13. 1] and 'unfitting affirmations' [13. 1].

Affirmations are 'unfitting', when we call God or the intelligent powers 'life' [12. 9] or 'light' [12. 8]. For life of this kind does not exist [there], in so far as such life arises through inhaling and exhaling; nor light which appears and causes objects to be seen. It is something above these. How much more appropriate to the intelligibles are negations through denials! For we say that they are invisible, and understand by this that they are not capable of being seen.

The discourse seems not to pry into or present the thing itself, that which does not appear. And yet, the words 'life' and 'light' seem to signify what is, and these in no way represent what God is.

44. 6 on 14. 18 (144A): *In the pure*: { . . . } When we speak of a 'lack of expressive rationality' [14. 20] among the incorporeal beings, we are not mocking them for their unintelligence, through our use of the shapes of lions and heifers and birds (e.g. the eagle), saying that the types and symbols of the irrational animals are appropriate to the heavenly orders. Rather, we are indicating mysteriously the difference between expressive rationality among them as compared with that among us. For we express ourselves in a rational fashion through the medium of language and through spoken images, moving the air in an articulate fashion, whereby speech passes from us into the ears of the

[5] *CH* 2. 3 (12. 14–20).

hearers, from body to body, as the divine Basil says in his work about the saying 'Attend to yourself'.[6] But rational expression is not like this there [i.e. among the celestial beings]. Rather, the angels, in so far as they are not endowed with a body, are able to pass in and out of one another, and in a way that is more clear than speech, in the process they can observe the thoughts of one another and in some sense converse with one another, silently sharing speech with one another.

44. 9 on 15. 2 (144B): *Matter:* ⟨ . . . ⟩ No wise reasoning denies that all matter also 'has its subsistence' [cf. 15: 3] from God. Even this bears in itself evidence of having being produced and adorned by God. Thus every orderly arrangement of matter has certain faint and dark 'echoes' [15. 4] of the intelligents. For just as the intelligents are capable of receiving the providential processions of God, to the extent that it is permitted them, and being a life, are enlivened by God who is beyond all life, and have powers capable of doing good and a certain transcendent movement; thus also *all* material things, taken as a whole and as individuals, are able (to the extent that it is granted them) to receive the providence of God in a manner that is appropriate to themselves and be enlivened and become life. 'Let the earth bring forth a living soul' [Gen. 1: 24], and again: 'Let the waters bring forth swarms of living souls' [Gen. 1: 20]. But also, all material things breathe forth beneficial activities for earthly creatures, as is shown by the benefits gained from plants and minerals. Moreover, material things have a corresponding movement, one which proceeds unto birth and destruction, and they receive an order which has been and will be assigned by God. But also, they can be illumined in the presence of the intelligent powers, as in the case of the angel who dazzled and illuminated its surroundings at the resurrection of the Lord [Matt. 28: 3, Luke 24: 4]. Matter has these things passively, not like the intelligent things which have them actively. Thus these material beings are said to have these according to a 'last echo'.

I will clarify the meaning of the last echo in the fourth chapter of *The Divine Names.*[7]

45. 4 on 15. 11 (144C): *Sun:* Malachi the prophet made mention of the 'sun of righteousness' [Mal. 4: 2]. The divine Peter said in his catholic epistle: 'Until the morning star rises in your hearts . . .' [2 Pet. 1: 19]. For this is the 'morning star' [15. 11]. Moses said: 'a fire in a bush, not consuming' [Exod. 3: 2], which is the fire 'illuminating harmlessly'

---

[6] Bas. *hom.* 3. 1 (PG 31: 197–200). Cf. *SchEH* 129. 6.
[7] *SchDN* 248. 1, 280. 1. Cf. *SchDN* 336. 4, *SchCH* 48. 2.

[15. 13]. Jeremiah spoke of 'water' [15. 13]: 'They have rejected me the fount of living water' [Jer. 2: 13], and others [have said] other things. And the Lord said: 'Out of his heart shall flow rivers of living water' [John 7: 38]. Solomon in the Song of Songs spoke of the 'myron ointment' [15. 16]: 'Your name is ointment poured out' [S. of S. 1: 2]. Among the twelve prophets, Hosea [Hos. 5: 14] and Micah [Mic. 1: 8, 2: 12, 5: 8] discuss in their works the things said of 'beasts' [15. 17] in the prophecies about God. David calls him a 'worm' [15. 20], 'I am a worm and not a human' [Ps. 22: 6], speaking about the person of the Lord. { . . . }

48. 2 on 16. 5 (145A): *Echoes*: By 'the last of the echoes of the things of God' [16. 4–5] in the creation he means what earlier he called the 'basest of the material ranks' [cf. 15. 2]. Why these things are called the 'last echo' will be discussed by us more fully in chapter four of *The Divine Names*.[8]

48. 7 on 16. 19 (145C): *And you, my child*: We should inquire why the great Dionysius calls the divine Timothy his 'child'. Either he says this—and this seems most likely—because he surpasses him in years and in his love of wisdom, for which reason he had been consulted by him, as is indicated by the books at hand.[9] For even if St Timothy was a believer before the divine Dionysius, as the Acts of the apostles indicates,[10] nevertheless the great Dionysius was more advanced in profane education. Or another option: he calls him child in imitation of the Lord, who said: 'Children, do you have anything to eat' [John 21: 5]? Or yet another option: because he calls those practising a blameless way of life in accordance with God's commandments 'children', as also Papias indicated in the first book of *The Sayings of the Lord*, and as did Clement of Alexandria, in his *Pedagogy*.[11]

3

49. 5 on 17. 6–7 (164D): *Completely uncontaminated by dissimilarity*: By similarity and equality and identity he means the one and that which makes [other things] one, and this in so far as it is simple and without mixture and without composition. By dissimilar and unequal

[8] *SchDN* 248. 1, 280. 1. Cf. *SchCH* 44. 9.
[9] Cf. *SchDN* 373. 1.
[10] Cf. Acts 17: 14, where Paul leaves Timothy and Silas behind before going on to Athens.
[11] Clem. *paed.* 1. 5 (GCS 12: 96–104); Papias, fr. 8 (ed. Bihlmeyer, 138), a fragment apparently not otherwise attested.

and alterity and mixed and subject to change he means that which is material. It should accordingly be understood that God is the one.

49. 7 on 18. 7 (165A): *Granting initiation*: I understand this to mean that someone enrolled in the clerical order ought not do anything greater than his own proper rank. Rather, he should only do and hand on through his teaching what is proper to his own worth: most certainly he should not reach beyond his own worth. For example, presbyters teach and present the gift [in the liturgy], but do not ordain; deacons teach but do not baptize—for they do not give the Holy Spirit, as not even the deacon Philip could do, as we read in the Acts of the holy apostles [Acts 8: 38]—or offer [the gifts in the liturgy], and so on. So also, those being initiated do only what is allotted, in order that what was said by the divine Paul might be rightly preserved: 'in whatever state each was called, let him remain' [1 Cor. 7: 24].

49. 12 on 18. 17 (165B): *Therefore . . . order*: Note the order and the function of the hierarchy.

Note also that those who approach must first through teaching be purified of the divisive admixtures of sin; then through knowledge of the divine Scripture be illuminated in the doctrines about the knowledge of God; and then be perfected through the 'washing of regeneration' [Titus 3: 5].

4

52. 7 on 20. 10 (177C): *Everything* [lit. **beings**]: Here he indicates all things in creation in brief through the word 'beings', both all intelligible and all visible things. For God made all things out of non-beings, so that they might enjoy his goodness. They enjoy it through his providence, as each one is fit, for the providence of God is the source of the essence of beings.

56. 1 on 21. 16 (180B): *Illustrious*: ⟨ . . . ⟩ 'Roles of conduct' [21. 17] refers to Joshua son of Nun, Gideon, and others [Josh. 5: 13–15, Judg. 6: 12–22]. 'From a profane life to the right way' [21. 17–18] refers to Cornelius the centurion, for he was the first to be converted from among the unbelieving Gentiles [Acts 10]. 'Sacred orders' [21. 18] refers to the thousand thousand in Daniel [Dan. 7: 10], the cherubim in Ezekiel [Ezek. 10], and the seraphim in Isaiah [Isa. 6]. 'Transcendent visions' [21. 19] refers to Paul, 'caught up into the third heaven' [2 Cor. 12: 2] and the Apocalypse of the divine John.

56. 6 on 22. 12 (180D): *Sacred ordinances of the Law*: Note that even the Law is an outline of the other divine ordinance, namely the divine Incarnation in Christ

Note also [22. 15] that the first ordinance was given through angels, as also St Stephen indicated by saying 'you received the Law as delivered by angels and did not keep it' [Acts 7: 53, 58].

57. 1 on 22. 25 (181B): *Gabriel*: Note that the angels were the first to be initiated in the things concerning the Incarnation, as is indicated by the facts about Gabriel, how he taught [Zechariah] about St John [the Baptist] [Luke 1: 19] and preached the good news to the Virgin that she would conceive of the Holy Spirit the enfleshed God Word [Luke 1: 26].

57. 2 on 23. 3 (181B): *The divine and human work of Jesus* [lit. the human theurgy of Jesus]: The Incarnation of Christ is a human theurgy, in which God while in the flesh did divine things. Observe how he here speaks of the 'human theurgy' of Jesus. Through the word 'human' he shows that he became a complete human; and through the word 'theurgy', that he is both God and human, the same [person] effecting the divine signs.[12]

A little later [23. 12] he uses the phrase 'without changing', for he remained what he was eternally.

Notice also [23. 4–5] how he says that in the holy Theotokos Mary 'was born the thearchic mystery of the ineffable formation of God'. By the expression 'formation of God' he shows that God was formed and thereby became human. As it is said: 'the Word became flesh' [John 1: 14]. The mystery of the Incarnation was thearchic in so far as God [$\Theta\epsilon\acute{o}\varsigma$] was the cause and source [$\grave{a}\rho\chi\acute{\eta}$] of those called gods (i.e. angels and the righteous), Jesus being the first whom he called 'God'.[13]

57. 3 on 23. 3 (181B): *To Mary*: { . . . } Note against the Nestorians and Acephalians, that he says Jesus is a 'transcendent cause' [23. 11], in so far as he is the maker of all.

Note also that he says he was born among us 'without change' [23. 12]. For these are not one and the same nature, although the same [one has] the two [natures].

Note also [23. 13–18] that he is both lawgiver and under the law, and that he is given orders by angels in so far as he is human, in the withdrawal into Egypt and in the return from there [Matt. 2: 13, 19–20], {and that the same is also the creator of the angels, for one and the

---

[12] Cf. *SchCH* 72. 6.
[13] For this etymology of 'thearchy', cf. *SchDN* 185. 6, 193. 1, 192. 7.

same Christ accomplished the great mystery of the economy in two natures. For it is said, 'who, though he was in the form of God, did not count equality with God a thing to be grasped, but emptied himself, taking the form of a servant' [Phil. 2: 6–7]. Behold, two forms. For he says here, 'he did not abandon' [23. 12], that is, he 'did not count equality with God a thing to be grasped', namely, he did not disdain as a human to obey even the angels, but 'obediently submitted to the wishes of God the Father as arranged by the angels' [23. 13–14]. For he himself arranged to administer the human race.}[14]

60. 1 on 23. 19 (181D): *Concerning the angel*: Note that the great Dionysius also speaks of the chapter in Luke concerning the angel who comforted the Lord [Luke 22: 43], and that the apostle Paul secretly passed it on as an oral tradition to him and to St Timothy, for Luke wrote his message with the help of [Paul].[15] That he received it secretly is clear from the saying 'I do not need to remind you of the sacred tradition' [23. 17–18].

Notice also the other interpretation [24. 2] where he said that Isaiah called [Jesus] an 'angel of great counsel' [Isa. 9: 6 LXX]. He says that to be named a 'begotten child' [23. 2] befits his flesh.

Note also why he is called an angel [24. 3–4]. { . . . }

5

60. 5 on 25. 5 (196B): *Reserve the 'angelic' order*: He says that only the final order of the intelligibles is rightly called by the name 'angels'. It holds differently in the case of the superior ones, of which he here names only some [25. 6–8]. In the next chapter he recounts in a mystical fashion all the nine orders; but now he simply though accurately says only that the higher orders understand whatever the inferior have learned through enlightenment and that they also know other things which are unknown to the inferior ones. Although this is the case, nevertheless at times all the intelligible orders are also called 'angels' through use of the name in a generic sense. This is why it says in Psalm 103: 'Bless the Lord, all his angels' [Ps. 103: 20], and in the 104th, 'who makest the winds thy angels . . .' [Ps. 104: 4]. The

---

[14] The bracketed materials are not present in Syr. They may have been omitted for their manifest dyophysite sentiments.

[15] John is here referring to a well-known tradition which goes back to the 2nd cent. See e.g. Werner Georg Kümmel, *Introduction to the New Testament* (Nashville, 1975), 147–8.

reasoning is not however reciprocal, for the inferior ones are not named after the higher ones.

Note also that the inferior [angels] are initiated into mysteries by the superior powers.

61. 4 on 25. 16 (196C): *Our own*: Having himself been filled with these contemplative mysteries, the sacred Dionysius reveals them, saying that the final order (i.e. that called 'angels'), like a pedagogue taking a child by the hand, uplifts the human hierarchs of the churches toward God, whereas the higher orders initiate into mysteries this lower order, our pedagogue, as well as those in higher grades, treating them all as inferior.

6

64. 4 on 26. 12 (200D): *Sacred-initiator*: When he refers to his 'sacred-initiator' he often means either the divine apostle Paul or St Hierotheus, as it was explained in *The Divine Names*.[16] Here I think he is speaking of none other than St Paul, for he alone was taken up into the 'third heaven' [2 Cor. 12: 2], and initiated into these things.

64. 7 on 26. 15 (200D): *Most holy (thrones)*: That one should take this first triadic and godlike source of order as the one which observes God conceptually and worthily [is clear] from Ezekiel [Ezek. 1: 26], who says that the throne is first, on which God is seen. Immediately next are the divine cherubim. According to Isaiah [Isa. 6: 1–7], the most holy seraphim stand in a circle contemplating God. These things indicate their high condition, next to God and beyond all others. These things are clarified in much the same way in the Revelation of St John the apostle, evangelist, and theologian [cf. Rev. 4: 2, 8].

64. 10 on 27. 1 (201A): *Authorities*: He lists the next two holy, triadic orders of intelligibles from the lower to the higher, for the dominions are first, followed by the powers and then by the authorities. But he here puts the authorities first and then places the dominions in the middle. As for the third ministering triad, the principalities are first, followed by the archangels and then by the angels. In the following chapter he does not recount them in this order; but here he proceeds from lower to higher.

The apostle mentions certain angelic orders in his letters to the Romans [Rom. 8: 38] and to the Ephesians [Eph. 1: 21], but he does

---

[16] See *SchDN* 228. 2, 236. 2.

not lay down this order. The great Dionysius thus shows that the divine apostle passed these things on to the saints in secret.[17]

7

65. 5 on 27. 13 (205B): *Similarity to what God is* [lit. **deiform habits**]: He ascribes 'deiform habits' to the divine minds. But one should not for this reason assume that the great Dionysius is saying that these virtues are present in the intelligibles as an accident, as they are in human beings. These virtues are not something present in a substrate or some sort of added quality. Accident and the substrate are excluded [from consideration], as well as every synthesis and the formlessness of matter. For if it were one thing in another, like an accident in a substrate, then that essence would not in and of itself be alive, nor would it be able to be deified in and of itself (to the extent that it is possible), through a single order which is preserved as one thing in another. Therefore, the habits which are said to be in them are essential and not like an accident in a substrate—and this, by reason of their immateriality. For this reason also the great Dionysius says below in the fourth chapter of *The Ecclesiastical Hierarchy* that habits among them are existential.[18]

65. 6 on 27. 13 (205B): *Conditions* [lit. **habits**]: Note that the divine powers have deiformity as a habit. A habit is an abiding quality.[19] For this reason it is here demonstrated that [angels] are endowed with free will, in so far as they have obtained their virtue by habit. Ammon of Adrianople presents this more fully in his treatises *On the Resurrection* which he wrote against Origen.[20]

65. 9 on 28. 7 (205D): *Defect*: He considers the thrones to be a certain lofty nature which God placed right next to himself. They in no way attend to material concerns: this is signified by the expression 'they do not give in to earthly matters' [cf. 28. 7]. 'Giving in' [ὕφεσις] is synonymous with 'yielding' [ἔνδοσις] and 'inclining' [νεῦσις] to what lies below it. Rather, the thrones have a nature which lifts them up to God, one which casts its attention upwards. ⟨ . . . ⟩

68. 1 on 28. 11 (205D): *They bear God*: Note that he also calls the rank of

---

[17] Cf. *SchCH* 60. 1.
[18] *EH* 4. 3. 9 (101. 12).
[19] Cf. *SchDN* 205. 2, 288. 13.
[20] For Ammon, see the notes to *SchEH* 176. 3.

the holy thrones 'god-bearing', in so far as it intelligibly bears the seated God. But observe! The blessed Basil of Cappadocia called the flesh [of Christ] 'god-bearing'.[21] We must therefore consider how this can be so. The flesh of the Lord was united in both essence and person to God the Word. For this reason the Fathers also said that [the Word] 'bore flesh' and that he was 'clothed in flesh'.[22] Is there anything strange then if also his flesh is said to be 'god-bearing'? It does after all bear God the Word by way of an inseparable union and is called and in fact is *his* flesh. In an ineffable and unthinkable manner these thrones have God in themselves by grace and for this reason they are called 'god-bearers'. { ... }

68. 6 on 29. 2 (208B): *Self-moved* [ταυτοκίνητον]: This saint says that their movement is ταυτοκίνητον in so far as it is without change or variation and is ever the same. Movements in their case are ceaseless intellectual activities, for they are minds which are unable to keep still. Note also the expression 'immutable love for God' [29. 2]. Concerning this, read the fourth chapter of *The Divine Names* and the eighth chapter of the present book.[23]

68. 7 on 29. 5 (208B): *'Contemplative'*: Note how it is that these holy orders are said to be 'contemplative'.

Note also that they do not acquire knowledge of God through symbols or through contemplating the Scriptures, as do we.

69. 4 on 29. 11 (208C): *God's working* [lit. **theurgic**]: Note that being similar to the Lord Jesus is theurgic (i.e. it causes those being made similar to be gods).[24]

Note also how these orders are made similar to Christ without mediation and apart from symbols. Rather, they received this from [Christ] himself.

69. 7 on 29. 16 (208C): *Analyse*: By 'understanding of varieties' [cf. 29. 16] he means an explanation of the complex sacred tradition which both interprets and clarifies. This type of understanding is needed by the lower orders, as he explains in what follows.[25] Humans also need it, but to a greater extent. It simply is not possible to understand these [varieties] apart from explanations which break down the varied

---

[21] See e.g. Basil, *de spir. sanc.* 12 (PG 32: 85), *epis.* 261. 2 (PG 32: 969).

[22] For 'to bear flesh' (σαρκοφορεῖν), see e.g. Ign. *ad Smyrn.* 5. 2 (SC 10: 158) and Clem. *paed.* 3. 1 (GCS 12: 237. 7). For 'clothed in flesh' (σάρκα ἐνδύσασθαι), see e.g. Hipp. *antichr.* 4 (PG 10: 752B).

[23] *DN* 9. 4 (209. 9), with *SchDN* 305. 9, *CH* 13. 4 (49. 6), with *SchCH* 101. 4.

[24] Cf. *SchCH* 57. 2, *SchDN* 185. 6, 193. 1, 192. 7.

[25] *CH* 7. 3 (30. 1–4).

wisdom of the holy contemplations—neither for us nor for those things which stand below the first three orders.[26] For this reason he says that the first member of each of the lower orders acts as hierarch [for its order], and that no other power [can do this], whereas God himself alone acts as hierarch for the hierarchy of those ranks which are highest, something which no other power [can do].

72. 5 on 30. 6 (209B): *Into the heavens (in a human form)*: {Note against the Basileans (i.e. the Nestorians)} that Jesus Christ, he who was raised according to his human [nature], is himself the Lord of all the intelligibles and the King of Glory.[27] Those who are being initiated learn this from those who say, 'Lift up the gates, O Principalities', and from those who ask, 'Who is the King of Glory'? and again from those who hear, 'The Lord of Dominions', and so forth [Ps. 24: 9–10 LXX].

Against the Acephalians and Eutychians, note that although he is the 'Lord of Dominions', he is nevertheless flesh and manifestly human, since the principalities one after another were astonished by this strange event.

72. 6 on 30. 7 (209C): *Divine work* [lit. theurgy]: Nicely does he call the economy [of salvation] for us a 'theurgy'.[28] For how true it is that all the works [ἔργα] effected in the economy of our Lord were of God [θεοῦ]: the holy birth, the healings, the signs accompanying his passion, and the resurrection.

73. 3 on 31. 7 (212A): *Circles*: He says that these first sources of order both stand still and rotate without intermediary around God. We should clarify how it is that they both stand still and are moved in a circle around God, as if in a dance. His starting-point for this is from Isaiah, who says first 'and the Seraphim stood encircling him, six wings to each one . . .', but then adds 'and with two they flew' [Isa. 6: 2]. But how do they stand and at the same time fly in a circle? I think we should understand this as follows.

Every mind which gives off light from God the cause of all, because it gives off its light only from the creator, is said to be moved around him as if around an axis. (Its movement, however, is not spatial, but rather intelligent and living.) Such a circular movement is an attribute of mind. Everything which thinks does so either because it is mind or because it in some sense participates in mind. For this reason, accord-

---

[26] Reading ὑποβεβηκότα for ὑπερβεβηκότα.

[27] The materials in brackets are not in Syr. A version is present in FA, but instead of 'Basileans' it reads 'Sabellians'.

[28] Cf. *SchCH* 57. 2.

ing as it is mind and thinks it can be said to be moved. This motion is thought to be circular inasmuch as it is reflexive, and being around him, in this manner he thinks himself and that which is before him, from which he gives off light. As then it was produced by an act of God's will, it will be around him (which is to say, around desire and love for God), as around an axis.

Secondary things are not united to those before them, but what happens is similar to a certain dance. The things which have been begotten, by their longing again to be in their own place, look at all sides of the one who generated them. That which has been returned intellectually to the things before it introduces the notion of a circular motion. Since, therefore, God is everywhere, those who everywhere follow along with him, out of their desire contemplate him eternally— they exalt in that one and dance around as if they were at a party.

Mind is said to be in itself and to strive toward itself. Whatever is in itself and seeks immortality, this has standing. In its being (which is being in an immortal fashion) it is understood to stand. In its striving toward itself, it is moved, not wishing to be dispersed in a sense into the things which are external to him [i.e. God] and into material thoughts. According as it is ταυτοκίνητον, it does not stand still but is moved—in accordance with an essence which is ever the same, it has standing but not motion. Therefore, the desire for God and the circular motion around him, as if around an axis, is an impulse natural to each mind. It is like circular motion around a sign or axis from which it subsists. Indeed, through a natural necessity each being dances its dance around God, inasmuch as it is desirous of being. Thus also all things are around the king of all; and because of that [king] all things [exist] and that [king] is the cause of all good things.

That which he said, that the first things dance 'without inter-mediary' [31. 7] around God (in so far as he has nothing before him)— this signifies that the second and third things (i.e. the perceptibles) analogously dance around God (as has been said), if only through intermediaries which are before them.

76. 7 on 32. 8 (212C): *A monad:* According to the author, not only does the Trisagion hymn [31. 21–2, citing Isa. 6: 3] and the voice praising God from his place [31. 19–20, citing Ezek. 3: 12] indicate that know-ledge and praise of God have been imparted to the inferior orders; but also, it signals something else in addition. The saying also indicates that we say that God is a henad and a thrice-hypostatic monad [32. 8–9] and that he provides providentially for all things, from the first to

the last things of the earth, encompassing all in a manner that is
ἀσχέτως [cf. 32. 12], which is to say, in a manner beyond being, containing them not through a corporeal providence, but through one that
is divine.

{The impious Evagrius also said that he is a henad and a monad in
the third chapter of his second century.[29] He is monad, since the divine
is simple and undivided: because of this he is a monad. Speaking
mathematically, a monad is simple and without composition. He is
'henad' because the holy Trinity is united with itself by nature, and
unites all those who draw near to it, according to the saying in the
Gospel, 'that they might be one, as we are one' [John 17: 11].}[30]

8

77. 5 on 33. 2 (237C): *Harsh* [lit. implacable] *dominion*: Here he
piously examines an error of those Greek philosophers who call a
certain three individual powers 'implacable', powers which proceeded
into existence from three other powers prior to them, but were not in
fact fashioned by God.[31] They also say that these implacable powers
are beneath those intelligible powers which precede them, restraining
them and in some sense resisting them, able to check those prior to
themselves and they themselves lest they fall into matter, and for this
reason weaker than those which preceded them, inasmuch as they
need to restrain themselves in order not to fall. This in brief is their
opinion.

The great Dionysius, however, wisely opposes all this. He says that
they were created by God and that they bear a 'resemblance' [33. 5]
to him in dominion, just as we also were created in his likeness [Gen.
1: 26]. He says further that by reason of their dominion they have
implacability against 'every defect' [33. 3]—in the sense that they cut it
off and sever it, not permitting desire for sensible things to overpower
themselves. [He does] not [mean this as those Greek philosophers do]
that they restrain those before them. ⟨ . . . ⟩

77. 7 on 33. 12 (240A): *Far from abandoning*: Note how he continually
says that the superior powers impart some of their own things to those

---

[29] Evagr. Pont. *keph. gnost.* 2. 3 (PO 28/1: 61, version S²).
[30] The materials in brackets are present in FA, though lacking in Syr. FA does not, however, refer to Evagrius as 'impious'.
[31] Omitting φῶτα.

after them and that the powers empower those which lay beneath them. We know that an angel was described as strengthening Daniel [Dan. 6: 22] and others, and, greater than all, even our Lord Jesus Christ himself, in so far as he was human, as it is written in the gospel of Luke [Luke 22: 42].

80. 7 on 34. 5 (240C): *Instructors*: Note that priests transmitted these things to the great Dionysius. { . . . }

9

85. 6 on 38. 11 (260D): *We ourselves*: Note in this passage more than any other how the inopportune and indiscriminate ignorance of some is curbed, those bold to say that these divine books were written by Apollinaris. From the people whom he mentions [in the body of these works] they do not infer the antiquity of the author, instead they say that Dionysius' greetings [at the beginning of these works] are spurious. [They do] not [recognize these works as authentic] even when he here says that he was converted from among the idolaters— and yet, Apollinaris was never one of them.[32]

88. 3 on 39. 7 (261B): *Took charge* [lit. by lot]: Note the interpretation of the words of the song of Moses: 'When the Most High gave to the nations their inheritance, when he separated the sons of Adam, he fixed the bounds of the peoples according to the number of the angels of God. For the Lord's portion is his people, and Jacob his allotted heritage' [Deut. 32: 8–9]. One must not suppose, he says, that the nations were divided up between different gods or angels. Israel did not obtain their God by lot, whereas [the nations obtained] other angels peculiar to themselves, so that the [latter] could not in any way serve God. It is as if we were to say: such and such a nation obtained such and such an angel and for this reason God does not care about [that angel's] nation, or for this reason the angel of that nation has not enough spare time for any other [nation] in God's presence. It is not the case that 'on an equal footing or even in a hostile manner' [39. 7–8] God received such and such a nation, and each angel in turn, its own nation—as it is written in Isaiah, the devil said that he has in himself mountains toward the north (i.e. the nations) and that he opposes God and is similar to the Most High [Isa. 14: 13–14 LXX]. [Instead we say

[32] That Dionysius is from the Greeks is also asserted in *SchCH* 32. 2. That Apollinaris was not the author of the corpus is also argued in *SchEH* 176. 4.

that] all things are servants of God who in turn rules them all. He honours those whom he knows and for this reason he is said to rule them, even if they have an angel standing over them as Israel has Michael [Dan. 10]. { . . . }

10

92. 2 on 41. 1–2 (273C): *Primary, middle:* Note that each of our minds has first and middle and last orders so that we might understand these three orders around God. We should understand this as follows: every mind has an essence, by which first of all it exists; then it has power, by which it endures, and finally it has activity, by which it piously does what is proper to itself. He clarifies these things in the next chapter.[33] { . . . }

13

96. 4 on 43. 21–44. 1 (300B): *Someone could well be puzzled:* Since this appears to contradict what has been said. For he said earlier that the lower ones are initiated by those [immediately] superior to them, not by those highest of all; in other words, that the third order is initiated by the middle order; the middle order, by the one higher than all.[34] [There is no real contradiction here], for these [two questions] were asked and resolved in different fashions.

97. 3 on 45. 15 (301C): *Throughout nature:* { . . . } We should understand that among the intelligibles virtues are not accidental, as they are among us, but that God is a living virtue, *per se* perfect and self-sufficient, because in a manner beyond being he has being and in order to give of himself he goes out into the intelligibles which exist from [his virtue] in so far as it is a cause.[35] For this reason God is fount of that virtue which is both living and deifies those who partake of it, according as it is permitted. But nevertheless, by reason of his providential care he goes out in a procession into the intelligibles which took their being from him, and does not refuse to be the peak and perfection of minds in this way.[36] Therefore it is not in an accidental fashion (as is the case with us) that the minds have virtue: for example, moderation

---

[33] *CH* 11. 2 (41. 20–42. 1).   [34] *CH* 10. 1 (40. 7–11).
[35] Cf. *SchCH* 65. 5.   [36] For 'peak', cf. *SchCH* 33. 10.

through discipline or through learning, or righteousness, or temperance through self-control, or courage through health of body and sinews. For virtue is not in these minds as one thing in another thing; rather, doing what is appropriate and ceaselessly attending to God and themselves, this among them is virtue 'which imitates God' [45. 20]. Nevertheless, he preserves the order (as if of one thing in another), as in the verse: 'Your soul lives in me',[37] which is to say, the communication of teaching.[38] The accident in a substrate (which does not exist) is there, for those are without composition and immaterial and their forms are alive, but not as in matter.[39]

101. 1 on 48. 9 (305B): *As for the powers of the second rank*: One should observe how he here says that each incorporeal power differs not a little in respect of its 'likeness to God' [48. 10]. The highest minds have a great deal of likeness to God, while the remaining minds have the remaining, lower [measure of likeness to God], as much as order requires. [This principle applies] right down to the lowest [minds]. More so even than these [is the measure of divine likeness possessed] by our souls, for our soul is left far behind all the minds.

Moreover, divine enlightenment, having been 'concentrated' [48. 11] or rather contracted, is received in accordance with each one's distance from God, divine enlightenment itself in some sense 'concentrating' its own manifestation into its 'unknown' and simple 'union' [48. 12]. The reason for this is that God himself is unknowable—unknowable, not because there is a certain subtle thought which we cannot know, but rather by reason of a certain unitary unknowing which simply and absolutely cannot be comprehended by us.[40]

101. 4 on 49. 6 (308A): *Preserves them immobile*: Note that God, the creator of absolutely all conceptual beings, both 'encompasses' [49. 5] the first beings and 'preserves' them in 'immutability' and 'unchangeability' [49. 6]. One should know that they are already 'immutable' in

---

[37] Cf. 1 Sam. 1: 26, 20: 3, 25: 26 (LXX).

[38] Reading τάξιν for τάξις.

[39] At its conclusion this scholion bears the following remark, not present in FA and clearly subsequent to John's labours: 'The one who wrote these marginalia understood these things. Keep in mind my remarks three folios back. Here also the expression "those who desire" (45. 19) supports my understanding [of angelic free will]. The fathers also understood it this way, and [the earlier scholiast] himself shows his approval of the free will of the angels, as you will shortly find.' This later scholiast is concerned with the free will of angels. He first refers his readers back to his prior comments on this subject, either *SchCH* 89. 4 or 88. 4 (neither of which is by John), notes another word in the corpus which supports his view, and then directs his readers to the coming comments of an earlier scholiast, meaning most likely *SchCH* 101. 4 (a scholion present in both FA and Syr and thus almost certainly by John).   [40] Reading ἀγνωσίαν for ἀθανασίαν, with FA.

respect of the principles of their existence: for example, in their immortality, in their life, the latter being that in accordance with which they
are endowed with being, and in their being light. In these respects they
are essentially immutable. But lest they be turned toward alien desires,
inasmuch as they are endowed with free will, God encompasses and
preserves them. The act of attending to him pertains to an intellectual
choice [on their part], whereas the act of persevering in this pertains to
the aid of God, inasmuch as all things stand in need of God's help.

15

105. 6 on 53. 8–9 (329D): *Powers of sense perception*: Note the difference
between the sense perception of irrational beings as compared with the
sense perception of rational beings (i.e. us humans). Irrational beings
have acute senses and it is through these that they survive even though
they are not endowed with reason. Our senses, however, are not so
good, for it is not through these that we survive, but rather through
our intellect. For this reason also, even after death we shall exist,
inasmuch as we are an intellectual soul. As for the angels, they do not
have sense perception: rather, our senses are a dim image [of their
superior ones]. { ... }

108. 5 on 54. 6 (332C): *The heart*: We take it for granted that the heart is
like a central point which receives life before [any other part of the
human].[41] The reason for our assuming this: the divine Basil said that
the heart was created first, that then the rest of the body was fashioned,
proceeding outwards as if from a central point, so that this life then
pervaded the whole of the body.[42] This happens because an innate heat
enlivens the body, or perhaps it is the spirit or even the blood itself—at
any rate, it is the heart which is the fount of all three of these. For this
reason certain people have thought that everything which is able to
impart life is primarily situated here, even if it exists everywhere in the
body and is not contained in a single place, not being circumscribed in
a place or contained by the body. The same holds in the case of the
invisible orders. After the fashion of servants they exercise their providential care either for everything at once or for each thing considered
individually. We should think of them as if they resided in the midst of
the heart, like the central point of the fount of life—although in fact

---

[41] Reading $\pi\rho o\epsilon i\lambda\eta\pi\tau\alpha\iota$ for $\pi\epsilon\rho\iota\epsilon i\lambda\eta\pi\tau\alpha\iota$.
[42] Bas. *hom in Ps.* 1. 3 (PG 29: 213D).

they are unrestrained and are not circumscribed in a place or in one of the bodily parts of those things which they encompass and for which they exercise their care at the bidding of God.[43]

109. 2 on 55. 1 (333A): *All things*: In the fourth chapter of *The Divine Names*, we have clarified fully the meaning of 'intelligible' and 'intelligent'.[44] But now the great Dionysius himself clarifies the meaning of these terms. The 'intelligible' is that which is thought. This is here rightly said to enlighten. The 'intelligent', on the other hand, is that which thinks. This is that which is enlightened. To summarize, the higher beings are intelligible and the lower beings are intelligent: that which thinks is subordinate to that which is thought. The divine nature 'intelligibly enlightens' [55. 1], whereas the angelic nature is 'intelligently enlightened' [55. 1].

112. 1 on 55. 19 (333C): *Instant* [lit. apart from time]: It is appropriate that he should use the expression 'apart from time'. In the case of beings endowed with sense perception, things are known in time and after the fact, whereas in the case of incorporeal and intelligible beings [acts of understanding] are accomplished 'apart from time' and eternally and without any delay. { ... }

112. 12 on 57. 8 (336D): *Tracks*: Note from this passage the character of the lion. For he says that the lion, when it wishes to elude hunters, walks and wipes out its tracks with its tail in order that they not be spotted. For this reason it is also said of God: 'Thy way was through the sea, thy path through the great waters, yet thy footprints were unseen' [Ps. 77: 19]. Like a passage through waters and the tracks of a lion, the journeys of God are not preserved.

18

113. 10 on 59. 10 (340B): *Regarding their transcendent*: { ... } It should be understood that the saints after their conversions were not embarrassed to use the titles which they had when they were still Greeks. For you can see here that he refers to himself as the 'Areopagite', even as the divine Justin signed his treatise *Against the Greeks* with the name 'Justin the Philosopher'.[45]

---

[43] Reading ἀκρατήτας for ἀκρατεῖς.

[44] *SchDN* 240. 3.

[45] The latter half of this scholion ('It should be understood . . . "Justin the Philosopher"') is found in Syr. but only at the beginning of the scholia on the *CH*, as a comment on the title. A nearly identical version which is not in the Syriac recension is found at *SchDN* 185. 6.

The Ecclesiastical Hierarchy

1

116. 2 on 63. 6 (372A): *Traditions*: Note that he received his understanding of hierarchy from tradition.

116. 5 on 63. 12 (372A): *Divine mind*: It should be noted against the Nestorians that a mind is also attributed to God.[1] ⟨ . . . ⟩

117. 2 on 64. 15 (372C): *Of angels*: Note that he is speaking of the nine orders and that now he says that he has already named them in *The Divine Hierarchy*.[2]

117. 11 on 65. 18 (373B): *The Conceptual* [lit. **Intelligible**]: It should be noted that his work *Concerning the Intelligible and the Perceptible* has not been found by us.

117. 14 on 65. 23 (373C): *Perfect* [lit. **most universal**]: By 'universal' he means those things which are more comprehensive. For this reason he says that (inasmuch as each and every order is called a 'hierarchy') the more primary and original 'total' [65. 24] of every hierarchy is another hierarchy. For example, the bishop is the hierarchy of the hierarchy of the presbyters (i.e. their order), as it is he who must know, purify, illuminate, and perfect. Similarly, the archdeacon is the hierarchy of the hierarchy of the deacons, as it is he who must know the liturgical activities. The same holds for the other ranks as well.

120. 2 on 66. 10 (373D): *Obvious (to itself)*: Note that the holy Trinity knows its own subsistence, as something 'obvious', even as we now say that it alone understands its own essence.

120. 9 on 67. 3 (376B): *Via the intellect* [lit. **intelligibly**]: One must understand how it is internally and not externally that the enlightenments of God move the divine minds. He says that God enlightens them 'intelligibly'. That which thinks is intelligent and that which is thought is intelligible, that which is thought being in some sense nourishment or sustenance for that which thinks.[3] Now then,

---

[1] The Dionysian text refers to Christ as a 'mind' (νοῦς).

[2] *The Divine Hierarchy* (i.e. *The Celestial Hierarchy*). Does this mean that the titles of the Dionysian texts were not yet fixed in John's time? Cf. *SchCH* 29. 1.

[3] Cf. *SchDN* 205. 2, 240. 3.

inasmuch as the incorporeal beings are minds, God, being himself intelligible and thought by them, to the extent that they can, internally enlightens them, the [incorporeal] mind thinking and being nourished in the process.

121. 5 on 68. 2 (377A): *Symbolical*: Note that the hierarchy among humans is symbolic and makes use of perceptible objects. { . . . }

2

121. 10 on 68. 22 (392A): *The sacred words*: He says that three things are needed for 'the starting-point of the commandments' [68. 21–2]: reception of the divine Scriptures, catechesis of the divine faith, and rebirth through divine baptism. He has rightly shown [69. 2–4] that the most honourable and distinguished movement of the mind is love for God, and that our divine creation (i.e. our rebirth through baptism, through which we begin to exist in a divine manner) is a certain beginning of love for God. Our creation from seed, even if it takes place only by way of the creator, God, is nevertheless physical, whereas the creation which comes from baptism is divine, for it is 'not of blood nor of the will of man' [John 1: 13]. In physical birth it is necessary first to come into being and only then 'to produce and experience' [69. 8, 10] appropriate things: for example, humans do their own sorts of things, whereas beasts in a similar way do what befits themselves. In the same way, in the divine rebirth through baptism is it necessary first to come into existence by God, and then to practise love for him and the other things required for right living.

124. 1 on 69. 3–4 (392A): *As our famous teacher*: He is speaking of the blessed Hierotheus, as he has often indicated in the preceding discussion.[4]

124. 3 on 69. 6 (392B): *Our divine existence*: That is, rebirth through baptism.

124. 21 on 71. 7 (393C): *To sing a hymn*: Note that hymns can be offered to God out of the entire Scripture, not only out of the Psalms of David. { . . . }

125. 6 on 71. 20 (396A): *Remove his garments*: Here [i.e. at this point in the baptismal ceremony] he does not remove all the clothing, but takes off a single cloak, as [Dionysius] shows in what follows [72. 9]. { . . . }

125. 7 on 72. 5 (396B): *He turns him eastward*: ⟨ . . . ⟩ Note that at

---

[4] e.g. *DN* 2. 9 (133. 13), with *SchDN* 228. 2, and *DN* 3. 2 (139. 17–18).

that time the deacons alone divested them for baptism, whereas the presbyters did the remaining rites, which now the deacons do—[all this] you can read a few lines earlier [72. 1].

In what follows you will also discover that by 'liturgists' he means the deacons, and by 'priests', the presbyters.[5]

128. 1 on 73. 8 (397A): *Rises once more to the contemplation of primary things*: What he means is as follows. The bishop is an image of the God of all. God remains eternally in his own unity and sameness and is inseparably grounded in himself; nevertheless, for the salvation of all, through providential processions he extends to all the enlightenments of his goodness and is present to all while yet not departing from his own foundation. In the same way, in symbolic imitation of God (inasmuch as that is possible), while remaining in his own state (i.e. the ecclesiastical source), in his providential love for humanity the bishop proceeds toward secondary things—that is, in his descent to the one being returned, he teaches him, anoints and seals him, and imparts the gift of baptism. Inasmuch as they are liturgical, all of these things are secondary to his source. When he has completed these secondary things, he returns to the altar. In this he symbolizes God: for the salvation of the one who approaches, in his providential care he goes out to secondary things, and yet he does not depart from doing his own things and from being among his own things (i.e. among the heights of the contemplation of God). ⟨ . . . ⟩

128. 5 on 74. 8 (397C): *In The Conceptual* [lit. **Intelligible**]: Note that he wrote a treatise on *The Intelligible and the Perceptible*. Note its contents as well.

128. 7 on 74. 15 (397D): *Intelligent beings*: He says that the intelligibles have two vices. They either fall away fully from the divine light on account of their love of vice. Or, they despise the measure of enlightenment which they have been granted and proudly attempt to reach beyond this, and because they are too weak to grasp something beyond their power, they completely fail to obtain even that measure of the unchanging divine light which had been granted them.

129. 6 on 75. 11 (400B): *Self-awareness*: Note that the first gift anyone receives from this precise teaching is the knowledge of oneself, in order to keep the injunction 'attend to yourself' [1 Tim. 4: 16]. The divine Basil also said this.[6] In this way he will imitate the angels who know themselves.

---

[5] *EH* 2. 2. 7 (72. 9–11), as well as *EH* 5 *passim* (104–14).

[6] Cf. Bas. *hom.* 3. 6 (PG 31: 212B), as well as *SchCH* 44. 6.

132. 3 on 77. 12 (401D): *Who, as God*: Note that Christ is God, against the Nestorians.

132. 9 on 78. 2 (404B): *Brings the soul into an invisible realm*: Some say that this invisible realm is Hades, that is, the unformed and invisible separation of the soul into places unseen by those endowed only with sense perception.[7]

132. 10 on 78. 4 (404B): *Change from its corporeal state*: Often the body is resolved not only into worms, but also into other animals. Observe that he also calls such a transformation 'change'. { . . . }

132. 11 on 78. 7–8 (404B): *The divine* [lit. thearchic] *death*: Note that he calls the Lord's three days in the grave a 'thearchic death'. Note also that he applies to the Word the Lord's saying, 'The ruler of this world is coming, and he will find nothing in me' [John. 14: 30]. By 'ruler of the world' [78. 10] and of the diabolical choices in humans he means Satan, 'who has the power of death', according to the apostle [Heb. 2: 14], who found no personal transgression in Christ, for 'he did no sin, nor deceit', as Isaiah said [Isa. 53: 9]. For this reason 'it was not possible for him to be ruled by death', as Peter said [Acts 2: 24], 'but he alone was pronounced free among the dead', according to David [Ps. 88: 5 LXX].

133. 2 on 78. 17 (404D): *How to recognize intelligently*: I suppose that it is by reason of his modesty that the great Dionysius is here silent, pretending that he does not know these things. For he was worthy of the spirit of foreknowledge, as he makes clear in his letter to the evangelist John.[8] Be that as it may, this passage seems to me to signify that those who have been deemed worthy of the Holy Spirit and have been united to him in purity (as the apostle says), inasmuch as they are wholly the 'sweet odour of Christ' [2 Cor. 2: 15]—such as these, I say, perceive his presence in their speaking in tongues, in their having received the gift of prophecy, in their working of cures, and in as many other things as were mentioned in the Acts and by the divine Paul.

It is also possible to understand this passage in another way. Those who understand spiritual things (inasmuch as they themselves are spiritual) and compare them to other spiritual things, will also understand the divine and spiritual sweet odour as follows. Paul says [2 Cor. 2: 14–15] that those who preach the Gospel are the 'sweet odour of

---

[7] There is here and in Dionysius (78. 2) a pun on 'Hades' (ἅδης) and 'unformed' (ἀειδής). According to Photius, cod. 234 (ed. Henry), 5: 100, Methodius in his *On the Resurrection* ascribed this pun to Origen.

[8] *EP* 10 (208–10).

Christ', inasmuch as they are being led 'from life' (i.e. from faith) 'to life' (i.e. to forgiveness through baptism) and make manifest the gift of the Holy Spirit and the kingdom of heaven through their divine deeds (i.e. their deeds which arise from that intelligible and sweet odour). For this very reason, in his Apocalypse the divine John saw a vision in which the prayers of the just were bowls full of incense [Rev. 5: 8]. On the other hand, sinful deeds are the foul odours of the devil, even as it is written in the Psalms [Ps. 38: 5], 'My wounds grow foul and fester because of my foolishness' (i.e. my sin). For this reason also Christ is said by the Scripture to be 'myron which has been poured out' [S. of S. 1. 2]. Moreover, the Lord 'smelled the fragrant odour' of the offering of the just man, Noah [Gen. 8: 21]. In the same way, the Gospel is for some (i.e. the believers) the fragrance of life, whereas for the unbelievers it is the fragrance of death: that is to say, for the unbelievers and the impious, it is a 'fragrance unto death' [2 Cor. 2: 16], inasmuch as it refutes their deeds and condemns them to Gehenna. It is like fine myron which at the same time both pleases humans and kills pigs, inasmuch as they cannot bear its sharp odour. He treats these things fully in the fourth chapter of this work which is on the myron.[9] { ... }

3

136. 1 on 79. 3 (424C): *Teacher of the sacraments*: He means St Hierotheus.

136. 5 on 79. 13 (424D): *The perfection, of the*: Note that it is impossible to be perfected without partaking of communion.

136. 16 on 80. 19 (425D): *Put*: This is in accordance with the custom which prevails in Rome. For only seven deacons serve the altar there. I suspect that he means by 'the chosen' [80. 18] these seven deacons, adding that the others perform another service.

Note also from this passage the antiquity of the father.

Note also that 'with the deacons the presbyters put the bread' [80. 18–19]. This takes place everywhere, whenever the deacons are few. But I suspect that this is what always happens in Rome, inasmuch as only seven chosen deacons serve the altar. Perhaps the seven chosen deacons were distinguished from the others by their excellent way of life.

[9] *EH* 4. 3. 4 (98. 23–99. 14).

136. 17 on 80. 21 (425C): *Universal*: Note that even then a certain symbol of faith was proclaimed, or rather an account of the faith and summary of it, which at that time they accepted.[10]

136. 20 on 81. 6 (425D): *And lifts into view*: That is, he makes manifest the things being praised (e.g. that Christ did this or that Christ did that). He also points up the divine gifts in these things (i.e. that they are for the forgiveness of sins, eternal life, and other such mysterious things). On the other hand, perhaps the meaning of the expression 'into view' is that the holy gifts are uncovered only after the prayers, having been covered until the time of communion. Or perhaps he is speaking of the lifting up and elevation of the single blessing of the divine bread, which the priest effects with the words, 'holy things for the holy ones'. You will discover which of these interpretations is more correct when he speaks of these things near the end of this chapter.[11]

137. 4 on 81. 24 (428B): *Reminds*: He is referring here to the fact that 'after supper, he took bread . . .' [cf. Luke 22: 19–20] and that his death is announced until he comes, according to the apostle [1 Cor. 11: 26] and the Lord himself, who said 'Do this in remembrance of me . . .' [1 Cor. 11: 24–5].

Note also that by 'original symbol' [81. 24] of the current mysteries he means the mysterious supper of the Lord, and that the partaking does not profit the one who partakes of the bread and the cup in an unworthy manner—or to be more accurate, it is received 'unto his judgement', according to the apostle [1 Cor. 11: 29, 34]. { . . . }

137. 7 on 82. 7 (428C): *From the effects (to the causes)*: That is, from the things done visibly to those which are invisible and mysterious, which are the causes and archetypes of the sensible deeds. By 'causes' he means those things which are causes derivatively.

Alternatively, by the expression 'from the effects to the causes' he means from the perceptible symbols to those which are intelligible and intelligent, that is, from those which are less perfect to those which are more perfect: for example, from the types to the image, and from that to the truth, even as the things of the Old Testament are shadows, those of the New, an image, and the state of the things to come, the truth.

---

[10] For Dionysius as a witness to the introduction of the Nicene Creed into the liturgy, see Ch. 1. The tenor of John's comments would suggest that he was aware of the novelty of the practice, though he was interested to note that a 'certain symbol' was recited in the apostolic age, if not the Nicene Creed itself.

[11] *EH* 3. 3. 12 (92. 15–20), with *SchEH* 148. 6, suggesting that the second interpretation is the more accurate.

140. 11 on 83. 22 (429D): *The beloved*: I think he means the Apocalypse of the divine John, or his Gospel, which is even more likely.

141. 13 on 86. 1 (433B): *Itself profane*: ⟨ . . . ⟩ Note that he classifies among the possessed those who impenitently remain subject to the seductions of the flesh (e.g. fornicators), those fond of shows, and those who do the like. When the divine apostle wrote of such people as these, he charged us not to eat with them [1 Cor. 5: 11]. He will clarify these things in what follows.[12] You should recognize that today we do not distinguish or differentiate such people with such accuracy.

141. 14 on 86. 12 (433C): *Not only will he never*: Note that someone united with God cannot be possessed by an unclean spirit.

141. 18 on 86. 23 (436A): *(Instability) of things* [lit. foreign things]: Note that our 'foreign things' are our propensity for sin, for sin is not of our nature, as is the propensity 'for every good work' [2 Cor. 9: 8], according to the apostle. Touching this same concern, in the Psalms we read: 'separate your servant from "foreign" things' [Ps. 19: 13]. From this you will understand the saying of the Lord: 'And if you are not found faithful in that of the "foreigner", who will give you yours' [Luke 16: 12]? Because of this, these foreign things are not termed 'beings', for they are not of nature, but are instead bastards; whereas acting in accordance with nature is a being and is not foreign to us. ⟨ . . . ⟩

144. 14 on 88. 7 (436D): *Completely (taking on our nature)*: { . . . } Against Apollinaris.

145. 4 on 88. 26 (437B): *The Word of God*: These words are from what is called the Wisdom of Solomon [Wisd. 5: 15]. { . . . }

145. 5 on 88. 27 (437B): *The intention*: One of the prophets has used the expression 'to call to memory before the Lord'.[13] [Dionysius] says that we should not understand this in the sense that God is being reminded of something through images which recall that thing, for such pertains only to those intelligent beings which are bound up in the flesh (i.e. us humans), whereas God's memory is his knowledge, through which he knows the perfect, those who are becoming deiform in him through their virtuous life and have been deemed worthy of a knowledge of him which cannot be forgotten. { . . . }

145. 10 on 89. 19 (440A): *The sacred (bath)*: Note that there was a washing in the law,[14] and that he has another treatise about the legal hierarchy. { . . . }

---

[12] *EH* 3. 3. 7 (86. 16–87. 11).
[13] We have been unable to locate the source of this quote.
[14] Omitting οὐ.

148. 6 on 90. 10 (440B): *And into view*: Back then the divine gifts remained covered for a longer period of time, until the moment of the holy communion. He also indicates this shortly.[15] { ... }

148. 13 on 91. 1 (441A): *Born* [lit. **beginning**]: Since we have the beginning of our subsistence from the earth, for our bodily nature is from it, it is right that after the fall we have an ending like the beginning, for we return to the earth. As it was said, 'You are earth, and you shall return to earth' [Gen. 3: 19].

149. 2 on 91. 9–10 (441A): *Providential gifts* [lit. **self-working providential care for us**]: Note the precision of his teachings, a precision that is expressed in a multitude of passages and fights against all heretics. On the one hand, that God's providential care for us was 'self-working' [αὐτουργός] implies that God the Word was one and the same, and not one in another, as some rave with Nestorius.[16] On the other hand, the phrase 'in a true sharing of *all* our properties, yet sinlessly' [91. 10–11] refutes the Manichaeans, the Eutychians, the Apollinarians, the Acephalians, and all other heretics at once.

149. 4 on 91. 16 (441B): *Not through overwhelming force*: Note that Christ conquered Satan not by force, but 'by an act of judgement and righteousness' [cf. John 16: 8]. Gregory of Nyssa also says this in his *Catechism*.[17]

149. 11 on 92. 21 (444A): *Simple, oneness (of Jesus)*: { ... } Note also the things pertaining to the economy [of salvation], and who is the one who will appear, and what is the breaking of the bread and its distribution.

149. 15 on 93. 15 (444C): *Holding to view*: { ... } He says 'utterly' [93. 16] [incarnate] since he took on both a rational soul and an earthly body. {Rightly does he speak of an unconfused Incarnation, for when he appeared as a human, he remained God and preserved the properties of each of the two natures.}[18] Note also that this is against the Apollinarians.

---

[15] Cf. *EH* 3. 3. 12 (92. 15–20), as well as *SchEH* 136. 20.

[16] Although it is not entirely clear in the English translation of Dionysius, the text in question (91. 8–12) states that the love for humanity of the thearchic goodness did not reject its 'self-working providential care for us' when it became incarnate without sin. John here argues that the adjective αὐτουργός as applied to the deity's providential care indicates that the divine and human natures in Christ were 'one and the same' (αὐτός). His reasoning seems to be based on the similarity of prefixes and on the fact that God the Word continued to exercise providential care even after the Incarnation. The arguments are somewhat similar to those of the extant fragment of his *Against Severus* (see Ch. 2).

[17] Gr. Nyss. *or. catech.* 23 (PG 45: 61–4).

[18] The material in brackets is present in FA, though not in Syr. Perhaps the

152. 2 on 93. 22 (444D): *Communion with God*: Note how we become 'partakers of the divine nature' [2 Pet. 1: 4] by being united with Christ.

152. 9 on 94. 10 (445A): *'Harmost'*: ⟨ . . . ⟩ The Spartans used the name 'harmost' [ἁρμοστής] to refer to their governors of subject cities, because he 'harmonizes' those governed so that they live according to the laws. For the same reason, the Athenians used the name 'harmost' [ἁρμοστήρ] with reference to those who disposed others to live well, as Plato the Comic clearly indicates in his drama *Ambassadors*.[19] Therefore Dionysius rightly calls the bishop who rules the Church a 'harmost'.

4

153. 6 on 97. 15 (476C): *The secret (beholders)*: Often in our comments on *The Divine Names* we have discussed the meaning of the terms 'intelligible' and 'intelligent' [cf. 97. 7, 13–15].[20] In this passage he also says the following: it is not through a teacher but through direct illumination that God reveals the mystery of contemplation and of the myron to the bishop, inasmuch as he is holy and akin to the divine light. For this reason, the covering of the divine myron does not include the bishop himself, but, as the apostle has said [2 Cor. 3: 18], with 'unveiled face' he contemplates the mysteries, whereas for those who are not perfect there is need of symbols. It is for this reason that the holy myron of God is covered with folds by the hierarch, who thus intervenes between the things of God and those of the laity and reveals the symbols through his interpretation.

He calls the bishops 'beholders' [θεωροί] because the Greeks use the name 'beholders' with reference to those who are nominated by all to inquire of God about the future, to offer sacrifices for them, and to propitiate God for them. { . . . }

157. 1 on 101. 22 (484A): *By the Father*: { . . . } Note the incomparable orthodoxy of the great Dionysius, how he has preserved the distinction between the deity of the Lord Jesus and his flesh. For although Jesus as

Monophysite translator excised it for its clear confesssion of two natures, in the very wording of the Chalcedonian formula. See also *SchCH* 57. 3 and the discussion of Christology in Ch. 4.

[19] Pl. Com. fr. 126 (ed. Kock, *CAF* 1: 634), otherwise unattested.
[20] e.g. *SchDN* 205. 2, 240. 3.

God sanctifies all things, as human he is 'sanctified by the Father, by himself' [101. 22–3], since he also is God, and 'by the Holy Spirit' [101. 22]. At the same time, the heavenly orders also know that 'their own source' [101. 23], their cause and creator, Jesus, although he is sanctified, nevertheless remains 'essentially unchanged' [102. 1], for he is God. { . . . }

157. 9 on 102. 20 (484C): *In human form*: Note here that Christ as human receives the Holy Spirit, inasmuch as he is sanctified, but that as God he gives it. { . . . }

5

161. 3 on 105. 19 (501C): *Half way*: Note how the ecclesiastical hierarchy is half-way between the heavenly hierarchy and the legal one, and how it shares in the two. { . . . }

165. 1 on 109. 7 (508B): *The hierarchical (ordinance)*: Note that the deacons at that time kept the doors. { . . . }

165. 3 on 109. 15 (508C): *But it is obvious that the order*: Note that the bishop also does the things of the subordinates.[21] { . . . }

165. 13 on 111. 5 (509C): *The announcement*: The proclamation in the case of ordinands is as follows. In the case of bishops: 'for the holy father, bishop N'. In the case of presbyters: 'for presbyter N'. In the case of deacons: 'for our brother, deacon N'. Such an announcement takes place when he proclaims during the ordination: 'the divine grace has put forward N. for such and such [a post]'.

165. 18 on 112. 9 (512C): *Consecrator*: As human, Christ also became the high priest. Note this against the Acephalians and Nestorians.

168. 4 on 113. 1 (513A): *It seems to me*: This passage from the Acts of the apostles [Acts 1: 26] I have found in some codices as follows: 'and they cast lots *for them*'. But in other codices I have found it this way: 'and they cast *their lots*'.[22] The reading 'for them' fits with what the divine Dionysius has here said, inasmuch as the lot is a sign which falls to the one to be selected—whether by revelation or by the activity of the Holy Spirit. For this reason, the great Peter said that the Iscariot 'obtained with us the lot of this ministry' [Acts 1: 17]. In the case of the apostles, however, it was not a lot such as is customary with us; rather, the allotting took place through the agency of the Lord who selected them.

---

[21] Cf. *SchCH* 29. 2.
[22] The second reading parallels Codex Bezae, see the discussion in Ch. 3.

6

169. 19 on 117. 26 (533D): *This is why many*: Note that this passage is against { . . . } the followers of Marcian, those who practise asceticism for just three years and then are indifferent for the remaining time of their life, so that without restraint they do every sort of unseemly deed.[23] Wallowing around in adultery, licentiousness, gluttony, incest, and generally in all dissoluteness, they say, amazingly, that they do such things without passion. They do not know that they are sick with passion and they do not feel it when they suffer afflictions both at their own hands and at the hands of the demons which dwell in them. Rather, they are like those who suffer an inflammation of the brain but are none the less happy and not at all distressed.

172. 1 on 118. 1 (533D): *Forbidden*: Note that monks are forbidden to do many things for which the laity have responsibility and authority, such as { . . . } associating with the military or market-place, and other things for which the laity are not condemned.

172. 11 on 119. 17–18 (537A): *Some heavenly*: Note that there is no 'injury' among any of the heavenly powers.[24] This is something opined by Origen and the like, who claim that each of the heavenly orders was allotted its name and rank in the measure that it turned away from God and that they were clothed in subtle bodies, in order to discipline them for turning away toward something lesser than God.[25] Rather, [we say that even now] they are pure and incorporeal minds, as they were created in the beginning. That the heavenly powers are incorporeal, you know well from earlier passages.[26]

We can interpret this passage in another way. After the demons fell, none of the heavenly minds was ever again ensnared [by evil]. [That they were again ensnared] is not mentioned by the divine Scripture or by the divinely wise fathers. This saint, however, by way of concession, seems to say it: namely, that they are holy and without any injury and

[23] This is a reference to the followers of Marcian the ascetic (*fl.* later 5th cent.). On him, Joseph Lebon, *Le Moine saint Marcien* (Louvain, 1968); Albert van Roey, 'Remarques sur le moine Marcien', *SP* 12/1 = TU 115 (1975), 160–72; J. Kirchmeyer, 'Le Moine Marcien (de Bethléem?)', *SP* 5/3 = TU 80 (1962), 341–59. For another (near contemporary) account of the followers of Marcian, Tim. CP *haer.* PG 86/1: 45–52.

[24] 'Injury' ($\lambda\acute{\omega}\beta\eta$) follows *CH* 119. 18 which refers to the angels as $\mathring{\alpha}\lambda\acute{\omega}\beta\eta\tau o\iota$.

[25] This description of the Origenist account of the fall is closely paralleled by Leon. Schol. *sect.* 10. 5 (PG 86/1: 1264–5).

[26] *DN* 4. 1 (144. 10), with *SchDN* 240. 3, *CH* 2. 2 (10. 17), *CH* 2. 4 (14. 24), *EH* 1. 2 (65. 9), *EH* 4. 6 (100. 6).

thus do not need any purification, but that *if* one of them is injured, then it passes over to the opposing powers, so that the remaining powers are not injured and similarly do not need purification. It is quite clear that this is what he is saying. For when he gives his own, true opinion in response to the hypothetical objection, he says 'if any' [119. 20] [of them is ensnared by evil. . . .] What he means is this: even if someone should grant that one of them erred, then it fell away from the choir of the [angels] . . . but I, he adds, do not say this, but rather the very opposite, that they remain eternally holy. [For if I did], I would myself fall from what has been established.

Let none of those initiated by Origen imagine that this passage supports his ill-considered opinion, when he claims that the heavenly minds are ever falling, turning away, and changing. In his *Peri Archon*, for example, Origen says: 'It is, I think, quite likely that everything which is endowed with reason is able to arise from some other being endowed with reason.' A little later he adds: 'After the end comes on all, again an emission and a fall take place.'[27]

Evagrius, in the 78th chapter of his second century, says: 'Each order of the heavenly powers consists either wholly from those below or wholly from those above, or from those above and below.'[28] And in the 19th chapter of the fifth century, he says: 'The psychic station arises from the angelic and archangelic station; the demonic and the human station, from the psychic station; and from the human station, again both angels and demons arise.'[29]

173. 1 on 120. 3 (537B): *Inferior beings*: ⟨ . . . ⟩ Note that the [angels] advance in knowledge, and that the [hypothetical objectors of Dionysius] do not say that demons are purified, because of those who claim that along with the saints even these are saved in the 'restoration' mythologized by them.[30]

---

[27] These two otherwise unattested fragments are situated toward the end of 1. 6. 3 in the edition of Gürgemanns and Karpp (228 n. 4).

[28] Evagr. Pont. *keph. gnost.* 2. 78 (PO 28/1: 91, version S²). This same passage was included in the canons of the Fifth Council against Origen (Mansi 9: 397).

[29] Evagr. Pont. *keph. gnost.* 5. 11 (PO 28/1: 181, version S²). This same passage was included in the canons of the Fifth Council against Origen (Mansi 9: 397).

[30] John seems to be projecting back to the 1st cent. the contemporary controversy over Origen and the *apokatastasis*.

7

173. 8 on 121. 10 (553B): *Among the unholy*: Concerning the death of
sinners, and what the Greeks think happens after death, whose
opinions he sets out. The more irrational of them (among them Bias,
not the Prienean but another one) say that the soul is not immortal, but
mortal and that it is dissolved in the same way as the body and passes
into non-existence.[31] There are others among them who are more
rational (like Plato and some others) who philosophize about an
immortal soul, saying that after death the body no longer subsists and
that for all eternity it never returns to the subsistence which it had.
This is what [Dionysius] means by the expression 'once for all' [121.
11]—which is to say, 'never to subsist again'. For he says that it is
unworthy for the material to live forever with the soul, in that the soul
alone exists immortally.[32] There are also heretics who say this, though
in a variety of different ways: for example, those descended from Simon
Magus, Menander, Valentinus, Marcion, and Mani. Even now there
are some who take their stand on the myths—not teachings!—of
Origen. See with whom they wish to be numbered, and what sort of
absurd opinions these men attach to the blameless faith of the
Christians, these men who are abominable to God and to right-thinking
people.

176. 2 on 121. 13 (553C): *Overlook*: Our Lord Jesus Christ has become
what the apostle calls a pledge and proof of the general resurrection
with the body [1 Cor. 15: 20; 2 Cor. 1: 22; Eph. 1: 14].

Note also that 'our life is now hidden in him' [Col. 3: 3] and that it
shall be made manifest in God in regeneration [Titus 3: 5, Matt.
19: 28].

176. 3 on 121. 15 (553C): *To the souls*: There were then certain heretics
like Simon Magus and his followers who claimed that souls will
have an ethereal body. One must know that Origen too says the same
thing in one of his works, whereas in other of his works he completely
denies this, teaching that every bodily nature passes into non-
existence.

Read what has been written about his views on the resurrection by
Methodius the holy martyr and bishop of Olympus Adrianople in

---

[31] Bias of Priene was one of the seven wise men of Athens, but John is careful to specify
his target as another Bias, the identity of whom we have been unable to determine.
[32] By 'he says', it would appear that John means Plato.

Lycia, and by Antipater the bishop of Bostra.[33] In that way you will learn of his [i.e. Origen's] monstrous and foolish fables.

176. 4 on 121. 19 (553C): *Perfect beatitude*: He says these things, hinting, I think, at Papias who was then bishop of Hieropolis in Asia and flourished in the time of the divine evangelist John. This Papias, in the fourth book of his *Exegesis of the Lord's [Sayings]*, asserted that there would be gustatory pleasures in the resurrection.[34] Later, Apollinaris believed in this teaching {(as is clear in his writing) which some call 'chiliasm'.[35] How, therefore, could these writings of St Dionysius, writings which oppose Apollinaris, be by Apollinaris, according to the idiocies of some?}[36] Irenaeus of Lyon also said the same in the fifth book of his *Against the Heretics*, and produced as a witness for what he was saying the aforementioned Papias.[37]

176. 6 on 122. 8 (556A): *Different regard* [lit. other eyes]: By 'other eyes' he means those of the mind, which is at last more pure so that it can look upon the things of Hades and begin to expect Gehenna, in which it had not previously believed. Therefore [this mind] does not bear death well and bewails it. { . . . }

177. 8 on 124. 13 (557C): *The catechumens*: There is nothing small in our mysteries, but all things are great. When they are compared to one another, however, they do differ in magnitude. The mysteries of the divine washing and of illumination and of communion are incom-

---

[33] The Greek text is here obviously corrupt. Syr. preserves what is probably the correct reading, mentioning first Methodius the martyr and bishop of Olympus in Lycia, and then Ammon the bishop of Adrianople. Cf. the comments of Ernest Honigmann, *Trois mémoires posthumes d'histoire et de géographie de l'orient chrétien* (Brussels, 1961), 38 n. 148. Methodius (d. 311) is best known for his work on the resurrection against Origen. Cf. Henri Crouzel, 'Les Critiques adressées par Méthode et ses contemporains à la doctrine origénienne du corps ressuscité', *Gregorianum*, 59 (1972), 679–716. As for Ammon the bishop of Adrianople in Thrace, he also is best known for his polemics against Origen on the resurrection. He probably died in the early 4th cent. John also mentions Ammon in *SchCH* 65. 6. As for Antipater of Bostra, he was the author of a refutation of Eusebius' apology for Origen. Of this text only fragments remain. He probably flourished in the mid-5th cent. As argued in Ch. 2, this scholion provides an approximate date for John's composition of the *Scholia*.

[34] Papias, fr. 9 (ed. Bihlmeyer, 138). John here clearly derives his knowledge of Papias from Iren. *haer*. 5. 33. 3–4 (SC 153: 411–21). Cf. *SchEH* 177. 13. See also Anton Baumstark, 'Zwei syrische Papiascitate', *OC* 2 (1902), 352–7.

[35] Chiliasm refers to the binding of the devil for a thousand years, leading to an earthly paradisiacal existence in which the risen martyrs shall reign with Christ. One of John's contemporaries associates the doctrine of chiliasm with the teachings of the godless Greeks: Ecumenius, *Com. on the Apocalypse* (ed. Hoskier), 213, on Rev. 20: 1–3.

[36] Bracketed materials not in Syriac, though FA has: 'How, therefore, could these writings of St Dionysius, writings which oppose Apollinaris, be by Apollinaris, according to the idiocies of some?' See the discussion in Ch. 5.

[37] Iren. *haer*. 5. 33. 3–4 (SC 153: 411–21).

parably greater than the things done over the dead. For this reason, he has referred to the things done over those who sleep as 'small' [124. 15]. Nevertheless, those who are still catechumens are not even worthy of these things.

177. 13 on 125. 17 (560B): *The words naming them:* ⟨ . . . ⟩ God refers to the pleasures there using expressions and names with which we are familiar, saying that there is no grief there or sickness, suffering or lamentations [Isa. 35: 10, 51: 11, Rev. 21: 4], but that there is light [Ps. 56: 13]. And yet, the good things there are not this, but are truly unknown and incomprehensible to us, for 'eye has not seen . . .' [1 Cor. 2: 9]. Rather, [God] gives examples of blessedness from what we know. { . . . }

177. 15 on 126. 8–9 (561A): *The prayers of the just:* Note that the prayers of the just benefit only those who are worthy of the mercies of God, whether living or dead. They do not benefit sinners and those worthy of condemnation, both here and after death.

180. 2 on 126. 13 (561A): *Which the sun bestows:* Be careful! Do not suppose that he claims that the sun gives its own lights. How can something without a soul give anything? An act of giving arises from an act of choice. Rather, he is using a rhetorical figure here, one which attributes the words and deeds of one person to another. It is as if the sun were to say: 'I give light to strong eyes.' And then someone with weak eyes says: 'Give to me too, for I am healthy.' And then, after receiving the ray, he loses even what he had seen before. In the same way also, a sinner suffers when he asks a holy man to pray for him, for the sinner is blind and when he receives the ray of the prayer of the holy man, he does not allow it to work and illuminate as it should. Rather, he procures darkness for himself, inasmuch as he does not devote himself to the gifts of God through a pure life, but leaves (i.e. withdraws from) the enlightening commandments of God. The sinner despises the law of God and profits nothing from the prayer of a holy man. In the fourth chapter of *The Divine Names*, he also shows that he thus understands the sun.[38]

181. 17 on 130. 3 (565B): *The entire person:* Note that by an 'entire person' he means one composed of a rational soul and a body, as is suggested by the expression 'in pure contemplation and understanding' [130. 1].

Note also that he refers to the 'whole salvation' [130. 4] of soul and body.

[38] *SchDN* 248. 1–2, 4.

One should pay careful attention to these two points so that you might understand the Incarnation of a rational soul and body when he elsewhere says that 'the transcendent Jesus *wholly* took on our human substance'.[39]

184. 4 on 130. 17 (565D): *The sacred tradition*: Note that even then there were some who made fun of our mysteries, especially the practice of infant baptism, inasmuch as infants who are not able to speak are presented by those who make the renunciations and confess the symbols for them. He defends against this scoffing, adding that not everything is known to all [cf. 1 Cor. 8: 7].

Note how even the angels are ignorant of many things.

[39] Cf. *DN* 2. 6 (130. 5–6).

The Divine Names

1

185. 6 on 108. 9 (588A): *What is beyond being:* ⟨ . . . ⟩ The divinity of the only God, which is hidden from all, is a 'thearchic power' [109. 4], because it is the source [ἄρχουσα] of those who are called gods [τῶν λεγομένων θεῶν], whether angels or holy persons, as also it is the creator of those who become gods by participation, in so far as it is in truth divinity itself, from itself and without cause.

188. 4 on 109. 3 (588A): *The superlative wisdom and truth of scripture* [lit. **most wise and true theology**]: Observe how he calls the Scripture of the divine Paul 'true theology', for it was he who said that enlightenment is clearly furnished by God 'according to the measure' of each one's capacity [2 Cor. 10: 13 or Rom. 12: 3]. The Lord also indicated this when he said to his more perfect disciples, 'To you it has been given to know the secrets of the kingdom' [Matt. 13: 11], and this, because they applied themselves more intently to the prophecies. The great Dionysius said that this was uttered not only respecting people, but also respecting the angels, whom following certain outside philosophers he was wont to call 'minds' [109. 4–5].[1] Some of the higher orders were called 'minds', in so far as they are essentially and completely mind, and understand singly all things which flow from God directly to them. For this reason also, all of the most holy Cherubim together are said to be covered with eyes.[2]

188. 6 on 109. 5 (588A): *Out of concern for our salvation* [lit. **in a preserving justice**]: He says that God reveals himself to each in proportion to their capacity, not because he begrudges the majority, but because he preserves justice in measuring out the knowledge of God, for justice is the appropriate granting to each in proportion to their merit. The knowledge of God is without measure, but we need measures. If it were revealed to us without measure, we would not be preserved, just as a bodily eye cannot receive the whole sun.

---

[1] Reading λέγεσθαι for διαλέγεσθαι.   [2] Cf. *SchMT* 417. 1.

189. 2 on 109. 7 (588B): *Just as the senses can neither grasp*: In this passage he establishes the incomprehensibility of the knowledge of God. If not even simple and formless things, even though they are beings, are subject to the senses (e.g. angels and souls are not subject to the bodily senses); how much more does God transcend the senses— God, I say, who is not being, but beyond being; not simple, but beyond simplicity; not mind, but even beyond mind; not henad, but even beyond henad; not circumscribed by a limit, but free from the circumscriptions of beings. When, therefore, you hear in the Scripture of a shape and form and face of God, think of God worthily by being uplifted beyond bodies. Likewise, when you hear of unity, do not think of a concourse of certain differences into unity. The present treatise does not concern such things; it concerns God, who is not the source of numbers, not even an uncompounded source, but is unified even beyond the simple beings.

189. 3 on 109. 13 (588B): *This source of all unity* [lit. a henad unifying every henad]: Henceforth, after distinguishing the things of God from all the things among beings, at last, in accordance with the limits of human speech—for one cannot escape these—he praises God by those very things from which he has distinguished him.

He calls him a 'henad' [109. 13], but adds 'unifying every henad' [109. 13], that is, the creator of all simple beings, such as angels and souls.

He calls him an 'unthinkable mind' [109. 14], which is to say, that which is not thought by any mind. For if like is known by like, it is necessary that, if he were mind, he be known by minds. But 'who has known the mind of the Lord' [Isa. 40: 13 LXX and Rom. 11: 34]? Accordingly, he is 'mind beyond mind' and 'name beyond every name' [Phil. 2: 9]. 'My name', he says, 'I did not speak to them' [Exod. 6: 3]. Thus also he is 'unnamed' [109. 15] to all.

Neither is he 'that which is' [109. 15]. For if he created beings from non-beings, he is not a being, but beyond beings. Even if he says, 'I am who am' [Exod. 3: 14], understand worthily that he is without beginning and end, and 'unsearchable' [Rom. 11: 33].

189. 4 on 110. 5 (588C): *Understanding . . . of itself*: God alone understands the things of God, since he with understanding properly knows himself as he is. But to all those outside he is not clearly known, namely, both what he is and how he is, for 'no one knows the Father except the Son, and no one knows the Son except the Father' [Matt. 11: 27]—since the Father knows his own venerable image (i.e. the

Son), he also knows himself. The same holds true with respect to the Holy Spirit, for 'no one knows the things of God, except the Spirit who is from God' [1 Cor. 2: 11]. All things, therefore, which this blessed man contemplated concerning God, he also understood to relate to the venerable Trinity.

192. 4 on 110. 16–17 (589A): *Venture toward an impossibly*: Rightly does he say 'impossibly'. Even if one were to attempt this, one would not succeed, but because one caused one's intellectual sight to grow dim, one would only fall away from the true light, since one obstinately received the whole sun with one's corporeal eye—that sun, I say, hinting at which, the divine and intelligible powers, the Cherubim and Seraphim, cover their faces, indicating that they do not strive after a contemplation which is above them and has not been granted to them [Isa. 6]. { . . . }

192. 5 on 111. 4–5 (589B): *Beyond thought*: From these things it is quite possible to overcome the madness of Arius and Eunomius, who made bold to quibble about the essence of the only-begotten, an essence which is in fact ineffable and beyond being itself.

192. 7 on 111. 5 (589B): [The Thearchy]:[3] He everywhere calls the all-ruling Trinity 'the Thearchy', since it is the source of those called gods, that is, angels and saints, as we have said.[4] The incomprehensible [nature] of that unnamable being is 'hidden' [111. 6]. A little later he asserts this same thing, when he uses the phrase 'with a prudent silence' [111. 6]; and a little earlier, when he said 'in a manner befitting the sacred' [110. 15].

193. 1 on 111. 17–112. 1 (589C): *The enlightenment of the illuminated*: Step by step, as if progressing to what is greater, he says that they are first illuminated and then perfected. To be perfected is to be led into perfection through the advance which comes about after baptism through right-living, so that one is able to say, 'I have finished the race, I have kept the faith' [2 Tim. 4: 7]. The venerable Trinity is rightly thought to be the source of such a rite [τελετή], since also it is the effective source of all perfection [τελείωσις]. Those advancing to perfection are wholly deified by becoming 'partakers of the divine nature' [2 Pet. 1: 4]. God is the Thearchy of such as these according to their capacity, since he is the source of those who have become gods. After this ascent they advance into simplicity by becoming equal to the angels through the resurrection, and according to the apostle, by no

---

[3] This phrase was not translated in the Paulist Press version.
[4] Cf. *SchDN* 185. 6.

longer having an ensouled body [cf. 1 Cor. 15: 44], that is, no longer subsisting and being moved through a soul. Rather they have a spiritual body, which is to say, through the Holy Spirit which is poured out upon them they are freed from the manifold diversity of thoughts and from the senses. Then they are united by being led into the henad of simplicity, as we said before, for he says the same elsewhere.[5] 'The company of those who believed were of one heart and soul' [Acts 4: 32].

193. 4 on 112. 11 (589D): *As a monad*: Here he makes clear what he especially wishes to signify by predicating 'henad and monad' [112. 11] of God. He says that the theologians said this in order to establish the undividedness of God. That which is distinguished by bulk and mass is such in so far as body is divided; that which is undivided has no share of body, but rather is even above every incorporeality.

Moreover, when God by thinking willingly established all things, this took place not like some mind divided into thoughts is multiplied, but having remained and remaining, he says, in the henad without division and dissipation he established and establishes the creation. For God 'is working still', as it is said in the Gospels [John 5: 17]. Therefore, he is beyond simplicity, since without division he transcends every simplicity.

193. 5 on 112. 13 (589D): *The diversity (of what we are)*: In the case of both the super-celestial worlds and this visible world, lower things turn toward higher things and the corporeal is established in the living, for 'in his hand are the depths of the earth' [Ps. 95: 4]. This also holds true with respect to the heavens, for 'in him are all things' [Rom. 11: 36]. In the case of us mortals, the opposite holds, for the soul turns toward the spirit in which are grounded the senses and thoughts through which we think about the objects of our inquiry—which spirit knows the things which are in man, according to the apostle [cf. 1 Cor. 2: 11]. Therefore, the soul, by turning toward that spirit, also turns toward the senses in it; and through them, to the body. Moreover, the conceptions in the mind are in some sense divided: by way of dissipation they advance into differences—from the first conception into the second conception, either better or worse. Therefore, he says that we, when we stretch upward toward God, are made an indivisible one by that henad, when our manifold differences are collected from dissipation into an enfolding and are made one supernaturally, that is, in a manner that is not sensible, but intelligent—when we are no longer

[5] *DN* 1. 4 (112. 11–12).

irreconciled to ourselves, but become one in form, even as 'he is one', as it is said in the Gospels [John 17: 22].

196. 1 on 112. 14–113. 1 (592A): *As a Trinity*: Note the 'thrice-hypostatic Trinity' [113. 1]. By 'fecundity' [113. 1] he means the paternal procession beyond thought unto the revelation of the Son and the Holy Spirit. Rightly does he say '*as* a Trinity' [113. 1], for not number, but glory is meant: 'the Lord God is one Lord' [Deut. 6: 4].

196. 4 on 113. 7 (592A): *A true share*: { . . . } See how he says that 'one of the hypostases wholly participated in us' [113. 7–8].[6] As the apostle said: 'in him the fullness of the Deity dwells bodily' [Col. 2: 9]. The word 'wholly' is also contrary to Apollinaris.[7] { . . . }

197. 1 on 113. 12 (592B): *Divine enlightenment* [lit. **theurgical lights**]: By 'theurgical lights' he means the teachings of the saints, in so far as they infuse the light of knowledge and cause those who believe to become gods.[8]

197. 2 on 113. 13 (592B): *By the hidden tradition of our inspired teachers*: Note that lofty matters and what is beyond the hearing of the masses, whether it relates to the theology or the economy of the life-giving God—all these things, I say, the divine apostles handed on in a hidden manner, when they revealed them secretly to the perfect.

Note also that the expressions 'without confusion' and 'without change', which he used [113. 11–12], are from the apostles, as also is the expression 'the whole man' [cf. 113. 7].

Accordingly, when the apostle wrote to the Thessalonians, he said

---

[6] Theodosius the Monophysite patriarch of Alexandria (d. 566), in his *Oratio theologica* (tr. Chabot, 50–1) was worried that this Dionysian passage might be wrongly interpreted to mean that the thearchy itself, rather than just one of its persons, was the subject of the Incarnation. He writes that certain theologians, who otherwise wish to avoid saying that the Father and the Spirit became incarnate, nevertheless fall into this error through their misuse of this passage. To prove his point, Theodosius appeals to *DN* 2. 6 (130. 5–11), which quite clearly states that it was the Word, not the thearchy, that became incarnate, stating also the explicit corollary that the Father and the Spirit did not enter the union. The context of this passage from Theodosius suggests that his unnamed opponents were in fact Chalcedonians. Theodosius, like Severus earlier, is on the defensive.

[7] For Monophysite appeals to this passage, see the discussion in Ch. 1. This same Dionysian passage, where it says that 'the simple Jesus became composite' (113. 9), was used by the Chalcedonian Ephrem of Amid (*sedit c.*527 to *c.*545) to show that the Chalcedonian expression 'one person' is equivalent to the more traditional Cyrillian expression 'one incarnate nature of the Word'. Ephrem appeals to 'St Dionysius the Areopagite' and pays close attention to his use of the word 'composite', which (he says) can be rightly applied to the hypostatic union, though no one but Apollinaris would dare to speak of a composite essence or a composite nature. Ephrem's text is no longer extant, but Photius (cod. 229 (ed. Henry), 4: 144) provides a summary of the passage in question.

[8] Reading θεούσας for θεούς.

that they must guard all that they heard 'either by word of mouth or by letter' [2 Thess. 2: 14]. When he wrote to Timothy, again he spoke of what had been 'entrusted' [2 Tim. 1: 12, 14] in secret. In the present text this is referred to as happening 'by means of revelation' [112. 9].

197. 3 on 114. 2 (592B): *In the sacred veils*: Note that one must place in a single rank both holy Scripture and the traditions of the bishops (whom he was wont to call 'hierarchs', since they rule over priests [ἄρχοντας τῶν ἱερέων], that is, elders and deacons and door-keepers, as he says in his treatise on our hierarchy).[9] Because of this single rank we also have faith in their doctrinal sayings.

From these oracles, he says, crass images are predicated of things which are beyond being, for the sake of our thought and mystagogy— in the case of God, when he appears as fire [Deut. 4: 24] and as an old man in Daniel [Dan. 7: 9, 13, 22] and as a man who wrestles with Jacob [Gen. 32: 24–9], and so forth; in the case of angels, like the Cherubim when they are in the form of wild beasts and various sorts of men and youths.

197. 5 on 114. 7 (592B): *When we are incorruptible*: Note that in the resurrection in addition to incorruptibility and immortality the saints will attain a Christ-like state, shining brighter than the sun, as also did the Lord when he was transfigured on the mountain [Luke 9: 28–36]— even as the apostle says concerning the saints, at that time they will be even as he is, and they 'will be always with the Lord' [1 Thess. 4: 16].

197. 6 on 114. 9 (592C): *The sight of God shining* [lit. **his visible theophany**]: Note that he calls even his divine body a 'visible theophany' so as to adapt his comment in the same way against both the Nestorians and the Acephalians, as well as against those who suppose that the Lord is neither now nor in the future with flesh.

Note also, on the one hand, what his 'visible theophany' is— ensouled flesh; on the other hand, what his 'intelligible' theophany [115. 1] is—that which will be intelligibly shared by us more perfectly at that time. { . . . }

200. 3 on 115. 11 (592D): *In a manner no words can describe, pre-existed*: You should make a special effort to understand the word 'pre-existed', for in what follows he makes clear all the other things [mentioned in this passage].[10] Moreover, from this it will be understood how the apostle says that we were in God 'before the foundation of the

---

[9] See *EH* 5. 1. 5 (107. 17–19). Cf. *SchCH* 29. 1 where John seems to qualify this etymology for 'hierarch'.

[10] Reading ἕτερα for ἔργα, with FA.

world' [Eph. 1: 4]. Now then, one must know that the production of all things depends upon him as cause and principle, since all beings are from him. Reasonably, just as all future things will happen through his unknowable act of will, they also pre-existed in him who knew both what he would produce and when he would produce it. Therefore, those things which before the ages were foreknown in him, 'pre-existed', for before the intelligibles were produced (i.e. the ages) and before every other creature, the things which will be were known to him, as it is said, 'He who knew all things before their generation' [Sus. 42], and again, 'Before I formed you in the womb, I knew you' [Jer. 1: 5].

201. 3 on 116. 4 (593B): *Apprehension* [lit. **touch**]: By 'touch' he here means intelligent comprehension, for when in understanding we intuit intelligible and immaterial things by means of the mind, we seem in some way to touch them and through the mind to perceive what sorts of things they are, as also we do through touching sensible objects. In the case of God, however, we do not touch him, even intelligently.

204. 1 on 116. 14 (593B): *The godlike unified minds who (imitate these angels as far as possible)*: He says that the godlike minds 'in imitation of the angels' (to the extent that they can) are led into union with the holy powers, which powers he has already called 'angels'. One must understand these godlike minds to be our theologians (i.e. our prophets and apostles). One must not suppose him to be speaking of angels (especially on the basis of the phrase 'in imitation of the angels'), for an angel does not imitate an angel, but what is less [imitates what is greater]. 〈 . . . 〉

204. 4 on 117. 4 (593C): *It is not a thing* [lit. **it is nothing**]: One must understand that God is 'nothing' as follows, namely, in so far as he is not a being, for the cause of beings is beyond beings. 〈 . . . 〉

205. 2 on 117. 12 (593D): *Divinely beneficent Providence*: With these words he refutes the ignorant opinions of those who dare to say that the creative faculty is in God by nature, as also weaving is in spiders, for he says that God produced the universe through his goodness alone.

None of the theologians dared to praise God on the basis of what he is (i.e. his essence), for this cannot be known. Rather, based on God's outward procession (i.e. his providence), they praise his providence over all things [or] 'his effects' [177. 13], that is, those things which subsist through him as cause.

All things desire divine providence through which they both exist and subsist, but intelligent and rational things do this mentally. As many things as (through being mind) think the higher intelligibles— these are called intelligences, for that which is thought is the intel- ligible, which is also the 'food' of the intelligent (i.e. that which thinks). Accordingly, as many things as (through their being intelligent, for mind thinks) are rational and apply themselves mentally to the provid- ence of God—these desire God according to their capacity.

As many things as are below the intelligences and have a sensible soul, I mean, beasts and all things with ensouled bodies but no reason, whose soul, because it is composed of the elements and material fire, has its existence in a material spirit—all these, I say, because they are driven to eat and drink by sense perception alone, suitably desire through sense perception the one who manages [the universe]. As it is said, 'These all look to thee, to give them their food in due season' [Ps. 104: 27]. You will find many such things in Job and David [e.g. Job 38: 39–21, Ps. 148].

There are other things, however, which have neither sense percep- tion nor a soul but only a certain vegetative or vital motion. Plants and grasses would fall into this class. Such as these subsist through their possession of this vital spirit alone, not being equipped with a faculty of sense perception. Through excessive dryness trees and the like can be deprived of this vegetative spirit through which they grow and flower. It is for these reasons that even such as these seem to desire divine providence in which they both subsist and flourish. Accordingly, in the 148th Psalm they are presented as praising God for his maintenance [Ps. 148 *passim*]. Therefore, although lacking soul and sense perception, even these things have a share in his ineffable providence, but only in so far as they are alive and are endowed with a certain 'habitual propensity' which is present in them as a potential. A permanent quality is said to be a habit. It is through this disposition and potential that it is called such a thing. Through this habit, there- fore, whatever participates only in this vegetative life in order to grow and move, essentially and habitually, but without a soul or sense per- ception, is said to desire the goodness of God.

209. 1 on 120. 2 (596C): *Their home*: He says that God is 'the home [ἑστία] of all things', because he is the dwelling place of all the saints. The Lord himself said this same thing: 'Remain in me' [John 15: 4]. Just as we are his 'temple' [1 Cor. 6: 19], according to the verse, 'I will live in them and walk around' [2 Cor. 6: 16], thus also he is our house. Rightly does he immediately add 'in a unity' [120. 3]. For when he said that God is all things and that in him are all things, someone might lower his mind to composition and fall away from the truth by supposing that all things are piled up inside God, or that God is all things by way of some sort of composition. It is for this reason that he immediately cures this absurd opinion, by saying 'unified', that is, in his unity.

Or to speak more properly, God is all things and in all things and yet remains beyond unity and simplicity, without division or mixture with beings. But also, he is 'unrelatedly' [120. 3] in all things, which is to say, held back or bodily circumscribed by nothing, but rather he is 'transcendently' [120. 3] in all things, for he is outside of all things, existing nowhere—he from whom are all things and who is in all, for from him all things hold together [cf. Col. 1: 17].

2

209. 11 on 122. 1 (636B): *Divine* [lit. thearchic]: In this chapter he fights especially against the Arians and Eunomians, both of whom maintain the inequality [of the Father and the Son], but also against the Nestorians and Acephalians.

By the 'entire thearchic subsistence' he means the divinity of the one holy and venerable Trinity, which divinity is known in three hypostases. For he customarily calls the revered Trinity the 'entire divinity'.[11] This Trinity, by revealing itself, what its entire divinity is, with a distinguishing of persons (i.e. a division), has made known to the saints, by revealing the properties of the three hypostases, that he is Father, Son, and Holy Spirit. The three are an entire divinity that is one and single.

One must know that 'subsistence' is not properly predicated of God. Rather, he is pre-subsistence, that is, before subsistence itself. But since all subsistence is from him, he is named after the things which appear through him, so that he is understood to be even beyond these.

212. 3 on 122. 7 (636C): *Rather than any part of it* [lit. not by parts]: Rightly does he say 'not by parts'. For the activities and all the hymns of theology are not assigned at random to one and only one of the persons of the divine Trinity, but rather they are common to the Trinity, except for the Incarnation alone, for this belongs only to the Son, as he says forthwith [125. 19–126. 2]. On the other hand, the characteristic properties of the three hypostases alone belong by part

[11] Cf. e.g. *DN* 2. 1 (122. 7–8, 11–12, 123. 2, 13).

and individually to each hypostasis. For example, 'Father' belongs to the Father and none other, thus also respecting the Son and the Holy Spirit.

212. 5 on 122. 11 (636C): *In all that he is:* Note that whoever says that the divine names are not common, impiously sunders the unity of the venerable Trinity.

212. 6 on 123. 3–4 (636C): *'Thus says the One who is':* One must note that {this St Dionysius}[12] accepts [as canonical or authentic] the Apocalypse of St John the evangelist. { . . . }

212. 8 on 123. 5 (637A): *That is in and (proceeds) from the Father:* Observe how he cites this passage [from Scripture], for it is not now said thus.[13]

213. 4 on 124. 8 (637C): *The unfailing* [lit. fount-like]: It is said in the Psalms, 'With you is the fount of life' [Ps. 35: 10], and in Jeremiah, 'They abandoned me, the fount of living water' [Jer. 2: 13]. Therefore God is called a 'fount', because he is like a certain womb and source and cause of all things which have appeared and come into being.

What some were wont to call 'universals' (i.e. kinds, wholes, or circumscriptions), in so far as they encompass the individual processions which are from themselves, holy Scripture calls the 'fount-like cause'. Moreover, because of the creative and unceasing nature of the things which subsist through the Holy Spirit and because the Holy Spirit is the cause of all beings, as it is said in Wisdom [cf. Wisd. 7: 21], rightly does he also theologize about it as a fount-like cause. The unceasing nature of creating—from this one can understand the saying, 'My Father until now is working, and I am working' [John 5: 17]. In the same way the Holy Spirit with the Father and the Son always works without ceasing. { . . . }

216. 1 on 125. 15–16 (640B): *These . . . in the sense of a superabundance:* He is praised through denial beyond thought, for from the things which are not contemplated of him he is transcendently worshipped. For example, he is not mortal, without end, not visible, not in need, and so on. These are names common to the Trinity.

'Things which can be assigned a cause' [125. 16] are as many things as flowed from him in creation, because he is the cause of all good—as it is written, 'All beauty belongs to him' (cf. Zech. 9: 17 LXX; Gen. 1: 31).

216. 2 on 125. 19 (640C): *Of the Father:* 'Transcendent' is understood to

[12] Bracketed material not in Syriac.

[13] In the Dionysian text, John 15: 26 is expanded to fit the argument. John seems to think that Dionysius' version represents a variant reading to the biblical text.

apply syntactically not only to the Father, but also to the Son and the Holy Spirit.

With respect to 'the distinguishing marks' [125. 19] of the holy Trinity (i.e. its names), he says that there is no 'interchange' and no 'sharing' [125. 20]. For the Father could not piously be called the Son; nor the Son, the Father; the same also with respect to the Holy Spirit.

216. 3 on 125. 21 (640C): *Jesus among us* [lit. according to us]: Note that God the Word alone became incarnate.

He says that [the Incarnation] is 'perfect' [126. 1]—against Apollinaris, since it is from an intelligent soul and our body. This he makes clear by saying 'according to us' [125. 21], which is also against Eutyches. It is also against Nestorius, because he speaks of 'the . . . unchangeable subsistence of Jesus' as God 'according to us' [125. 21–126. 1].[14]

Note also that he says that his mysteries in humanity are 'real' [126. 2]—hunger, thirst, walking on water, passing through closed doors to his disciples, raising the dead, the passion itself, and so on.

216. 7 on 126. 13 (641A): *The differentiations*: He calls the enhypostatic and venerable subsistences 'differentiations', that is, the unspeakable radiance of the Son from the Father and the inconceivable procession of the Holy Spirit from the Father.

216. 10 on 127. 1 (641A): *Its wholly belonging to the conceptual realms* [lit. its all-known]: We should explain how God is unknown and all-known and how we receive knowledge of him in unknowing, for God is known through unknowing.

Do not understand unknowing as that which occurs through ignorance (for that is a darkness of the soul), neither as an ignorance which knows, for an ignorant person does not know. Truly it is a type of knowledge. And yet, the known is known through unknowing. Through this unknowing, thoughts which were multiplied and scattered are brought back to unity in a manner beyond thought and are again enfolded, although they are not yet one. In this way, after transcending every thought about God, we become simple. And then, by being in a state of unknowing and remaining without judgement in the stability of unity, and by firmly standing in unity, we do not know that we do not know. In other words, by not knowing any other thing, we, as if we were ignorant, do not know, being unable to learn those things of which we are ignorant, but being ignorant of those things which are not piously known by the rational creation. Having remained

---

[14] John has added the expression 'as God' in order to make this passage refute Nestorius.

in this unknowing, we become a form of that which is before all things: on the one hand, having cast off all forms and thoughts, on the other hand, grounded in a speechlessness greater than all speech, while not even knowing that we do not know. At that time, again having turned away from the speechless silence, and descending from silence into speech, knowing that we do not know, we then hold back from seeking what is unknown.

Again, God is 'all-known' [127. 1], because what he is is known from his munificent providence and from his creative acts: from the former, that he is saviour; from the latter, that he is creator. ⟨ . . . ⟩

Note that the divine hypostases are in one another according to a certain remaining and rest [127. 2–3]. As it is said, 'I am in the Father, and the Father is in me' [John 10: 38]. The apostle speaks in the same way of the Holy Spirit [cf. Rom 8: 9].

220. 1 on 127. 4 (641B): *The light from all the lamps*: The whole mind of the father [i.e. Dionysius] is thus disposed. He is giving an example regarding the holy Trinity. He says that it is like what happens when three lamps or candles are kindled in a temple or house. On the one hand, the hypostases are distinguished (i.e. separated) from one another, for they are different lamps. On the other hand, they have a communion of nature and activity, a communion which is united by the light and inseparable. In the air of the house no one is able to distinguish and say what sort is the light of this candle and what sort of that one.[15]

After saying these things, he passes from the things of the Trinity to an account of the economy and the glorious departure of God the Word from the Father. As [God the Word] himself said: 'From my Father I have come, and to my Father I return' [John 16: 28]. He explains this as follows: 'But if somebody were to take even one of the lamps out of the house, all of its light would also leave with it—none of the illumination of the other lamps is drawn with it, nor is its own light left behind for the others' [127. 13–15]. When the Son went from the Father and dwelt in the world, he brought with himself neither the

---

[15] This passage was used by Leontius of Byzantium (d. *c.*543) in his *Against the Nestorians and the Euthychians* 1. 7 (PG 86/2: 1304C–1305A) in a discussion of the sort of union wherein entities are in one another but are not mixed with one another. For Dionysius the analogy of light was applied to the persons of the Trinity. Leontius, however, applies it to the unity of natures in Christ. Similarly, at 1. 4 (PG 86/2: 1288) Leontius examines how the deity is not more present in the one nature of the Trinity than in the three persons. He appeals to *DN* 2. 10 (134. 11), but this time transfers Dionysius' Christological reference to the Trinity.

Father nor the Spirit, nor did he leave anything of his own with them when he went forth, but he effected the indivisible departure from his remaining.

221. 1 on 128. 14–15 (641D): *Of unions and of differentiations:* Now he theologizes concerning the ineffable procession of the holy Trinity into three hypostases, saying that God the Father, moved apart from time and out of love, went into the differentiation of hypostases, although beyond union and simplicity remaining without parts and diminution in his own wholeness, while his own radiance (i.e. his living image) went into subsistence, and while the all-holy Spirit proceeded from the Father reverently and beyond eternity, just as the Lord taught by mystagogy [John 15: 26]. For the cause and fount of all was multiplied through goodness into the thrice-hypostatic thearchy. Gregory the theologian also says these things in his treatises against Eunomius.[16]

The divine differentiation also happens in another way—the procession of God into the multiplicity of the visible and invisible creation through the abundance of his goodness. This creative providence and goodness is common to the thrice-hypostatic and differentiated Henad. ⟨ . . . ⟩

221. 8 on 130. 5 (644C): *In our favour:* Here again when he treats of the economy, he applies this to God the Word without any participation by the Father or the Holy Spirit, apart from the will alone [130. 8–9].

Note also the accurate explanation of the economy, that God the Word who is beyond being took on being 'without change' [130. 11] since he remained God and 'wholly' [130. 6] took on being from us for our sake. That is, he in truth had a body and rational soul.

Note also that God the Word is in truth the one who 'suffered' [130. 7], that is, in the flesh.

Note also that his 'human theurgy' [130. 7] is all the things of the economy.

Note also that the Father did not share in these things, neither the Holy Spirit, except in their good pleasure at the Incarnation and in their willing of it, as well as in their working with God the Son in effecting the divine signs [130. 8–10].

Note also that these things are especially against the Nestorians, Acephalians, and Phantasiasts.

224. 7 on 132. 1 (645B): *The originating source [lit. fount]:* Note the reverent and awe-inspiring names of the immaculate Trinity, namely, that the Father is 'the fount of the Godhead' [132. 1] and the Son and

---

[16] Cf. Greg. Naz. *or.* 29. 2 (SC 250. 178–81).

the Holy Spirit are 'shoots of the divine-begetting Divinity' [132. 2], that is, the Father, as well as 'divine offshoots, the flowering and transcendent lights' [132. 2–4].

Moreover, he says that shoots are spoken of in the Scripture in Zechariah's (the eleventh prophet's) vision of the olives [Zech. 4: 3, 12].[17] The Septuagint speaks of 'two shoots of the olive'. Others interpreters translate it as 'scions and shoots'.

'Lights' are mentioned when it is said, 'Father of lights' [Jas 1: 17] and 'light from light'.[18] ⟨ . . . ⟩

225. 3 on 133. 5 (648A): *The most evident idea in theology*: Note that he calls the things relating to the Incarnation 'theology'.[19]

Note also that he says that the taking flesh of the Lord Jesus for our sake is a 'god-making' [133. 6]. These things are directed especially against Nestorius, namely, saying that he took on being after a human fashion.

Observe how he says that the body of the Lord Jesus was 'formed from virgin blood' [133. 8–9].[20]

Note how he says that certain angels are oldest and that one of them is premier [133. 7]. The divine John speaks of elder angels in the Apocalypse [e.g. Rev. 7: 11–13]. We read in Tobit that there are seven premier angels [Tobit 12: 15], as well as in the fifth book of Clement's *Hypotyposes*.[21] He was wont to call the three highest orders 'the oldest angels'—Thrones, Seraphim, and Cherubim—as he often signifies in his treatise *The Celestial Hierarchy*.[22] Here he says that the manner of the Incarnation is accessible not even to the highest of the angels [133. 6–7].

228. 2 on 133. 13 (648A): *Teacher*: He is hinting at his teacher, St Hierotheus, as he straight away makes clear, for after Paul he was aided by him. He says that perhaps that man, because he 'suffered divine things' [134. 2], was thus inspired. The letter to the Hebrews explains what it is 'not only to learn, but also to suffer' [134. 1–2]—'He learnt obedience through what he suffered' [Heb. 5: 8]. One who suffers learns his lesson by experience. Just as one who is struck knows better

---

[17] Dionysius does not mention Zechariah by name.

[18] A reference to the Nicene Creed?

[19] 'Theology' was often used in patristic Greek to refer to the doctrine of the Trinity, while 'economy' was applied to the doctrine of the Incarnation.

[20] This passage was twice cited by Severus against the Julianists (writing between 518 and 528). See Ch. 1 for a discussion of the issue at stake.

[21] Clem. fr. 5 (GCS 17: 196). This fragment is otherwise unattested.

[22] *CH* 11. 2 (42. 10), 12. 2 (42. 18).

than one who only hears but is never struck—he knows better, I say, what is such a pain, and would better understand what sort of thing grief is. Thus also he who is initiated through revelation interprets divine things more divinely. { . . . }

229. 5 on 135. 5 (649A): *Without himself undergoing change*: Note that he participated in us 'without change and confusion' [135. 5], as well as 'without passion' [135. 6].

Note also that 'in our natural things' he remained 'beyond nature' [135. 7]; that 'in the things according to being' he remained 'beyond being' [135. 8]; and that he had 'our things beyond us' [135. 8–9]. For example, birth from a virgin and sinlessness, saying and doing all things in the power of God, walking on water, and the like.

Note that no one theologizes as well as he does concerning the economy, against the Nestorians, Acephalians, and Phantasiasts.[23]

232. 2 on 136. 18 (649D): *A thought . . . by whom I*: That is, the apostle Paul, their common teacher and guide, for through him he came to believe, as we know from Acts [Acts 17: 34].

One must also note that St Hierotheus was also instructed by St Paul.

232. 3 on 137. 2 (649D): *For although there are many so-called*: Even if there are 'many gods and lords' [1 Cor. 8: 5], nevertheless there is one true God and Father and one true Lord Jesus. This verse indicates that the cause of all, the creative divinity, produced the so-called gods and lords through an undivided and unscattered gift of the name of his own divinity and lordship, although his divinity was not cut up into parts of divinities, like gold into many coins; nor do the many gods complete his divinity, in the way that the many forms complete the one world. Rather, God is said to be 'multiplied' only by reason of his willing production of beings, his providential processions—being multiplied but remaining an undivided one, just as the sun emits many rays but remains in unity, for it is also said of 'the sun of righteousness' [Mal. 4: 2] that it is daily divided and not consumed. ⟨ . . . ⟩

3

236. 5 on 140. 14 (681B): *As second . . . scriptures*: Note that one must believe the writings of St Hierotheus to be secondary holy Scriptures.

236. 8 on 141. 6 (681C): *That source of life*: Perhaps by 'source of life

---

[23] Cf. *SchDN* 221. 8.

which bore God' he means the body of the holy Theotokos who at that time fell asleep.

Note also the expression 'James, the brother of God' [141. 7].

Note also that this divine man was present with the apostles Peter and James [141. 5].

236. 10 on 141. 10 (681D): *That divine frailty* [lit. **thearchic weakness**]: Here he means by 'thearchic weakness' the willing condescension of the Son into flesh apart from sin. Because he was ignorant of sin in every way, he was deemed worthy to become sin [cf. 2 Cor 5: 21] apart from sin for our sake (although he did not depart from what was his own), so that through his adoption of us he might lead back to our original freedom we who were slaves of sin. Being rich in divinity, he became poor in a rich-like poverty, by supernaturally taking up our flesh, so that we might be made wealthy in his divinity. Although he was in the form of God and God in his essence, through an overflow of his goodness he put on the form of a slave [cf. Phil. 2: 7]—the Word who is simple, enhypostatic, and without change became flesh [cf. John 1: 14].

In addition to these, he put on each of his fleshly and poor actions: the manger, his flight into Egypt, indifferent concourse with harlots and publicans, the calling of poor fishermen, his homelessness, his extemporaneousness, the fact that his whole fleshly life was everywhere unplanned, the dishonourable death on a cross—'For cursed is everyone who hangs on a tree' [Gal. 3: 13]—the fact that he was numbered with wicked robbers, the piercings of nails, the lance wound in his side, the slaps on the face, the spittings, the vinegar, the bitter drink, the crown of thorns, the mockery and laughter, the genuflections, the cheap funeral and grave.

What is wiser and by far stronger than men, by reason of the economy—as it were, the foolishness and weakness of God [cf. 1 Cor. 1: 25]—was shown forth by the very strong and very wise victory of the stronger, by being unspeakably declared to all creation by an ineffable silence through his deeds. Even if he was 'crucified in weakness he none the less lives in power', according to the divine Paul [2 Cor. 13: 4].

On the same passage. It is right that he should speak of 'thearchic weakness'. Through his willing condescension to us, having submitted to all things even 'unto death, death on a cross' [Phil. 2: 7], he himself took on our weaknesses, and suffered for us, and we have all been healed by his stripes [Isa. 53: 5].

The suffering is said to be his own, according to the voice of Peter which says, 'Christ suffered for us in the flesh' [1 Pet. 4: 1]. And, 'If they had known, they would not have crucified the Lord of glory' [1 Cor. 2: 8]. For this reason the Jews are called 'Lord-killers'.

4

240. 2 on 144. 1 (693B): *Think of how it is with our sun*: Let no one suppose that the great Dionysius judges the things of God wholly on the example of the sun. Rather, you should understand these things as follows. The sun, since it is not something other than light, does not have light as an accident, as if it were something other [than light], or in the manner of a soul by choosing beneficent action does it receive light from within and give it to all things. The opposite is the case. Being neither equipped with a soul, nor having choice, it acts beneficently (for it lacks reason); neither receiving light from another (for it is this very light and that which gives light). In this manner it is necessary to think this alone also of God, namely, that God does not have the good accidentally, as if it were a certain added quality, as we have virtues. Rather, God himself is the essence of the good, even as light is the essence of the sun. In so far as God is the good itself, he extends the splendour of goodness to all by treating beneficently those who are being enlightened. For this reason he speaks of the example of the sun, as it is a dim and rather opaque image of the wholly incommunicable archetype. For if images had the truth, they would no longer be examples, but archetypes.

240. 3 on 144. 6 (693B): *Intelligible and intelligent beings*: Properly speaking the one is intelligible and the other intelligent. The intelligible is like a certain 'food' for the intelligent, since what is thought (i.e. the intelligible) is greater and is conceived before that which thinks (i.e. the intelligent).[24] Therefore, the orders which are higher and lie close to God are properly called 'intelligible', whereas those which lie below are [properly called] 'intelligent', in so far as they think those which are above. But just because the things which are thought are intelligibles, one must not suppose that they do not think. For these also think, since they are minds and the created essences of life and of the highest mind. But also, activities and essences are there substantial. For every motion and rest are there substantial, being both

[24] Cf. *SchDN* 205. 2 and *SchEH* 120. 9.

living powers and beyond flux and bodily variation. Therefore, they are thought (in so far as they are immaterial), but think beings (in so far as they are incorporeal and transcendent minds), being enlightened from above as to the rational principles of beings and transferring these rational principles secretly to the lower angels by way of thought and revelation. ⟨ . . . ⟩

241. 6 on 145. 4 (696B): *The angelic*: By 'angelic purifications' he means, for example, the purifications of Isaiah [Isa. 6: 6–7] and Ezekiel [Ezek. 3: 3] who in ecstasy ate the scroll. By the angels' 'power to perfect' [145. 4] he means, for example, the case of Daniel and the angel who interpreted [the vision] [Dan. 10–12] and the case of the shepherd who perfected Hermas, as we read in *The Shepherd*.[25] Moreover, he explains how the angels themselves are purified and perfected in *The Celestial Hierarchy*.[26]

244. 1 on 145. 10 (696C): *The souls*: Note that the other souls after the angels are below them, and that they are immortal in so far as they were created as 'essential lives' [145. 12], and that souls fit for angelic life are guided by the angels. We can also read about this in *The Shepherd*.[27]

248. 1 on 147. 12 (697C): *A distant echo of the Good*:{ . . . } Rightly does the divine Dionysius straightaway cure the error of those things said of the sun. For he says that the soulless sun is a clear image of the goodness of God—calling the creature of the creator an image.

He here introduced the phrase 'a distant echo', which in the following chapter he explains in a better way.[28] We must say what this 'distant echo' is. It is just as if someone by shouting and crying out said something and those standing near by (if they possess healthy ears) hear both the sound and what was said, whereas those standing off a little, as much as they are separated, by so much do they hear the voice more weakly, whereas those separated by a great distance receive only a distant and obscure part of the echo, so as to hear a meaningless sound and not understand its significance. It can be concluded that the light of the sun [as compared] to the true [light] is such that the difference is beyond comparison.

248. 2 on 148. 3 (700A): *For the origin*: Do not think that the sun is the cause of generation or life or increase or perfection with respect to any being—as also no other element is, even if it happens to be necessary

---

[25] Herm. *mand. passim*, but especially 12. 6 (SC 53: 208).
[26] Cf. *CH* 7. 2 (28. 23–29. 24); *EH* 6. 3. 6 (119. 16–120. 12).
[27] Herm. *passim* (SC 53).
[28] *DN* 4. 20 (166. 1, 167. 5), and 6. 1 (191. 5).

[for existence] like water. For we can live for some time without sun and water, even if not perfectly. Rather, God knew that cold is completely infertile, whereas moderate warmth effects generation, and that plants and seeds stand in need of heat, as also do all bodies which have life, whether sensitive or vegetative. The sun 'cleanses' [148. 4] many things, so that they are whitened, for example, clothes and other things; it also 'rejuvenates' [148. 5] cold seeds. For this reason God caused the sun to have such a nature that it might do all the above-mentioned things from the creator, having received the ability not by its own choice or power. St Dionysius says this perfectly, just as he explains himself below at the end of the fifth and sixth chapters.[29] Accordingly, think well and do not distort!

248. 4 on 148. 6 (700A): *It was this light*: Note that the sun, 'though unformed' [148. 6], enlightened even the three days before its creation, that the first-created light was transformed into the sun on the fourth day, and that he speaks of the triad of days, even as the great Basil clearly says in his *Hexaemeron*.[30] Do not ignore that what was said before did not concern the sun but the first-created light which was transformed into the sun.

249. 2 on 148. 15–16 (700B): *All things desire it*: Observe how he classifies all the types of beings, and note the king of all whom also all beings desire. He speaks first of 'intelligent beings' and then of 'logical beings' [148. 16]. Intelligent beings are those not mixed with bodies, like all the super-celestial powers. Human souls are logical inasmuch as they are related to a body, as in the case of a man given over to sense perception. For if, according to the apostle [cf. Rom. 7: 22–3], the inner man alone acts (i.e. the soul), having no relation to the body, then the man would be intelligent and would not be called logical like every other animal composed of body and soul.[31]

He says that 'the intelligent and logical beings desire' God 'gnostic-ally' [148. 16], in so far as this desire is in them by nature, so as to know the king of all and participate in his goodness, since their soul is gnostic and logical. Rightly is it also called a 'desire for the good'. Irrational animals desire life (and thus the good) through their faculties of sense perception. Beings without sense perception (e.g. plants and creatures without souls or life) naturally desire the good, certainly not so that they might know it, but so that they might remain, which is to say, only by natural desire are they held together in existence by the good.[32]

---

[29] *DN* 5. 8 (188. 3–4), 6. 3 (192. 15–193. 4).
[31] Reading λογικός for λογικῶς.

[30] Bas. *hex*. 6. 2 (SC 26: 330–5).
[32] Cf. *SchDN* 205. 2.

249. 3 on 149. 2 (700B): *Makes all things a 'sum'*: 'Sum' [ἀολλῆ], that is to say, 'gathered together'.

Note that it is called 'sun' [ἥλιος] because it makes 'sums' [ἀολλῆ] and because it 'brings together scattered things' [149. 2].

Note also that he denies that the sun is God, even if he says many things which seem to be contrary to this, which are easily distorted.[33]

249. 4 on 149. 5 (700C): *The old myth* [lit. **according to the word of antiquity**]: 'According to the word of antiquity', either because the divine Dionysius and Timothy were Greeks, as is clear from the Acts of the holy apostles, or because he means the foolishness of the Greeks, for they used to call the sun 'old' and 'ancient', as in comedy.

252. 7 on 151. 19 (704A): *From this beauty*: 'Behold, all things are very beautiful' [cf. Gen. 1: 31]. Zechariah says the same thing [Zech. 9: 17 LXX]. Anything which is beautiful came into being from the uncaused beauty, for through beauty the conjunctions of the elements came about, which he calls 'harmonies' [152. 2]. Also through it perdures the well-ordered binding together of beings, the so-called 'friendships and communions' [152. 2] of all virtuous and rational creatures, which are in some sense thoughts with God, as the church of the first-begotten in heaven and on earth. Among irrational creatures there are herd-like associations. Among things without souls there are habitual sympathies for one another. Therefore, 'all things have united to beauty' [152. 2–3], by having been restored to their cause by participation in it.

253. 1 on 152. 4–5 (704A): *Of all as Goal* [lit. **limit**]: God is called 'the limit of all' in so far as he holds together all [Col 1: 17], in so far as he holds all in safety [Ps. 104: 5 LXX], in so far as all were brought into being for his sake [John 1: 3] and lack nothing for perfection. For this reason, he is called the 'source' of all, as cause, thus also a 'means', in so far as he grants a sustaining order, also an 'end', in so far as beings reach their limit in his will, by which also they are restored, just as also he calls him 'perfecting' [152. 5], in so far as he is beginning and end, according to the divine John in the Apocalypse [Rev. 21: 6], and 'paradigmatic' [152. 6], in so far as he possessed beforehand in himself the predeterminations of all things which will be, even before he produced them, as the apostle says, 'whom he predetermined . . .' [Rom. 8: 30]. For St Dionysius thinks of these paradigms as the providential predeterminations in God of what will be, even before they were

---

[33] Reading εἶπε for εἴπομεν.

produced, that is, before they were defined and distinguished by the singular foreknowledge of God which encompasses all things. You will also find these things in the fifth chapter.[34] { . . . }

256. 2 on 152. 22 (704C): *All rest*: He speaks of three types of rest and motion which also he enumerates, that is, of minds, souls, and bodies. It is necessary to understand these matters accurately.

Minds rest and are moved, as both Isaiah and Ezekiel say *vis-à-vis* the Seraphim and Cherubim [cf. Isa. 6 and Ezek. 10], and since they ascend and descend, as Moses says [cf. Gen. 28: 12].

To be returned ceaselessly to God and to be founded in their reaching out for him, even if they depart and descend to inferior creatures, because of their providence for those who are receiving their aid—this is to rest firmly in their nearness to God and to be moved to serve those who receive good from them. It can also mean that they are moved by thinking of higher beings and they rest by being thought by inferior being, as intelligibles, while remaining in their own sameness, in so far as they have their own garrisons and their own resting places. They dwell in themselves, having turned in upon themselves and being unscattered by those things which are foreign to piety. Moreover, all inferior beings are returned to the superior. The motions of minds and souls are round and circular, as Ezekiel says [Ezek. 1: 15–17], since they went forth from themselves and returned to themselves without having left themselves.

The above-stated principles apply to incorporeal beings, whereas in the case of bodies rest and motion are understood differently. Matter remains (in the substrate), but is moved into the diverse kinds of bodies which arise from it, bodies both with and without souls.

257. 4 on 153. 7 (705B): *Then it moves in a spiral fashion*: You see from this how great is the difference between the soul and the intelligibles. The latter 'intellectually and unitedly' [153. 18], that is, according to a gathered intuition, think the high and divine illuminations which are revealed according to their measure.[35] But the soul 'rationally and discursively' [153. 18] thinks them, that is, being divided into parts and being taught by participation. For the mind, by descending into conceptions, is as it were divided and stands in need of discursive reason with many examples in order to represent the object of its thought (i.e. the transcendent). Accordingly, the soul functions 'through mixture and discursively' [154. 1], even when it thinks. For

---

[34] *DN* 5. 8–9 (188. 3–13).
[35] For 'gathered intuition', cf. Plot. *Enn.* 3. 8. 9. 21–2, 4. 4. 1. 20.

this is proper to the soul, even when from without it is led to the higher things, for it is ascending from things which are foreign.

260. 2 on 154. 14 (705C): *The universal one and the many* [lit. **manifold**]: How will the universal one and the manifold be understood? Posit the whole world to be a great plant.[36] In some way it lives in all its animate parts (e.g. its stem and its roots) and in the parts of its parts (e.g. its branches and twigs and leaves). For [this is true, especially] if you suppose with me that each of these is in some sense a living being complete in itself, and this, because it preserves its unity and order in the whole, according to which unity and order the tree lives both in itself and in its parts.

Whatever sort of life it may have—intelligent things intellectually and rationally, irrational things sensibly, things without soul and breath vegetatively and habitually[37]—it lives in itself, just as I said that each part lives in the whole through motion, the parts in the universals. [Posit this and] you will know the kinship and yoke of all to the one and to the manifold, to the extent that each lives as it should, as we have said. ⟨ . . . ⟩

260. 4 on 155. 1 (705D): *Whether such source be exemplary*: An 'exemplary' cause or 'source' is that in relation to which generated beings are generated. It is either an idea (i.e. thought perfect in itself, eternal thought of the eternal God), or an eternal paradigm which is present in nature, that in relation to which generated beings are generated. For ideas and paradigms are incorporeal.

A 'final' cause or 'source' [155. 2] is that for the sake of which generated beings are brought to perfection. Alternatively, a final cause is that which is inseparable from its effect. Alternatively, it is something immanent from which generated beings are generated (e.g. the matter of the universe, though God also produced this).

An 'efficient cause' [155. 3] is that which is separated from its effect (e.g. God and everything by which generated beings are generated).

261. 4 on 156. 1 (708B): *Let no one imagine*: Note that one must not ascribe to God inconsistent names, unless indeed they be contained in the divine Scripture, as even now he says concerning 'eros'. { . . . }

264. 1 on 156. 17 (708D): *And the same happens with our intelligent powers*: { . . . } By 'intelligent powers' he means those thoughts which are lower and which are a scattering of the mind. When the soul wishes to rise up to God and as much as possible be united to him, its eye

---

[36] For a similar use of the plant metaphor, Plot. *Enn.* 3. 8. 10.
[37] Cf. *SchDN* 205. 2.

(i.e. the mind itself) must turn away from individual things and jump upward to the more universal things. (Thoughts are individual things, as we have said.) For then the mind, having become whole and having turned within, having further become a unity and simplicity, will be able to receive the divine rays, and this, through praiseworthy unknowing—not an unknowing through ignorance but one which knows that it does not know the incomprehensible things concerning God. It will know by enjoying the divine rays. This happens not through sensible eyes (for it will not comprehend by these) but by a state of the mind without eyes.

268. 4 on 161. 1 (713A): *When we talk of yearning* [lit. eros]: Understand how the great Hierotheus philosophized the best things concerning praiseworthy eros. First he says that it is 'divine' [161. 1], since in an exalted manner and apart from cause God is the first cause of heavenly eros. For if eros is itself charity, as has been said,[38] and it is written that God is charity [1 John 4: 8], then clearly God is the eros (i.e. the charity) which unifies all.

After this he moves on to the angels—whence also he speaks of 'angelic eros' [161. 1]—where especially one can find the divine eros of unity. For there is nothing discordant or rebellious in them.

Then, after the angels, he speaks of 'intelligent eros' [161. 1] such as is found among the theosophs of the church. To such as these Paul says, 'So that you might think the same thing . . .' [Phil. 2: 2].[39] And the Lord says to them, 'So that they might be one as also we are one' [John 17: 11]. These things concern true Christians, but also all people in whom is the law of friendship. (Previously he referred to the logical souls as 'intelligent', naming them after the divine mind.)[40]

He called the eros of irrational beings 'psychic eros' [161. 1], a type of friendship based on the faculties of sense perception but without using the mind. By this erotic power birds fly in flocks (e.g. swans, geese, cranes, ravens, and the like). Footed creatures are also such (e.g. deer, cows, and the like). So also are swimming creatures (e.g. tunny-fish, kephaloi, and the like). From this source even non-gregarious animals are moved to gather together with those of the same kind.

The eros of creatures without soul or sense he calls 'natural eros' [161. 2], because they, being sustained by the Creator, love him

[38] *DN* 4. 12 (158. 9–12).
[39] Reading φρονῆτε for λέγηται.
[40] *DN* 4. 11 (156. 9–16), cf. *SchDN* 264. 1.

according to their habitual tendency (or quality). Therefore, through this living (or natural) motion even these are returned to God.

269. 1 on 161. 6 (713B): *The many ... from the One:* We said above that intelligents think and intelligibles are thought and that without doubt the intelligents are surpassed by the intelligibles.[41] Whence also those things which are thought are the 'food' of those things which think. Now then, the intelligents have eros for the intelligibles, in so far as they are being returned to them, even those which are in some sense above them. But also, the intelligibles have providential eros for the intelligents, and this by granting them reciprocal aid. Let it be acknowledged therefore that the eros of such beings is above the eros of sensible beings. ⟨ ... ⟩

272. 1 on 162. 7 (716A): *Even that which is not wishes for a place in it:* Since he said that even non-being somehow desires the good and wishes to be in it (which also you will find that he said a few pages earlier)[42]—granted that it is being declared on the basis of Greek doctrines, for he is fighting against the Greeks especially, as well as the Manichaeans who are pre-eminent in bad doctrine—it is necessary to explain in greater detail why it is called non-being and why it is pious and necessary that there be one principle of beings.

This it is right to think, for God is this [one principle]. For if there were diverse principles, they would be altogether infinite in number. If then God is this one principle, thus also he is true being and the good itself.

Reason will also of necessity discover the opposite of what has been said. For where there is a beginning there will also without doubt be an end. And if there is being, then there will also be non-being. And if there is good, then there will also be evil. But since existing things are beings and forms, non-being is formless and beingless, contemplated by reason alone. Accordingly, the ancients called this non-being 'formless matter', which they also called the 'end shame'.[43]

Matter is called 'non-being', not because it is absolutely nothing, but because it does not exist. For God is true being and the good itself. For even matter was produced by God from non-beings—but not as some suppose, as something formless and shapeless. For this reason matter is not the source of sensibles, but rather that which fills them, an end and

---

[41] *SchDN* 240. 3.

[42] *DN* 4. 7 (152. 10–12).

[43] For matter as 'formless', cf. Proc. *In Alc.* 189. 17 and 318. 3, *In Prm.* 999. 24 and 1119. 7–8; Simpl. *In Ph.* 9. 211. 16, 10. 1333. 6. For matter as 'end shame', cf. Plot. *Enn.* 1. 8. 5. 23.

a sediment[44] of the things which are. Therefore, it is neither an image of God (as are rational beings) nor a reflection[45] of true being. The sensible reflection of the real intelligible world, because sensible, is not without matter; on the other hand, it is greater than matter, because in some way it participates in form. Therefore, matter will never be manifested apart from form and qualities (i.e. states). For when is there fire without heat or light or white colour; or water without cold or moisture or dark-blue colour? Similarly the earth and air.

For this reason he says that matter contemplated by reason is without form and quality and shape [cf. 162. 8].[46] For from this come visible and invisible things, which is to say, from things which were not they were produced by God, though not because there was some underlying matter first formless and only then ordered, as the divine Moses has taught [Gen 1: 1–2]. Thus, on the one hand, [non-being] is in God, in so far as even matter was created by him. On the other hand, it is understood to be beyond being in him, in so far as that one as good holds together all things. These things you will find inserted here and there in what follows.[47]

276. 1 on 164. 4 (716D): *Where does evil come from*: From here, after putting forward an objection, he expounds it at great length, as if it were probable.[48] For if we do not grant that there is something contrary to the beautiful (i.e. evil), then virtue is not recognized as good, but rather all things are indistinguishably mixed together, since virtue is not praised and its contrary is not blamed, just as apart from the law there is no sin [Rom. 4: 15, 7: 7].[49]

Now, the objector replies, unless we grant that evil is the opposite of the good, the good itself will be contrary to itself in those who sin by a lack of good. But even before the activity of virtue of a virtuous person we see in his soul that evils are distinguished from virtue. For, on the one hand, when the reasonable part of the soul does its proper activities, in none of its goods is it fettered. On the other hand, when the irrational part of the soul, which is mixed with matter and body, conquers, then the rational part is fettered and prevented from acting properly. Therefore, the irrational part is corrupted by intermixture with matter. The rational part, however, not by being mixed with

---

[44] For matter as 'sediment', cf. Plot. *Enn.* 2. 3. 17. 24, as well as *SchDN* 312. 1.

[45] For matter as 'reflection', cf. Plot. *Enn.* 1. 8. 3. 37, 2. 4. 15. 23.

[46] But see *DN* 4. 28 (174. 6).

[47] *DN* 4. 20 (166. 9–11).

[48] For a full discussion of this scholion, see Ch. 5.

[49] Reading ἀρετῆς for ἀρετῇ.

matter, but by inclining towards matter (i.e. yielding to the irrational and not overcoming it) is corrupted, just as when it is dark and the eye is thus hindered from seeing.

He is not demonstrating whether absolute evil subsists. For it is not 'evil for something' (i.e. absolute evil), but rather, even vice exists by being a species and accident of the evil. By the additions it turns into this or that particular [evil]: for example, injustice of the soul is wickedness. And again, the species of injustice [stand in relation] to the matter of desire: for some happen with respect to money and others with respect to honours. Also, by additions the species of evil come about also from the parts of the soul: cowardice or audaciousness from the appetitive part, boldness or silliness from the desirous part. Species of evil also come from the activities: for example, cowardice is a lack with respect to impulse, audaciousness is an excess with respect to impulse, and licentiousness with respect to experiencing. Therefore it has become clear how in the soul (even before activities) evils are distinguished from virtues through there being rational and irrational parts of the soul. He shows that these things of the irrational part are another law which attacks us in our minds, as the apostle says [Rom. 7: 23], and by not being overcome imprison the rational part, as we have shown.

277. 1 on 164. 20 (717B): *Hence evil*: { . . . } If corruption is evil and corruption corrupts even evil, how will there be absolute evil when it corrupts itself? For if evil resides in matter, it is quite clear that it is easily corrupted, but it is still matter: and this corrupts itself. For this reason matter is said to be 'without being' in comparison to the being of the God which is beyond being, in so far as it is itself corruptible and does not always exist, and is said to be 'formless' in comparison to the form of God, as Moses called the Creator Word [Gen. 32: 30 LXX]. In addition, matter is called 'non-being' in comparison to the divine subsistence in its being.

280. 4 on 166. 16–167. 1 (720B): *That which is totally bereft of the Good*: His object is to prove that simple and absolute evil is not a being. He says that nothing among beings and in creation is completely without a share of the good. For that which has no share in the good, in so far as it also was not created by the good, does not even exist. What else is a creator? But neither can something subsist, if in its accidents it does not share in a state or quality of the good. Many things deprived of an added state or quality remain in subsistence: for example, heated iron, having participated in the highest heat, after the fire has been

extinguished, remains what it was; and water of itself is said to be an element without quality, but when it penetrates the earth, from that source it is qualified, and nevertheless having partaken it ceases from the quality and yet subsists; thus also with respect to frozen and cold things, when the cold is gone, they still subsist; but also with respect to those things which have no share in life (e.g. trees, stones, and stars), and with respect to those things which have no share in mind (e.g. cattle)—all these things, I say, nevertheless subsist. (God, because he is beyond being, transcends even being, and none the less he exists and pre-exists.) But it is not possible to speak thus of the good. For unless they participate in the quality of the good, in which they subsist, they cannot subsist. 'For in him we live and are', as the apostle says [Acts 17: 28]. ⟨ ... ⟩ { ... }

281. 4 on 167. 16 (720D): *For that which totally lacks a share*: The intention of the divine Dionysius is clear from many things, as he fights against the opinions of certain Greeks concerning evil.[50] For he says that evil is not a being. For in no way could absolute evil be essential, unless it were completely without a share in the good through the complete lack of it. It is not possible to find this anywhere, not even in formless matter itself, even if this seemed good to some of the Greeks. For that which was wholly produced by God, even if dimly and in the lowest manner, participates none the less in the good. Moving on, he proves this perfectly in the tenth chapter of this problem.[51] For if evil were mixed with the good (i.e. it is partly non-being through a slight lack of the good and partly also being[52] because its creator wholly exists), then it would not be evil. For evil is not in just any lack, but in a complete lack of the good. Therefore that which lacks the good only slightly[53] is not evil. For it can also be perfect as to its nature. For it is something defective as to the good, but perfect as to its nature: which is to say, it is good and in no way evil, though participating in a lack as to the first good.

That which is not completely without a share in the good, but is closer to evil, is not completely evil, as also that which is less near the good has something of the good and is invested with being from it and invests with being its own privation in its wholly participating in the

[50] For a full discussion of this scholion, see Ch. 5.
[51] By 'tenth chapter' is meant not the present divisions of the text of chapter 4 of *The Divine Names* but an older division which can still be found in FA. This would correspond to *DN* 4. 28.
[52] Reading καὶ ὄν for μὴ ὄν, with FA.
[53] Reading ὀλίγῳ for ὀλίγον, with FA and Plotinus.

good.[54] For if there were purely and completely an absence of the good, then it is clear that there would be neither 'universal good nor mixed good nor self-evil' [168. 5–6]. For where the good is not, neither is there anything in the nature. How then will there be evil if it is not invested with being by another? Take away bodies and light, and there will be no shadows. { . . . }

285. 3 on 169. 1 (721D): *That two opposites*: Note these things, for he is in especial contest with the Manichaeans, who thoughtlessly assert a dyadic source of their [two] contrary [principles]. The science of numbers refers divisible numbers to a 'limit', and this by positing the monad as source of every number and the dyad as source of just even numbers. Now then, whatever is a 'source' is that which is most simple in each genus. How then will the dyad be the source of all? For the dyad is not a simple source, but a composite one. Surely then, a source arising from composition does not make [other things] simple. How then could it be called a source? For before this composite source there will be a proper source, the one, by which the dyad is perfected, while the monads are composite. It is clear then from all sides that the doctrine of two sources is inconsistent.

288. 7 on 170. 6 (724B): *The punishment*: As an aside, he anticipates the opposition of certain heresies which ascribe to evil the angels who punish at the command of God, as well as the punishment itself. Immediately and in a most wise and fitting manner he brings these objections to naught. From the priests who debar and exclude the polluted and profane from the church on account of their profane and polluted deeds, he indicates that neither are these evil because they punish the polluted.[55] May it not be! It is said, 'He does not bear the sword for nothing, for he is a minister of God, an avenger who brings wrath upon the one who practises evil' [Rom. 13: 4]. Note then his solution. For he dissolves the many questions of those who ask whether public executioners and rulers are from God.

288. 13 on 170. 22 (724D): *Some failure*: Note that by 'corruption' he means an errant and inharmonious motion of nature contrary to order.[56]

---

[54] Reading μετέχεσθαι for μάχεσθαι and omitting ἐκ. Cf. *DN* 168. 4–5.

[55] Reading ἀπειργόντων for εἰργόντων with *DN* 4. 22 (170. 8).

[56] Leontius of Byzantium (d. *c.*543) in the unpublished florilegium attached to book 2 of his *Against the Nestorians and Eutychians* appeals to Dionysius' parallel discussion of the nature of corruption at *DN* 4. 25 (173. 6–7) and uses it against the followers of Julian. The passage in question would have been of great use to Leontius for its clear definition of corruption and could thus form a starting point for his debates with the Julianists over whether Christ's body was itself subject to corruption. For the text of this passage from

You find this also in Ezekiel concerning the devil, 'Your understanding was corrupted along with your beauty' [Ezek. 28: 17].

In order to refute the Greeks and Manichaeans, he says that not even demons are evil by nature. Then he presents and refutes their suppositions, saying first that demons do not corrupt beings [170. 16], for beings as beings do not pass over into non-existence, and then that, even if this is so, not for all nor of all is corruption evil,[57] as in the case of beasts, reptiles, deadly plants, and the like.

One must next inquire whether demons corrupt potentiality or actuality [170. 16–17]. To begin with, we must briefly explain what potentiality and actuality are. One must know that the corruption of a potentiality is such only with respect to its actuality, even as a habit is such only with respect to its proper actuality. (A habit is a certain permanent quality.)[58] This can be illustrated as follows. Fire has the potential to impart heat: this ability to heat is its habit or quality. What is in accordance with its habit or quality is its actuality—as when a certain body is heated by it, for here we see the actuality of the habit of the fire being brought to fulfilment. In other words, the potentiality has within itself its own actuality, for the actuality of the potentiality is that which is being brought to fulfilment from within itself (for the potentiality is comprehended according to what it effects). Actuality is therefore the corruption of potentiality.

Now then, just as potentiality pertains to [a creature's] being, so also with regard to actuality. An actuality which is 'contrary to order, symmetry, and harmony' [170. 20–1] is a weak procession. In this, by wrongfully progressing, they are not able to remain as their capacity, activity, and being dictate. If the weakness were total, as we have said,[59] and not just a partial weakness of the things which have been mentioned, then it would also corrupt the substrate in which reside the potentiality and the actuality. Neither its potentiality nor its actuality, nor for that matter its being or even corruption itself, would be left— and this, in so far as those things to which the corruption pertains are also destroyed. The activity of the intelligible and intelligent minds is to act in accordance with nature, that is, to stretch upward to God, whereas the capacity of the human mind is to descend into thoughts.

Leontius, David B. Evans, 'Leontius of Byzantium and Dionysius the Areopagite', *BS* 7 (1980), 28.

[57] The latter paraphrases Dionysius' statement οὐδὲ τοῦτο παντὶ καὶ πάντῃ κακόν (170. 18–19).

[58] Cf. *SchDN* 205. 2, *SchCH* 65. 5.

[59] *SchDN* 281. 4.

As has been said, if they are wrongfully moved, they lack the good.[60] Therefore, there is nothing evil by nature.

293. 2 on 172. 10 (725C): *What is not really there*: We should explain how those things which desire what is not desire evil. God is a being, though also beyond beings. Since God is also the truth, the truth is thus a being. Rightly then, falsehood which opposes the truth is not a being.[61] For it is completely outside of God, being not even an image of the truth, having nothing good from God. When [what is not] persuades certain individuals that it is in fact something, it will be a dark and dim idol of the things which exist. It is in actuality an idol and in actuality falsehood, that is, really and truly falsehood. Whence also in actuality it is non-being, in so far as it is not a being—it is truly non-being. Just as in the case of things which exist falsely and are wholly this falsehood, the falsehood, when it is taken away, takes away every essence of the thing; in the same way also, the lover of falsehood (like the demons) loves that which is not and does not remain in being, that is, in the truth, as the truth itself says [John 8: 44a]. Demons, as Jesus said [John 8: 44b], being false and the fathers of falsehood, do not exist and they desire that which is not, since they also desire evil falsehood.

293. 3 on 172. 14 (728A): *Can become evil*: { . . . } We also said above in the fifth chapter[62] that there is not a complete privation of the good in beings, since there would also be complete corruption, even of corruption itself, but rather privation takes place through a partial lack of the good. For this reason, neither does the soul have complete evil, rather it will have and not have. Also, the good is essential, whereas evil is from without.

Someone might also argue as follows: evil is merely an impediment for the soul, [which impedes] its natural activity. Now then, though this impediment is external, this impediment will none the less be responsible for the production of evil deeds, even as the soul is hindered from seeing when it is dark.

To this one must respond as follows: on the basis of the principles already laid down it is clear that such an impediment produces evil, but is not evil itself. For vice is not absolute evil, but merely a species of evil, even as virtue is something which helps to produce good, but is not for all that the absolute good.[63]

---

[60] *DN* 4. 22 (170. 6–8).
[61] For 'God is a being . . . not a being', cf. Plot. *Enn.* 1. 8. 6. 44–7.
[62] *SchDN* 281. 4, 288. 13. 'Fifth chapter' corresponds to *DN* 4. 23 in FA.
[63] This scholion is heavily dependent on Plotinus, see our discussion in Ch. 5.

297. 4 on 173. 20 (728D): *Cause of evil in the soul*: Because certain philosophers say that to do evil arises from the irrational part of the soul which is mixed with matter and body, when the soul inclines towards it, as he explained above,[64] the divine Dionysius solves the problem very well from the other types of being, those which are incorporeal and in no way mixed with a body, which erred even apart from a body by means of a lack of the good.

297. 7 on 174. 7 (729A): *Even the capacity to be effected*: It is fitting to explain in brief the opinions of those who say that matter is non-being, and how they call it non-being, so that also the syllogisms of the divine Dionysius might be understood.[65]

They call matter 'non-being' for the following reason. They say that being [τὸ ὄν], which is in the intelligible orders, came from the first [creature] which is under being. Since that is beyond being, this being from it was called 'being other than being' according to a declension. This being about which they are speaking, they name 'the matter of the intelligibles', matter contemplated by reason alone, which they also call 'form' and 'life', as if it is the substrate of intelligible beings.

But they also speak of the matter of sensibles as lacking all things which are in the intelligibles. It is neither form nor life. This came, they say, from being which they say came from that which is first and beyond being. As a result, they do not say that it is being, but non-being, since it is other than being.

They say that it is necessary that the declension proceed even as far as the 'last regions of being' [ἔσχατοι], and for this reason they say that matter is other than being and other than the beautiful (as it is not beautiful).[66] They say that in actuality it is nothing, or rather, that it is deprived of all things accidental to it (e.g. form and quality). For it neither shapes itself into form (like heaven, earth, air, water, animals, and stars), nor does it effect anything, rather it is disposed to these by another. Therefore, in so far as it is not in itself a being (i.e. form and quality) but is these only potentially (i.e. it can be borne into form and quality, but it is not in actuality one of these), suitably is it non-being, not existing in itself in actuality. Therefore also, in so far as it is without form and quality and is non-being and lacking all things, it was called evil by them.

Solving these objections, the divine Dionysius says: how will matter

---

[64] *DN* 4. 23 (170. 12–172. 11).
[65] John is here apparently thinking of Plotinus' doctrine of two matters (cf. *Enn.* 2. 4).
[66] Cf. Plot. *Enn.* 1. 8. 7. 19–20.

do evil, matter which is completely non-being in actuality (for to do is the part of actuality), matter which is not even 'able to suffer anything' [174. 7], matter which only exists in itself? For it is disposed to form and quality by another for our sake. Therefore, because it exists in itself, it does not suffer. If you call it non-being, in so far as it is completely nothing, it will be neither evil nor good. But if it is some being, it is either from God or from itself or from another source—and it and God exist. But if matter is necessary, in so far as it fills[67] the world, how is matter evil? After all, [recall] the definition of the necessary: eternal, true, and in some sense useful, even as virtue is useful. Therefore, evil is one thing and necessity another.

300. 1 on 174. 17 (729B): *Evil qua evil:*[68] Overturning the opinions of those who say that matter is evil, he says: how then is the growth of things from the earth (i.e. plants and animals) begotten of matter and nourished? For these also are composed of both form and matter. How then does evil itself beget and nourish and not immediately corrupt and become corrupted? For this is the habit of evil.

But neither, as we said above that some say,[69] does matter drag souls into evil through the irrational part of the soul, matter which is mixed with the irrational part of the soul through the body. For many have overcome such a part of the soul, as in the case of the saints of God.

Some of the Greeks say that heaven and the stars are not corrupted since they come from a very pure matter, whereas those things proximate to corruptible bodies come from sedimentary and course matter—necessarily such matter came down, matter which is lowest in the declension of creatures—and therefore the lower things are corrupted and unstable, not able to rest and stay firmly in themselves (like heaven and the stars). If then they came into being of necessity in this way, how is matter evil, since (in our opinion) it has necessity in itself? Therefore, matter is in no way evil.

305. 3 on 177. 10 (732D): *It is a defect:* Wonderfully has he shown that evil lacks a hypostasis [177. 1], by demonstrating that it is a privation of order and nature. The privation is not a self-hypostasis, as we said

---

[67] Reading συμπληρωτική for συμπληρωτικόν, with FA.

[68] This scholion was passed over by Suchla in her collation of the scholia. Internal criteria suggest that it is by John of Scythopolis, namely, the statement, 'But neither, as we said above that some say, does matter drag souls into evil through the irrational part of the soul, matter which is mixed with the irrational part of the soul through the body.' For this see *SchDN* 297. 4 (by John). The scholion is present in its entirety in FA.

[69] *SchDN* 297. 4, cf. *SchDN* 276. 1.

above,[70] but rather it is the absence of what ought naturally to be present.[71] Thence also he speaks of what relates to privation as 'sin' [177. 11], that is, a certain failure to hit the mark and a certain falling away from what is fitting, and as 'without end' [177. 11], that is, missing the end, from the metaphor of shooting arrows. For just as those who hit their end (i.e. the target at which they aim, which is called an end) do well; thus also those who shoot outside the target sin. Accordingly, he says that evil is in no way anything.

305. 9 on 178. 11–12 (733B): *The popular notion that Providence*: Note how he rebukes those who ask: 'Why did God not make us in such a way that, even if we wished, we could not sin?' This is the same as asking: 'Why did he not make us without mind and reason?' For to be 'led to virtue' [178. 12] by necessity neither shows us to be in control of our own affairs nor does it allow our intelligent 'nature' [178. 13] to exist (i.e. our intelligent soul). For take away our free will and we will be neither an image of God nor a rational and intelligent soul—in reality our 'nature will be destroyed' [178. 13], in so far as it is not what it must be.

We should understand that by 'self-moving' [178. 14] he means those endowed with free will and those who rule themselves. He does not mean things which move themselves (e.g. animate beings, in opposition to immobile things, e.g. houses and mountains), or things incapable of independent motion (e.g. stones and trees). For while speaking of virtue, he treats those things which are self-moving, the providence of which he says is fitting: for example, providence which is through the law and the prophets [or] providence through beneficial acts, as also the apostle makes clear when he speaks among the Athenians [Acts 17: 25–7].

5

308. 7 on 180. 9–10 (816B): *That being in its transcendence*: The ancients called God 'the one', not because he is the source of numbers, but because he transcends all things and because none of the things after him is connumerated with him, but also because he is uncompounded and simple.[72]

---

[70] Cf. *SchDN* 301. 1.
[71] For a similar definition of privation, see Plot. *Enn.* 1. 8. 11. 10.
[72] It is unclear why John comments on the one, for such language is absent from the beginning of *DN* 5.

He does not present what the essence of God is. For 'essence' is not properly predicated of God, in so far as he is beyond being.

309. 3 on 181. 5 (816B): *To all living things, and yet is beyond them*: It should be noted how, when he speaks about angels and humans, he calls the angels 'intelligibles', and our souls 'intelligents', as we have often presented above when we explained the meanings of 'intelligible' and 'intelligent'.[73] Now, however, since he is speaking primarily of God, rightly does he call the angels (as well as us) 'intelligents' [181. 5], in so far as they also by the act of thinking of God, to the extent that they are able, are nourished by the thought and are returned to divine wisdom, even as are human souls. By 'the sensibles' [181. 6] he means irrational beings. None the less, all animate beings share in divine wisdom—both because of their natural stirrings (as the divine Basil shows in his *Hexaemeron*), but also because all things came into being in wisdom, as it is said, 'You made all things in wisdom' [Ps. 104: 24].[74]
{ . . . }

312. 1 on 181. 14–15 (816C): *With their own share*: { . . . } The cause of all things is one, and not many; and rightly does one divinity, the holy and blessed Trinity, produce all things, and not many creative divinities. He says this not so as to waste words, but in order to attack the wise men of the Greeks and the heretics who follow Simon. Such as these speak of the gods as 'world-makers', adding that, inasmuch as they have declined, so much do they also produce the weaker things of creation, even until 'the sediment of all', as they say, that is, matter.[75]

316. 4 on 183. 18–20 (820A): *Being in itself is*: It must not be thought that these things are said of the cause of all. Rather, they concern those things which subsist through his act of creation, that is, the intelligibles, intelligents, sensibles, and the rest.

As we have already said, God is before being: indeed, he is pre-existent.[76] (Being is like a certain reflection of a cause which subsisted beforehand.) Now then, God is called both pre-existent and existent, and this, in so far as he is the cause of all and in so far as all things are from him. Conceptually speaking, being subsists as a result of its participation in his pre-existence, not because God was divided into

[73] *SchDN* 240. 3, *SchCH* 109. 2, *SchEH* 120. 9. Cf. *SchDN* 205. 2.
[74] Cf. Bas. *hex*. 9. 3–4 (SC 26. 489–503). Cf. *SchDN* 205. 2.
[75] For 'world-makers', cf. Dam. *Pr*. 270; Proc. *In Prm*. 902. 31; and *Theo. Arist*. 43. For the 'sediment of all', meaning matter itself, cf. Proc. *In Alc*. 181. 17 and *In Tim*. 2. 44. 8, 2. 65. 24, 2. 232. 1; Plato, *Phaedrus* 109 C 2; Plot. *Enn*. 2. 3. 17. 24. Cf. *SchDN* 272. 1.
[76] Cf. *SchDN* 185. 6.

existence and pre-existence, but because his will which led all beings into being is said to pre-subsist in God.

Since this divine will preordained the creation into existence, God is rightly thought to be a source of being 'older' [183. 19] than the other things of God in which beings participate. For first something is, and then it is life and wisdom. Accordingly, the invisible and exalted minds first participate in being, and in this way in life and wisdom. For just as in our case first some prime matter subsists, from which we are; so also in the case of incorporeal minds, being itself (like matter) is thought to be the form of each through life, through which [being] they are given substance for life and wisdom and likeness.

We have explained 'likeness' [cf. 183. 20] and 'sameness' above, those powers which uplift us to God.[77] Through these powers, those beings which are proximate to him are made like unto him. Those things which are right behind these proximate beings, in so far as they also participate in being—these participate in these powers by way of declension.

By 'the sources of beings' [184. 6] one must understand the first beings to subsist in creation. These are called 'sources', not because beings are from them (as if they were elements), but because, as has been said, they are prior to the things which follow them.[78] For example, in the case of intelligibles, the thrones are the source of creation—and in the same way for the rest. In the case of the sensibles, heaven and earth are the source of creation: for 'in the beginning God created the heaven and the earth' [Gen. 1: 1]. For these are the first created sensibles.

We can understand these things in another way. The ideas and paradigms, which are the self-complete and eternal thoughts of the eternal God, as we have said,[79] are conceptualized as being like the elements, sources, and immaterial and incorporeal matter of the things which participate in those ideas—for example, the incorporeal created orders.[80] For 'life itself and wisdom itself' [183. 19–20] and order itself and the rest are paradigms in God, in which creatures participate, just as straight lines drawn to the [circumference of a] circle [participate] in a point or a centre [cf. 185. 4–7].

320. 3 on 184. 18–19 (820C): *From it and in it are*: We should understand these things as follows.[81] 'The absolutely transcendent Good-

---

[77] *SchDN* 256. 1.   [78] *DN* 5. 5 (184. 6–7).   [79] *SchDN* 253. 1.

[80] Omitting καί after μετεχόντων, with FA.

[81] Most of this scholion is a loose paraphrase of Plot. *Enn.* 5. 9. 5–8.

ness' [184. 17], being mind and wholly act, by turning to itself, exists in actuality, not in potentiality (first being mindless and then becoming mind in actuality). For this reason, it is alone a pure mind, not receiving its thought from without, but wholly thinking from itself.

If its essence were other than itself and what it thinks were other than itself, then its essence would be unthinking. But if it has something, it has it from itself and not from another. But if it thinks from itself and out of itself, then it is what it thinks. Therefore, since it is mind, it truly thinks beings, in so far as it is.

If then by thinking itself it thinks beings, it is beings. For it will think these either as beings from another, or as beings in itself, in so far as they are from it. Now then, it is impossible to think that they are from another. (For where are there beings among the sensibles? The sensibles are not beings, in so far as they are subject to change, generation, and corruption.) Therefore, it thinks itself in itself.

Since God is also the creator of beings, he will think them in that which does not yet exist. But he is the archetype of this universe. And these things he thinks not by receiving types from another, but by himself being the paradigm of beings. Thus, he is neither in a place, nor are things in him, as if in a place. But he has them, in so far as he has himself and is one with them—since all things, on the one hand, exist together and exist in the indivisible in him; and since, on the other hand, they are distinguished indivisibly in the indivisible.[82] Accordingly, his thoughts are beings, and these beings are forms.

But one must not understand thoughts in such a way that when he thinks of something, he becomes this something, for it is necessary that what is thought precede this thought, so that by thinking it he might create it. But he thinks beings, in so far as he thinks himself and is joined to the things which are within himself. Thought for him is generation for beings.

That which exists in them, this is form and idea. He, being wholly mind, is wholly understanding. The things which are from him and in him are minds like unto the contemplations of understanding. They are both together and distinguished in him—even as there are many understandings together in the soul which remain unmixed and act outwardly one by one, when it is necessary; even as the soul has together within itself all the potentials according to which it cares providentially for the body, and nevertheless it puts these forward unconfusedly at the proper time. It does this, on the one hand, by

---

[82] Reading ἓν ὄν for ἑνών, with Plot. *Enn.* 5. 9. 6. 2.

activating the natural potential of the body by which it grows, increases, and does what is proper for generation; on the other hand, by activating the sensible potential of veins, arteries, flesh, and nerves, by which potential we comprehend the sensibles; and [by activating] the opining [potential] by which it judges the sensibles; and [by activating] the imaginative [potential] by which it imagines the sensibles; and [by activating] the representative [potential] by which it shapes [images]; and [by activating] the [potential] of memory by which it remembers; and [by activating] the appetitive [potential] by which a living being desires and moves in respect of place; and so on for the potential of likening, anger, and desire (by using the body in its irrational part it has these potentials). After death, mind alone will act, whereas those will cease.

324. 1 on 185. 18 (821B): *For that Source is the beginning of everything*: If that through which generated beings are generated is a cause, then rightly do all things pre-subsist in the cause of all, as in an idea and a paradigm (as we have said), together and uniformly.[83] This also applies to contraries, in so far as they are said to be contemplated in God.

How he can speak of 'unitedly' [185. 18] and 'contraries' [185. 18], you will understand as follows. That which has been ordered has a divided form, as in the world there are stars here and a person there; and again, fire here and water there.[84] Contrary beings, if they were generated together, are corrupted. But in the thoughts of God all beings are both together and unconfused—and not in a place, for they are neither bodies nor in bodies, but in the eternal thoughts which are paradigms. For this reason, God is the source of all things, for whatever subsists before its effect is a source.

In addition to the other things, he is the 'order' [185. 20] of those things in so far as they have been ordered. Order is the act of assimilating all beings to one another and the symmetry which is the cause of the communion of each part of the universe with the other parts.

Moreover, God is 'every stability' [185. 22] and 'every motion' [185. 22–3] of beings. These things should be understood differently [in the case of different sorts of beings].

In the case of intelligibles and intelligents, their nature, in so far as it is a source of movement and stability (i.e. of rest, since they are the same), signifies an activity. For motion resulting in divine service and the teaching of subordinates is an activity which imparts life, whereas

---

[83] *SchDN* 253. 1, 316. 4.
[84] This sentence is derived directly from Plot. *Enn.* 5. 9. 9. 14–16.

rest and stability, in so far as they are eternal and unchanging, signify that the minds are doing what is proper and are being filled with divine things.

In the case of beings with sense perception, their nature, in so far as it is a source of motion and stability (i.e. rest), signifies, with respect to motion, an act of production which results in being, and with respect to stability (i.e. rest), either a cessation or change which takes place through the corruption of being.[85]

God is said to be these things, because he is a cause which transcendently exists. In the case of God, 'motion' is a providential procession in goodness toward the things which are from him and through him. 'Stability' for God is always to exist in the same way and unexplainably to possess his unknowable rest and unchangeable freedom from disturbance.

One must note that he called the intelligible powers 'aions' [186. 14], in so far as they participate in the aion. There is a passage in Scripture which says: 'For the things which are seen are temporal, but the things which are not seen are aions' [2 Cor. 4: 18].

The things 'which exist in others' [186. 3] are, for example, holiness, immortality, and blessedness, for such as these are in the intelligible and intelligent beings. They are 'said [to exist] conceptually' [186. 3] in the intelligibles and us, as gods and lords and 'angels powerful in strength' [Ps. 103: 20], as well as humans by participation.

329. 1 on 188. 5 (824C): *The exemplars* [lit. **paradigms**]: In the preceding we have already explained the definition of paradigms (which they also call 'ideas')—namely, that he says an idea (i.e. a paradigm) is an eternal production of the eternal God which is complete in itself.[86] Here the great Dionysius is explicating Scripture when he calls the ideas 'pre-definings' [188. 8] and hints at the divine Paul who says in his letter to the Romans that, 'Whom he pre-defined, these he also called' [Rom. 8: 30], and elsewhere that, 'He pre-defined us in his will' [Eph. 1: 5]. He says here that the paradigms and ideas are 'an act of will' [188. 9] and 'a pre-defining' [188. 8].

Moreover, he introduces the blessed Clement bishop of Rome, whom the apostle mentioned [Phil. 4: 3].[87] This Clement said that 'in

---

[85] Reading τήν before εἰς, with FA.

[86] *SchDN* 316. 4. Cf. *SchDN* 320. 3.

[87] John follows the tradition recorded, e.g. by Eus. *h.e.* 3. 4. 9 (SC 31: 101), which identifies Paul's Clement as the third bishop of Rome. It would appear that this identification was first suggested by Origen, *Jo.* 6. 54 (GCS 10: 163). The expression τὸν Ῥώμης ἐπίσκοπον, although bracketed in Migne, is present in FA.

beings there are more originative paradigms' [188. 11–12] of those things which are in a sense 'relative' [188. 11].

What is being said can be clarified as follows. There is a certain opinion which likens all things to a line. The upper part of the line is assigned to the intelligibles; the lower part, to the sensibles. To the 'more originative' of these (i.e. the individual intelligibles) belong the first and upper part; to the things derived from the intelligibles, what follows that. It holds thus for the others according to the descent of the line.

Such an opinion wishes to show that all things are not of the same worth, but that some are derived from others—even as the lower forms are derived from the universal sources in creation, which universal sources he says are 'more originative'. Therefore, he says that the sacred Clement says that there are also in creatures more generic paradigms (i.e. ideas) of those things which are 'relative', which is to say, of lower forms which subsist in relation to some higher pattern—for example, materal fire in relation to aetherial fire.

The great Dionysius, however, says that these are not properly ideas, but rather the thoughts of God, for even if paradigms are said to be in creation, they are not to be worshipped, as Moses says [Exod. 20: 5].

He does not indicate where St Clement said these things.

332. 1 on 188. 12 (824D): *Does not proceed according to the proper*: The blessed Clement followed a certain opinion which says that even in the generation of sensible beings there are certain primal causes: for example, the activities (i.e. the acts which bring into being) of the intelligibles (i.e. the incorporeal angels) have primal causes, [that is], the ideas and thoughts of God. With regard to these ideas, because they are paradigmatic, the intelligibles are like primal activities which impart happiness and function as leaders.

In the case of sensibles, the above-mentioned opinion says that the form which is in matter is a primal cause which imparts happiness and acts as a creator. For it says that the rational principle of the nature in generation, by which the sensibles are given form, is such an originative form.[88]

It may be that the blessed Clement seemed to have said this. It is not possible, however, to say that these are properly paradigms or originative ideas (i.e. primal causes). For these are not from themselves, but rather from the thoughts of God, who alone ought to be worshipped.[89]

---

[88] Reading ἀρκτικόν for ἀρκτέον, with FA.
[89] Reading ἑαυτῶν for αὐτῶν, with FA.

332. 4 on 189. 3 (825A): *All duplication*: Since some said that the ideas and paradigms are self-subsistent beings, he now smites those Greeks, saying: if the ideas should not exist simply and unitedly, in so far as they are the super-simple thoughts of a super-simple and super-united God, then God would be a compound of a paradigm and himself, which he called 'duplication'. { . . . }

6

336. 4 on 191. 4 (856B): *From this Life souls*: After the life of the angels he places in order the life of our souls, in so far as rational beings are also immortal. After rational souls he then introduces the life of the sensible and nutritive (i.e. vegetative) soul (i.e. the soul of irrational beings and plants), which he also says exist 'after the manner of a lowest echo' [191. 5], an expression which we have often explained above.[90]

The lives of irrational beings and plants are not divine, but are from a material fire and spirit. The words of David [to which Dionysius alludes 191. 6–8] refer only to these 'lowest' (as it is said) living beings: 'Thou dost take away their spirit, they expire, and return to their dust. Thou dost send forth thy Spirit, they are created; and thou dost renew the face of the earth' [Ps. 104: 29–30]. The great Dionysius applies these divine oracles only to the sensible soul and vegetative life. He does not think that such is the case with regard to the life of the intelligibles or our life. For God, after creating this life in its essence for immortality, would not take away from the intelligibles and from our souls their life, since they would be not even beings [if this were to happen]. Moreover, David is speaking about living beings which are renewed from the earth, and certainly not of these [angels or human souls].

As for the life of the demons who willingly departed, he adds that even this remains indestructible, since God who created them wills this, even though they revolted against God. 'For the gifts . . . of God are irrevocable' [Rom. 11: 29], God who from the beginning made them immortal. { . . . }

337. 2 on 191. 15 (856D): *With their composite nature*: It is amazing how he teaches all doctrines in a correct manner! In this passage, as he hands on the mode of the resurrection, he declares that we are a

---

[90] *SchDN* 248. 1. Cf. *SchCH* 44. 9, 48. 2.

mixture.[91] We are a mixture in so far as we are mortals composed of immortal soul and mortal body.

At the same time, he says that the essential life of the soul is less than the angelic beings. [This can be inferred] from the fact that he also names it 'life in the form of angels' [191. 15], but not 'angelic life'—in other words, not angelic *per se*, but something like it.

He also says that we are in part rational souls, and at the same time, that we are wholes, of body and soul.

He also says that our bodies are immortalized in the resurrection, asserting that the doctrine of the resurrection seemed unbelievable 'to antiquity' [192. 3], which is to say, to the foolish opinion of the Greeks, because they thought that the resurrection of matter was 'contrary to nature' [192. 4]. Foolishness is called antiquity! Although the fact of the resurrection is beyond nature, that is, with respect to the present manner of life which is supported by nourishment, excretion, and sicknesses, none the less, with respect to God, nothing is either contrary to nature or beyond nature, since he is the cause of every life.

337. 5 on 192. 9 (857A): *The faulty* [lit. **contradicting**] *arguments . . . Simon*: He says that the arguments of Simon contradict our doctrine which says that our bodies will rise again and be granted immortality—in so far as the fact is contrary to nature. Some who spoke against Simon, also refuted him concerning these things, namely, Irenaeus, Origen, Hippolytus, and Epiphanius.[92] The great Dionysius, however, in a divine manner puts an end to what is said by Simon, namely, that the resurrection of bodies is contrary to nature. Since nothing is contrary to God, how is anything contrary to nature? The fact that someone thought to contrive demonstrations from those things which are merely visible and sensible—demonstrations, I say, which are contrary to the cause of all, which is incomprehensible and unseen to all, that is, contrary to God—this is what is truly contrary to nature! How shall opinions and thoughts overturn that which is beyond every sensation and thought?

[91] Reading μικτούς for θνητούς.
[92] Cf. Iren. *haer.* 1. 23 (SC 264: 312–20), Or. *Cels.* 1. 57 (GCS 2: 109) and 6. 9 (GCS 3: 81), Hipp. *haer.* 6. 2–15 (GCS 26: 134–41), Epiph. *haer.* 21 (GCS 25: 238–45). None of these authors explicitly raises the question of the resurrection in their criticisms of Simon Magus. One does find it in *Hom. Clem.* 2. 29 (GCS 42: 47).

7

340. 4 on 193. 10–11 (865B): *The light* [lit. sun] *of . . . instructor*: Note that he says that the apostle Paul was the sun of himself and St Hierotheus.

Note how the father understood the saying of the apostle, for Chrysostom and the other fathers understood it to apply to the cross.[93]

340. 5 on 193. 14 (865B): *It is customary for theologians*: The custom of which he speaks is for the theologians to apply privations to God in an opposite sense.[94] We can understand this as follows. These theologians desire to represent the divine light as much as is possible. But because he is unapproachable and unseen and because it is not possible to apply to him anything (whether immaterial or sensible), they named him 'darkness'. As it is said: 'He made darkness his hiding place' [Ps. 18: 11]. The apostle said the same: 'He dwells in unapproachable light' [1 Tim. 6: 16], for that to which nothing can approach is similar to the darkness which transcendently does not see.

Again it is said: 'Knowledge of you is too wonderful for me; it is high, I cannot attain it' [Ps. 139: 6]—just as the wholly incomprehensible and unknowable knowledge of God is likened to an unknowing which exists beyond every creaturely knowledge, for the unknowing regarding God of those wise in divine things is not an absence of learning, but a knowledge which knows in silence that God is unknowable.

In the same way, the theologians also call the Incarnation of God the Word 'an emptying' [cf. Phil. 2: 7], and yet it is full, or rather beyond fullness of wisdom, power, and salvation.

Moreover, they name the victory of the cross 'the weakness of God', because by death the evil and invisible powers of the devil were destroyed; and instead of death the resurrection of the dead and the kingdom of heaven were offered.

In this manner also the understanding of God which transcends every human wisdom and understanding is God's foolishness [cf. 1 Cor. 1: 25].[95]

---

[93] In reference to 1 Cor. 1: 25, cited at *DN* 193. 11. For Chrysostom's use of this passage, see e.g. *hom. in I Cor.* 4. 3 (PG 61: 34), *hom. in Rom.* 3. 3 (PG 60: 413), *hom. in II Cor.* 29. 3 (PG 61: 599).

[94] John seems to be using ἀντιπαθῶς ('in an opposite sense') as synonymous with the Dionysian word ἀντιπεπονθοτῶς (193. 14). John understands by 'theologians' the writers of Scripture.   [95] Cf. *SchDN* 340. 4.

You can understand what is being said if you think of the heretics and the Greeks, both of whom imagine that by means of sensible syllogisms they have proved that the Incarnation of God which was dispensed even unto death is impossible. With such as these in mind, the most divine Paul with his head in a whirl cried out: 'O the depths of the riches and the wisdom of God, how unsearchable are his judgements' [Rom. 11: 33]. Accordingly, could the method which surpasses every created wisdom be equal to words of foolishness not taught by God? For the mystery cannot be explained with words or sensible demonstrations, unless faith precedes.

344. 2 on 194. 16 (868A): *Neither reason*: Here he clarifies quite well how the greatness beyond wisdom of the incomprehensibility regarding God is the foolishness of God [1 Cor. 1: 25]. Because we are confined to the sensible, he says, when we examine the doctrine of the immateriality and supersubstantiality (if I might use that word) of God, we err because we measure these by sensibles.

It is like what happens when some people examine the teaching of the holy Trinity who alone is to be worshipped and hear about the thrice-hypostatic theology without part and division. Straightaway their head begins to whirl because they attend to bodies in need of place and extension, saying: how can there be three hypostases in themselves and they be indivisible? Indeed, they do not know how to be foolish in the sensibles, in order that they be wise in divine things.

There are a myriad of other such things which the Lord intends, when he says: 'If I told you earthly things and you do not believe, how shall you believe if I tell you heavenly things?' [John 3: 12] And the divine Paul says: 'The natural man does not receive the things of the spirit' [1 Cor. 2: 14], for they are foolishness to him. Therefore, the spiritual things which must be pursued are 'the foolishness of God' among men [1 Cor. 1: 25]. { . . . }

345. 3 on 195. 8 (868B): *Theirs is*: He says that the angels have an intelligent power and activity which derives from the supernatural wisdom of God. From it the divine angels by participation have the power of intelligent activity, by which they think themselves and beings, understanding by way of vision even the ideas which he said are the thoughts of God. Therefore, they have this intelligent activity as something brought in from without, from God as a cause; and they understand beings in a manner which far transcends souls, because souls understand beings from beings themselves and intuit forms, which is to think and encircle all things in a more discursive fashion.

The angels by an innate likeness to God understand the multitude of creation singly. They are not divided into the scattering of the variation of beings (i.e. into sensibles), as are rational souls. To some extent souls are worthy of that, in imitation of the angels, when by winding together the thought of the many into one they have all things together and unconfusedly distinguished within themselves. Nevertheless, souls have thinking as something brought in from without, whereas the angels think from themselves and in themselves, in so far as they are godlike.

These things also hold concerning the intelligibles.

As for how God thinks, you have what is here, as well as what is above near the end of the fifth chapter.[96]

What we said concerning souls, namely, that after the fashion of the angels by winding the many into one they think—especially in the resurrection they will have [this] perfectly, when again being in their bodies they will obtain the perfect knowledge of beings. { . . . }

348. 6 on 196. 21 (869B): *The example of light*: The example is faultless! Imagine that someone were to suppose this visible light to be furnished with mind and reason, that we were to inquire of it whether it knows darkness, and that it were to say that it knows it even before darkness comes into being, not according to some experience—for how could light know darkness? For if it is light, it will not be darkness—but rather, in so far as it is light. Therefore, it also knows that if it reduces its own light, no one will see. In the same way, God has 'knowledge of all things causally within himself' [196. 18–19], not because he obtained this by experience, since God would thus be posterior to knowledge, or would have been at some time unknowing.

Note that darkness is an effect, in so far as it comes to subsist from the privation of light. This is against the Manichaeans.

349. 4 on 197. 14 (869C): *The angels*: That the angels know earthly matters, not by intuiting sensibles through sense perception (as we do), but through a transcendent power—I think this is clear from diverse oracles: as, for example, in Tobit where it is said that the divine angel Raphael told the son of Tobit to take the gall of the fish which had risen, since it would take away the white spots in his eyes from the sparrow dung [Tobit 2: 10, 6: 8], for one should not suppose that he learned the cure from experience.[97] But also, the angel in Judges, who

---

[96] Cf. *SchDN* 320. 3.

[97] Lit. 'from suffering'. Cf. Dionysius' comments on Hierotheus, who learned divine matters, not by inquiry, but by suffering (*DN* 2. 9 (134. 2), with *SchDN* 228. 2).

in the presence of Gideon cast fire from the rock for the sacrifice, did not know by sensation that fire was capable of burning (as we do), but rather in a higher manner [Judg. 6: 20–1].[98] Thus also with respect to the rest.

If someone should ask how the devil and his angels will experience the eternal fire, he will be answered in the fitting place.[99] { . . . }

349. 5 on 197. 17 (869C): *This is something we must inquire into*: He is examining how we know God. He says correctly that the nature of God, what he is, is never known by any created thing, neither in understanding, nor in vision, for by these we intuit the incorporeals. Rather, God is known from the order of creation, for if, as the apostle says [cf. Rom. 1: 20], the beauty of created things reveals the author of generation (i.e. the maker of generated beings), then suitably the order of beings is the knowledge of the one who grants order. After all, beings (i.e. forms) and individual creatures (e.g. the angelic orders and all sensibles) are images and likenesses [Gen. 1: 26] of the divine ideas, that is, paradigms of the things in God, which paradigms are the eternal thoughts of God, through which and in accordance with which all things whatsoever were in him (because they are not other than he) and what was produced came into being.

In the same way, the most divine John in the Apocalypse said [Rev. 4: 11] that a certain one of the elder angels said to him that all things were and had come into being, meaning the ideas, because all things which had come into being were the images and likenesses of the ideas (i.e. the paradigms). For the intelligents are images of the intelligibles; and the lower, of the higher.

By 'the removal of all' [198. 1] these things—for God is removed from beings, because he is none of the things created by him, but unspeakably transcends all these—God is known 'transcendently' [198. 2].

353. 3 on 198. 21 (872C): *God . . . as 'Logos'*: He is speaking here of God the Logos, explaining why he is called Logos, what this name signifies, and that there is one reason why he is named Logos, to wit, because he has in himself the causes of all beings, for the rational principles of every nature are in him, as he is the cause of every creature—for 'through him are all things' [Rom. 11: 36, cf. 1 Cor. 8: 6, Heb. 2: 10].

The ideas and paradigms are in him, not [as if] they are different from him, but because they are the eternal thoughts and the rational

---

[98] Reading τρόπῳ for προσφόρῳ.
[99] Perhaps a reference to *EP* 8. 6 (188. 9–192. 2).

principles which make all things. [The eternal thoughts and the rational principles] are a nature, for a nature is a rational principle which has a cause and a nature, as the natures of beings are not random and pointless.

He says that he is the Logos, both because he extends through all things without hindrance, and because he encompasses all things even unto the very limits, as in the letter to the Hebrews, 'For the Word is living and active . . .' [Heb. 4: 12].

353. 5 on 199. 8 (872C): *If knowledge unites*: God the Word himself, Christ Jesus (whom the discourse here treats), in order to explicate the nature of true knowledge and show that knowledge truly unites knowers and the known, says: 'And I know my sheep and I am known by my own; just as the Father knows me, I also know the Father' [John 10: 14–15].

When knowledge knows that which it wishes to know, it is united to what is known, no longer having doubt about it, nor being divided through doubt into other thoughts, and thus being unstable and becoming ignorance, because it is not persuaded that it knows. In the same way, the faithful, when they have been united by knowledge to Christ who is known (who is God the Word) and have established their faith in him, when they have a faith in the things known which is most steady and unshaken, namely, that they know God and are known by God—the faithful, I say, on the one hand, stand apart from ignorance (which we said separates and divides and shakes them sometimes to this and sometimes to that doubt, because it does not know what it is necessary to know); on the other hand, they stand in firmness, having been fully persuaded by faith that they know and are united through this to what is known.

Now then, according to the apostle, he who is in the darkness of ignorance, shaken by error, is borne about by every wind of the deceit of men [Eph. 4: 14].[100] They are like those who are 'tossed about' on the open sea by waves—the apostle also says these things [Eph. 4: 14]. They believe that the gnostics are mad, as also Festus said to Paul when he preached divine knowledge, 'You are mad, Paul' [Acts 26: 24].[101]

The real gnostic Christian, inasmuch as he knows Christ in truth and through him has obtained divine knowledge—I mean, a unitary knowledge of the truth (simple and uncompounded knowledge is

---

[100] Reading σκότῳ for σκοπῷ.

[101] We use the word 'gnostic' here to denote a Christian who knows.

unitary)—on the one hand, the real gnostic Christian abandons the world, because he is not enamoured of worldly knowledge and the error of the unfaithful; on the other hand, he knows himself to be sober and freed from many-errored faithlessness. Every day they die for the sake of truth, not only at all times being in danger of death because of the truth, but also all the time dying to ignorance, but living to knowledge and giving witness that they are Christians.

8

360. 7 on 203. 5 (893B): *Elymas the magician has this to say*: The antiquity of the saint can be seen from this passage, for he knows what Elymas the magician said, even he who opposed St Paul in Cyprus. Mention of him can be found in the Acts of the holy apostles [Acts 26: 24].

Similarly, Arabia has many like Elymas who say to us (we who say that Jesus Christ, God the Word, suffered for our sakes in the flesh, but not in his divinity): 'Unless you grant that he suffered in his divinity, as he willed, you make God powerless, by asserting that he cannot suffer in his divinity if he should so will.'[102]

In response to them, we should say that God, as he considered the passion, did not will something contrary to nature, in order that his naturally impassible divinity might suffer. { . . . }

361. 1 on 203. 12 (893B): *Denial of the true self* [lit. denial of himself]: That which I was saying, to wit, that Eymas the magician scoffed at the divine Paul when he said that God cannot deny himself, and at the fact that it could not be shown by Paul that God is able to do what he wills, that is, deny himself—this the great Dionysius refutes in a most philosophical manner.

---

[102] John seems to refer to certain people who hold an extreme form of theopaschism wherein God could or perhaps even did will to suffer, not only in his flesh, but also in his divinity. But the controversy turns not so much on the question of the suffering of the divinity of Christ, as upon the question of whether God the Word could will this. In this regard, it is reminiscent of the Phantasiast controversy, where a key question was whether Christ willed to undergo suffering or whether this happened by nature—and yet, it is hard to imagine any Phantasiast subscribing to patripassianism! See e.g. M. Jugie, 'Gaianites', *DTC* 6/1 (1947), 999–1014. As for Arabia, this could be either the province of Arabia, or the peninsula itself, including the heavily Christianized south. It is known that the Phantasiasts had made strong inroads in both the Ghassanid areas of the province and in southern Arabia (see e.g. R. Aigran, 'Arabie', *DHGE* 6 (1924), 1226, 1246). Still, it is not certain who is the object of John's censure here.

He says that God is truth and that 'the truth is a being' [203. 12], but that falsehood (because it lacks a hypostasis) is not even a being. If God were to deny himself [2 Tim. 2: 13], then the truth, by having been falsified, would become not-being. How could this happen? ('To be unable', as it is applied to God, is a sign of his ineffable power.) For it is like saying that God is able to cause himself not to be God, or rather, to proceed into non-subsistence—which, apart from being impossible, is also blasphemy. Further, how will it be said that he who is is he who is not? Accordingly, God is unable [to deny himself]. That is, that the not exist is impossible, or rather, that he not exist is inadmissible.[103] Therefore, it cannot happen that God not be able (i.e. that God be unable). For just as light *qua* light cannot become darkness, thus also for God these things are impossible through his unsurpassable truth.

In this way, God 'does not know not-knowing by way of privation' [203. 16], even as God did not learn by experience what is. He does not know what this not-knowing (i.e. this unknowing) is. He does not know unknowing by way of privation, for unknowing is a privation, not a hypostasis: rather, it comes from outside the essence in which the privation resides, for it is a lack of what ought to be present. Therefore, God is deprived of unknowing and he has never known unknowing. For unless we say that God does not know unknowing by way of privation, then not-knowing will be found to be of his essence. Moreover, his unknowing would be essential and God would be found to be darkness (for unknowing is darkness).

In this way you will understand in a lofty manner the saying: 'It is impossible that God be false' [Heb. 6: 18], as well as the saying, 'The Son is unable to do anything by himself, unless he sees the Father doing it' [John 5: 19], which is like saying, 'It is impossible, if the Father wills one thing, that the Son will another.' For there is one will in the one and only venerable Trinity according to its divinity. { . . . }

9

368. 8 on 207. 8 (909B): *Divinely named*: He says very wise things concerning the divinely named images, transferring them from the Greeks to the truth. For they used to make certain things like statues, having neither hands nor feet, which they used to call 'Hermes'. They used to make them with hollow doors, like cupboards in a wall. Within they

---

[103] Reading ἀνεγχώρητον for ἀναχώρητον, with FA.

then placed images which they worshipped as gods, and closed the Hermes from without. Thus the Hermes appeared to be worthless, but within they had the ornaments of their gods. Thus also here you will understand that some of the scriptural names of the real, true, and only God are not worthy to be said of God: for example, smallness and sitting, etc. But when the names are explained and interpreted in a manner worthy of God, they have images and divine types of the glory of God within.[104]

369. 2 on 207. 10 (909C): *God is called great*: Although he interprets the titles predicated of God, it is none the less necessary to clarify these with scriptural testimonies.

He is called 'great' where it is written, 'Great is our Lord and great his strength' [Ps. 147: 5]. There are many other similar passages in the Scripture. That he is 'small' [208. 1] is signified by the third book of kingdoms where he says to Elijah the prophet, 'Behold, a sound of a slight breeze, and there is the Lord' [1 Kgs. 19: 12], for this signifies that he is in some sense surrounded by the breeze, that is, by slightness and smallness.

That he is the 'same' you have in the passage cited here [by Dionysius], as well as in the saying, 'I am and I do not change' [Mal. 3: 6]. That he is 'different' [208. 2] you find when he appeared to Ezekiel like a man from fire and ember [Ezek. 1: 26–7], and elsewhere, 'His eyes are like lamps' [Dan. 10: 6], and what John says in the Apocalypse, 'Like the form of bronze and a furnace' [cf. Rev. 9: 2].

You find 'likeness' [208. 3], when he says that he created humans according to his likeness [Gen. 1: 26], and 'unlikeness' [208. 4], in Isaiah when he says, 'By what do you name me, says the Lord' [Isa. 40: 25], since he has no likeness.

You find 'standing' [208. 5] and 'motionless' [208. 5], when he says to Moses concerning the rock, 'Here did I stand, before you were here' [Exod. 17: 16], and the like; and 'sitting' [208.5], where Baruch says, 'You sit forever and we are forever destroyed' [Baruch 3: 3], and again, 'You sit upon the Cherubim' [Ps. 99: 1]; and 'moved' [208. 6], as when he says, 'And he ascended on the Cherubim and flew' [Ps. 18: 10], and again, 'Come, descending and let us mix up their languages' [Gen. 11: 7], and, 'He bent the heavens and descended' [2 Sam. 22: 10].

These will do for now; but in the individual explanations what is necessary will be clarified.

---

[104] For this scholion, cf. Henri-Dominique Saffrey, 'Nouveaux liens objectifs entre le Pseudo-Denys et Proclus', *RSPT* 63 (1979), 6–11.

369. 3 on 208. 15 (909C): *This greatness is infinite*: The reason for this is that God has a wholly perfect limit, being both beyond perfection and beyond infinity, as it is written, 'And of his kingdom there will be no end' [Luke 1: 33]. But also, he is beyond every number, for even if God should be called 'one' and 'the one', none the less he is beyond the one. For 'the one' properly signifies a relation *vis-à-vis* the many numbers which are from it, and it is in some sense a source of the multitude of numbers. Nevertheless, God is also worthy to receive the name of 'the one' from the things which are from him, since the one is simple, indivisible in itself, and uncompounded. But also in this way he is super-unified, which is to say, he is beyond the one. Therefore, it is said, 'And of his understanding there is no number' [Ps. 147: 5].

372. 3 on 209. 14 (912C): *He is unborn* [lit. ungenerated]:[105] Note in how many senses the word 'ungenerated' can be understood: (i) either what has not yet come into being, but will come into being, as Sarah said, 'He has not yet come into being for me' [Gen. 18: 12], or (ii) like that which is imperfect, like the tower in Chalanē,[106] or (iii) [not having come] from something, like 'Paul, an apostle not of men' [cf. Gal. 1: 1], or (iv) [not having become] such and such, like Justus one of the twelve [cf. Acts 1: 23], or (v) that which in no way exists, such as the many things about which the Greeks speak prodigiously (Scylla and Chimera and the like). 'Ungenerated' is predicated of God properly and 'without qualifications' [210. 1].

Another comment on the same. When he says that God is ungenerated, he purifies the name of its blasphemous implications, saying: do not understand the expression to mean that God has been generated (in the sense that he has another above himself [who caused this generation]), in order that through the agency of this prior being he came to be such and such (e.g. creator, good, spirit, fire, or some such thing).[107] Rather, do not suppose him to be ungenerated, nor in any way a being, nor in generation, nor something else. In what follows he explains how we should understand the word 'ungenerated'. He makes these comments against the Arians and the Eunomians who

[105] Here and in what follows, reading ἀγένητον for ἀγέννητον, following Suchla's edition of *The Divine Names*. For another treatment of this passage, Anast. S. *hod.* 22. 3. 40–8 (CCSG 8: 298–9), citing as his source Dionysius the bishop of Alexandria.

[106] The identity of 'the tower in Chalanē' is not certain, but it could be a reference to the tower of Babel, a supposition which accords well with John's intended point. In Gen. 10: 10 a certain city, Chalannē, is mentioned as being in the land of Sennaar, and in Gen. 11: 1–4 it is said that 'the tower' was built in the land of Sennaar.

[107] Reading γένηται for γέρνηται.

blaspheme God through their use of the words 'generated' and 'ungenerated'.

373. 1 on 210. 1 (912C): *Fully unbegotten* [lit. everything ungenerated]:[108] He says that God is 'above everything ungenerated'. These words suggest that he himself is also claiming that there is something in creation, posterior to the holy Trinity, that is itself ungenerated. We should clarify what is here being stated.

To begin with, it is clear that the divine Dionysius was eager to lead to the truth all things said in error by the philosophers who at that time flourished in Ephesus, where also Ionian philosophy first arose—and this, because St Timothy was bishop there.

[Dionysius] was aware that there were certain philosophers who taught that all the intelligibles were also immortal and that all the generated intelligents were also ungenerated ('generated', because they subsisted from God as cause by way of the procession of enlightenment; 'ungenerated', because they proceeded not in time, but eternally, that is, in the aions). (We ourselves have said above that the sensibles have time, whereas the intelligibles have the aion, whence also they are called eternal.)[109] These philosophers, [to summarize,] said that they were enlightened by way of procession and that they are ungenerated.

On the other hand, [Dionysius] was aware of other philosophers who claimed that this visible world was both generated and ungenerated. It is 'generated', inasmuch as in this universe, [this visible world] either proceeds from the one to the many (that which concerns the generation of formal animals, plants, and the rest), or from the many to the one (which is to say, when it proceeds to corruption for the dissolution of the elements). At the same time, they say that this same world is 'ungenerated' (i.e. eternal), inasmuch as, in their opinion, it never ceases from the motions which result in generation and the restorations which result in corruption.

The great Dionysius explains how it might sometimes be called 'ungenerated', either as I have said or as the Greeks. Do not understand this to apply to God: the other things are said to be 'ungenerated' after the manner of a cause, whereas God is such apart from causes and 'without qualifications' [210. 1]. For what cause is there for God who excels all things in absolute simplicity?

376. 6 on 211. 10 (913B): *(That difference) in God:* The ancients used to call the cause of the sympathy of the universe and of its providence and

---

[108] Reading πᾶν ἀγένητον for παναγέννητον, following Suchla's edition of *The Divine Names*.   [109] *SchDN* 324. 1.

preservation 'unity and sameness and equality and similarity'—which they also called 'the one'. They used to use the names 'difference and dissimilarity' to refer to the creative providence which [proceeds] into divisibles (both those subject to change or those subject to the senses) and into beings (i.e. the intelligibles)—and this, because they understood the names by analogy with what is being signified, as also we have said above in a different way.[110] Some spoke of 'sameness' and 'difference' (i.e. the same and different form and privation); others, of limit and infinity. { ... }

377. 1 on 211. 13 (913C): *God . . . as 'similar'*: We cannot refer to ourselves as 'similar', for our bodies are composed of similar and dissimilar parts, as also Aristotle shows at the beginning of his work on *The Generation of Animals*.[111] God, on the other hand, is what he is in a wholly similar manner, since in fact divine Scripture says that he, although he is the same eternally and without change, is dissimilar to all things. 'Who among the gods is similar to you, O Lord' [Ps. 86: 8]. And again: 'To whom shall you liken me, says the Lord' [Isa. 40: 25]. And again: 'I have multiplied visions and been likened in the hands of the prophets' [Hos. 12: 10], that is, I myself [have been likened] to myself, as Irenaeus says in his *Contra Haereses*.[112]

380. 3 on 212. 16 (916B): *Regarding the divine attributes of 'resting'* [lit. the divine standing]: He understands standing and sitting as the same thing. By 'standing' he does not mean the notion of becoming erect after reclining in a seat. Rather, he uses the word 'standing' to refer to the unshaken and unmoved firmness of God, even as to be seated is to be in an ineffable kingdom and in an enduring and incomprehensible repose. To be sure, in the Scripture he is said to arise from a seated state, as in the verse, 'Arise, O Lord, go before them' [Ps. 17: 13], and again, as if changing from standing to sitting, in the verse, 'Because you mounted your horses' [Hab. 3: 8 LXX], and, 'Your horsemanship is salvation' [Hab. 3: 8 LXX], and again, 'He mounted his Cherubim and flew away' [Ps. 18: 10], and especially, 'You sat upon your throne, you who judge justice' [Ps. 9: 4], and, 'God sat on his holy throne' [Ps. 47: 8]. { ... }

---

[110] *SchDN* 256. 1.
[111] Arist. *gen. anim.* 715ᵃ8–11.
[112] Cf. Iren. *haer.* 4. 20. 6 (SC 100: 644).

10

385. 1 on 214. 9–10 (936D): *'Omnipotent' and 'Ancient of Days'*: God appeared to Daniel as a hoary old man with a head white like wool, for which reason he is called the 'ancient of days' [Dan. 7: 9, 13, 22]. He is younger than a hoary old man when as a man he appeared to Abraham with the angels [Gen. 18: 1–8], and as a youth [cf. Mark 16: 5].

In his contemplations, [Dionysius] resolves these things as follows. God is an old man in so far as all things are from him and after him (thus they are younger than him), whereas, he is a young man in so far as he does not grow old in his flourishing and steadfast blessedness.

If you should speak of both together (i.e. of old and young at the same time), he says that this signifies that God remains eternal though pervading 'all things' [215. 17] 'from the beginning' [215. 16] and 'progressing unto the end' [215. 18], which end is younger than the beginning.

After this, he introduces the opinion of the divine Hierotheus, for I reckon that it is of him that he speaks when he mentions his 'sacred-initiator' [215. 18], which is to say, his teacher.

385. 4 on 216. 3 (937C): *Absolutely uncreated* [lit. ungenerated]:[113] Above, in the fifth chapter, we have discoursed at length upon eternity and time. Now we should clarify the subject of the present inquiry. He says that Scripture not only calls God 'eternal', as when it speaks of 'God the eternal who founded the ends of the earth' [Isa. 40: 28]. (He says that God is 'absolutely ungenerated' [216. 3] in so far as he is this apart from any cause.) But also, it uses the word 'eternal' to refer to those things which have a share in incorruption, whose essence is unvarying, whether meaning the angels or the upper heavens. This can be seen in the following verses: 'He established these for eternity and for an eternity of eternity' [Ps. 148: 6], and, 'The things which are unseen are eternal' [2 Cor. 4: 18]. (By 'unvarying' [216. 4] he means those things which remain as they were when they came into being.) By 'eternal gates' [216. 5] he means either the heavens or the angels which are established in them like gate-keepers [Ps. 24: 7, 9].

Moreover, [Scripture] refers to old things as 'eternal', as in the verse, 'I have recalled eternal years' [Ps. 77: 5]. At the same time, it refers to time as 'eternity', as in these verses: 'Until the consummation of eternity' [Matt. 28: 20], and, 'That he might take us from the

---

[113] Reading ἀγένητα for ἀγέννητα, with Suchla's edition of *The Divine Names*.

present evil eternity' [Gal. 1: 4]. Vice versa, it refers to eternity as 'time', as in the following verse: 'I will raise him up on the last day' [John 6: 54]—for it is eternity, not a day, which concerns the resurrection—and again, 'The God of this eternity has blinded the thoughts of unbelievers' [2 Cor. 4: 4]. There are still other verses which call time 'eternity': 'The days of eternity' [Mal. 3: 4], and, 'The Moabites and the Ammonites will not enter the house of the Lord until the tenth generation unto eternity' [Deut. 23: 3], for by ten generations he means eternity. { . . . }

388. 4 on 216. 16 (940A): *Simply co-eternal with God*: { . . . } He says that one must not suppose that 'the things called eternal' [216. 16–17] are for this reason 'co-eternal with God who is before eternity' [216. 16]. We said above that the eternal is not properly eternity itself, but rather that which participates in eternity.[114] For this reason, it must be said that the intelligibles properly both exist (in so far as they have become immortal) and are eternal (in so far as they remain without end by the will of God), inasmuch as they were also produced by God and did not exist beforehand. By using words in their proper sense, he securely transfers the haughty ideas of the Greek philosophers to piety. Accordingly, he says that the incorporeal powers created by God are beings and eternal, but certainly not coeternal with God, as the Greeks say in their silliness, when they assert, 'at the same time God, at the same time all'.[115]

As for these 'generated beings' [216. 19], by which he means terrestrial bodies (which they name both 'generation' and 'corruption' in so far as they are founded in matter)—these are all the more crass sublunary beings. There are also mediate beings, that is, beings between eternal and generated beings (the latter being the more crass terrestrial bodies which often pass into and out of existence, in generation and corruption). These mediate beings are bodies and to some extent share in both eternity and time. Heaven and all the stars are mediate, for these are bodies, even though they are extremely tenuous and totally without mixture in matter. The apostle speaks of 'heavenly and earthly bodies' [1 Cor. 15: 40], and then, in order to make clear what sort they are, he adds, 'The glory of the sun is one thing, the glory of the moon another, and the glory of the stars another' [1 Cor. 15: 41].

The highest heaven and the earth came into being in eternity, for they were created before that created light which is also called 'day', as

---

[114] Cf. *SchDN* 385. 4, as well as *SchDN* 324. 1.
[115] This phrase is also used in *SchEP* 569. 9.

Moses says [Gen. 1: 5]. The firmament and the stars [came into being] in temporal dimensions. Although they are bodies and temporal (for they are tangible and visible), they will be eternal through their participation in eternity, even as our bodies will be transformed into incorruptibility. This is made clear by the apostle when he speaks about how the shape of this world is passing, but not the world [1 Cor. 7: 31]. The Psalms also speak of these mediate beings: 'He established them for eternity and for an eternity of eternity, he placed the ordinance and it shall not pass away' [Ps. 148: 6].

Note therefore that the stars, the sun, the moon, and heaven are very tenuous bodies, but that they became immortal by the will of God, as also our bodies become immortal after the resurrection. { . . . }

11

392. 3 on 218. 4 (949A): *Scattered in some endlessly:* Now he refutes the great errors of the Greek philosophers, transferring these errors to piety. Many of these philosophers do not agree with one another. Some of them say that all things were begotten of contrariety and war through strife and quarrel. Others say that all things were created from friendship and concord alone. In so far as they do not think of God in an appropriate fashion, this man, by transferring their coinages to correctness, establishes God as both the creator and the uniter of the universe. He does this by understanding 'the intestine war of the universe' [217. 9] to relate to the natural discord of corporeal, material, and sensible beings with the incorporeal, immaterial, and intelligible beings. For the former are dissimilar to the latter beings and in discord with them. 'For the flesh desires against the spirit, and the spirit against the flesh' [Gal. 5: 17].

Not only this, but also still other philosophers say that all sensibles (i.e. bodies) are infinite and are corrupted unto infinity. They add that the mixture of all things (which he calls 'infinity') gives rise to difference, separation, and parts; and that this results in this mixture's being decomposed and broken down. Further, they say that, as a result, all things are destroyed and corrupted, except for simples (i.e. the elements)—and this, as distance between them grows greater, a process which not only purges these mixed objects of things which are discordant and foreign, but which also eventually severs concordant objects which are naturally united to one another and causes them to be dissimilar and different from one another. They refer to that which does not permit wholes to be united as a 'war'.

As I have said, the great Dionysius, inasmuch as he is a friend of truth, says that God brings to naught such a natural war. ⟨ . . . ⟩ In place of intestine war, God gives to all peace, harmony, and concord; he holds together and reconciles all things in himself, as the apostle says [cf. Col. 1: 20]. Moreover, he will reconcile the heavenly with the earthly. In this way, he will unite the powers which are set in command over individuals and which take care of them out of their love for their inferiors, and he will return all things to himself, guiding them like a steersman and holding all things together.

393. 1 on 218. 7–8 (949A): *The sacred Justus gives . . . 'ineffable'*: { . . . } The Acts of the holy apostles make mention of this St Justus, when it says that he was also called Joseph [Acts 1: 23]. Now then, it is more likely that [Justus] wrote something than that [Dionysius] employed unwritten traditions. This also establishes the antiquity of St Dionysius and the fact that he flourished with the apostles themselves and others of the apostolic age.

Note that even these divine men used the phrases of philosophers, as when they referred to the peace of God as 'ineffability' [218. 8] and 'motionlessness' [218. 9].

397. 2 on 220. 2–3 (952B): *The individuality of each thing*: Note what he means by 'individuality', namely, each thing's being as it is by nature and remaining as it was when it came into being. These things are against the Acephalians, who do not even understand the nature of individuality. [Dionysius] examines in detail and clarifies the meaning of individuality.

397. 8 on 220. 20 (952D): *Completely unstable*: In a wonderful manner he brings to naught the opinions of the Greeks and such heretics as the Valentinians and Manichaeans, who suppose matter to be a source which bears in itself contraries to the things of God. They say that matter is 'instability' [220. 20], waywardness, 'infinity, and unboundedness' [220. 21]—and all these things, perpetually. This is shown to be truly and completely false. For there neither is nor has come to be anything which is not from that by which it was produced, and which through its having been set in order by God was endowed with form and in this way obtained providence from God in order that it might continue as it had been produced.

12

405. 1 on 225. 20–226. 1 (972B): *'Holy ones', and 'kings'*: This blessed man was deemed worthy of divine inspiration![116] How piously and religiously does he mystically interpret ideas which for some have resulted in polytheism! He says that those sources which stand above the lower beings are called 'saints, kings, lords, and gods' on account of their excellence. The same holds for those most excellent of men, for they also are named in this fashion. Likewise, those teachers among us who excel in virtue are said to have virtue within their souls in a singular fashion: through their teaching, they impart to others the virtues, with the result that the virtue which is being imparted is subject to multiplication in relation to the different number of those who are being taught. In a similar fashion, if more intensely and more divinely, we should contemplate the immaterial orders. The lower orders participate in the gifts of God by way of those orders which are higher and nearer to God. It is like a bowl which 'overflows' [225. 16] and gushes forth. Nearby vessels are filled first as they receive what falls their way. Eventually these also overflow with the result that lower vessels are filled in turn. But what happens depends upon the number of receiving vessels and their difference sizes. In other words, the contents of the original bowl are subject to dissipation, inasmuch as the first vessels hold in themselves through the unity of fullness what originally had fallen their way from the original bowl. { . . . }

13

409. 6 on 228. 7 (980B): *The entire thearchy*: The holy and venerable Trinity is the 'entire thearchy'. Through the ineffable unity of its nature, it is called both 'the one' [masculine] and 'the one' [neuter].

412. 1 on 228. 18–19 (980C): *The one cause of all*: ⟨ . . . ⟩ After wonderfully explaining on the basis of natural principles the nature of numbers, he adds that even if the supreme deity is praised as a monad and a trinity, it is in fact neither a trinity nor a monad—at least not such as is known through numbers, 'whether by us or by some other' [229. 6]. Rather, God both is and is said to be beyond every mind, for by saying what he is not, we understand what God is.[117]

---

[116] Reading ἐπιπνοίας for ἐπινοίας.

[117] The Chalcedonian Job the Monk (wr. *c*.550), in his *Tract on the Incarnation* (*apud*

413. 1 on 229. 8 (981A): *The fruitfulness of God* [lit. **divine-begetting**]:
He says that the name 'Trinity' signifies a 'divine-begetting'. (In order
that the venerable manifestation of the ineffable hypostases might be
represented, number was invented, as Basil and the divine Gregories
say.)[118] By way of analogy, he refers to the Father as 'fertile', inasmuch
as he is Father of the venerable Son and fount of the co-venerable Holy
Spirit. Now then, 'fertility' [229. 11]—or any other name applied to
human beings or to the intelligible powers—does not accurately represent the things of God as they are, for these are hidden from all. For
how is it possible to name God after a being, in so far as he is not a
thing, but rather is beyond all beings?

413. 3 on 229. 16 (981A): *In our urge to find some notion:* { . . . }
Negations (i.e. denials and privations) are not predicated of God in an
absolute sense by the theologians. For, as they say, such negations are
not thought, but are transcendently contemplated.

As for the names 'immortal', 'invisible', 'incorruptible', 'without
lack', and 'without sin', no one with a share in wisdom could accept
these in the common manner—nor for that matter any other such
things which are said of God. Rather, by abandoning the things
signified, [Dionysius] lifts his eyes to silent and more divine thoughts.
For this reason, he rightly refers to these as the more divine names of
God.{ . . . }

Photius, cod. 222 (ed. Henry), 3: 176–7) was likewise attracted by Dionysius' tendency to
downplay the correlation between God's nature and his names, his tendency to relativize, if
you will, the names by which God is known.

[118] Although the Cappadocians often discussed number as it touches upon the doctrine of
the Trinity, we could find no passages where they claim that number was invented so that
the hypostases of the Trinity might be represented.

The Mystical Theology

1

417. 1 on 142. 4 (997B): *sightless minds:* They [i.e. certain angels] do not have a lot of sensible eyes. Rather, their essence, in so far as it is a living mind, is wholly a sharp-sighted eye. It is also for this reason that Scripture refers to them as 'many-eyed' [Ezek. 1: 18 and 10: 12].

417. 2 on 142. 6 (997B): *Leave behind you everything perceived:* One and the same thing is being signified pleonastically. For the ancients used to refer to perceptible beings as 'non-beings' [142. 7], inasmuch as they partake of every change and are not eternally the same, whereas they used to use the name 'beings' [142. 7] to refer to the intelligibles, in so far as they are eternally immortal by the will of their maker and their essence does not change. We have often discussed these things in our comments on *The Divine Names*.[1]

417. 5 on 142. 10 (1000A): *Ray of divine shadow:* Here also, by 'shadow' he means that which is completely incomprehensible.

417. 7 on 142. 15 (1000A): *If beyond such people:* Before this [142. 12–15], he discussed those who believe in the name of Christ, but have not come to the more perfect knowledge, who measure the truth instead by their own opinion, not knowing the difference between what are only called beings and what rightly are beings, between beings and him above all beings and thus beyond being itself. Such as these, in so far as they are 'uninformed' [142. 12] about loftier matters, suppose that that shadow among us which hides God, which conceals him from sight—they suppose, I say, that that shadow is the true darkness. How truly do many even among us suffer this delusion, inasmuch as they do not know that the unsurpassed light darkens every sight. If there are such as these among us, he says, what should we say of the idolaters who in no way partake of the mysteries and stand in awe of images? It is right to say, therefore, that the intelligibles are beings, whereas the perceptibles only bear the name of 'beings'.

---

[1] Cf. *SchDN* 205. 2, 240. 3.

'Beyond such people' [142. 15] means the faithful who are caught up in the corruptible.

420. 2 on 143. 8 (1000B): *The divine Bartholomew (says):* Note also from this passage that these divine writings are authentic works of the great Dionysius. In addition to the comments here, in earlier books he made mention of the pronouncements of certain men who were contemporaries of the apostles.[2] Now in the same way he brings up the pronouncement of the divine Bartholomew, as 'says' denotes. If it was what [Bartholomew] had taught without writing [and thus handed down through the tradition], [Dionysius] would have said 'said'.

Note that he presents the pronouncement of St Bartholomew, how the Word of God is both vast and minuscule.

421. 1 on 144. 9 (1001A): *Breaks free of them:* One should understand the meaning of this passage as follows. After contemplating the place where God stood and 'breaking free from the things seen' [144. 10]—that is, all perceptible objects—and 'from what sees' [144. 10]—that is, all rational objects, in other words, all intelligible and intelligent beings, and with them our own souls—Moses then entered 'into the darkness' [144. 10]—that is, the unknowing about God—where, after 'shutting out all cognitive perceptions' [144. 11–12], he 'entered into the intangible and invisible' [144. 12] mind, a mind beyond 'all cognitive perceptions' of the transcendent God. In this way, after being 'united with unknowing and inactivity' [144. 14–15], Moses in unknowing knew everything. By 'inactivity' I do not mean Moses' own mind's inactivity with regard to God, nor another mind's inactivity in knowing neither itself nor any other thing, but rather that Moses was united with 'the completely unknown' [144. 13–14] of every knowledge of him 'who is beyond all' [144. 12–13].

Note how he understands unknowing as 'darkness' [144. 10].

He explains here how God is known through unknowing. We also have discussed this more fully in our comments on the second chapter of *The Divine Names*.[3]

It is necessary to know that in Exodus where it is written that Moses entered into the darkness where God was, the Hebrew text has *araphel* [Exod. 20: 21]. The Septuagint renders *araphel* as 'darkness' [γνόφος], as do Aquila and Theodotion.[4] Symmachus, however, translates

---

[2] See *SchDN* 236. 8 on Peter and James at *DN* 3. 2 (141. 7), *SchDN* 360. 7 on Elymas at *DN* 8. 6 (203. 5), and *SchDN* 393. 1 on Justus at *DN* 11. 1 (218. 8).

[3] *SchDN* 216. 10.

[4] Aquila was a 2nd-cent. convert to Judaism. His translation of the Hebrew Bible was very literal and eventually ousted the Septuagint in Jewish circles. It was, moreover, used by

araphel as 'fog' [ὁμίχλη].⁵ The Hebrew says that *araphel* is the name of the firmament into which Moses went, for they [scil. the Jews] speak of seven firmaments, which they also call heavens.⁶ They also give names to them which we need not mention now. I have also read about the seven heavens in the *Dialogue between Jason and Papiscus* written by Aristo of Pella.⁷ In the sixth book of his *Hypotyposes* Clement of Alexandria says that St Luke wrote down this [dialogue].⁸

In his letters [Dionysius] has also rather divinely philosophized about this darkness, how it is contemplated in divine unknowing.⁹ In the fifth one he has discussed this most fully.¹⁰

2

424. 1 on 145. 7–8 (1025B): *We should praise the denials*: { . . . } In our comments on *The Divine Names* we have thoroughly considered the nature of these assertions and denials.¹¹

3

424. 3 on 146. 2 (1033A): *How the divine and good nature*: Note the contents of his work, *The Theological Representations*. Observe the resources of its theology, containing as they do every divine and

---

Origen in his *Hexapla*. Theodotion was another Jewish translator of the 2nd cent. His version was also used by Origen in the *Hexapla*.

⁵ Symmachus is said to have been a 2nd-cent. Ebionite. His translation of the Hebrew Bible was used by Origen in the *Hexapla*.

⁶ Although it is tempting to identify 'the Hebrew' here mentioned with Philo, this can hardly be so, for Philo says quite explicitly that the cloud into which Moses entered was the immaterial conceptions of the immaterial God, see e.g. *post.* 14–15 (LCL Philo 2: 334–7). There is no place in his corpus where the cloud is identified with the firmament. Jewish speculations concerning the heavens in antiquity spoke of between two and ten heavens, most commonly positing seven, for which biblical proof-texts were supplied and names given (see *TDNT* 5: 511). Patristic authorities were somewhat critical of the theory of the seven heavens, cf. Or. *Cels.* 6. 21 (GCS 3:91), Or. *prin.* 2. 3. 6 (ed. Gürgemanns/Karpp, 318–320), Clem. *strom.* 4. 25 (GCS 15: 318), and Bas. *hex.* 3. 3 (SC 26: 200).

⁷ Aristo was a 2nd-cent. apologist. It is John alone who claims that he was author of this dialogue.

⁸ Clem. fr. 11 (GCS 17: 198–9). This fragment is otherwise unattested. For ἀναγράψαι as 'write down', cf. Clem. fr. 8 (GCS 17: 197), where it is said that the evangelist Mark 'wrote down' (ἀναγράψαι) what Peter preached.   ⁹ *EP* 1 (156. 5), with *SchEP* 528. 2.

¹⁰ *EP* 5 (162. 3–10).

¹¹ *SchDN* 216. 10.

enlightened knowledge and orthodoxy. It knows how 'the divine nature is one' [146. 2]—certain more recent fathers have proposed *homoousion*—how it is 'triune' [146. 3]—which we call 'thrice-hypostatic'. It knows the properties of the persons and what they signify—that is, 'Fatherhood and Sonship' [146. 3]. It knows the nature of the sanctifying power and 'theology of the divine Spirit' [146. 4], how it is said that 'my heart overflows with a goodly theme' [Ps. 45: 1], and how it is said of the adored Spirit that he 'proceeds from the Father' [John 15: 26]. It knows how 'in the Father, in themselves, and in each other' [146. 5–6] the Son and the Spirit are in 'an abiding without departure' [146. 6–7], and this, coeternally [146. 6], without division and without separation.

It is necessary to know that 'abiding' and rest are the same thing and that motion is not the same thing as abiding. It is thus that he says of the divine nature, that although it is eternally in an unmoving abiding, [its persons] seem to be moved as they proceed in and out of one another.

425. 2 on 146. 7 (1033A): *How Jesus, who is above individual being:* Note that this is against the Nestorians and the Acephalians.

425. 8 on 147. 10 (1033C): *From the most exalted:* Since the intelligibles are the henads of God beyond mind and God himself is one or rather beyond the one, suitably has [the argument] 'been contracted' [147. 13], in so far as it is both without parts and without multiplicity. As for things inferior to God, the more they descend to the sensibles, the more they consort with things which are divided and dispersed, and because of these multiplied objects they themselves are multiplied and end up being divided like the sensibles.

'To the humblest' [147. 10], that is, from *The Theological Representations*.

425. 11 on 147. 17–18 (1033C): *Affirmation upon which everything else depends* (lit. hypothetical affirmation): An affirmation is a positive assertion wherein a universal or a contradiction or a combination or a comparison [is predicated of the subject]. For example, God is life or God is goodness. A hypothetical [statement] is a positive assertion which signifies either a universal or some contradiction or a combination. Thus, a 'hypothetical affirmation' in the case of God is that 'God is life and goodness rather than air or stone' [147. 19–20].

As for 'denials' [147. 18], these are negations and the opposite of assertions. For a hypothetical assertion, as it is said, is said to be an affirmation. For example, God is life or air. But a negative denial is that God does not get drunk or go on a rampage.

In the case of the assertions we begin with those things which are more characteristic [147. 17]. Life and goodness are more appropriate to God than are air or stone. In the case of the denials we ascend from the lowest things [147. 15–16]. For example, that God is signified by no word and is not conceivable is more appropriate to God than that he is not drunk or on a rampage. Thus we generally begin the denial from what is secondary. For example, 'God is not drunk' [is said] rather than 'God is not speakable', and 'God is not on a rampage' rather than 'God is not conceivable'.

'Drunkenness' [κραιπάλη] [147. 20] is a bout of excessive drinking. It is like a καραπάλη, that is, something which 'shakes' [πάλλουσα] or violently moves the 'head' [κάρα].

'Wrath' [μῆνις] [147. 20] is not a trifling anger, but a lasting one.

It is necessary for us to understand all these bodiless denials by ascending from the perceptible to the intelligible, not basely but by supplying in thought (in the case of each of the things mentioned) what the blessed Dionysius said. For God is none of the things said which we ourselves know or conceive, and none of the said things which all the conceptual powers know. For all the said things are altogether from God, and his gifts. How can he who provides for them properly be from them?

We have discussed all these things thoroughly in our comments on *The Divine Names*.[12] For all these things, as accidents, are in the beings of those after God. But God is both beyond being, and their cause, therefore also beyond them. { ... }

5

429. 1 on 149. 8 (1048A): *Neither one nor oneness:* { ... } Note that not even divinity is the essence of God, even as not even one of the things mentioned here or its opposite [are the essence of God]. Thus, God is none of these things, inasmuch as these are not his essence, but the glory which lies about him. This was also argued by Sextus, the ecclesiastical philosopher.[13] { ... }

429. 3 on 150. 2–3 (1048A): *Beings do not know:* He says that 'beings do not know' [150. 2–3] God, the cause of all things. Not to know God is

---

[12] e.g. *SchDN* 480. 2, 4.
[13] Claimed as author of a collection of Christian philosophical maxims based on an earlier set of Neopythagorean maxims. The text in question is found at *sent.* 23 (ed. Chadwick, 14).

manifest destruction. But he immediately clarifies this when he says, 'as he is' [150. 3], that is, no being knows God in respect of that which he is (i.e. his incomprehensible essence which is itself beyond essence or the subsistence in which he subsists). As it is said, 'no one knows the Son except the Father, and no one knows the Father except the Son' [Matt. 11: 27]. Dionysius probes the flip side of this when he goes on to suggest that God himself 'does not know beings as they are' [150. 3].[14] What he means is that God does not apprehend sensible objects sensibly or beings as beings. This does not befit God. [We] human beings know what sensible objects are through sight or taste or touch, whereas we grasp the intelligibles through learning or teaching or enlightenment. God, however, does not know beings in these ways, rather he has a knowledge appropriate to himself. This is suggested in the following verse: 'the one who knows all things before their generation' [Sus. 42]. This verse means that God knows beings not through an account of their generation (i.e. sensibly), but through a different type of knowledge. As for the angels, they know these things through their minds alone and in an immaterial fashion, not as we do, sensibly. We can thus conclude that God knows beings in a special way that is higher even than this, and certainly not by apprehending beings. {. . .}

On the same text. Note that no one knows the pure Trinity as it is, which is to say, there is nothing like it, such that it also might know it as it is. We know what humanity is, since we are humans. But we do not know what the subsistence of the pure Trinity is, for we are not of its essence. In the same way, God does not know beings as they are, like we do, for he is not a being, nor does he exist as they do.

Even if God is spirit or is thus called the Holy Spirit, still he is not 'spirit' as known to us or the angels [149. 9].

Above he stated that [God] is not 'light' [149. 6] or 'truth' [149. 8], but here he says again that [God] is 'neither darkness nor light, neither error nor truth' [150. 4–5]. Why is this? It may be that he is attempting to say the following. He speaks first of absolute light, [in which] there is no error (even as [there is no error] among the angels), [rather] there is truth which is of itself unconditioned and without cause.[15] As for the later passage, [he is saying] that [God] is not a relative being, that is, he has not changed from darkness into light, in some sense, from potential light into actual light (light and darkness are co-dependent), for [God]

---

[14] Deleting materials bracketed in Migne's text (καὶ . . . ἐστίν).

[15] Reading πλάνην for πλάνη. Still, John's meaning is not entirely clear.

is neither darkness nor great light. In the same way, he has not changed into actual truth from potential error, [that is], from the opposite. For all these things are posterior to him, inasmuch as they have proceeded providentially from him. { . . . }

The Epistles

1

528. 1 on 156. 2 (1065A): [Comment on title]: Based on the other people with whom this divine man associated—among them, the apostles themselves—I conjecture that this Gaius is the one to whom the divine evangelist John wrote his third letter [3 John 1].

In the sixth chapter of *The Ecclesiastical Hierarchy* he said that the monks are called 'therapeutae'. He also discussed there how they are constituted—not clergy, but none the less above the laity. Philo the Jew seems to have admired them in his treatise on *The Contemplative Life* (i.e. *The Suppliants*), calling them 'therapeutae' and discussing their way of life near the end of that book.[1] Read Philo's comments.

528. 2 on 156. 5 (1065A): *But not in terms of deprivation*: Darkness is dissolved by light and 'the more so as there is more light' [156. 1]. Unknowing, which is itself darkness, recedes in the presence of knowledge and the more so as there is more knowledge. He says that we should not understand this in the normal sense, such that the unknowing regarding God is like unknowing in terms of a lack of understanding. This is a point which we ourselves have also made.[2] Rather, [you should understand this as follows]: the more one is illuminated by God and attains to a knowledge of beings (i.e. of the intelligible and the intelligent beings), so much the more, ascending to the knowledge about God, one will know the incomprehensibility (i.e. the unknowing about God), that God is light and knowledge beyond all things known. Moreover, in silence one will honour the speechlessness about God.[3] Therefore, the unknowing about God is discussed not in terms of a

---

[1] Philo, *vit. cont. passim* (LCL Philo 9: 112–69). Contrary to what John here says, the way of life of the therapeutae is discussed throughout the text in question, not just at its end. It may well be that John is citing Philo based only on what he has read in Eusebius. See *h.e.* 2. 17 (SC 31: 72–7). This may account for John's error, for Eusebius gives his most detailed description of their way of life near the end of his own summary of Philo's account. It should further be noted that John, like Eusebius before him, considered the ascetics described by Philo to be Christians.

[2] Cf. *SchCH* 101. 1.

[3] Cf. *DN* 1. 3 (111. 6).

privation of knowledge, but in terms of an excess [cf. 156. 5] and overflowing of every knowledge, because one knows that which is incomprehensible and unknowable for all, even for oneself. These things were also discussed in the first chapter of *The Mystical Theology* and in the second chapter of *The Divine Names*.[4]

2

529. 3 on 158. 3 (1068A): *How could it be that he who surpasses everything*: He has discussed these things often in *The Divine Names*, though in a different way. He interpreted them especially near the end of the eleventh chapter of that book,[5] saying: how is the cause of all both divinity and goodness, as well as that which gives substance to divinity [and goodness] and also beyond these? You should understand this as follows. You ask how God is beyond the source of divinity. Here is the answer. If you understand by 'divinity' not God himself but the gift of God by which we are deified, you have the solution. For God in and of himself and as a transcendent being is beyond the 'thearchy' which is given and bestowed by him, namely theosis. Interpret the other attributes similarly. Then he continues the argument: if the gift of God is the source of our deification, it is clear that the cause of every source—being itself a source or rather beyond every source—is thus also beyond so-called divinity ot thearchy. For God has the good, not as a superadded condition, as we do, but as something unconditional, whereas we have it as a condition, the reason for this being that we are changeable, whereas he is unchangeable.

3

532. 1 on 159. 3 (1069B): '*Sudden*': I think that Gaius asked about the prophetic [statement] of the prophet Malachi, which reads: 'The Lord whom you seek will suddenly come to his temple, and the angel of the covenant in whom you delight' [Mal. 3: 1]. That this is what was asked seems clear from what follows: 'the Word of God uses this term' [159. 4–5]. Here he theologizes marvellously about our Lord Jesus Christ. Note how he etymologizes 'suddenly'.

---

[4] Cf. *SchMT* 421. 1 and *SchDN* 216. 1, 216. 10.
[5] Cf. *DN* 11. 6 (221. 13–223. 14).

Note also the expression 'Christ was endowed with being after the fashion of a human being' [159. 6].

4

532. 3 on 160. 3 (1072A): *You ask how it could be that Jesus:* ⟨ . . . ⟩ Note the word 'here' [160. 4], that is, in the economy—for even apart from [the Incarnation], he is said to be a human as the cause of humans, as the maker of humans.

532. 4 on 160. 4 (1072A): *Not as the cause of humans:* Africanus also said this in his *Chronographies.*[6] For God is named after all the things which are from him, since he is in all things. But in the economy he is said to be a human inasmuch as he was endowed 'with the whole being' [160. 5]. As it is said: 'in him the whole fullness of deity dwells bodily' [Col. 2: 9].

Note the whole of this letter, since it is against every heresy, old and new.

533. 1 on 160. 11 (1072B): *And superior to the human condition:* It is human [to be born] of a woman; it is beyond human, of a virgin. { . . . }

533. 2 on 161. 5 (1072B): *Has the force of a negation pointing toward transcendence* [lit. has the power of negation pre-eminently]: Here too he uses the term 'pre-eminently' [ὑπεροχικῶς] in order to distinguish [negations in the case of Christ from those] which arise from privation.[7] He immediately explains what he means. In our comments on the third chapter of *The Mystical Theology* we have already discussed the nature of affirmations.[8] How in the case of our Lord Jesus Christ affirmations have the power of a pre-eminent negation—this can be explained using a human example. If we affirm of Christ that he is human and that in his human [nature] he is from a virgin mother, nevertheless this has the power of negation, a power that is hidden and beyond mind. For the hearer will say: he is not human, since he is from a virgin, but he is beyond the human, even if he is human in other things. [Dionysius] interprets this as well, commenting that to say he is human affirmatively means that he is not human negatively, but is beyond the human. { . . . }

---

[6] No parallel could be found in the extant fragments of Africanus.
[7] For a similar use of ὑπεροχικῶς, *EP* 1 (156. 5) with John's comments (*SchEP* 528. 2).
[8] Cf. *SchMT* 425. 11.

533. 3 on 161. 8 (1072C): *Not by virtue of being God that he did divine things:* { . . . } How he did divine works but not as God—this is manifest in the example of his physically walking upon the water [Matt. 14: 25]. It was of God to harden the water, but it was not of God to walk along on fleshly feet, neither were the flesh and bones of his feet of the deity. Again, it was of God to make a virgin conceive, but it was not of the deity to have a face and the other human members. In a similar fashion, the same thing can be shown from the opposite, for he did human things but not as a human. He was human from a virgin, but this was not as a human. For what sort of human is from a virgin? Again, it was human to walk with one's feet, but to do so on water, was not human. For what sort of human has ever done this?

536. 1 on 161. 9 (1072C): *Something new:* Let no one foolishly say that he calls the Lord Jesus θεανδρίτης. For he did not speak of a θεανδριτική [energy]—the adjectival derivative of ὁ θεανδρίτης—but of a θεανδρική activity, in some sense a compound activity of God and man. Whence he also speaks of God as 'humanized' [161. 9], which is to say, God who had become a human being. He called this mixed activity alone a θεανδρική [activity]. For he acted as God alone when he, although absent, healed the centurion's child [John 4: 46–52]; but as human alone, although he was God, in his eating and passion. He accomplished other miracles as a mixture, as when he healed the blind through an anointing [Mark 8: 23, John 9: 5] and stopped a flow of blood by his touch [Luke 8: 43–4].[9]

6

536. 3 on 164. 5 (1077A): *For it could happen:* { . . . } Note that one should not refute the opinions of others, but should strengthen one's own, that one should not write against an opinion or cult which does not seem good, but rather for the truth. The next letter clarifies what he means by this.

[9] For Severus' use of this passage in his third letter to John the Hegumen, see our discussion in Ch. 1. This Dionysian passage was also invoked by Themistius (*fl.* mid-6th cent.), founder of the Monophysite sect of the Agnoetes. He interpreted 'theandric' to mean that Christ's energy was not two things, but one and the same in so far as it is of one and the same. See the fragment of his *Epistle to Marcellinus and Stephen* (Mansi 10: 981a). For one interpretation of this scholion, Henri-Dominique Saffrey, 'Un lien objectif entre le Pseudo-Denys et Proclus', *SP* 9/3 = TU 94 (1966), 98–105. Cf. also Jaroslav Pelikan, 'The Odyssey of Dionysian Spirituality', in *Pseudo-Dionysius: The Complete Works* (Mahwah, NJ, 1987), 19–21.

7

536. 5 on 165. 3 (1077B): [comment on title]: This Polycarp became
the bishop of Smyrna in Asia, after having been a disciple of St John
the evangelist, as Irenaeus says in the third book of his *Against So-
Called Knowledge.*[10] His life culminated in martyrdom through fire.
The same divine Polycarp also has letters to the Philippians.[11] This
letter of the blessed Dionysius contains many marvels and oddities
regarding the solar eclipse which took place during the crucifixion of
Christ.

537. 2 on 166. 7 (1080A): *The sophist Apollophanes*: Concerning
Apollophanes the Sophist, who was a companion of the great
Dionysius and reviled him when he became a Christian. { . . . }

537. 6 on 167. 9 (1080C): *Because of this, the sun*: He here recounts the
story of Joshua son of Nun [Josh. 10: 12–14], reminding St Polycarp of
this, so that he might use it against Apollophanes. He bids [Polycarp]
to tell [Apollophanes] the following: learn how, when the sun and
moon were diametrically opposed to each other, with the sun already
setting, God stopped those lights in their place, a stoppage which took
place in accordance with the unspeakable power of God, their cause.
He also held the whole immobile along with those two lights: neither
the heaven nor the other stars moved in their course, rather they stood
unmoving with those two lights. The course and motion of the whole
stood at rest not just for a short time, but for an entire day, so that
Joshua son of Nun had a twofold day of twenty-four hours [of day-
light], as Jesus ben Sirach says clearly in his hymn of the fathers [Sir.
46: 4].

Then [Dionysius] adds: if Apollophanes should say that it could not
happen, for the heaven and other stars did not stand still along with the
two lights, but rather they were moved, while [the sun alone] stood
still, tell him that it would be better for him to return to the true God
and to the knowledge of him who moves the heaven which contains the
lights, while holding immobile the lights which are contained. For it is
a mark of even greater power that, while the heaven and other stars are
being moved, God should keep the sun and moon from moving and

[10] Iren. *haer.* 3. 3. 4 (SC 211: 108–10), the same passage is found in Eus. *h.e.* 4. 14 (SC
31: 179–80).

[11] Perhaps John knew about Polycarp's letters to the Philippians from Iren. *haer.* 3. 3. 4
(SC 211: 114), the same being cited in Eus. *h.e.* 4. 14 (SC 31: 179–80). Eus. *h.e.* 5. 20. 8 (SC
41: 63), again citing Irenaeus (*To Florinus*), also speaks of Polycarp's letters.

from being borne along with the motion of the whole, a motion with which they always used to be carried along.

541. 3 on 169. 3 (1081A): *In Heliopolis*: He is probably speaking of Heliopolis in Egypt, for he was still studying at the time.[12]

541. 5 on 169. 4–5 (1081B): *And from the ninth hour*: Note here the solution to a difficulty in the Gospel of Luke [Luke 23: 44–5]. No one has yet explained the strange and marvellous manner of the eclipse, except this author alone. When the divine Luke says that during the crucifixion of the Lord there was darkness from the sixth hour, inasmuch as the sun was eclipsed, there has been a great deal of controversy as to how he could call this an eclipse, for at that time the moon was in its fourteenth day and there was thus no conjunction of the sun and moon. Just about all exegetes, being far removed from these events, have supposed that the sun simply lost its rays for three hours, that is, until the ninth hour.

The strange manner of the eclipse is here discussed. He says that the moon was in its fourteenth day—'for it was not a time of convergence' [169. 4]—that at the sixth hour it overtook the sun from the east,[13] and that it intercepted the solar disc and passed [between it and the earth], moving in an easterly direction. It is thus that the moon came and intercepted the sun, passing [between] it [and the earth before] proceeding to reverse course, so as to overshadow the entire disc. If there had been a normal eclipse, both the eclipse and the restoration would have had to begin on the same edge [of the sun]. For example, when the moon passes between the sun [and the earth], it is from the east first that it blocks the eastern edge of the solar disc, as it begins to pass between it [and the earth]. It is also on its eastern edge that the disc of the sun begins to be restored, as the moon moves on toward the west and uncovers first that part of the sun which it had first covered over when it overtook it, that is, its eastern part. During the saving passion it did not happen in this way, but in just the opposite way. Coming 'from the east' [169. 7], the moon passed between the sun [and the earth] and blocked the whole of it. Afterwards, it did not proceed onward toward the west, but rather it reversed course again toward the east and laid bare first of all the western edge of the solar disc, for it was moving back toward the east, toward the opposite perimeter of the sun.

---

[12] As opposed to Heliopolis in the Lebanon.

[13] Dionysius in fact says that the eclipse began in the ninth hour and lasted until the evening (169. 5). Here John seems rather to be following the text of Luke, which speaks explicitly of the eclipse lasting from the sixth to the ninth hour.

As a result, we can say that the eclipse and its restoration did not both begin on the same edge of the sun.

Phlegoñ the Greek chronographer mentioned this eclipse in the thirteenth book of his *Chronographies*, in the 103rd Olympiad, saying that it did not occur in the usual way, though he did not say in what respect this was so.[14] Moreover, our Africanus in the fifth book of his *Chronographies* recorded this eclipse, as also did Eusebius Pamphili.[15]

8

544. 1 on 171. 3 (1084B): [Comment on title]: This Demophilus was a monk, as the title indicates, for by 'therapeutae' he means the monks.[16] He rebelled against his presbyter and was quite vexed at him for having received a certain repentant sinner. It is for this reason that he first expelled the penitent and then put the priest out, taking his place as a self-ordained presbyter.

Note that these evils also took place in those times. ⟨ . . . ⟩

544. 4 on 171. 13 (1085B): *Personal pride*: { . . . } By θεόκριτος [172. 1] he does not mean someone by that name, but someone who has been fittingly selected [κρινόμενος] by God [θεός] to have a position of authority.

545. 1 on 172. 8 (1085B): *Why was David, father of God*: Note that he calls David 'father of God' because of Christ. { . . . }

545. 8 on 174. 7 (1088A): *They have only to make a backward turn and there he is*: ⟨ . . . ⟩ It is amazing how he says that [Christ] 'as a whole [embraces] them as wholes' [174. 7]. In this he puts to shame the heretics of that time, who used to say that only the soul is saved by God, not the body. By 'as a whole' he means the Lord who by taking both soul and body has saved us 'as wholes' [composed] of both soul

---

[14] Jacoby, *FGrHist*. 257F16 (=fr. 15, ed. Müller, *FGH* 3: 607). John was probably getting this material from Phlegon at second or third hand. It was often cited by earlier patristic authorities: e.g. Or. *Cels*. 2. 33 (GCS 2: 159–60), see also below for Africanus and Eusebius, both of whom place this event in the 203rd Olympiad (not as in John in the 103rd). This same Dionysian passage was of decisive import for John Philoponus who, after referring to Luke, Plegon the Chronographer, and Eusebius, also appealed to the authority of Dionysius in order to establish that the eclipse took place in a way contrary to nature and thus that it could be dated to the nineteenth year of the reign of Tiberius. See Jo. Phil. *opif*. 2. 21 (ed. Reichardt), 99. Cf. the parallel passage at *opif*. 3. 9 (ed. Reichardt), 129.

[15] Afric. *chron*. fr. cited at PG 10: 87–9. The fragment shows that Africanus himself cited Phlegon. Eus. *chron*. a. 19 Tiberii imp. (Latin version, GCS 24: 174–5; Armenian version, GCS 20: 213), also cites Phlegon. For John's use of Africanus, cf. *SchEP* 532. 4.

[16] Cf. *SchEP* 528. 1.

and body.[17] There were then heretics who followed Simon, as Irenaeus and Hippolytus indicate.[18] So also, those who follow Origen have the same opinion. ⟨ . . . ⟩

548. 2 on 175. 14 (1088C): *It is not permitted that a priest*: Note that even if a presbyter sins, he must not be corrected by deacons or monks, nor for that matter by the laity—except of course in the case of heresy. Presbyters are after all above the order of monks and liturgists (i.e. deacons). If this is the case, how much more is it not to be permitted that bishops be accused by anyone.

548. 6 on 176. 11 (1088D): *The rank (of sacred initiators)*: Concerning the ecclesiastical ranks, and what is the service of the monks, for by 'therapeutae' he means monks.[19] He also discussed these things in *The Ecclesiastical Hierarchy*.[20]

549. 6 on 179. 11–180. 1 (1089D): *What may even be a work of justice, except worthily*: Note what it is 'to pursue the just things justly', which Moses said [Deut. 16: 20 LXX], and that it is not permitted to pursue just things in an unworthy manner. You will understand the meaning of this from what follows. Origen explicates this quite well in the tenth of his homilies on the Lamentations of Jeremiah.[21]

552. 1 on 183. 13 (1093C): *Let hierarchs bow to the apostles*: Note that the apostles and successors of apostles are greater even than bishops, and that each one should only be corrected by someone more holy than himself. { . . . }

552. 4 on 184. 10–11 (1093D): *In a double sin*: Note what he means by a double sin, that is, when the one who sins is unaware that he has done so. This is from Jeremiah, as he shortly makes clear: 'the people have sinned twice; forsaking me the fount of life . . .' [Jer. 2: 13].

552. 11 on 186. 14 (1096C): *Our most divine (master)*: ⟨ . . . ⟩ { . . . } By 'master' he means St Paul the apostle, since it was he who ordained him high priest of the church of the Athenians, as it is written in the sacred *Apostolic Constitutions*.[22]

553. 8 on 188. 9 (1097B): *Once I was in*: { . . . } Note this story which treats of the ineffable compassion of our Lord Jesus Christ and penitents. He also speaks about the sanctity of the divine Carpus. This

---

[17] For a similar formulation, Greg. Naz. *ep.* 101. 15 (SC 208: 42).
[18] Iren. *haer.* 1. 23 (SC 264: 312–20), Hipp. *haer.* 6. 2–15 (GCS 25: 238–45).
[19] Cf. *SchEP* 528. 1, 544. 1.
[20] See *EH* 6.
[21] For a very close parallel, see the fragment cited at GCS 6: 279.
[22] *Const. App.* 7. 46. 11 (SC 336. 110). Cf. *Prol.* 17C. Eusebius also recorded that Dionysius became bishop of Athens. See *h.e.* 3. 4. 10 (SC 31: 101).

is the Carpus whom the apostle mentioned in his second letter to Timothy [2 Tim. 4: 13].

553. 9 on 188. 12 (1097C): *In the preliminary* [προτέλειους] *sacred prayers*: The term προτέλειος used to be used by the Athenians in reference to the prayers and sacrifices which precede the rite of marriage.[23] This was because they used to refer to the wedding as a τέλος, inasmuch as it fulfils [τελειοῦν] human life. This can also be seen in many of the comedies. At any rate, they used to consider marriage to be a certain mystery.[24] They used to use the verbs προτελίζεσθαι and προμνεῖσθαι—both of which mean 'being purified beforehand'—to refer to the state of being ready for a mystery, as Cratinus shows in his drama, the *Pulaia*.[25] But above all, they used to refer to the mysteries of a certain of their so-called gods as a τέλος and as a τελετή, and this because it perfects the initiates and leads them into perfection. The great Dionysius applies the impious words of the Greeks to the true mystery when he uses the adjective προτέλειος to refer to those most perfect prayers which precede the mystery of communion and request purification and an uncondemned partaking of the perfect and perfecting gift of the sacrifices. { ... }

556. 1 on 189. 2 (1097C): *Amidst the joyful* [ἰλαρίων] *days*: The pagans had certain days which were called *hilaria*. Some of these *hilaria* were private, such as when someone got married or bore a son; others were communal and public, as when a king upon his inauguration would declare a number of days to be public *hilaria*. It was forbidden to mourn during these days, but rather every day there would be public spectacles and sacrifices. As for the mourners, they would have to leave off their mourning, watch the spectacles, and participate in the endless feasting—and this, for the entire period of days designated as *hilaria*. There was also a particular feast of the Romans which was called a *hilaria*.[26] It was to honour the mother of their gods—or more properly, their demons. Demophilus speaks of it in his work, *Sacrifices and Feasts among the Ancients*.[27]

---

[23] See e.g. Plato, *leg.* 774E.

[24] John here seems to be arguing that even if his first etymology is not quite correct, still, because marriage was thought by the Athenians to be a mystery, it was thus a τέλος or sacred rite. Cf. *SchCH* 32. 10.

[25] Crat. Com. fr. 180 (ed. Kock, *CAF* 1: 67), otherwise unattested.

[26] Cf. Jul. *or.* 5. 168d and Dam. *Isid.* 131.

[27] We have been unable to identify either work or author. Of the various authors in antiquity named 'Demophilus', none is credited with a work of this or similar title, nor is the work itself independently documented. Perhaps it was a portion of *On the Lives of the Ancients* by Damophilus. Cf. *Suidas* (ed. Bernhardy), 1: 1169–70, s.v. 'Damophilos'. To

557. 3 on 191. 2 (1100B): *Into the pit*: Note how the devil casts humans into the outer darkness, which he here calls the 'pit' (i.e. the chasm), either by deceiving them or by pushing in those who obey him. This takes place when he receives the wanton as his co-workers in deceiving others, such as the idolatry of the man who was deceived in this account. In his vision he sees certain men among the serpents (i.e. among the demons), men who are winding themselves about those conquered by the devil. May the Lord free us from such men!

557. 4 on 191. 5 (1100B): *By evil*: Note the expression 'by evil' (i.e. by sin), which we rightly call evil born of free choice. When he refers to them as 'unwilling' and 'ravaged' [191.6], one should not suppose that he is positing a certain coercive power (i.e. the devil), such as that affirmed by the Manichaeans and Messalians. Rather, because we are persuaded to do something evil, we give space to the deceiver to attack us continually. The deceiver receives from us his power over us. On the other hand, he will be powerless if we do not obey him, since the aid of God is near and supports us, even as the rest of the story indicates.

9

557. 9 on 193. 2 (1104B): [Comment on title]: This is the Saint Titus who was a companion of the apostle and was appointed by him as the bishop of Crete, as is said in the letter which the divine Paul wrote to this same Titus [Titus 1: 4].

560. 4 on 195. 2 (1105A): *Domain of the mind*: { . . . } The expression 'armour of barbarians' [195. 6] is perhaps derived from this verse: 'in a golden vest' [Ps. 45: 10 LXX]. Or perhaps from that which says: 'gird your broadsword upon your thigh, O mighty one' [Ps. 45: 3], for the broadsword is a barbarian weapon, as the historian Phylarchus records.[28] ⟨ . . . ⟩

561. 2 on 195. 8 (1105B): *Well-laid feasts*: { . . . } Concerning the Song of Songs, note that it was considered holy by these holy men, for Theodore of Mopsuestia disparaged it, with great foolishness.[29]

compound the issue, the letter receiving this scholion is addressed by Dionysius to a monk named 'Demophilus'.

[28] Jacoby, *FGrHist.* 81F57 (= fr. 58, ed. Müller, *FHG* 1: 352–3), some parallels with another fragment *apud* Plut. *Cleom.* 26, but otherwise unattested. Cf. the discussion in Ch. 3.

[29] Theodore appears to have rejected allegorical interpretations of the Song of Songs, treating it instead as a secular love poem. See Dimitri Z. Zaharopoulos, *Theodore of Mopsuestia on the Bible* (Mahwah, NJ, 1989), 49–52. For a criticism of Theodore's under-

561. 4 on 197. 10 (1105D): *The ineffable*: He refers to the tradition of Scripture as being 'ineffable and mysterious' [197. 10]. He himself interprets the meaning of these terms when he further qualifies [the tradition of Scripture] as 'symbolic' [197. 11]. It is symbolic in so far as it delivers its oracles by means of symbols. [The tradition of Scripture] is also 'initiatory' [τελεστική] [197. 11] in so far as it hands on the rites [τελεταί] of the mysteries in a symbolic fashion through the agency of the clerical tradition. This ineffable (i.e. symbolic) tradition, he says, is 'intertwined with the spoken word' [197. 12], that is, the 'ineffable and mysterious' [tradition of Scripture is] also [intertwined] with symbols which permit of vocal expression. Whatever is true and at the same time not to be made public is hidden in these symbolic shadows, even as the true passover was hidden in the shadows of the Law, as it is said: 'For Christ, our paschal lamb, has been sacrificed' for us [1 Cor. 5: 7].

The second part of the scriptural tradition is 'open and evident' [197. 10–11]—it is not [made manifest] through symbols. He also calls [this part of the tradition] 'philosophical and demonstrative' [197. 11–12]. It, for example, hands on [knowledge] of ethics, of the physical world, and of the act of creation. This more open [part of the scriptural tradition] has a certain 'persuasiveness' [197. 13], as well as the truth itself bound up with what is being said. For this reason, it is also 'demonstrative'.

The symbolic [part of the scriptural tradition] does not have [such] persuasiveness. Instead, it has a certain divine activity, unapparent and yet active, which 'establishes' [197. 13] or in some sense 'founds' in Christ those souls which are receptive to the mysteries and contemplative, and this, through enigmas which are mysterious (i.e. symbolic), that is, through mysteries which cannot be taught with words. Rather, [this activity] enlightens the mind and brings it into an understanding of the ineffable mysteries through silence and through a revelation of the enlightenments of God. { . . . }

565. 2 on 198. 6 (1108A): *Human life*: { . . . } Notice how marvellous are his teachings about the soul. He mentions its 'undivided' [198. 6] part, which he also calls 'impassible' [198. 8]. This is the most pure part of the soul. One could say that it is its 'bloom' [ἄνθος], that is, its mind.[30] The mind is the rational part of the soul, that by reason of which the soul is also intelligent, that through which, even apart from symbols,

standing of the Song of Songs by one of John's contemporaries, see Leont. B. *Nest. et Eut.* 2. 16 (PG 86/1: 1365D).

[30] Cf. *SchDN* 194. 13.

the soul can look with understanding upon mysteries which are 'simple' [198. 8] and in a sense naked. Its 'divided' [198. 7] part, which he also calls 'passible' [198. 9], is that power of the soul which is united to sensible objects through the spirit which stands midway between the soul and the body. In this spirit are established the powers of sense perception and of those thoughts which are occasioned by sense perception. This part of the soul is passible in so far as it is borne downward into an attachment to perceptible objects through the act of perceiving them. This part of the soul, he goes on to say, is not pure like its mind. Apart from mediation, it cannot look upon those things which are divine, understandable, and intelligible. Rather, it stands in need of a more coarse intermediary which is able to guide it to those things which are simple and undivided. This is what symbols are able to do, making use of divided objects (i.e. of objects which are sensible and only apparent) in order to guide [the soul] to those objects which are ineffable.

565. 5 on 198. 13 (1108B): *Some image guiding them to a conception*: As when the divine Athanasius represented the persons of the adored Trinity as trees, and the other saints in other ways.[31] { ... }

568. 3 on 199. 2 (1108B): *Social*: One part of philosophy is practical; another, theoretical. Practical philosophy is further subdivided into the common, which is also called political (e.g. a concern for laws), and into the private or ethical. Between these there stands the concern for the proper running of a household. As for theoretical philosophy, one part of it is called physical. This treats of objects which are perceptible and subject to change. This is also called cosmological. Another part of it is contemplative and theological. This deals with those objects which are intelligible and eternal. It is this aspect of philosophy which he here treats. Between the physical and contemplative parts there stands that which is concerned with eternal, sensible objects (e.g. astronomy and mathematics). Scripture does not [explicitly] mention the latter, but the Hebrews have it in Deuteronomy.[32]

569. 2 on 199. 12–13 (1108C): *The transcendent lights*: By the expressions 'lights transcendent, intelligible, and divine' [199. 13] he means the pure and holy Trinity. By 'intelligibles' [200. 2] he means the higher angels. We considered their differences fully in *The Divine Names*.[33]

---

[31] See e.g. Ps. Ath. *def.* 1. 8 (PG 28: 540).
[32] The meaning of this last sentence is obscure.
[33] Trinity: *SchDN* 220. 1, 221. 1, 224. 7. Angelic intelligences: *SchDN* 240. 3.

569. 9 on 202. 2 (1109B): *Neither a beginning nor an end*: He says that
the providence of God was 'without beginning' [202. 2]. This is not
because God exercised his providence over coeternal beings, according
to the fools who say 'at the same time God, at the same time all'.[34]
Rather, it is because without any beginning the providence of God
existed before every creation, even before beings were produced in the
ideas (i.e. paradigms) of God, that is, in his eternal conceptions.
Whatever would be produced was prefigured in these ideas and conceptions of God. We have explained in our comments on *The Divine
Names* how the divine Paul called these ideas 'predestinings'.[35] ⟨ . . . ⟩

572. 4 on 202. 12–13 (1109C): *Never going out of itself*: { . . . } To say of
God that he is 'ever resting and ever moved' [203. 2–3] refers to his
providential activity, 'in his permanence' [203. 4]. 'Never resting and
never moved' [203. 3] refers to his permanence, 'in his providing' [203.
4]. We have often discussed this in *The Divine Names*.[36]

10

573. 7 on 208. 2–3 (1117A): [Comment on title]: This letter befits its
sacred antiquity and is worthy of the disciple whom Jesus loved. It is a
letter of greeting. One can deduce from his seventh letter to St
Polycarp that the great Dionysius was around 90 years of age when he
wrote these lines. For in his letter to St Polycarp he said that while in
Heliopolis of Egypt he observed the unnatural eclipse of the sun which
occurred during the saving crucifixion of Christ, in the eighteenth year
of the reign of Tiberius. It was in the fifteenth year of Tiberius that the
Lord Jesus began his preaching, as is shown by the gospel according to
Luke. After preaching for three years and a few months, our Lord and
God willingly endured the passion. This was in the eighteenth year of
Tiberius. Tiberius reigned a total of around twenty-three years, so that
from the saving passion until the end of the reign of Tiberius there
were about six years. St John the evangelist was exiled to the island of
Patmos, one of the Cyclades, toward the last year of the reign of
Domitian. Domitian reigned a total of fifteen years and five months.
Between the seventeenth year of Tiberius when the eclipse occurred
and the last year of Domitian's reign, there were thus a total of sixty-

---

[34] This same phrase is used in *SchDN* 388. 4.
[35] Cf. *SchDN* 329. 1 with reference to Rom. 8: 29–30.
[36] *SchDN* 380. 3, 381. 1, 381. 2.

four years and around seven months. Let us suppose that the divine Dionysius, when he saw the eclipse during the crucifixion of the Lord, was 25 years of age, as we can gather from the fact that he was still studying at the time.[37] Thus, all told he must have been around 90 years of age. Irenaeus recounts the exile of St John by Domitian in the third and fifth books of his *Against Heresies*,[38] where he also explained the chronology, as does Clement of Alexandria, in his book *Can a Rich Man be Saved?*[39]

576. 2 on 209. 8 (1117C): *The sun of the gospel*: He rightly refers to this divine John as 'the sun of the Gospel'. This is what he is saying: 'I, although rightly criticizing and upbraiding those who reckon that they have limited you in a place, you who are the sun of the Gospel—I none the less pray that they sober up and run to you, so that they be enlightened and thus saved. Even as those who think that they have enclosed the sun in a place have gone mad, so also have these gone mad who reckon that they have limited the light of your Gospel with you on the island of Patmos.'

576. 3 on 209. 11 (1117C): *So far as I am concerned, no one can:* ⟨ . . . ⟩ Note that the great Dionysius was also a prophet. This is clear from the fact that he states that God had revealed to him, as well as to St John, that in a short time he would be recalled from exile on Patmos. This is in fact what happened. As we have just stated, John was exiled to Patmos shortly before the last year of the reign of Domitian, when Domitian launched his persecution.[40] Then around the time of this emperor's death, the evangelist John saw the divine Apocalypse.

---

[37] Cf. *SchEP* 541. 3.

[38] Cf. Iren. *haer.* 3. 3. 4 (SC 211: 114), saying only that John remained with the church of Ephesus until the time of Trajan, 5. 30. 3 (SC 153: 384).

[39] Clem. *q.d.s.* 42. 1–3 (GCS 17: 187–8). Eusebius also linked these very same passages from Irenaeus and Clement in his discussion of the exile of John, see *h.e.* 3. 23 (SC 31: 126–9).   [40] *SchEP* 573. 7.

APPENDIX
Collation of the Scholia

We here present a collation of Migne's edition of the *Scholia* with Syr. We our-selves were responsible for collating *The Celestial Hierarchy*, *The Ecclesiastical Hierarchy*, *The Mystical Theology*, and the *Epistles*. In order to facilitate access to the scholia as a whole, however, we have also included a summary of Suchla's collation of the scholia on *The Divine Names*. In what follows, the symbol '—' indicates that the scholion is not present in the Syriac recension, whereas 'Syr.' shows that the whole of the scholion is present. If only part of the scholion is present, we indicate this with the symbol 'S/G', followed in brackets by the line numbers of those parts of the scholion which are *not* in Syr.

SchCH		
29. 1 Syr.	36. 2 —	41. 2 S/G [1–13]
29. 2 Syr.	36. 3 S/G [9–16]	41. 3 —
29. 3 Syr.	37. 1 —	41. 4 Syr.
32. 1 —	37. 2 —	41. 5 —
32. 2 S/G [5–6]	37. 3 —	44. 1 —
32. 3 —	37. 4 —	44. 2 —
32. 4 S/G [2–12,	37. 5 Syr.	44. 3 —
14–16]	37. 6 —	44. 4 —
32. 5 Syr.	37. 7 Syr.	44. 5 —
32. 6 —	37. 8 —	44. 6 S/G [1–5]
32. 7 —	37. 9 —	44. 7 —
32. 8 S/G [1–3]	37. 10 Syr.	44. 8 —
32. 9 —	37. 11 Syr.	44. 9 Syr.
32. 10 Syr.	40. 1 —	45. 1 —
33. 1 —	40. 2 —	45. 2 —
33. 2 S/G [3–6]	40. 3 —	45. 3 —
33. 3 —	40. 4 —	45. 4 S/G [16–26]
33. 4 S/G [1–4]	40. 5 —	48. 1 —
33. 5 Syr.	40. 6 S/G [6–8]	48. 2 Syr.
33. 6 —	40. 7 —	48. 3 —
33. 7 Syr.	40. 8 —	48. 4 Syr.
33. 8 —	40. 9 Syr.	48. 5 —
33. 9 —	40. 10 —	48. 6 Syr.
33. 10 S/G [20–3]	40. 11 —	48. 7 Syr.
36. 1 —	40. 12 S/G [5–8]	49. 1 Syr.
	41. 1 Syr.	49. 2 —

49. 2 —
49. 3 —
49. 5 Syr.
49. 6 —
49. 7 Syr.
49. 8 —
49. 9 —
49. 10 —
49. 11 —
49. 12 Syr.
52. 1 —
52. 2 —
52. 3 —
52. 4 Syr.
52. 5 —
52. 6 —
52. 7 Syr.
53. 1 —
53. 2 —
53. 3 —
53. 4 —
53. 5 —
53. 6 —
53. 7 —
53. 8 —
53. 9 —
53. 10 —
56. 1 Syr.
56. 2 —
56. 3 —
56. 4 —
56. 5 —
56. 6 Syr.
56. 7 —
56. 8 —
56. 9 —
57. 1 Syr.
57. 2 Syr.
57. 3 S/G [1–6, 14–25]
57. 4 —
57. 5 —
60. 1 S/G [13–28]
60. 2 —

60. 3 —
60. 4 —
60. 5 Syr.
61. 1 —
61. 2 —
61. 3 —
61. 4 Syr.
61. 5 S/G [1–6]
64. 1 —
64. 2 —
64. 3 —
64. 4 Syr.
64. 5 —
64. 6 —
64. 7 Syr.
64. 8 —
64. 9 —
64. 10 Syr.
65. 1 Syr.
65. 2 Syr.
65. 3 —
65. 4 —
65. 5 Syr.
65. 6 Syr.
65. 7 —
65. 8 —
65. 9 Syr.
68. 1 S/G [15–17]
68. 2 Syr.
68. 3 Syr.
68. 4 —
68. 5 —
68. 6 Syr.
68. 7 Syr.
68. 8 —
69. 1 —
69. 2 —
69. 3 —
69. 4 Syr.
69. 5 —
69. 6 —
69. 7 Syr.
72. 1 —

72. 2 —
72. 3 Syr.
72. 4 —
72. 5 S/G [1–2]
72. 6 Syr.
72. 7 —
72. 8 —
72. 9 —
72. 10 Syr.
72. 11 —
72. 12 —
72. 13 —
73. 1 —
73. 2 —
73. 3 Syr.
76. 1 Syr.
76. 2 —
76. 3 —
76. 4 —
76. 5 —
76. 6 S/G [6–10]
76. 7 S/G [11–20]
77. 1 —
77. 2 —
77. 3 —
77. 4 —
77. 5 Syr.
77. 6 —
77. 7 Syr.
80. 1 —
80. 2 Syr.
80. 3 S/G [3–4]
80. 4 Syr.
80. 5 —
80. 6 —
80. 7 S/G [2–5]
80. 8 —
80. 9 Syr.
80. 10 —
80. 11 —
80. 12 —
80. 13 —
80. 14 —

80. 15 —	92. 3 —	100. 13 —
80. 16 —	92. 4 S/G [5–13]	100. 14 —
80. 17 —	93. 1 —	100. 15 —
81. 1 —	93. 2 —	100. 16 —
81. 2 —	93. 3 —	100. 17 —
81. 3 —	93. 4 —	100. 18 —
81. 4 —	93. 5 —	100. 19 —
81. 5 Syr.	93. 6 —	101. 1 Syr.
81. 6 S/G [3–12]	93. 7 —	101. 2 —
84. 1 Syr.	93. 8 S/G [2–3]	101. 3 —
84. 2 —	93. 9 Syr.	101. 4 Syr.
84. 3 —	96. 1 —	101. 5 —
84. 4 Syr.	96. 2 —	101. 6 —
84. 5 —	96. 3 —	101. 7 —
84. 6 —	96. 4 Syr.	101. 8 Syr.
84. 7 —	96. 5 —	104. 1 —
84. 8 —	96. 6 S/G [1–5]	104. 2 —
84. 9 Syr.	96. 7 Syr.	104. 3 —
84. 10 —	96. 8 Syr.	104. 4 Syr.
84. 11 Syr.	96. 9 —	104. 5 —
84. 12 —	96. 10 —	104. 6 —
84. 13 —	96. 11 —	104. 7 —
84. 14 —	96. 12 —	104. 8 —
85. 1 —	97. 1 —	104. 9 —
85. 2 —	97. 2 —	104. 10 —
85. 3 —	97. 3 S/G [1]	104. 11 —
85. 4 —	97. 4 —	104. 12 —
85. 5 —	97. 5 —	104. 13 —
85. 6 Syr.	97. 6 —	104. 14 —
85. 7 —	97. 7 —	105. 1 Syr.
85. 8 —	97. 8 Syr.	105. 2 —
88. 1 —	100. 1 Syr.	105. 3 —
88. 2 —	100. 2 —	105. 4 Syr.
88. 3 S/G [22–7]	100. 3 —	105. 5 —
88. 4 —	100. 4 —	105. 6 S/G [9–16]
89. 1 —	100. 5 —	105. 7 —
89. 2 —	100. 6 —	108. 1 —
89. 3 Syr.	100. 7 —	108. 2 —
89. 4 —	100. 8 —	108. 3 —
89. 5 S/G [3–5]	100. 9 —	108. 4 —
89. 6 —	100. 10 —	108. 5 Syr.
92. 1 —	100. 11 —	108. 6 —
92. 2 S/G [8–26]	100. 12 —	108. 7 —

108. 8 —
108. 9 —
109. 1 —
109. 2 Syr.
109. 3 —
109. 4 —
109. 5 —
109. 6 —
109. 7 —
109. 8 —
112. 1 S/G [4–5]
112. 2 —
112. 3 —
112. 4 —
112. 5 —
112. 6 S/G [1–2, 4–5, 7–8]
112. 7 —
112. 8 —
112. 9 —
112. 10 —
112. 11 —
112. 12 Syr.
112. 13 —
113. 1 —
113. 2 —
113. 3 —
113. 4 —
113. 5 —
113. 6 —
113. 7 S/G [1–5]
113. 8 —
113. 9 Syr.
113. 10 Syr.

SchEH
116. 1 —
116. 2 Syr.
116. 3 —
116. 4 —
116. 5 Syr.
116. 6 Syr.
116. 7 Syr.

116. 8 —
117. 1 —
117. 2 Syr.
117. 3 —
117. 4 —
117. 5 —
117. 6 —
117. 7 Syr.
117. 8 —
117. 9 Syr.
117. 10 Syr.
117. 11 Syr.
117. 12 —
117. 13 —
117. 14 Syr.
117. 15 —
120. 1 Syr.
120. 2 Syr.
120. 3 Syr.
120. 4 —
120. 5 —
120. 6 S/G [1–4]
120. 7 Syr.
120. 8 —
120. 9 Syr.
120. 10 —
120. 11 Syr.
120. 12 —
121. 1 S/G [1–2]
121. 2 —
121. 3 —
121. 4 —
121. 5 S/G [1–2]
121. 6 —
121. 7 —
121. 8 —
121. 9 —
121. 10 Syr.
124. 1 Syr.
124. 2 Syr.
124. 3 Syr.
124. 4 —
124. 5 —

124. 6 —
124. 7 —
124. 8 —
124. 9 —
124. 10 —
124. 11 —
124. 12 —
124. 13 —
124. 14 Syr.
124. 15 Syr.
124. 16 —
124. 17 —
124. 18 —
124. 19 —
124. 20 —
124. 21 S/G [1–3]
125. 1 —
125. 2 —
125. 3 Syr.
125. 4 —
125. 5 —
125. 6 S/G [1–3]
125. 7 Syr.
125. 8 —
125. 9 —
125. 10 S/G [8–10]
125. 11 Syr.
125. 12 —
128. 1 Syr.
128. 2 —
128. 3 S/G [1–2]
128. 4 —
128. 5 Syr.
128. 6 —
128. 7 Syr.
128. 8 —
129. 1 —
129. 2 —
129. 3 —
129. 4 —
129. 5 —
129. 6 Syr.
129. 7 —

129. 8 —	136. 20 Syr.	144. 2 —
129. 9 —	137. 1 —	144. 3 —
129. 10 —	137. 2 —	144. 4 —
129. 11 —	137. 3 Syr.	144. 5 —
129. 12 —	137. 4 S/G [1–10]	144. 6 Syr.
129. 13 —	137. 5 —	144. 7 —
129. 14 —	137. 6 —	144. 8 —
129. 15 Syr.	137. 7 Syr.	144. 9 —
129. 16 —	137. 8 —	144. 10 —
129. 17 —	140. 1 —	144. 11 —
129. 18 —	140. 2 —	144. 12 —
132. 1 —	140. 3 —	144. 13 —
132. 2 —	140. 4 —	144. 14 S/G [2–3]
132. 3 Syr.	140. 5 —	144. 15 —
132. 4 —	140. 6 Syr.	144. 16 Syr.
132. 5 —	140. 7 Syr.	144. 17 —
132. 6 —	140. 8 —	145. 1 —
132. 7 —	140. 9 Syr.	145. 2 Syr.
132. 8 Syr.	140. 10 Syr.	145. 3 —
132. 9 Syr.	140. 11 Syr.	145. 4 S/G [1–2]
132. 10 S/G [1–4]	140. 12 —	145. 5 S/G [1–9]
132. 11 Syr.	140. 13 —	145. 6 —
133. 1 S/G [1–8]	140. 14 —	145. 7 —
133. 2 S/G [1–36]	140. 15 —	145. 8 S/G [11–20]
136. 1 Syr.	141. 1 —	145. 9 S/G [3–4]
136. 2 —	141. 2 —	145. 10 S/G [1–3]
136. 3 —	141. 3 Syr.	145. 11 —
136. 4 Syr.	141. 4 —	148. 1 —
136. 5 Syr.	141. 5 —	148. 2 —
136. 6 —	141. 6 —	148. 3 —
136. 7 —	141. 7 Syr.	148. 4 —
136. 8 —	141. 8 Syr.	148. 5 —
136. 9 Syr.	141. 9 Syr.	148. 6 S/G [1–3]
136. 10 —	141. 10 —	148. 7 Syr.
136. 11 —	141. 11 —	148. 8 —
136. 12 Syr.	141. 12 —	148. 9 —
136. 13 —	141. 13 Syr.	148. 10 —
136. 14 —	141. 14 Syr.	148. 11 —
136. 15 —	141. 15 Syr.	148. 12 —
136. 16 Syr.	141. 16 —	148. 13 Syr.
136. 17 Syr.	141. 17 Syr.	148. 14 —
136. 18 —	141. 18 Syr.	148. 15 —
136. 19 —	144. 1 Syr.	148. 16 Syr.

148. 17 —
148. 18 —
149. 1 Syr.
149. 2 Syr.
149. 3 —
149. 4 Syr.
149. 5 —
149. 6 Syr.
149. 7 —
149. 8 —
149. 9 —
149. 10 —
149. 11 S/G [4–7]
149. 12 —
149. 13 —
149. 14 —
149. 15 S/G [3–4, 7]
152. 1 —
152. 2 Syr.
152. 3 —
152. 4 —
152. 5 —
152. 6 —
152. 7 —
152. 8 —
152. 9 Syr.
152. 10 —
152. 11 —
152. 12 —
152. 13 —
152. 14 —
152. 15 —
152. 16 —
152. 17 —
152. 18 —
153. 1 —
153. 2 —
153. 3 —
153. 4 Syr.
153. 5 Syr.
153. 6 S/G [1–17]
153. 7 —
153. 8 —

153. 9 —
153. 10 —
153. 11 —
153. 12 —
156. 1 —
156. 2 —
156. 3 —
156. 4 —
156. 5 —
156. 6 —
156. 7 —
156. 8 —
156. 9 —
156. 10 —
156. 11 —
156. 12 —
156. 13 —
156. 14 —
156. 15 —
156. 16 —
156. 17 —
156. 18 —
156. 19 —
156. 20 —
156. 21 —
156. 22 Syr.
156. 23 —
157. 1 S/G [2–12]
157. 2 —
157. 3 Syr.
158. 4 —
158. 5 —
158. 6 Syr.
158. 7 —
157. 8 Syr.
157. 9 S/G [1–3]
157. 10 —
157. 11 —
160. 1 —
160. 2 —
160. 3 —
160. 4 —
160. 5 —

160. 6 —
160. 7 Syr.
160. 8 S/G [1–2, 4–6]
160. 9 —
160. 10 —
160. 11 —
160. 12 —
160. 13 —
160. 14 —
161. 1 Syr.
161. 2 —
161. 3 S/G [1–3]
161. 4 —
161. 5 —
161. 6 —
161. 7 —
161. 8 —
161. 9 —
161. 10 —
161. 11 —
161. 12 —
161. 13 —
161. 14 —
164. 1 —
164. 2 Syr.
164. 3 —
164. 4 —
164. 5 —
164. 6 —
164. 7 —
164. 8 Syr.
164. 9 —
164. 10 —
164. 11 Syr.
164. 12 Syr.
164. 13 —
164. 14 Syr.
164. 15 —
164. 16 —
165. 1 S/G [1–2]
165. 2 —
165. 3 S/G [1–2]
165. 4 —

165. 5 S/G [1–2]
165. 6 S/G [1]
165. 7 —
165. 8 —
165. 9 —
165. 10 —
165. 11 —
165. 12 —
165. 13 Syr.
165. 14 —
165. 15 —
165. 16 —
165. 17 —
165. 18 Syr.
165. 19 —
168. 1 —
168. 2 —
168. 3 —
168. 4 Syr.
168. 5 —
168. 6 —
168. 7 —
168. 8 —
168. 9 —
168. 10 —
168. 11 —
168. 12 —
168. 13 —
168. 14 —
168. 15 —
168. 16 —
168. 17 —
169. 1 Syr.
169. 2 Syr.
169. 3 Syr.
169. 4 Syr.
169. 5 Syr.
169. 6 —
169. 7 —
169. 8 —
169. 9 —
169. 10 Syr.
169. 11 —

169. 12 S/G [1]
169. 13 —
169. 14 S/G [1–2]
169. 15 —
169. 16 —
169. 17 —
169. 18 —
169. 19 S/G [1–2]
172. 1 Syr.
172. 2 —
172. 3 —
172. 4 —
172. 5 —
172. 6 —
172. 7 —
172. 8 —
172. 9 —
172. 10 —
172. 11 Syr.
173. 1 Syr.
173. 2 —
173. 3 —
173. 4 —
173. 5 —
173. 6 —
173. 7 Syr.
173. 8 Syr.
176. 1 —
176. 2 Syr.
176. 3 Syr.
176. 4 S/G [1–7,
    11–14]
176. 5 —
176. 6 S/G [1–5]
176. 7 —
177. 1 Syr.
177. 2 —
177. 3 —
177. 4 Syr.
177. 5 —
177. 6 —
177. 7 Syr.
177. 8 Syr.

177. 9 Syr.
177. 10 —
177. 11 —
177. 12 —
177. 13 S/G [1–8]
177. 14 Syr.
177. 15 Syr.
180. 1 —
180. 2 Syr.
180. 3 —
180. 4 —
180. 5 —
180. 6 —
180. 7 Syr.
180. 8 —
180. 9 —
181. 1 S/G [1–3]
181. 2 —
181. 3 —
181. 4 —
181. 5 —
181. 6 —
181. 7 —
181. 8 —
181. 9 —
181. 10 S/G [1–2]
181. 11 —
181. 12 —
181. 13 —
181. 14 Syr.
181. 15 —
181. 16 —
181. 17 Syr.
184. 1 S/G [2–4]
184. 2 —
184. 3 —
184. 4 Syr.
184. 5 —
184. 6 —
184. 7 —
184. 8 Syr.
184. 9 —
184. 10 —

SchDN	197. 6 S/G [8–12]	212. 6 S/G [3–8]
185. 1 —	197. 7 —	212. 7 —
185. 2 —	200. 1 Syr.	212. 8 Syr.
185. 3 —	200. 2 —	212. 9 —
185. 4 Syr.	200. 3 Syr.	212. 10 Syr.
185. 5 Syr.	200. 4 —	212. 11 —
185. 6 Syr.	200. 5 —	212. 12 —
188. 1 —	201. 1 —	213. 1 —
188. 2 —	201. 2 S/G [26–7]	213. 2 —
188. 3 Syr.	201. 3 Syr.	213. 3 —
188. 4 Syr.	201. 4 Syr.	213. 4 S/G [17–18]
188. 5 Syr.	201. 5 —	213. 5 —
188. 6 Syr.	201. 6 —	213. 6 S/G [4–6]
189. 1 —	201. 7 Syr.	213. 7 Syr.
189. 2 Syr.	204. 1 Syr.	213. 8 —
189. 3 Syr.	204. 2 —	213. 9 —
189. 4 Syr.	204. 3 —	216. 1 Syr.
189. 5 Syr.	204. 4 Syr.	216. 2 Syr.
192. 1 —	205. 1 —	216. 3 Syr.
192. 2 —	205. 2 Syr.	216. 4 —
192. 3 —	208. 1 —	216. 5 —
192. 4 S/G [8–10]	208. 2 Syr.	216. 6 Syr.
192. 5 Syr.	208. 3 —	216. 7 Syr.
192. 6 —	208. 4 —	216. 8 —
192. 7 Syr.	208. 5 Syr.	216. 9 —
192. 8 —	208. 6 —	216. 10 Syr.
192. 9 —	208. 7 —	220. 1 Syr.
193. 1 Syr.	209. 1 Syr.	220. 2 —
193. 2 —	209. 2 —	220. 3 S/G [8–9]
193. 3 —	209. 3 —	220. 4 Syr.
193. 4 Syr.	209. 4 —	221. 1 Syr.
193. 5 Syr.	209. 5 —	221. 2 —
196. 1 Syr.	209. 6 —	221. 3 —
196. 2 Syr.	209. 7 —	221. 4 —
196. 3 —	209. 8 —	221. 5 —
196. 4 S/G [1–8]	209. 9 —	221. 6 —
196. 5 —	209. 10 —	221. 7 —
196. 6 —	209. 11 Syr.	221. 8 Syr.
197. 1 Syr.	212. 1 —	224. 1 —
197. 2 Syr.	212. 2 —	224. 2 —
197. 3 Syr.	212. 3 Syr.	224. 3 —
197. 4 —	212. 4 —	224. 4 Syr.
197. 5 Syr.	212. 5 Syr.	224. 5 —

224. 6 Syr.
224. 7 Syr.
225. 1 —
225. 2 —
225. 3 Syr.
228. 1 —
228. 2 S/G [12–28]
228. 3 Syr.
229. 1 —
229. 2 Syr.
229. 3 —
229. 4 —
229. 5 Syr.
229. 6 —
229. 7 —
232. 1 —
232. 2 Syr.
232. 3 Syr.
233. 1 —
223. 2 —
223. 3 Syr.
233. 4 S/G [3–4]
233. 5 —
233. 6 —
233. 7 —
233. 8 —
236. 1 —
236. 2 Syr.
236. 3 —
236. 4 —
236. 5 Syr.
236. 6 —
236. 7 Syr.
236. 8 Syr.
236. 9 Syr.
236. 10 Syr.
237. 1 —
237. 2 —
237. 3 —
237. 4 —
237. 5 —
237. 6 —
237. 7 —

237. 8 —
237. 9 —
237. 10 —
240. 1 —
240. 2 Syr.
240. 3 Syr.
241. 1 —
241. 2 —
241. 3 —
241. 4 Syr.
241. 5 —
241. 6 Syr.
241. 7 —
244. 1 Syr.
244. 2 —
244. 3 —
244. 4 —
244. 5 —
244. 6 Syr.
244. 7 Syr.
244. 8 —
244. 9 Syr.
245. 1 —
245. 2 —
245. 3 —
245. 4 —
245. 5 —
248. 1 S/G [1–5]
248. 2 Syr.
248. 3 —
248. 4 Syr.
249. 1 —
249. 2 Syr.
249. 3 Syr.
249. 4 Syr.
249. 5 —
249. 6 Syr.
249. 7 Syr.
252. 1 —
252. 2 Syr.
252. 3 Syr.
252. 4 Syr.
252. 5 S/G [3–10]

252. 6 Syr.
252. 7 Syr.
253. 1 S/G [19–20]
253. 2 —
256. 1 S/G [26–8]
256. 2 Syr.
257. 1 —
257. 2 Syr.
257. 3 Syr.
257. 4 Syr.
257. 5 —
257. 6 Syr.
257. 7 —
260. 1 —
260. 2 Syr.
260. 3 Syr.
260. 4 Syr.
260. 5 Syr.
261. 1 S/G [7–8]
261. 2 —
261. 3 —
261. 4 S/G [4–6]
261. 5 —
261. 6 —
264. 1 S/G [1–2]
264. 2 Syr.
264. 3 —
264. 4 —
264. 5 —
264. 6 —
264. 7 —
265. 1 Syr.
265. 2 —
265. 3 —
265. 4 Syr.
265. 5 —
265. 6 —
265. 7 —
265. 8 —
265. 9 —
265. 10 —
265. 11 —
265. 12 —

265. 13 —
265. 14 —
265. 15 —
268. 1 —
268. 2 —
268. 3 —
268. 4 Syr.
269. 1 Syr.
269. 2 —
269. 3 —
272. 1 Syr.
272. 2 —
272. 3 Syr.
272. 4 —
273. 1 —
273. 2 —
273. 3 Syr.
276. 1 Syr.
276. 2 —
276. 3 —
276. 4 Syr.
277. 1 S/G [1–2]
277. 2 —
277. 3 —
277. 4 Syr.
277. 5 —
280. 1 Syr.
280. 2 Syr.
280. 3 —
280. 4 S/G [47–54]
281. 1 —
281. 2 —
281. 3 S/G [10–13]
281. 4 S/G [33–41]
284. 1 —
284. 2 —
284. 3 S/G [5–16]
285. 1 —
285. 2 —
285. 3 Syr.
285. 4 —
285. 5 —
285. 6 Syr.

288. 1 —
288. 2 —
288. 3 —
288. 4 —
288. 5 S/G [5–6]
288. 6 —
288. 7 Syr.
288. 8 —
288. 9 —
288. 10 —
288. 11 —
288. 12 —
288. 13 Syr.
289. 1 —
289. 2 —
289. 3 —
289. 4 S/G [5–10]
292. 1 —
292. 2 Syr.
292. 3 —
292. 4 —
292. 5 —
292. 6 —
292. 7 —
292. 8 Syr.
292. 9 —
292. 10 —
292. 11 S/G [1–10]
293. 1 —
293. 2 Syr.
293. 3 S/G [1–5]
296. 1 —
296. 2 —
296. 3 Syr.
296. 4 —
296. 5 Syr.
297. 1 —
297. 2 —
297. 3 Syr.
297. 4 Syr.
297. 5 —
297. 6 —
297. 7 —

301. 1 S/G [8–12]
301. 2 —
301. 3 —
301. 4 Syr.
301. 5 —
301. 6 —
301. 7 Syr.
301. 8 Syr.
304. 1 —
304. 2 Syr.
304. 3 —
304. 4 —
305. 1 —
305. 2 —
305. 3 Syr.
305. 4 —
305. 5 Syr.
305. 6 —
305. 7 —
305. 8 —
305. 9 Syr.
308. 1 —
308. 2 —
308. 3 Syr.
308. 4 Syr.
308. 5 —
308. 6 —
308. 7 Syr.
308. 8 —
309. 1 —
309. 2 —
309. 3 S/G [15–17]
309. 4 —
309. 5 —
309. 6 —
312. 1 S/G [1–6]
312. 2 —
312. 3 Syr.
313. 1 —
313. 2 —
313. 3 Syr.
316. 1 Syr.
316. 2 —

316. 3 —
316. 4 Syr.
317. 1 —
320. 1 —
320. 2 —
320. 3 Syr.
321. 1 —
321. 2 Syr.
321. 3 —
321. 4 —
321. 5 —
324. 1 Syr.
324. 2 —
325. 1 —
325. 2 —
325. 3 Syr.
325. 4 —
325. 5 —
325. 6 —
325. 7 —
328. 1 Syr.
328. 2 —
329. 1 Syr.
329. 2 —
332. 1 Syr.
332. 2 —
332. 3 Syr.
332. 4 S/G [7–9]
332. 5 —
332. 6 —
332. 7 S/G [17–18]
333. 1 —
333. 2 —
333. 3 —
333. 4 —
336. 1 —
336. 2 S/G [8–9]
336. 3 —
336. 4 S/G [28–30]
337. 1 —
337. 2 Syr.
337. 3 —
337. 4 —

337. 5 Syr.
340. 1 —
340. 2 S/G [14–16]
340. 3 —
340. 4 Syr.
340. 5 Syr.
341. 1 —
341. 2 —
341. 3 —
344. 1 S/G [10–15]
344. 2 S/G [20–4]
344. 3 Syr.
345. 1 —
345. 2 —
345. 3 S/G [28–33]
348. 1 —
348. 2 —
348. 3 —
348. 4 —
348. 5 —
348. 6 Syr.
349. 1 —
349. 2 S/G [1–4]
349. 3 —
349. 4 S/G [16–21]
349. 5 Syr.
352. 1 —
352. 2 S/G [1–12]
352. 3 Syr.
352. 4 —
353. 1 —
353. 2 Syr.
353. 3 Syr.
353. 4 Syr.
353. 5 Syr.
356. 1 —
356. 2 —
356. 3 —
356. 4 —
356. 5 Syr.
356. 6 —
356. 7 S/G [1–2]
356. 8 Syr.

357. 1 —
357. 2 S/G [36–8]
357. 3 —
360. 1 S/G [1–4, 5–6]
360. 2 S/G [1–10]
360. 3 —
360. 4 —
360. 5 —
360. 6 Syr.
360. 7 S/G [13–14]
361. 1 S/G [40–3]
361. 2 —
361. 3 S/G [1–2]
364. 1 S/G [12–20]
364. 2 Syr.
364. 3 —
365. 1 —
365. 2 —
365. 3 —
365. 4 —
365. 5 Syr.
365. 6 —
365. 7 —
365. 8 —
368. 1 —
368. 2 —
368. 3 —
368. 4 —
368. 5 —
368. 6 Syr.
368. 7 —
368. 8 Syr.
369. 1 —
369. 2 Syr.
369. 3 Syr.
372. 1 —
372. 2 Syr.
372. 3 Syr.
373. 1 Syr.
373. 2 —
373. 3 —
373. 4 Syr.
376. 1 —

376. 2 —
376. 3 —
376. 4 —
376. 5 S/G [5–7]
376. 6 S/G [12–17]
377. 1 Syr.
377. 2 —
377. 3 Syr.
377. 4 —
380. 1 S/G [23–5]
380. 2 —
380. 3 S/G [15–16]
381. 1 Syr.
381. 2 Syr.
381. 3 —
384. 1 —
384. 2 —
384. 3 S/G [10–11]
384. 4 Syr.
384. 5 —
384. 6 S/G [9]
385. 1 Syr.
385. 2 S/G [1–2]
385. 3 Syr.
385. 4 S/G [27–32]
388. 1 —
388. 2 —
388. 3 —
388. 4 S/G [1–2, 47–55]
389. 1 —
389. 2 —
392. 1 —
392. 2 —
392. 3 Syr.
393. 1 S/G [1–3]
393. 2 —
393. 3 —
393. 4 —
393. 5 Syr.
393. 6 —
393. 7 S/G [10–14]
393. 8 —

393. 9 Syr.
396. 1 —
396. 2 —
396. 3 S/G [7–8]
396. 4 —
396. 5 Syr.
397. 1 —
397. 2 Syr.
397. 3 —
397. 4 —
397. 5 Syr.
397. 6 —
397. 7 —
397. 8 Syr.
397. 9 —
397. 10 S/G [9–13]
400. 1 —
400. 2 —
400. 3 —
400. 4 —
400. 5 —
400. 6 —
400. 7 S/G [1–4, 5–9]
400. 8 —
401. 1 —
401. 2 —
401. 3 Syr.
401. 4 —
401. 5 —
401. 6 —
401. 7 —
404. 1 S/G [6–17]
404. 2 Syr.
404. 3 —
404. 4 —
404. 5 Syr.
404. 6 —
404. 7 S/G [9–11]
405. 1 S/G [25–9]
405. 2 —
405. 3 Syr.
405. 4 —
408. 1 —

408. 2 Syr.
408. 3 —
408. 4 Syr.
409. 1 S/G [7–8]
409. 2 S/G [5–6]
409. 3 —
409. 4 —
409. 5 S/G [3–8]
409. 6 Syr.
409. 7 S/G [4–10]
412. 1 Syr.
412. 2 —
412. 3 —
412. 4 —
413. 1 Syr.
413. 2 —
413. 3 S/G [1–7, 16–24]
413. 4 Syr.
416. 1 —
416. 2 Syr.
416. 3 Syr.
416. 4 —
416. 5 —
416. 6 —

SchMT

416. 1 —
417. 1 Syr.
417. 2 Syr.
417. 3 —
417. 4 —
417. 5 Syr.
417. 6 —
417. 7 Syr.
417. 8 —
420. 1 —
420. 2 Syr.
420. 3 —
420. 4 —
420. 5 —
420. 6 —
420. 7 —

420. 8 —
421. 1 Syr.
421. 2 —
421. 3 —
421. 4 —
424. 1 S/G [1–7]
424. 2 —
424. 3 Syr.
425. 1 —
425. 2 Syr.
425. 3 —
425. 4 —
425. 5 —
425. 6 —
425. 7 —
425. 8 Syr.
425. 9 —
425. 10 —
425. 11 S/G [38–40]
428. 1 —
428. 2 —
428. 3 —
429. 1 S/G [1–4]
429. 2 —
429. 3 S/G [1–6,
    32–41, 65–6]

SchEP
528. 1 Syr.
528. 2 Syr.
529. 1 —
529. 2 —
529. 3 Syr.
529. 4 —
529. 5 —
532. 1 Syr.
532. 2 Syr.
532. 3 Syr.
532. 4 Syr.
532. 5 —
532. 6 —
532. 7 —
533. 1 S/G [2–4]

533. 2 S/G [17]
533. 3 S/G [1–17]
536. 1 Syr.
536. 2 —
536. 3 S/G [1–18]
536. 4 —
536. 5 Syr.
537. 1 —
537. 2 S/G [4–5]
537. 3 —
537. 4 —
537. 5 S/G [1–18]
537. 6 Syr.
540. 1 —
540. 2 —
540. 3 —
541. 1 —
541. 2 —
541. 3 Syr.
541. 4 —
541. 5 Syr.
544. 1 Syr.
544. 2 —
544. 3 —
544. 4 S/G [1–2]
545. 1 S/G [2–6]
545. 2 Syr.
545. 3 —
545. 4 —
545. 5 —
545. 6 —
545. 7 —
545. 8 Syr.
545. 9 —
545. 10 —
548. 1 Syr.
548. 2 Syr.
548. 3 S/G [1–3]
548. 4 —
548. 5 —
548. 6 Syr.
548. 7 —
548. 8 —

548. 9 —
548. 10 —
548. 11 —
549. 1 —
549. 2 —
549. 3 —
549. 4 —
549. 5 S/G [5]
549. 6 Syr.
549. 7 Syr.
549. 8 —
549. 9 —
549. 10 —
549. 11 —
549. 12 —
549. 13 —
549. 14 —
549. 15 —
549. 16 —
549. 17 —
552. 1 S/G [4–5]
552. 2 —
552. 3 S/G [4–7]
552. 4 Syr.
552. 5 —
552. 6 —
552. 7 —
552. 8 —
552. 9 —
552. 10 —
552. 11 S/G [6–10]
553. 1 —
553. 2 —
553. 3 —
553. 4 —
553. 5 —
553. 6 —
553. 7 —
553. 8 S/G [1–3]
553. 9 S/G [18–19]
556. 1 Syr.
556. 2 —
556. 3 —

556. 4 —
556. 5 —
557. 1 —
557. 2 Syr.
557. 3 Syr.
557. 4 Syr.
557. 5 —
557. 6 Syr.
557. 7 —
557. 8 Syr.
557. 9 Syr.
557. 10 —
557. 11 —
557. 12 —
560. 1 —
560. 2 —
560. 3 —
560. 4 S/G [1–37]
561. 1 Syr.
561. 2 S/G [1–19]
561. 3 Syr.
561. 4 S/G [27–8]
564. 1 —
564. 2 —

564. 3 —
564. 4 —
564. 5 —
565. 1 —
565. 2 S/G [1–4]
565. 3 —
565. 4 —
565. 5 S/G [4–6]
568. 1 S/G [1–3]
568. 2 —
568. 3 Syr.
568. 4 —
569. 1 —
569. 2 Syr.
569. 3 —
569. 4 —
569. 5 —
569. 6 —
569. 7 Syr.
569. 8 Syr.
569. 9 Syr.
569. 10 Syr.
572. 1 S/G [1–3]
572. 2 —

572. 3 Syr.
572. 4 S/G [1–8]
572. 5 —
572. 6 —
572. 7 —
572. 8 —
572. 9 —
572. 10 —
572. 11 —
572. 12 —
572. 13 —
573. 1 —
573. 2 Syr.
573. 3 Syr.
573. 4 —
573. 5 —
573. 6 —
573. 7 Syr.
573. 8 —
576. 1 —
576. 2 Syr.
576. 3 Syr.

BIBLIOGRAPHY

PRIMARY SOURCES

Classical sources are cited by author and name of work, followed by a reference to the passage in question according to the traditional divisions of the text. For full bibliographical information on the standard editions of these classical texts, the reader may want to consult Luci Berkowitz and Karl A. Squitier, *Thesaurus Linguae Graecae Canon of Greek Authors and Works*, 3rd edn. (New York: Oxford University Press, 1990). (Abbreviations for classical and most Christian sources can be found in the introductions to LSJ and Lampe.) Those Christian and Jewish sources which are located in standard text series (i.e. GCS, LCL, PG, PL, PO, SC, CCSG, ACO, Mansi) have been cited as above, except that following the reference to the passage in question we have included in parentheses the series name, as well as volume and page numbers. The works of Dionysius are cited from the new edition of Günter Heil, Adolf Martin Ritter, and Beate Regina Suchla (PTS 33 and 36). Other Christian sources (Syriac and Greek) are cited according to the following editions and translations.

ANDREW OF CAESAREA, *Studien zur Geschichte des griechischen Apokalypse-Textes*: I. *Der Apokalypse-Kommentar des Andreas von Kaisareia: Text*, ed. Josef Schmid (Munich: Karl Zink, 1955).

Die Apostolischen Väter, ed. K. Bihlmeyer, rev. F. X. Funk (Tübingen: C. B. Mohr, 1924).

CYRIL OF SCYTHOPOLIS, *Life of Sabas*, in *Kyrillos von Skythopolis*, ed. E. Schwartz (TU 49/2; Leipzig: J. C. Hinrichs Verlag, 1939).

Doctrina patrum de incarnatione Verbi, ed. Franz Diekamp (Münster: Aschendorff, 1907).

ECUMENIUS, *The Complete Commentary of Oecumenius on the Apocalypse*, ed. H. C. Hoskier (Ann Arbor: University of Michigan, 1928).

NICHOLAS OF METHONE, *Nicholas of Methone: Refutation of Proclus' Elements of Theology*, ed. Athanasios D. Angelou (Corpus philosophorum medii aevi: Byzantinoi philosophoi, 1; Leiden: E. J. Brill, 1984).

ORIGEN, *Vier Bücher von den Prinzipien*, ed. Herwig Gürgemanns and Heinrich Karpp (Texte zur Forschung, 24; Darmstadt: Wissenschaftliche Buchgesellschaft, 1976).

PHILOPONUS, JOHN, *De opificio mundi*, ed. Gualterus Reichardt (Leipzig: Teubner, 1898).

PHOTIUS, *Bibliothèque*, 8 vols., ed. and tr. René Henry (Paris: Société d'édition 'Les Belles Lettres', 1959–77).

PSEUDO-CAESARIUS, *Pseudo-Kaisarios: Die Erotapokriseis*, ed. Rudolf Riedinger (GCS, unnumbered; Berlin: Akademie-Verlag, 1989).

PSEUDO-DIONYSIUS, *Pseudo-Dionusius: The Complete Works*, tr. Colm Luibheid and Paul Rorem (The Classics of Western Spirituality; Mahwah, NJ: Paulist Press, 1987).

——— *Über die Mystische Theologie und Briefe*, tr. Adolf Martin Ritter (Bibliothek der griechischen Literatur, 40; Stuttgart: Anton Hiersemann, 1994).

SERGIUS OF RESH'AINA, in P. Sherwood (ed. and tr.), 'Mimro de Serge de Rešayna sur la vie spirituelle', *L'Orient syrien*, 5 (1960), 433–57; 6 (1961), 95–115, 121–56.

SEVERUS OF ANTIOCH, *Severi Antiocheni liber contra impium grammaticum*, ed. and tr. I. Lebon (CSCO (Syriac), vols. 45/46 (= bk. 3. 2), 50/51 (= bk. 3. 1), 58/59 (= bks. 1 and 2).

——— *Sévèrus d'Antioche: La Polémique antijulianiste*: IIA. *Le Contra Additiones Juliani*, ed. and tr. R. Hespel (CSCO (Syriac), vols. 124/125).

——— *Sévèrus d'Antioche: La Polémique antijulianiste*: IIB. *L'Adversus Apologiam Juliani*, ed. and tr. R. Hespel (CSCO (Syriac), vols. 126/127).

——— *The Sixth Book of the Select Letters of Severus Patriarch of Antioch in the Syriac Version of Athanasius of Nisibis*, 2 vols. in 4, ed. and tr. E. W. Brooks (London: Williams and Norgate, 1902–4).

SEXTUS, *The Sentences of Sextus: A Contribution to the History of Early Christian Ethics*, ed. Henry Chadwick (Cambridge: Cambridge Univeristy Press, 1959).

STEPHEN BAR SUDAILE, *The Book Which is Called The Book of the Holy Hierotheos*, ed. and tr. F. S. Marsh (London: Williams and Norgate, 1927).

Suidae lexikon graece et latine, 2 vols., ed. G. Bernhardy (Halle: Schwetschke, 1843–53).

THEODORET, *Theodoret of Cyrus: Eranistes*, ed. G. H. Ettlinger (Oxford: Clarendon Press, 1975).

THEODOSIUS I, *Oratio theologica*, ed. and tr. I.–B. Chabot, in *Documenta ad origines monophysitarum illustrandas* (CSCO (Syriac), vols. 17/52, 40–79 (text), 26–55 (translation)).

ZACHARIAH OF MITYLENE, *The Syriac Chronicle Known as that of Zachariah of Mitylene*, tr. F. J. Hamilton and E. W. Brooks (London: Methuen, 1899).

SECONDARY SOURCES

AIGRAN, R., 'Arabie', *DHGE* 6 (1924), 1158–1339.

AMANN, É., 'Job', *DTC* 8/2 (1925), 1486–7.

——— 'Scythes (Moines)', *DTC* 14/2 (1941), 1746–53.

——— 'Thémistius', *DTC* 15/1 (1946), 219–22.

——— 'Théopaschite (Controverse)', *DTC* 15/1 (1946), 505–12.

AVI-YONAH, M., 'The Bath of the Lepers at Scythopolis', *IEJ* 13 (1963), 325–6.

BACHT, HEINRICH, 'Die Rolle des orientalischen Mönchtums in den kirchen-politischen Auseinandersetzungen um Chalkedon (431–519)', in Aloys Grillmeier and Heinrich Bacht (eds.), *Das Konzil von Chalkedon*, vol. ii (Würzburg: Echter-Verlag, 1953), 193–314.

BARDY, GUSTAVE, 'L'"Expositio Fidei" attribuée à saint Ambroise', in *Miscellanea Giovanni Mercati*, vol. i, Studi e testi, 121 (Vatican: Biblioteca apostolica vaticana, 1946), 199–218.

——'Jean Philopon', *DTC* 8/1 (1947), 831–9.

——'Sur une citation de saint Ambroise dans les controverses christologiques', *RHE* 40 (1944/5), 171–6.

BAUMSTARK, ANTON, *Geschichte der syrischen Literatur* (Bonn: A. Marcus und E. Weber, 1922).

——*Lucubrationes Syro-graecae* (Leipzig, 1894).

——'Zwei syrische Papiascitate', *OC* 2 (1902), 352–7.

BEIERWALTES, WERNER, 'Johannes von Skythopolis und Plotin', *SP* 11/2 = TU 108 (1972), 3–7.

——*Proklos: Grundzuge seiner Metaphysik*, 2nd edn. (Frankfurt am Main: Klostermann, 1979).

——and KANNICHT, RICHARD, 'Plotin-Testimonia bei Johannes von Skythopolis', *Hermes*, 96 (1968), 247–51.

BEULAY, ROBERT, 'Joseph Ḥazzāyā', *DS* 8 (1974), 1341–9.

BIENERT, WOLFGANG A., *Dionysius von Alexandrien: Zur Frage des Origenismus im dritten Jahrhundert*, PTS 21 (Berlin: Walter de Gruyter, 1978).

BINNS, JOHN, *Ascetics and Ambassadors of Christ: The Monasteries of Palestine 314–631*, Oxford Early Christian Studies (Oxford: Oxford University Press, 1994).

BREYDY, M., 'Les Témoignages de Sévère d'Antioche dans l'exposé de la foi de Jean Maron', *Mus.* 103 (1990), 215–33.

BROCK, SEBASTIAN, 'The Conversations of the Syrian Orthodox under Justinian (532)', *OCP* 47 (1981), 87–121.

CAPELLE, BERNARD, 'Alcuin et l'histoire du symbole de la messe', *RTAM* 6 (1934), 249–60.

——'L'Introduction du symbole à la messe', in *Mélanges Joseph de Ghellinck*, vol. ii, Museum Lessianum: Section historique, 14 (Gemboux: Éditions J. Duculot, 1951), 1002–27.

CASTAGNO, ADELE MONACI, 'Il problema della datazione dei Commenti all'*Apocalisse* di Ecumenio e di Andrea di Cesarea', *AAST* 114 (1980), 223–46.

CLARK, ELIZABETH A., *The Origenist Controversy: The Construction of an Early Christian Debate* (Princeton: Princeton University Press, 1992).

CORSINI, EUGENIO, 'La questione areopagitica: Contributi alla cronologia dello Pseudo-Dionigi', *AAST* 93 (1958/9), 128–227.

——*Il trattato 'De divinis nominibus' dello Pseudo-Dionigi e i commenti neoplatonici al Parmenide* (Turin: Giappichelli, 1962).

281

Bibliography

CROUZEL, HENRI, 'Les Critiques adressées par Méthode et ses contemporains à la doctrine origénienne du corps ressuscité', *Gregorianum*, 59 (1972), 679–716.

DALEY, BRIAN, 'The Origenism of Leontius of Byzantium', *JTS* NS 27 (1976), 333–69.

DIEKAMP, FRANZ (ed.), *Analecta Patristica: Texte und Abhandlungen zur griechischen Patristik*, Orientalia Christiana Analecta, 117 (Rome: Pont. Institutum Orientalium Studiorum, 1938).

——*Die Origenistischen Streitigkeiten im sechsten Jahrhundert und das fünfte allgemeine Concil* (Münster: Aschendorff, 1899).

DILLON, JOHN, 'Plotinus at Work on Platonism', *Greece & Rome*, 39 (1992), 189–204.

DOWNEY, GLANVILLE, 'Ephraemius, Patriarch of Antioch', *ChH* 7 (1938), 364–70.

DRAGUET, RENÉ, *Julien d'Halicarnasse et sa controverse avec Sévère d'Antioche sur l'incorruptibilité du corps du Christ* (Louvain: P. Smeesters, 1924).

DRÄSEKE, JOHANNES, 'Prokopios' von Gaza "Widerlegung des Proklos"', *BZ* 6 (1897), 55–91.

EVANS, DAVID B., 'Leontius of Byzantium and Dionysius the Areopagite', *BS* 7 (1980), 1–34.

FLUSIN, BERNARD, *Miracle et histoire dans l'œuvre de Cyrille de Scythopolis* (Paris: Études Augustiniennes, 1983).

FRANK, RICHARD M., 'The Use of the *Enneads* by John of Scythopolis', *Mus.* 100 (1987), 101–8.

FREND, W. H. C., *The Rise of the Monophysite Movement* (Cambridge: Cambridge University Press, 1972).

FRITZ, G., 'Pierre le Foulon', *DTC* 12/2 (1935), 1933–5.

FROTHINGHAM, A. L., *Stephen Bar Sudaili the Syrian Mystic and the Book of the Holy Hierotheos* (Leiden: E. J. Brill, 1886).

GERO, STEPHEN, 'Hypatius of Ephesus on the Cult of Images', in Jacob Neusner (ed.), *Christianity, Judaism and Other Greco-Roman Cults: Studies for Morton Smith at Sixty*: part 2, *Early Christianity*, Studies in Judaism in Late Antiquity, 12 (Leiden: E. J. Brill, 1975), 208–16.

GODET, P., 'Basil de Cilicie', *DTC* 2/1 (1932), 463–4.

GOUILLARD, JEAN, 'Hypatios d'Éphèse ou du Pseudo-Denys à Théodore Studite', *REB* 19 (1961), 63–75.

GRAY, PATRICK T. R., *The Defense of Chalcedon in the East (451–553)*, Studies in the History of Christian Thought, 20 (Leiden: E. J. Brill, 1979).

——'Forgery as an Instrument of Progress: Reconstructing the Theological Tradition in the Sixth Century', *BZ* 81 (1988), 284–9.

——'"The Select Fathers": Canonizing the Patristic Past', *SP* 23 (1989), 21–36.

GRILLMEIER, ALOYS, 'Éphrem d'Amid', *DHGE* 15 (1963), 581–5.

——in collaboration with Theresia Hainthaler, *Christ in Christian Tradition*: vol. ii, *From the Council of Chalcedon (451) to Gregory the Great (590–604)*: part 2,

The Church of Constantinople in the Sixth Century, trans. John Cawte and Pauline Allen (Louisville, Ky.: Westminster John Knox Press, 1995).

GRILLMEIER, ALOYS, in collaboration with Theresia Hainthaler, *Christ in Christian Tradition*: vol. ii, *From the Council of Chalcedon (451) to Gregory the Great (590–604)*: part 4, *The Church of Alexandria with Nubia and Ethiopia after 451*, trans. O. C. Dean Jr. (Louisville, Ky.: Westminster John Knox Press, 1996).

GUILLAUMONT, ANTOINE, 'Étienne Bar Soudaili', *DS* 4/2 (1961), 1481–8.

—— *Les 'Képhalaia Gnostica' d'Évagre le Pontique et l'histoire de l'origénisme chez les Grecs et chez les Syriens*, Patristica Sorbonensia, 5 (Paris: Éditions du Seuil, 1962).

HARNACK, ADOLF VON, *Geschichte der altchristliche Literatur bis Eusebius*, 2 vols. in 4 (Leipzig: J. C. Hinrichs, 1958).

HATHAWAY, RONALD F., *Hierarchy and the Definition of Order in the Letters of Pseudo-Dionysius: A Study in the Form and Meaning of the Pseudo-Dionysian Writings* (The Hague: Martinus Nijhoff, 1969).

HAUSHERR, IRÉNÉE, 'Doutes au sujet du "Divin Denys"', *OCP* 2 (1936), 484–90.

—— 'L'influence du "Livre de Saint Hiérothée"', in Irénée Hausherr (ed.), *De doctrina spirituali christianorum orientalium*, Orientalia Christiana, 30 (Rome: Pont. Institutum Orientalium Studiorum, 1933), 176–211.

HELMER, SIEGFRIED, *Der Neuchalkedonismus: Geschichte, Berechtigung und Bedeutung eines dogmengeschichtlichen Begriffes* (Bonn: Rheinische Friedrich-Wilhelms Universität, 1962).

HIPLER, FRANZ, *Dionysius, der Areopagite: Untersuchungen über Aechtheit und Glaubwürdigkeit der under diesem Namen vorhandenen Schriften* (Regensburg: Georg Joseph Manz, 1861).

HONIGMANN, ERNEST, *Évêques et évêchés monophysites d'Asie antérieure au VIe siècle*, CSCO 127, Subsidia 2 (Louvain: Imprimerie orientaliste, 1951).

—— 'Juvenal of Jerusalem', *DOP* 5 (1950), 211–79.

—— *Trois mémoires posthumes d'histoire et de géographie de l'orient chrétien*, Subsidia hagiographica, 35 (Brussels: Société des Bollandistes, 1961).

IRMSCHER, JOHANNES, 'Teodoro Scitopolitano: De vita et scriptis', *Augustinianum*, 26 (1986), 185–90.

JUGIE, M., 'Gaianites', *DTC* 6/1 (1947), 999–1023.

—— 'Le Récit de l'histoire euthymiaque sur la mort et l'assomption de la Sainte Vierge', *EO* 25 (1926), 385–92.

KARALEVSKIJ, C., 'Antioche', *DHGE* 3 (1924), 563–703.

KIRCHMEYER, J., 'Le Moine Marcien (de Bethléem?)', *SP* 5/3 = TU 80 (1962), 341–59.

KITZINGER, ERNST, 'The Cult of Images in the Age before Iconoclasm', *DOP* 8 (1954), 85–150.

KOCH, H., 'Proklus als Quelle des Pseudo-Dionysius Areopagita in der Lehre vom Bösen', *Philologus*, 54 (1895), 438–54.

—— *Pseudo-Dionysius Areopagita in seinen Beziehungen zum Neuplatonismus und*

Mysterienwesen, Forschungen zur christlichen Litteratur- und Dogmengeschichte, 1/2–3 (Mainz: Franz Kirchheim, 1900).

KÜMMEL, WERNER GEORG, *Introduction to the New Testament*, trans. Howard Clark Kee (Nashville: Abingdon Press, 1975).

LAMOREAUX, JOHN C., 'Episcopal Courts in Late Antiquity', *JECS* 3 (1995), 143–67.

—— 'The Provenance of Ecumenius' Commentary on the Apocalypse', *VC* 52 (1998), 88–108.

LEBON, Joseph, 'La Christologie du monophysisme syrien', in Aloys Grillmeier and Heinrich Bacht (eds.), *Das Konzil von Chalkedon*, vol. i (Würzburg: Echter-Verlag, 1951), 425–580.

—— 'Encore le pseudo-Denys et Sévère d'Antioche', *RHE* 28 (1932), 296–313.

—— 'Éphrem d'Amid, patriarche d'Antioche (526–544)', in *Mélanges d'histoire offerts à Ch. Moeller*, vol. i (Louvain: Bureau du Recueil, 1914), 197–214.

—— *Le Moine saint Marcien*, Spicilegium sacrum Lovaniense, 36 (Louvain: Spicilegium sacrum Lovaniense, 1968).

—— *Le Monophysisme Sévèrien* (Louvain: J. van Linthout, 1909).

—— 'Le pseudo-Denys l'Aréopagite et Sévère d'Antioche', *RHE* 26 (1930), 880–915.

LOOFS, FRIEDRICH, *Leontius von Byzanz und die gleichnamigen Schriftsteller der griechischen Kirche* (Leipzig, 1887).

MERCATI, GIOVANNI, *Notizie di Procoro e Demetrio Cidone, Manuele Caleca e Teodoro Meliteniota ed altri appunti per la storia della teologia e della letteratura bizantina del secolo XIV* (Vatican: Bibliotheca apostolica vaticana, 1931).

MEYENDORFF, JOHN, *Imperial Unity and Christian Divisions: The Church 450–680 A.D.* (Crestwood, NY: St Vladimir's Seminary Press, 1989).

MOELLER, CHARLES, 'Le Chalcédonisme et le néo-chalcédonisme en Orient de 451 à la fin du VIe siècle', in Aloys Grillmeier and Heinrich Bacht (eds.), *Das Konzil von Chalkedon*, vol. i (Würzburg: Echter-Verlag, 1951), 637–720.

NAUTIN, PIERRE, *Lettres et écrivains chrétiens des IIe et IIIe siècles*, Patristica, 2 (Paris: Éditions du Cerf, 1961).

O'DALY, GERARD, 'Dionysius Areopagita', *TRE* 8 (1981), 772–80.

PELIKAN, JAROSLAV, 'The Odyssey of Dionysian Spirituality', in Colm Luibheid and Paul Rorem (trans.), *Pseudo-Dionysius: The Complete Works* (Mahwah, NJ: Paulist Press, 1987), 11–24.

PERRONE, LORENZO, *La chiesa di Palestina e le controversie christologiche, dal concilio di Efeso (431) al secondo concilio di Constantinopoli (553)*, Testi e ricerche di scienze religiose, 18 (Brescia: Paideia Editrice, 1980).

PITRA, JEAN BAPTISTE, *Analecta Sacra*, vol. iv (Paris, 1883).

REES, SILAS, 'The *De Sectis*: A Treatise Attributed to Leontius of Byzantium', *JTS* 40 (1939), 346–60.

RICHARD, MARCEL, 'Léonce de Jérusalem et Léonce de Byzance', *MSR* 1 (1944), 35–88.

RICHARD, MARCEL, 'Notes sur les florilèges dogmatiques du Ve et du VIe siècle', in *Actes du VIe congrès international d'études byzantines (Paris, 27 juillet–2 août 1948)*, vol. 1 (Paris: École des hautes études, 1950), 307–18.

——'Le Traité "De Sectis" et Léonce de Byzance', *RHE* 35 (1939), 695–723.

RIEDINGER, RUDOLF, 'Akoimeten', *TRE* 2 (1978), 148–53.

——'War der Kompilator der Erotapokriseis des Pseudo-Kaisarios ein Severianer?' *Helikon*, 8 (1968), 440–3.

RIST, JOHN M., 'Plotinus on Matter and Evil', *Phronesis*, 6 (1961), 154–66.

——*Plotinus: The Road to Reality* (Cambridge: Cambridge University Press, 1967).

——'In Search of the Divine Denis', in W. S. McCullough (ed.), *The Seed of Wisdom: Essays in Honour of T. J. Meeks* (Toronto: University of Toronto Press, 1964), 118–39.

ROQUES, R., 'Denys l'Aréopagite', *DS* 3 (1957), 244–86.

——'Denys le Pseudo-Aréopagite', *DHGE* 14 (1960), 265–86.

ROREM, PAUL, *Biblical and Liturgical Symbols within the Pseudo-Dionysian Synthesis*, Studies and Texts, 71 (Toronto: Pontifical Institute of Mediaeval Studies, 1984).

——'The Doctrinal Concerns of the First Dionysian Scholiast, John of Scythopolis', in Y. De Andia (ed.), *Denys l'Aréopagite et sa postérité en Orient et en Occident* (Paris: Études Augustiniennes, 1997), 187–200.

——*Pseudo-Dionysius: A Commentary on the Texts and an Introduction to their Influence* (New York: Oxford University Press, 1993).

——and Lamoreaux, John C., 'John of Scythopolis on Apollinarian Christology and the Pseudo-Areopagite's True Identity', *ChH* 62 (1993), 469–82.

ROUECHÉ, CHARLOTTE, *Aphrodisias in Late Antiquity*, Journal of Roman Studies Monographs, 5 (London: Society for the Promotion of Roman Studies, 1989).

SAFFREY, HENRI-DOMINIQUE, 'Le Chrétien Jean Philopon et la survivance de l'école d'Alexandrie au VIe siècle', *REG* 67 (1954), 396–410.

——'Un lien objectif entre le Pseudo-Denys et Proclus', *SP* 9/3 = TU 94 (1966), 98–105.

——'Nouveaux liens objectifs entre le Pseudo-Denys et Proclus', *RSPT* 63 (1979), 3–16.

SALAVILLE, L., 'Hénotique', *DTC* 6/2 (1947), 2153–78.

SCHER, Addai, 'Joseph Ḥazzāyā: Écrivain syriaque du VIIIe siècle', *Académie des inscriptions et belles-lettres, Paris: Comptes rendus des séances* (1909), 300–7.

——'Joseph Ḥazzāyā: Écrivain syriaque du VIIIe siècle', *RSO* 3 (1910), 45–63.

SHELDON-WILLIAMS, I. P., 'Henads and Angels: Proclus and the ps.-Dionysius', *SP* 11/2 = TU 108 (1972), 65–71.

SHERRY, E. J., 'The Life and Works of Joseph Ḥazzāyā', in W. S. McCullough (ed.), *The Seed of Wisdom: Essays in Honour of T. J. Meeks* (Toronto: University of Toronto Press, 1964), 78–91.

SHERWOOD, P., 'Sergius of Reshaina and the Syriac Versions of the Pseudo-Denis', *SE* 4 (1952), 174–84.

SIDDALS, RUTH M., 'Logic and Christology in Cyril of Alexandria', *JTS* NS, 38 (1987), 341–67.

SLIPYI, JOSEF, 'Die Trinitätslehre des byzantinischen Patriarchen Photios', *ZKT* 44 (1920), 538–62; 45 (1921), 66–95, 370–404.

SOLIGNAC, AIMÉ, 'Pierre le Foulon', *DS* 12/2 (1986), 1588–90.

SPEIGL, JAKOB, 'Das Religionsgespräch mit den severianischen Bischöfen in Konstantinopel im Jahre 532', *AHC* 16 (1984), 264–85.

STEEL, CARLOS G., *The Changing Self: A Study on the Soul in Later Neoplatonism* (Brussels: Paleis der Academien, 1978).

STIGLMAYR, JOSEF, 'Das Aufkommen der Pseudo-Dionysischen Schriften und ihr Eindringen in die christliche Literatur bis zum Lateranconcil 649: Ein zweiter Beitrag zur Dionysios-Frage', *Jahresbericht des öffentlichen Privatgymnasiums an der Stella matutina zu Feldkirch*, 4 (1894/5), 3–96.

—— 'Der Neuplatoniker Proclus als Vorlage des sog. Dionysius Areopagita in der Lehre vom Übel', *HJ* 16 (1895), 253–73, 721–48.

—— 'Der sog. Dionysius Areopagita und Severus von Antiochien', *Scholastik*, 3 (1928), 1–27, 161–89.

—— 'Die "Streitschrift des Prokopios von Gaza" gegen den Neuplatoniker Proklos', *BZ* 8 (1899), 263–301.

—— 'Über die Termini Hierarch und Hierarchie', *ZKT* 22 (1898), 180–7.

SUCHLA, BEATE REGINA, 'Eine Redaktion des griechischen Corpus Dionysiacum Areopagiticum im Umkreis des Johannes von Skythopolis, des Verfassers von Prolog und Scholien: Ein dritter Beitrag zur Überlieferungsgeschichte des CD', *NAWG* (1985), 4: 177–93.

—— 'Die sogenannten Maximus-Scholien des Corpus Dionysiacum Areopagiticum', *NAWG* (1980), 3: 31–66.

—— 'Die Überlieferung von Prolog und Scholien des Johannes von Skythopolis zum griechischen Corpus Dionysiacum Areopagiticum', *SP* 18/2 (1989), 79–83.

—— 'Die Überlieferung des Prologs des Johannes von Skythopolis zum griechischen Corpus Dionysiacum Areopagiticum', *NAWG* (1984), 4: 176–88.

—— 'Verteidigung eines platonischen Denkmodells einer christlichen Welt: Die philosophie- und theologiegeschichtliche Bedeutung des Scholienwerks des Johannes von Skythopolis zu den areopagitischen Traktaten', *NAWG* (1995), 1: 1–28.

VAN ESBROECK, MICHEL, 'Peter the Iberian and Dionysius the Areopagite: Honigmann's Thesis Revisted', *OCP* 59 (1993), 217–27.

VAN ROEY, ALBERT, 'Remarques sur le moine Marcien', *SP* 12/1 = TU 115 (1975), 160–77.

VON BALTHASAR, HANS URS, 'Das Problem der Dionysius-Scholien', in *Kosmische Liturgie*, 2nd edn. (Einsiedeln: Johannes-Verlag, 1961), 644–72.

VON BALTHASAR, HANS URS, 'Das Scholienwerk des Johannes von Scythopolis', *Scholastik*, 15 (1940), 16–38.

VON SCHÖNBORN, CHRISTOPH, *Sophrone de Jérusalem: Vie monastique et confession dogmatique*, Théologie Historique, 20 (Paris: Éditions Beauchesne, 1972).

WESTERINK, L. G., 'Proclus, Procopius, Psellus', *Mnemosyne*, 3rd ser. 10 (1942), 275–80.

WIDENGREN, G., 'Researches in Syrian Mysticism: Mystical Experiences and Spiritual Exercises', *Numen*, 8 (1961), 161–98.

WRIGHT, WILLIAM, *Catalogue of Syriac Manuscripts in the British Museum, Acquired since the Year 1838*, vol. ii (London: Longmans, 1871).

ZAHAROPOULOS, DIMITRI Z., *Theodore of Mopsuestia on the Bible: A Study in his Old Testament Exegesis* (Mahwah, NJ: Paulist Press, 1989).

INDEX